Family Group Conferencing

MODERN APPLICATIONS OF SOCIAL WORK

An Aldine de Gruyter Series of Texts and Monographs

SERIES EDITOR

James K. Whittaker, *University of Washington*

Paul Adams and Kristine E. Nelson (eds.), **Reinventing Human Services: Community-and Family-Centered Practice**

Ralph E. Anderson and Irl Carter, with Gary Lowe, **Human Behavior in the Social Environment: A Social Systems Approach (Fifth Edition)**

Richard P. Barth, Mark Courtney, Jill Duerr Berrick, and Vicky Albert, **From Child Abuse to Permanency Planning: Child Welfare Services Pathways and Placements**

Gale Burford and Joe Hudson, **Family Group Conferencing: New Directions in Community-Centered Child and Family Practice**

Dana Christensen, Jeffrey Todahl, and William C. Barrett, **Solution-Based Casework: An Introduction to Clinical and Case Management Skills in Casework Practice**

Marie Connolly with Margaret McKenzie, **Effective Participatory Practice: Family Group Conferencing in Child Protection**

Kathleen Ell and Helen Northen, **Families and Health Care: Psychosocial Practice**

Marian F. Fatout, **Models for Change in Social Group Work**

Mark W. Fraser, Peter J. Pecora, and David A. Haapala, **Families in Crisis: The Impact of Intensive Family Preservation Services**

James Garbarino, **Children and Families in the Social Environment (Second Edition)**

James Garbarino and Associates, **Special Children-Special Risks: The Maltreatment of Children with Disabilities**

James Garbarino and Associates, **Troubled Youth, Troubled Families: Understanding Families At-Risk for Adolescent Maltreatment**

Roberta R. Greene, **Human Behavior Theory: A Diversity Framework**

Roberta R. Greene, **Human Behavior Theory and Social Work Practice (Second Edition)**

Roberta R. Greene, **Social Work with the Aged and Their Families (Second Edition)**

André Ivanoff, Betty J. Blythe, and Tony Tripodi, **Involuntary Clients in Social Work Practice: A Research-Based Approach**

Susan P. Kemp, James K. Whittaker, and Elizabeth M. Tracy, **Person-Environment Practice: The Social Ecology of Interpersonal Helping**

Jill Kinney, David A. Haapala, and Charlotte Booth, **Keeping Families Together: The Homebuilders Model**

Gary R. Lowe and P. Nelson Reid, **The Professionalization of Poverty: Social Work and the Poor in the Twentieth Century**

Robert M. Moroney and Judy Krysik, **Social Policy and Social Work: Critical Essays on the Welfare State (Second Edition)**

Peter J. Pecora, Mark W. Fraser, Kristine Nelson, Jacqueline McCroskey, and William Meezan, **Evaluating Family-Based Services**

Peter J. Pecora, James K. Whittaker, Anthony N. Maluccio and Richard P. Barth, with Robert D. Plotnick **The Child Welfare Challenge: Policy, Practice, and Research (Second Edition)**

Norman A. Polansky, **Integrated Ego Psychology**

John R. Schuerman, Tina L. Rzepnicki, and Julia H. Littell, **Putting Families First: An Experience in Family Preservation**

Madeleine R. Stoner, **The Civil Rights of Homeless People: Law, Social Policy, and Social Work Practice**

Albert E. Trieschman, James K. Whittaker, and Larry K. Brendtro, **The Other 23 Hours: Child-Care Work with Emotionally Disturbed Children in a Therapeutic Milieu**

Harry H. Vorrath and Larry K. Brendtro, **Positive Peer Culture (Second Edition)**

Betsy S. Vourlekis and Roberta R. Greene (eds.), **Social Work Case Management**

James K. Whittaker and Associates, **Reaching High-Risk Families: Intensive Family Preservation in Human Services**

Family Group Conferencing

New Directions
in Community-Centered Child
and Family Practice

EDITORS

Gale Burford · Joe Hudson

ALDINE DE GRUYTER
New York

About the Authors

Gale Burford
Professor and Director, Department of Social Work,
University of Vermont.

Joe Hudson
Professor in the Faculty of Social Work, University of Calgary.

Aldine de Gruyter
A division of Walter de Gruyter, Inc.
200 Saw Mill River Road
Hawthorne, New York 10532

This publication is printed on acid-free paper CCC

Library of Congress Cataloging-in-Publication Data

Family group conferencing : new directions in community-centered child and
family practice / editors, Gale Burford and Joe Hudson.
    p. cm.
    Includes bibliographical references and index.
    ISBN 0-202-36121-7 (cloth : alk. paper)—ISBN 0-202-36122-5 (pbk. :alk.
paper)
    1. Family social work. 2. Social work with children. 3. Child welfare. 4.
Family counseling. 5. Family—Decision making. 6. Social networks. I. Burford, Gale. II. Hudson, Joe.

HV697.f3635 2000
362.82—dc21

                                       00-038041

Manufactured in the United States of America
10 9 8 7 6 5 4 3 2 1

Gale and Joe dedicate this book to
Gale's sister Mary Jane
and her children
Jessi, Zeke, and Morning Star

Contents

SECTION III

INTRODUCTION: COMPARATIVE PRACTICES

SECTION IV

INTRODUCTION: EVALUATING FAMILY GROUP CONFERENCES

Foreword

Contemporary North American child welfare exists in a global context. Concerns about the prevention of child maltreatment, "permanency planning," "risk assessment" in child protection, and "family support" in its numerous forms, increasingly define what has become a common agenda for policymakers, senior administrators, researchers, and practitioners in most industrialized countries. The recent exponential growth of technology means that service innovations once considered "local" now find their way rather rapidly into what has become an international discourse on innovative practice. Thus, "patch" programs of geographically based integrative services from the United Kingdom are "imported" to the United States at the same time as "family preservation" strategies are "exported" to a wide range of venues from western Europe to Australia. No doubt each of these "transplants" will be altered by their new host cultures sufficiently to allow for their "rediscovery" after a decent interval has passed.

Whether the resultant services will be simply "old wine in new bottles," or improvements on the original innovation, remains to be seen. Critical perspectives are much needed both to set the cultural/historical context for looking at new and promising ideas in services, as well as to appreciate the incremental enhancements they have acquired. Key questions for planners and practitioners include:

- What was the specific cultural context within which the service innovation arose and what are the cultural requisites that sustain it at present in its culture of origin?

- What modifications will likely need to be made if the innovation is to be adopted in another country or culture?

- What is the valuative and empirical-evidential base for the innovation, and what questions should inform the next generation of studies on its efficacy?

- What are the points of potential conflict and complimentarity between the service innovation and the existing service continuum?

- What will likely be the key issues in implementation, and what "network of champions" will be there to sustain the innovation during the critical phase of its introduction?

- By what outcome measure(s) will the innovation be adjudged a success?

These and related questions are particularly germane for the subject of this present volume, Family Group Conferencing. Since its origins in the Maori culture in New Zealand, Family Group Conferencing in one form or another has attracted widespread attention in North America, western Europe, and Australia both as a "front end" (preventive) service, and also as a culturally sensitive intervention for children, youth, and families already deeply enmeshed in the service system. Among its features of interest are its blending of lay and professional helping, its focus on family "empowerment," its cultural relevance, and its creative use of the group process. Contributors to the Burford and Hudson volume offer a rich menu of topics that, taken together, illuminate the landscape where Family Group Conferencing originated in addition to providing a snapshot of its potential applications.

A careful reading of Burford and Hudson will yield in ample measure a perspective on what could perhaps be called the most intriguing child welfare innovation to arise in the last quarter century. As seasoned researchers and program developers they have chosen their contributors wisely, and the resultant volume is perhaps the most comprehensive statement on Family Group Conferencing to appear in the international literature of social work and child welfare. It will serve as a valuable sourcebook for practitioners, planners, and students of child welfare. The authors offer a rich and diverse array of critical perspectives that will aid immensely in understanding the potential strengths and limitations of this intriguing innovation. The authors strive to balance in their various selections aspects of policy, practice, and research perspectives. All who work with, plan services for, or conduct research on services for children and families will find something of substance in this volume. It is particularly timely for the U.S. context where critics from differing philosophical perspectives are increasing their calls for a total overhaul of the child welfare system. This richly detailed and provocative volume by Burford and Hudson and their colleagues provides both a stimulus and a catalyst to this debate.

James K. Whittaker
The University of Washington

Acknowledgments

We are indebted to the chapter authors and thank them for the hard work, cooperation, and tolerance demonstrated in working with us to meet deadlines. We are also very thankful to Dean Gayla Rogers of the Faculty of Social Work, University of Calgary. Dr. Rogers supported this project by making available her administrative staff person, Elsie Johnson. We owe Elsie many thanks for skillfully and quickly preparing the final manuscript, keeping track of communications with authors around the world, and making innumerable edit changes. She is a gem.

At the University of Vermont, Department of Social Work, office staff assisted in addition to their regular work. Susan Haggerty, Ann Pond, and Dianne Pratt moved chapters, release forms, and author's biographies literally around the world and particularly Dianne helped chase down final hour details from authors.

Gale thanks his friend and colleague, Leon Fulcher, for introducing him to New Zealand and family group conferencing. Daughter Jaime made very helpful editorial suggestions about the Introduction. Gale's wife Kathy did a wide range of behind-the-scenes organizational tricks including getting a new computer set up in St. John's, Newfoundland, so the work could continue over Christmas holiday period 1999.

Finally, we thank those at Aldine de Gruyter and in particular Mai Shaikhanuar-Cota for timely and substantive assistance in bringing the book to print.

Contributors

Paul Adams Professor and Associate Dean, Mandel School of Applied Social Sciences, Case Western Reserve University

Paul Ban Independent social worker, Melbourne, Australia.

Gordon Bazemore Professor, Department of Criminal Justice; Director, Community Justice Institute, Florida Atlantic University

Jennifer L. Boland Research Consultant, Casey Family Services, Vermont

John Braithwaite Professor and Head of the Law Program, Research School of Social Sciences, Australian National University

John D. Burchard Professor, Department of Psychology, University of Vermont

Sara N. Burchard Associate Professor, Department of Psychology, University of Vermont

Gale Burford Professor and Director, Department of Social Work, University of Vermont

Judy Cashmore Honorary Research Associate, Social Policy Research Centre, University of New South Wales

Cynthia M. Collea Social Worker, Casey Family Services, Vermont

David S. Crampton Program Evaluator, Kent County Evaluation Project, University of Michigan School of Social Work

Gill Crow   Consultant Clinical Psychologist, Community
                                 Health Sheffield, and Research Fellow,
                                 University of Sheffield

Linda Crozier   Children Services Trainer, Ulster Community
                                and Hospitals Trust, Family Resource Centre,
                                James Street, Newtownards, Northern Ireland

Judith Daly   Casey Family Services, Vermont

Mike Doolan   Chief Social Worker, Department of Child Youth
                                and Family, Wellington, New Zealand

Don Fuchs   Dean, Faculty of Social Work, University
                                of Manitoba

Nathaniel Green, Sr.   Pastor, Christ Unity Baptist Church, Modesto,
                                California; Coordinator, Family Group
                                Conference of West Modesto King Kennedy
                                Neighborhood Collaborative

Ruth H. Hale   Social Worker, Casey Family Services, Vermont

Thomas E. Hill   Team Leader, Casey Family Services, Vermont

Joe Hudson   Professor, Faculty of Social Work, University
                                of Calgary

Wendy Lewis Jackson   Program Director, Children and Family Services,
                                The Grand Rapids Foundation

Susan P. Kemp   Associate Professor, School of Social Work,
                                University of Washington

Ted Keys   Family-based Services Program Coordinator,
                                Oregon Department of Human Services, State
                                Office for Services to Children and Families,
                                Portland

Patricia Kiely   Manager, Burnside Family Work Program;
                                Registered Psychologist; Coordinator, Family
                                Decision Making Project, Sydney, Australia

Teri Kook   Chief of Child Welfare Services, Stanislaus
                            County Community Services Agenc

Catherine Love   Lecturer, counseling programs, Massey
                            University, Palmerston North; researcher, trainer,
                            and family therapist, the Family Centre,
                            Wellington, New Zealand

Anthony N. Maluccio   Professor, School of Social Work, Boston
                            College.

Peter Marsh   Professor, Child and Family Welfare, University
                            of Sheffield

John M. McDonald   Director, Transformative Justice Australia

Lisa Merkel-Holguin   Manager, National Center on Family Group
                            Decision Making, Children's Division of the
                            American Humane Association

David B. Moore   Director, Transformative Justice Australia

Paul Nixon   Commissioning Officer-Family Group
                            Conferences, Hampshire County Council Social
                            Services Department, Winchester, Hampshire,
                            England

Joan Pennell   Professor and Director, Social Work Program,
                            North Carolina State University

Pam Phillips   Manager Operational Policy, Department of
                            Child, Youth and Family, Wellington, New
                            Zealand

Kay M. Pranis   Restorative Justice Planner, Minnesota
                            Department of Corrections

Anna M. Rockhill   Research Analyst, Child Welfare Partnership,
                            Portland State University; Chief Investigator of an
                            exploratory study of decision-making dynamics
                            within Family Unity Meetings, Portland, Oregon

Rupert Ross   Assistant Crown Attorney, Kenora, Ontario

Jackie Sieppert   Associate Professor, Faculty of Social Work,
                                   University of Calgary

Paul Sivak   Child Welfare Training Project,
                                   Coordinator/Lecturer, California State University

Jeanne B. Stinchcomb   Associate Professor and Coordinator, Master of
                                   Justice Policy and Management Program,
                                   Department of Criminology and Criminal Justice,
                                   Florida Atlantic University

Barry Stuart   Chief Judge, Territorial Court of Yukon

Knut Sundell   Research Director, Bureau for Research and
                                   Development, Stockholm Social Services
                                   Administration

Elizabeth M. Tracy   Associate Professor, Mandel School of Applied
                                   Social Sciences, Case Western Reserve University

Yvonne A. Unrau   Assistant Professor, Department of Social Work,
                                   Illinois State University

William M. Vesneski   Evaluation Consultant, Npower/Innovation
                                   Network, Inc.

Ted Wachtel   President, Community Service Foundation,
                                   Bethlehem, Pennsylvania

Charles Waldegrave   Psychologist, family therapist, Anglican priest,
                                   social policy analyst, researcher, and Pakeha
                                   (European) Coordinator of the Family Centre in
                                   Wellington, New Zealand

Marie Overby Weil   Professor, University of North Carolina,
                                   Chapel Hill

James K. Whittaker   Professor of Social Work, University
                                   of Washington

General Introduction: Family Group Conference Programming

GALE BURFORD and JOE HUDSON

This book presents current information on family group conferences (FGCs) and related child welfare practices. The chapters are organized in four parts according to major themes addressed. Part I deals with the origins of conferencing and major set of value assumptions underlying practice. Part II presents the principles of conferencing, relating these to social work theory, child welfare practice, and related programming efforts, including wraparound, patch, circles, and working with social support networks. Chapters in Part III present information on current national and state conferencing practices. Included are chapters on such countries as Sweden, New Zealand, Australia, England and Wales, the United States, Northern Ireland, as well as the states of Oregon, North Carolina, and California. Part IV presents an approach for evaluating family group conference programs, along with case studies of evaluation practice.

Conferencing and the Coordinator

The core idea of a family group conference in child welfare is a meeting of all family members, child protection officials, and other persons involved with the family to plan for the care and protection of children seen to be at risk of abuse and neglect. Family group conferences amount to a partnership arrangement between the state, represented by child protection officials; the family; and members of the community, such as resource and support persons; with each party expected to play an important role in planning and providing services necessary for the well-being of children. A family group conference coordinator plays the critical role of helping identify persons to be invited to the conference, preparing them for the conference, bringing them together, making sure the conference runs well through its different stages, monitoring the implementation of conference plans, and reconvening conferences as necessary.

A key task of the coordinator is to help ensure that conferences truly reflect a partnership between state officials and family members, with responsibility shared, respect demonstrated, full information disclosed, negotiations conducted in good faith, and decisions jointly arrived at. Family group conferences should not be seen as a way of state officials abdicating their child protection responsibilities. While noting the many nuances and difficulties involved in working out true conference partnerships, the chapter authors assume that a balance can be struck between the interests of child protection and family support. This means using family group conferences to support families in caring for their children, as well as building stronger links between the family and children when out-of-home care is necessary.

A central premise of family group conferences is that families with children seen to be in need of care and protection do better when decisions affecting them have been arrived at by respecting the integrity of the family unit, focusing on strengthening family and community supports, and creating opportunities for parents and other adults, including extended family members, to feel responsible for their children. Family members should have an active voice in matters affecting them. This elementary notion is all too often lost sight of in child protection work, yet it is the core of good social work practice. Unless families have voice, the safety and well-being of their children will likely be jeopardized and their capacity diminished for dealing with problems of abuse and neglect. Characteristics of family group conferencing are the same democratic processes that create and sustain healthy communities. Building from this perspective, this book focuses on family group conferencing within a context of services and supports for children and families situated in communities. Included in the services and supports covered in this book are social networking, wraparound services, patch programming, and circle processes.

A strong theme running through these chapters is the great deal of effort involved in family group conferences for all participants. Properly run conferences are a far cry from a dispassionate family polling process in which views are obtained on what might be done about the children. Conferences involve face-to-face interactions, honest communications about what has happened to the children, and struggles to come up with ways of addressing the safety concerns identified. Conferences widen the circle of people who know what was done in the family, putting responsibility on family members to prepare a safety plan that can then be presented, discussed, modified as necessary, and supported by child protection officials.

Evidence and Expectations

A growing body of evidence attests to a high level of interest in family group conferences in a number of countries. The approach has attracted keen interest from policymakers, researchers, and practitioners. A substantial number of programs have been implemented and an accumulating body of evaluation evidence has been compiled to show that children can be kept safe and a culture of cooperation fostered between families and state child protection officials. Studies carried out on programs in Australia, Canada, England, New Zealand, Sweden, and the United States show considerable consistency in findings. Many are reported in the chapters of this book. Overall, the research reports show that:

- Considerable effort is required to adequately prepare family members and professionals for conferences, but having done this work, conferencing can be carried out safely without violence to participants.
- When offered the opportunity, families, including extended family members and significant persons involved with the families, do participate in family group conferences.
- Families are able to make decisions and come up with plans for the care and protection of their children.
- Family plans are most often accepted by child protection officials including aspects of the plan that address measures for keeping the children safe.
- A large proportion of family group conference plans involve the participation of extended family members who assume responsibilities for carrying out planned activities.
- A high proportion of plans for children who require placement apart from their parents or from the people who have been abusing them recommend placement within the extended family.
- Family members report satisfaction with their influence in family group conference decision-making.
- Family members and professionals report satisfaction with the fairness of their family group conferences.
- Child protection workers who participate in conferences see service coordination as a major benefit of family group conferences.

While there is ample evidence available on conferencing practices in various countries, as with any practice innovation, there is a danger of setting grandiose expectations that will inevitably fall short of what can feasibly be delivered. Several points need to be considered about what can reasonably be expected from family group conferences. These are addressed in more detail in the chapters that follow. A critical point concerns the appropriate comparison to be used in assessing conferencing practice. Most reasonably this would be the actual performance of the current child protection system and the extent to which families are satisfied with the services provided, feel they have been treated fairly and respectfully, and have had adequate opportunities to express their views, participate in decision-making, and have their children safely provided for. Current practice is the benchmark against which family group conference programs should be compared, not some ideal standard.

Another point lending some caution to excessive expectations for conference practices is the plausibility of expecting a single family group conference to bring about dramatic, positive change in family functioning. Families with children coming to the attention of child protection authorities commonly have long-standing and serious problems in living. To expect these problems to dissipate following a family group conference is unrealistic, and holding such a view amounts to setting up conferencing practices for failure. What may be more realistic, and also in line

with good child protection practice, is to plan and hold a series of regularly scheduled family group conferences running throughout the active life of the family's
involvement with child protection authorities. In this way, for those families requiring follow-up conferences, the practice can become institutionalized as an accepted way of doing child welfare work with an increased likelihood of substantive change occurring. Additionally, families will more likely feel supported and
assisted in the difficult work of protecting and caring for their children. Routiniz-
ing conferences in this way fits with case review requirements of many child protection authorities. Therefore major procedural changes would not be so much required as changes in the way procedures are carried out to reflect principles of
family group conferences.

Necessary conditions for successful family group conference programs are
identified in these chapters. An obvious, but often ignored condition is that adequate human and financial resources are available, accessible, and used. Chapters
in Parts II and III, describing conferencing principles and implementation, deal
with this point, and it is clear that unless necessary resources are marshaled to plan,
hold, and follow up conferences, the aims of family group conferences are not
likely to be achieved.

Trained coordinators are a critical resource required for successful conferences
and they need sufficient time to adequately prepare participants about the purpose
of the conference and the process to be followed. Conferences take time to plan,
hold, follow up, and monitor plan completion, and the coordinator's job is labor
intensive. Sufficient time must be available to concentrate on the many and varied tasks involved. Not least of these is getting and maintaining the support and
participation of another important conference resource, child protection officials.
These officials play important roles in referring families to conferences, attending
and participating in them, giving clear assessment information to the families, as
needed, and supporting and assisting families to obtain necessary services and supports to complete plans for the care and protection of their children.

The coordinator's job is to facilitate a process. The plan coming out of a conference is best seen as a tool enabling the family to achieve care and protection
goals. Conference plans can and should be changed in light of different circumstances and the family group conference reconvened to deal with new situations.
This means that FGC plans are monitored and followed up. In addition to technical knowledge about child protection, coordinators must believe in the importance
of collaborative work, respect and have genuine affection for people, and be willing and able to serve as convener, group worker, community developer, as well as
scribe and gopher, attending to the many detailed arrangements necessary for holding family group conferences.

Another condition for successful conference programs noted in these chapters
is that families feel respectfully involved, have voice in decisions affecting them,
and have a sense of control over their destinies. Families must have a sense of ownership of the plan coming out of a family group conference, and private family time

at the conference is important for achieving this. A related condition for successful conferences is that professionals recognize that their work is worthwhile only when it is carried out in a collaborative manner with families. This means seeing conferences as places where all parties participate as equals and where different views are considered, even when they conflict. All parties must feel free to express their views openly and not withhold information germane to the conference.

Another condition noted in these chapters is that conferences must facilitate linkages between family members, child welfare agencies and officials, and community members, agencies, and associations. Families implicated in child protection systems likely lack necessary resources, and connections need to be made to persons both within and outside the extended family who can assist in bringing services and supports to bear on family needs. In this way, conferences serve as community connectors, brokering between and within extended families to identify and obtain necessary services and supports.

ORIGINS AND CONTEXT FOR FAMILY GROUP CONFERENCES

Family group conferences made their first legislated appearance with the implementation in 1989 of New Zealand's Children, Young Persons, and Their Families Act. International interest in the New Zealand legislation can be traced to the unprecedented acknowledgment by that government that their practices toward children and families were not culturally appropriate. Family group conferences were proposed as part of the solution. Indigenous groups in other parts of the world who had voiced similar sentiments to those of the New Zealand Maori took notice: state interventions into matters having to do with children and young people need to be understood and developed within a context of family, community, and culture. This view fit with the aspirations of indigenous groups in other parts of the world who had been working to gain recognition for their cultural practices. Their desire to have greater influence over matters of child and family welfare, education, justice, language, and land use to protect their cultures was seen to be represented by the New Zealand legislation.

News that family group conferences were also to be used with majority culture families in New Zealand also raised considerable attention within and outside the country. Many noted that the approach was well grounded in commitments to social justice, human rights, and an orientation to helping people draw on their own strengths and have voice in decisions affecting them. Involving people in constructing solutions that fit for their families, social networks, and communities was seen to help develop their capacities. These ideas resonated with community-minded social workers who long supported the idea that lasting solutions to problems are ones that grow out of, or can fit with, the knowledge, experiences, and desires of the people most affected. Here in the New Zealand model was an example of a policy that sought to bring officials mandated to protect children and young people together with the extended family to work toward common goals. In youth corrections, family group conferences brought justice professionals, offenders and their families, and victims together to plan for solutions that held offenders accountable, while also setting things right with victims and communities. The New Zealand family group conference model dealt with offenses not simply as acts between the offender and state, but also saw injuries to the victims and a rupture to the families and communities as essential considerations in restoring a balance. In this approach, the role of law and the processes of social justice were seen to hold promise for a reasonable balance within a democratic society.

Family group conferences have appeared at a time when relations between the state and citizens, as well as between professionals and the people served, are continuing to evolve through a crucial stage of reexamination. A renaissance of interest is developing in strengthening communities, rebuilding neighborhoods, involving families in decision-making, seeking a wider variety of approaches to solving disputes, and preempting the escalation of problems through preventive services. Expressions of these interests are apparent in government efforts at restructuring services in health, education, social welfare, and justice, as well as in developments reflecting a wide range of communitarian concerns. These include self-help, mentoring, and mutual aid, conflict resolution and transformation, community policing, and partnership building in which people take more active roles in developing the capacities of localities and communities.

THEMES FOR THE BOOK

There were many challenges in compiling this book. In setting a context for this wide-ranging collection of chapters, a number of themes were identified and used in selecting authors and topics, leaving open opportunities to identify others as the work progressed. With growing interest in family group conference programming and implementation experience in different countries, this book needed to include an international slate of authors. This introduces variation in the legal, cultural, and ethnic contexts in which the model's conceptualization, practice, and evaluation are occurring. The ideas and needs driving interest in FGCs and related practices are complex and of considerable magnitude. They involve redrawing the boundaries between the formal and informal helping systems, and necessitate gaining understanding in a wider construction of social, legal, and cultural context than has historically been the case with the use of more individualized, expert-dependent models of assessment and intervention. As will be seen from the description of implementation experiences, contextual, relational, or ecological understandings underpin everything when the focus is shifted to partnerships between formal and informal helpers. The emergence of FGCs is considered as part of widespread efforts towards civic renewal and the selection of authors and themes should reflect this.

Substantive Theory in Social Work and the Social Sciences

Authors have also been included with a view to linking FGCs with other substantive theory, practice and research findings in social work, as well as authors experienced with community-centered models of child and family practice. As is often the case, there is a sense that practice has outrun the development of relevant theory. An aim of this book is to link rapidly growing practice of FGC with like-minded theories of intervention, particularly those that locate work with children and families in a community context.

A central theme of this book is the need to link the protection of children with the enhancement of family and community well-being. This is not easy at the best of times but the pressure of the media spotlight and the horrible examples of harm done to children at the hands of both birth parents and substitute caretakers has all too often meant social workers becoming targets of recrimination. Widespread dissatisfaction with the child protection system is obvious. Evidence suggests that these systems are overwhelmed with the number of children referred, and the safety and well-being of children compromised. The practice of social work in many child protection systems has been reduced to a highly proceduralized, adversarial, and even antagonistic process that does not serve the kind of decision-making required in addressing the highly complex situations confronting workers. People working at all levels in the child protection system are so caught up in protecting themselves that they are resistant to change. A bunker type of philosophy of "us against them" all too often prevails. Child protection workers are criticized for the way they make decisions, the way they carry out investigations, and the type and duration of services they offer to children and families. Much child protection practice has little resemblance to the research literature on "what works."

No lack of criticism has been slung at anyone trying to change the situation. Major efforts to test approaches aimed at keeping families from breaking up have been castigated for further placing children in harm's way, despite research demonstrating that many children benefit from efforts to keep families together. Other efforts to slow drift in foster care, and seek earlier and permanent placements for children have met similar attack, despite supporting evidence. The debates affecting child protection have become so vitriolic as to polarize the very people who should be working together to ensure that quality services of various types are available to children and families, including early intervention and prevention programs, family preservation and reunification, quality out-of-home and substitute care, adoption, and treatment services. We believe that FGCs have the potential to bring relevant partners to the table and to do so in a way that represents sound, theoretically driven, quality practice that advances social justice and the exercise of human rights.

The Building Blocks of Participatory Democracy

Chapter authors were also invited to participate when they were able to locate the origin and development of family group conferences in a value-based commitment to human rights, social justice, and culturally competent practice. This purpose for the book grew out of an interest in the ways FGCs are being viewed, in some circles, as part of a larger movement toward civic renewal, particularly as expressed by proponents of restorative justice.

Proponents seem to hold the view that the development of local and meaningful structures in which citizenship can be meaningfully exercised has not kept pace with the growth of government and its displacement of responsibilities once held by families and local communities. The effect has all too often meant that governments have eroded citizenship. Individuals feel alienated from having a say. This is experienced as a disconnection between people's expectations of participation and what actually happens to them. Going to court to settle a dispute is an example. Similarly, schools have become so large and impersonal that many students report feeling alienated. Functions once held by the family and communities that gave all individuals social as well as economic value have been taken over by the state. In this view, children in postindustrial society have lost economic value to families to such an extent that they are relegated to the role of consumers: having lost productive roles in families, children are deprived access to avenues of once-important learning for roles as citizens. Also consistent with this view is the notion that we have become a culture dependent on experts. It is a common dissatisfaction in postindustrial society that people feel alienation from important decision processes and roles that validate worth, including economic roles, which make a vital contribution to identity in small groups, communities, and social networks. The solution is to find ways to build cooperative social relations that promote democratic principles including reciprocity and trust.

FGCs are thought by some to be a good example of a structure that interfaces between the mandated rule of law and the social justice of families and communities. At the same time, proponents of the use of FGCs, like proponents of restorative justice, have continued to work on the outskirts of mainstream practices. Few child welfare systems have "mainstreamed" family group conferences into systemwide practice. We were interested in finding authors who could discuss the dilemmas that emerge in implementing programs and the extent to which bureaucratic processes and the social justice aspects of conferencing are compatible. For the purposes of this book, we were interested in identifying authors knowledgeable about program sponsorships and what roles will be found for practitioners and advocates of FGCs and whether these will be new or familiar ones like "group worker" or "community development worker" and how these practices will fare when they are developed through government supported, quasi-private, or nongovernmental partnerships.

Another major consideration in identifying chapter authors was based on our commitment to multiple-methods, multiple-indicators; evaluation and research including those with an empirical orientation. We believe that no single approach can shed light on the complex questions that need to be addressed in the area of child protection. Hence, while evaluation strategies must be sensitive to process, context and the subjective experiences of the participants, they must also take into account the changing evidential basis demanded to justify programs. This is in line with growing demands for holding human service systems more accountable and stresses the inclusion of empirically derived measures of program integrity, progress, and outcomes to demonstrate the extent to which programs are carrying out their public charge.

Section I   Introduction: Origins and Philosophical Framework

JOE HUDSON and GALE BURFORD

Chapters in this section describe the origins of conferencing and circles, along with the broad set of assumptions underlying their practice. Chapter 1 by Rupert Ross describes the indigenous origins of conferencing practices in North America. Rupert Ross is well-known for his writings on indigenous ways of settling conflicts and provides a sensitive account of his learnings about the worldview of indigenous cultures. His respect for indigenous ways of knowing is particularly impressive given his professional training and experience as a prosecuting attorney in the formal legal system. Chapter 2 by Catherine Love complements the first chapter by outlining elements of traditional Maori culture, providing an overview of Maori involvement with state child protection and justice systems, and examining the history and operation of family group conferencing in New Zealand. Catherine Love traces the origins of contemporary family group conferences in Maori culture, contrasting these practices with Western approaches for dealing with children and families. Key issues in the operation of contemporary New Zealand conferencing practices are identified; many of these are addressed in subsequent chapters.

Chapter 3 by John Braithwaite traces the recent development of restorative practices from roots in indigenous cultures, through more contemporary dispute resolution and mediation processes. Key conferencing lessons learned from indigenous practices are discussed and the argument is made for extending restorative practices to everyday life in families, work places, and peer groups, with the aim of rebuilding democracy. This is what Braithwaite calls a "civic republican program," one in which citizens actively participate and take responsibility for themselves, their families, and their communities. In Chapter 4, Kay Pranis picks up on themes addressed by Braithwaite, particularly in respect to the potential of conferences and circles to build and strengthen healthy communities by citizens taking responsibility. Kay Pranis writes from her long experience working with communities to design and implement conferencing and circle processes in both child welfare and justice systems. An important point raised is that conferencing has the potential to strengthen communities if the values underlying the practices are consistent with caring and respect for all participants. Unless conferencing practices demonstrate such values, family group conferences and circles can become the latest in a long line of quick-fix methods to be tried, to fail, and to be subsequently rejected. The important lesson about restorative practices and the use of conferences and circles is not so much the method used, as the spirit in which the practices are carried out. Values are more basic than technique or method.

Chapter 5, the final chapter in this part, by David Moore and John McDonald, deals with conferencing processes, the nature of programs used to deliver these processes, and basic practice principles. Moore and McDonald emphasize, like Pranis and Braithwaite, that conferencing processes are fundamental to building healthy democratic communities and see these as amounting to conflict resolution processes. Like Braithwaite and Pranis, they argue that democracy is undermined by dependence on professional classes for analyzing and solving community problems. Conferencing is seen as offering the potential to move responsibility and authority back to community members and demonstrate democracy in action, with people having a voice in decisions affecting their lives. Moore and McDonald elaborate on this theme in discussing central questions about conferencing, before turning to principles underlying conflict transforming processes. A number of major themes are addressed in these chapters and can be touched upon here.

Conferencing as a Process for Conflict Resolution

All chapters underscore the view that conferencing and circles are ways of resolving conflict or, in Moore and McDonald's terms, transforming conflicts. Family group conferences and circles amount to programs for delivering the processes. As Ross notes, the focus in conferences is on relationships between people, and the aim is one of enhancing and developing positive relationships—wider, stronger, and more positive links between people in families and communities. Emphasizing mutual responsibility, the aim of conferencing processes is to change wrong relationships based on power, fear, anger, and control. Ross and Love describe indigenous ways of seeing and knowing as amounting to making connections between all forms of life. Moore and McDonald use the metaphor of ecology, contrasting it with a metaphor of individual pathology. Kay Pranis notes that unless we address the web of relationships in which people are embedded, it is futile to try and change individuals. Family conflicts and failures of responsibility lead to children going to state care and the response should be one of building relationships, emphasizing mutual responsibility, promoting collaboration between formal and informal resources in the family, community, and state. Conferencing and circles are seen as important ways of empowering people, allowing them to take active responsibility for resolving and transforming conflicts.

Functions of Conferencing

Most generally, these chapters see circles and conferences as vehicles for teaching people how to be democratic citizens. Pranis and Braithwaite describe how a conferencing process can clearly articulate and reinforce norms and expectations, along with a sense of mutual responsibility. In contrast, state practices controlled by professionals all too often teach passive responses. The aim of conferencing processes is one of empowering people to take active responsibility for themselves, their family, and community.

Conferencing Values

These chapters emphasize a common set of values underlying conference and circle processes. Braithwaite emphasizes values of democratic deliberation; mutual respect and caring; nondomination with space for all to have a say and take responsibilities. In a similar vein, Moore and McDonald emphasize such rules of participatory democracy as fair rules, fair play, and fair outcomes; participation, deliberation, equity, and nontyranny. The role of the conferencing coordinator is one of abiding by these values and, according to Moore and McDonald, demonstrating characteristics of transparency and openness, clarity of communication in the language of the participants, and respect for all participants. While emphasizing ways in which conferencing processes can strengthen families and communities, all chapters make the point that conferencing can also weaken families and communities, depending on the manner and extent to which caring and respect are demonstrated. This can occur in cases when conferencing programs emphasize what Moore and McDonald call "agency-specific procedures" at the expense of values of participatory democracy. The result of such a process, as Pranis notes, can simply amount to new ways of doing old things that have effects of disconnecting, disempowering, and labeling people.

Role of State Agencies

These authors agree on the role of state professionals as essentially one of safeguarding the conferencing process in ways true to democratic principles, helping the parties come together to work on themselves and each other, and guiding the parties into using the conferencing process to change relationships. State officials are seen as contributing to conferences and circles by facilitating a process so the parties become authors of their own recovery. As Catherine Love stresses, this does not mean disempowering conference participants by officials making decisions about where and when the conference will take place, who will be invited to attend, and the decisions to be made.

Policy and Practice Issues

Several issues related to conferencing policy and practice are dealt with in these chapters and many of them are addressed in more detail in later sections. One practice issue addressed is the extent conferences and circles are appropriate ways of dealing with particular categories of problems. Braithwaite and Moore and McDonald hold the view that conferencing as a way of communicating can be expanded to a variety of problems affecting people, including homelessness, school failure, and family violence. Given their views on conferencing as a way to deal with conflict between people, they see the potential of conferencing and circles serving a diverse range of programs and settings. To achieve this, Braithwaite wants to institutionalize conferencing as a way of revitalizing the civic republic, so that affected citizens have opportunities to participate in settling their disputes, including spouse abuse. Speaking to the concerns of feminists, the point is made that conferencing and circle processes address power imbalances by having support people stand in with the affected parties. This issue is addressed in the second section, by Joan Pennell and Gale Burford in their discussion of the Newfoundland and Labrador family violence conferencing project.

While acknowledging the important place of culture, Moore and McDonald take argument with the notion that conferencing applies uniquely to people of indigenous heritage. Such a view is seen by them as ahistorical and divisive, setting up a hierarchy of moral authority, and likely to result in the marginalization of conferencing programs. A related issue addressed in these chapters is the possibility of conferencing being used by the majority to dominate, diminish rights and protections, and lead to the use of harsh practices. Several arguments are made in response. Moore and McDonald, for example, argue that if the conferencing focus is on the conflict between people, anger is more likely to be addressed and transformed, not ignored and displaced. Braithwaite agrees, while cautioning that just as Western justice systems have much to learn from indigenous traditions, so indigenous practices have something to learn from contemporary legal systems. There is an important place for legal safeguards.

Another issue touched on concerns the location of conferencing coordinators and whether they should be institutionalized in government agencies staffed by professionals. These authors generally argue against such a practice. Several chapters in Part II deal in greater detail with this issue, pointing to the advantages and limitations of different approaches for organizing conferencing programs.

1 Searching for the Roots of Conferencing

RUPERT ROSS

I remember listening to a Cree grandmother from Saskatchewan passing some of her teachings on to a group of aboriginal youngsters. At one point she startled everyone by slapping her thigh and exclaiming, "You know, I think I finally figured out what it means to live a good life." Her words caught me by surprise, because I'd seldom heard Elders tell anyone what to think, say, or do.

"Maybe," she told us, "you know you're living a good life when you get to my age, and you look back maybe five years or so, and you find yourself saying 'Boy, I sure didn't know too much . . . way back then!'"

I enjoy the picture of life she gave me, the sense that I will always be given deeper questions as I stumble along. Her teaching suggested something else as well: If I acknowledge that every five years or so I'll probably change my advice to myself, why would I try to give anyone else advice along the way? Instead, all I can do is tell my stories as best I can. If others happen to find them useful in some way, within *their* unique experience of life, well, great.

So that's the spirit in which I'll try to write.

Next, a couple of confessions. First, I am not aboriginal, and I cannot see the world through well-educated aboriginal eyes. I can only share my experience of watching aboriginal people approach issues from unique, often startling, perspectives. It must also be said that the very way I analyze and describe them will be shaped by the fact that the foundations of my thought and language are Western, not aboriginal. So be wary!

Second, the conferencing and healing processes I have observed coming from aboriginal people do not seem to be context-restricted. Instead, they are considered effective ways to respond to *all* the social problems that confront us. In fact, the Western insistence that everything be subdivided into separate criminal, civil, family, child welfare, and other specialties is sometimes seen as part of the problem!

My contribution does not therefore involve describing how conferencing works in any particular context. Instead, I want to describe the odd way I was introduced to these processes, and how that introduction made it impossible for me to see them simply as *techniques*. Instead, they came to me as necessary manifestations of a fundamentally different way of looking at Creation, and at the place of human creatures within it. Family group conferencing was a gift from the aboriginal people of New Zealand, the Maori, and I was instantly struck by the degree to which their vision of the source of individual, family, and community problems paralleled that of the aboriginal peoples of Canada. I was also struck by the degree to which both groups had evolved similar strategies for dealing with them.

It is because I sense that these strategies derive their power from the world-views that shaped them that I am worried: if Western justice professionals don't understand what shaped them in the first place, we'll quickly bend them *out* of shape. If that happens, if we Westernize them, consciously or unconsciously, I suspect that their power will be substantially eroded.

It was a Mi'kmaw Elder on Canada's Atlantic Coast who sent me on this particular journey. I was just beginning a three-year, cross-Canada search for what aboriginal people described as their "healing" approach to justice, distinguishing it from the adversarial, punitive system of which I was a part. My plan was to head directly into aboriginal communities doing healing work, study their "techniques," and then report back to my superiors. She, however, seemed to be talking about a different approach. She kept emphasizing how much she had learned, in her own lifetime, listening to the Elders, the philosophers, and the medicine people, gaining a sense of how they approached Creation. She spoke about going into ceremony, watching to see what was considered worthy of celebration, what was understood to give human creatures the strength needed to live good lives. After a while, it came to me: she was afraid that I would never come to an understanding of aboriginal notions of justice unless I first gained some sense of aboriginal notions of the workings of Creation. If I didn't begin there, she hinted, I might never get beyond my own Western justice eyes.

I thank her. Without her guidance I would have missed the essence of everything I saw. With her guidance, I set out on the strangest journey of my life, constantly being given things that refused to "link up" in any patterned way.

I remember, for instance, being told that Western and aboriginal scientists might approach the study of a plant in very different ways. The Western scientist might focus most of her attention on understanding and naming all the parts and properties of the plant, figuring out its root, stem, and leaf patterns, how it took in water, sunlight, and nutrients, how it reproduced, its life expectancy, and so forth. The aboriginal scientist, by contrast, would likely focus most of her attention on understanding what role that plant played in the meadow. She would examine how it held soil when the rains came, what plants flourished close to it, what birds, animals, and insects were attracted to it, how it was useful to them, what kinds of conditions it needed to remain healthy enough to fulfill their roles, that sort of thing. It's not that the two scientists paid *no* attention to the concerns of the other, it's just that their emphasis was different. They "saw" the plant in a different way.

I had no idea how a teaching like that might relate to justice, but I couldn't shake the Mi'kmaw grandmother's encouragement. I built a special shelf in my memory, labeled it "Indian Puzzles," and stuffed that plant-in-the-meadow story up there, hoping that one day I might figure out the connection. Everywhere I went it was the same!

I was told that Western and aboriginal cultures hold opposite views about the importance of human creatures in Creation. The Bible put us right at the top of the heap, set on earth to rule all the fishes in the sea, and so forth. Aboriginal teachings, by contrast, present an opposite hierarchy. Mother Earth (with her life-blood, the waters) plays the most important role in Creation, for without the soil there would be no plant realm. Without the plants there would be no animal realm, and without soil, water, plants, and animals there would be no us. Within this "reverse hierarchy," human creatures are the least essential and the most dependent. No longer masters of Creation, we are its humble servants. It was not how I was used to seeing myself!

It got worse. I remember an Elder saying: "Your people seem to think that law comes from books. That's not the way my people understand it." He turned toward a window, pointed out to dense bush, and announced *"That's* where law comes from!" All I could think of was "Whoa! I know what kind of law is out there: The Law of the Jungle! Where we all live in dog-eat-dog anarchy, acting like *animals* toward each other! Isn't that exactly what man-made Law is designed to control?" I didn't say that, of course, because I'd often heard him giving his teachings, and he always spoke of values like respect, love, caring, sharing, and humility. How did he get those values from the bush? Which one of us was missing something, and why did I think it was me?

One more. At the opening of an aboriginal justice conference in the mountains of Alberta, a large shell was brought around, filled with smoldering sweetgrass. Each of us wafted that beautifully scented smoke over our heads, eyes, ears, mouths, chests, and thighs, asking for its assistance to think, see, hear, speak, and feel only in respectful ways during our time together. The discussion leader then started talking about language differences, explaining that aboriginal languages were not as much noun-centered as they were verb-centered, trying to capture not the thing-aspect of Creation but the pattern, flow, and function aspect. He held that shell in his hands and told us that in aboriginal languages it would be "called" differently at different times. It could be a sacred vessel at one calling, a vessel bringing candy at another, or a vessel receiving cigarette butts at another. It depended on its relationship to the speaker and to the occasion. To call it, as European languages did, by one name for all occasions was seen as a "poorer" way to speak of the world. Once again, I was being given the impression that Indian eyes saw a more fluid, transforming, and interconnecting reality when they surveyed Creation, but I wondered why we were being reminded of that at a justice conference!

Then, one beautiful August day, a very small event hit me in a very large way. I came across an Ojibway grandmother hitchhiking in northwestern Ontario. I gave her a lift and, knowing that a lot of the old people gathered blueberries to raise a little cash, asked her how the blueberry crop was that summer. She immediately replied "Oh, I was at the garbage dump last night, and there were SIXTEEN BEARS out there!" I knew immediately that was an answer to my question. Bears thrive on blueberries, and a failed blueberry crop causes hungry bears to converge on the nearest dumps in search of food. Conversely, a bumper crop means all the bears are way back in the blueberry patches sporting huge purple grins!

But it was the automatic way she answered that got to me. I could feel all the teachings I had jammed onto my Indian Puzzles shelf doing little two-steps around each other, like they were finally organizing around a theme. I had asked about one thing, but had received an answer that referred to a totally separate thing instead.

It started coming: things weren't separate to her at all, not the way they were to me. Instead, all things acted within complex webs of relationships. Whatever happened with one thing rippled out to touch and affect all other things. If you talked about one, you were talking about all. And any point of reference would do.

It moved a little further. To her, the real essence of Creation lay in what was going on *between* things. That's where her attention went, to all the relationships that bind things together so strongly that a question about blueberries gets an answer about bears!

As I chewed that over, other connections started jumping out. The plant-in-the-meadow teaching, for instance, where the well-educated aboriginal eye sees not the plant in isolation but the vast web of relationships connecting it with all the other things that make up the meadow. Go a little deeper and the meadow becomes less a collection of things than it is a complex of ever-modifying relationships. If, that is, the eye learns to focus between, rather than on.

Relationships. It was suddenly clear where the "reverse hierarchy" came from. If your "way-of-knowing" focuses on relationships, it will be "natural" to see that the relationships between human, animal, plant, and earth/water aspects of Creation are fundamentally relationships of *dependency,* with us at the bottom. Identically, if your "way-of-knowing" focuses on things and their properties, human creatures will "naturally" stand out as near the top, given our unique powers of communication, movement, toolmaking, and the like. And from that lofty vantage point it would only be "natural" for us to put the deaf, dumb, immobile, and stupid plant world right down at the bottom of the heap, just one small step above "dirt."

Relationships. The naming of the shell showed the same emphasis. It was the relationship between it, the person using it and the occasion of its use that shaped the way it would be called at any moment. Change any part of the dynamic and the naming changes with it. Aboriginal languages, I have been told, can enter with ease into the subatomic world, where transformation, force, and pattern—dynamic relationship!—are understood to be the essence of existence. I often hear aboriginal speakers complain that the noun-dominated English language doesn't let them capture "the poetry" in Creation.

Relationships. Looking between, among, and around, not at. When the Elder pointed out the window to the bush, it was not things he directed me toward, but relationships. What he saw, what his teachings helped him observe, was a totality defined primarily by healthy, sustaining, *symbiotic* relationships between all the things out there. While bears need fish need frogs need insects need algae need water needs sunlight, and so forth, they are not so much linear chains of dependency as they are interwoven mutualities of such complexity that no one can truly "know" what will happen if one element changes its contribution to—its relationship with the—mix. All we can say is that they are all necessary to each other, to us, and to the relationships that sustain us all together—or they wouldn't be there.

In the Elder's language, we are all sacred. And the fundamental law to be discerned from observing the symbiotic dynamism of the natural order is: *the law of respect*. Each makes essential, and essentially unique, contributions to the maintenance of a healthy whole. And every "contribution," whether positive or negative, touches all. Within this vision, matter is little more than the medium through which patterned forces manifest themselves. It is those patterned forces, however, which are the essence of Creation.

And how does all this relate to justice and child welfare?

A Cree grandmother once explained why she worried about the court's determination to cart abusive men off to jail. "I know you do this to protect the women and children," she said, "but to protect us in your way, you'd have to keep them there forever. Since you don't, could we try our way instead?" Unable to think of a comeback, I asked what she meant by "her way." Her teachings, she said, suggested that people who abuse others must have learned somewhere that relationships are things built on values like power, fear, anger, and control. That's how abused children can become abusive adults, because they remain in exactly the same kinds of power-based relations they grew up in. The only thing that changes is that *they* now have the power. Whenever they use it the same way on others, their own pain comes flooding back to them and a deep sense of shame gets added to the mix. Because that way of relating is all they know, however, they can't see a way out. A sense of desperation sets in as well, adding fuel to the fire. "It's our job," she said "to teach them about relationships based on good values instead, like respect and caring."

She then asked what kinds of relationships existed in our jails (I took it as a rhetorical question), and she worried that their men would come home with an even stronger experience of relationships based on power, fear, and anger. "So that's why we are concerned," she added, "because maybe your jail system makes it harder for us to teach better ways, not easier."

And there it was. Her eyes focused not on separated offenders and victims, but on the relationships that ensnared them. She didn't try to describe a particular man or woman, but the relationships that tied them together. She didn't try to put labels on anyone, but looked instead for what it was in the relationship that made both of them less than they otherwise might be. And the question she asked was not "How can we change him or her?" but "How can we change the relationships that keep them in such unhealthy patterns?"

Had I not been forced to struggle my way through plants and meadows, bears and blueberries, and a host of Indian Puzzles I haven't even mentioned, I doubt that I'd have heard what she was really talking about. She was talking about the *between* world she had been taught to look for, not the *thing* world I grew up in— and it makes a world of difference.

For instance, we believe that we can deal effectively with people strictly as individuals. The accused stands alone in the prisoner's box, whether at trial or at sentencing, and it is his or her behavior *as an individual* that occupies the spotlight. Conferencing proceeds on the understanding that it is everyone's "way-of-relating" with others that has the greatest impact on individual behavior. In aboriginal terms, discord means there are "disharmonies" in those ways of relating, disharmonies that must be investigated by all, understood by all, and reshaped with the contributions of all.

We also seem to believe that individuals can simply *choose* to alter their behavior. We threaten people with punishment because we believe that our threats will force them to make better choices. We also regularly ship troubled youngsters off to treatment facilities, hoping that a few more skills will enable them to make better choices. When they go right back to making "poor" choices within days of returning home, however, we scratch our heads and wonder: did they just get *poor* treatment, or not *enough* treatment—or is this just a truly *bad* kid? By contrast, the relational analysis begins with the proposition that in many cases the tide of dysfunctional relations swirling around individuals is simply too powerful to resist, no matter how skilled and determined the person might be. If progress is to be made, then all of those relationships must be brought into the circle so that everyone can see the need to make better choices *together*.

Then there is our determination to focus almost exclusively on acts. It is particular acts that must be carefully alleged, then proven in court "beyond a reasonable doubt." Those same acts then largely determine the court's response, because we believe that "the punishment must fit the crime." In aboriginal processes, those disruptive acts achieve significance primarily as signals of relational disharmonies, and it is those disharmonies that are quickly moved to center stage. Conferencing shows a similar thrust: once the act is acknowledged and its impact made clear, attention frequently turns toward locating and remedying the relational disharmonies that spawned it. People who entered the conference with anger and mistrust begin to connect in healthier ways. Offenders often volunteer offers of compensation, and victims often make suggestions to help offenders deal with the problems in better ways. While the criminal act may have brought them together, it is often the promise (and feel!) of healthier relations that sends them on their way.

And this leads me to the proposition that has startled me the most: justice in the relational world may not be about "stuff" at all, whether it is work done, dollars paid back, or years served in jail. And the reason is just as startling: in the relational world, the "crime" is not primarily a physical thing, no matter how much we try to define it that way. A couple of illustrations may be helpful.

I remember a woman talking about how her life had been changed by her rape some twenty years earlier. To this day, she told us tearfully, whenever her grandchildren try to crawl up on her knee, she still feels so dirty that she pushes them away. They do not know why, and they wonder if there's something wrong with them. In relational terms, her rape has diminished her capacity to be a part of warm relationships with those grandchildren, and it has made them wonder how loved they will be in life. While the act was twenty years ago, the relational dysfunctions it spawned continue to spread and infect.

And it is not just relationships with other people that suffer. Victims of violent crime frequently report that they can no longer relate to their houses, neighborhoods, or even their towns in the same way. Trust has been replaced by fear, openness by guardedness, comfort with deep suspicion, security with menace. They are no longer able to relate in healthy ways to the physical surroundings that once felt like "home."

My experience with victims suggests that what they really need are processes that encourage them to tell their offenders how much their lives have been changed, to present them with emotion-centered pictures of all the relational disfigurements now afflicting them. No lawyers please, no careful words to sugarcoat the message. Just "Here is how my life has changed!"

I learned about that from a man whose teenage daughter had been raped and killed. He set up a series of jailhouse meetings with her killer. He needed to tell that man what it *felt* like, every day, to come down to the breakfast table and see that she was not there. His surviving daughter went too, needing to tell him about the huge hole in her world, now, and forever, caused by the loss of her sister. As I listened, it seemed that justice for those two survivors did not come from the life-sentence imposed on the killer. It didn't begin to emerge for them until they had swamped that man with so many stories of loss and deprivation that he too started to cry. It was at that moment, when the killer's hard face cracked and tears flowed, that justice seemed to begin for them.

It was a powerful story for me. It underlined, in a way no academic treatise ever could, that our lives are made precious by the relationships that nourish us. If that's accurate, then our search for processes intended to give victims the justice they require must focus primarily on their emotional and spiritual dimensions, and it must seek to make offenders emotionally aware of the damage they have done. I was reminded of something Robert Yazzie, chief justice of the Navajo Tribal Court, said about traditional Navajo Peacemaking processes. "The most important piece of paper in Peacemaking is . . . the Kleenex, because until I know how you feel, and you know how I feel, we'll never move *beyond* those feelings." The comparison with my own justice system was startling—as soon as a victim or witness starts to cry, the court takes a recess to let everyone "collect themselves," so we can "get back to business." In relation-centered processes, hurt *is* the business.

It also seems important for victims to learn that the person who hurt them is a human being, not just "a criminal." Having the offender's friends and families in the circle is often critical, because their expressions of regret and remorse, often powerfully expressed, put a human face on the offender's life. If that face does *not* emerge (and it seldom does in the courtroom), many victims continue to be haunted by the image of nightmare creatures lurking behind every tree and around every corner, and can never move "beyond" the original injury.

I don't suggest for a moment that justice for victims should be the only concern of a justice system. I do suggest, however, that our failure to contemplate the relational dimension of crime has two consequences: we fail virtually all victims virtually all the time, and we routinely let offenders "off the hook" by never forcing them to take emotional responsibility for what they've done.

I am also concerned that our adversarial, punitive, and fact-centered system regularly fails offenders as well.

As I mentioned, we attach the label "criminal" as fast as we can, stigmatizing them not only to the community, but also to themselves. As Braithwaite has argued so powerfully, that kind of shaming only increases antagonism and escalates alienation. Relational justice tries to move in the opposite direction, to convince people that they are more than their antisocial acts, that they can learn how to respond in better ways to the pressures that affect them day to day. In relational terms, we want them to believe that they too can enjoy respectful and caring relationships. The more powerful healing circles actually give them the *experience* of those relationships, so respectful, open, and caring are the healers. When I marvel at how caring their processes appear to be, toward offenders as well as victims, they look at me in wonder. They are too polite to ask out loud, but I can hear the questions: "How can you bring about respect if you show disrespect? Caring if you punish? Trust if you ambush? Faith if you condemn?" In their view, the values you hope to teach must be the values demonstrated by the process itself.

At the same time, relational processes regularly show us something the courts routinely miss: many offenders simply don't know how they've hurt someone. A youngster who thinks he "only" ran into a house and stole a bottle of rum seems genuinely shocked to discover how fearful the householders have become, how they wake up sweating with every strange sound in the night. A purse snatcher who "only" pushed his victim to the side and ran away seems stunned to hear that she is now too frightened to go anywhere alone, that she now looks at *every* strange man approaching her as a possible attacker. Conferencing shows us that offenders need to hear those things, to be forcefully shown the relational damage they have done. Until that happens, they will continue to minimize their behavior and resist any demands for significant change.

Relational processes also give offenders something else denied them in the courtroom: the opportunity to survive emotion-centered encounters with their victims. Until they face whatever emotional outpouring is out there, waiting for them, they can never hope to put their crime behind them. We have to give them

ways to "clean the slate" as far as their victims are concerned if we want healthier attitudes to start emerging. When victims move out of their anger and start expressing genuine forgiveness instead, the impact on offenders can be dramatic:
many make heartfelt commitments to prove themselves *worthy* of that forgiveness
by changing their behavior for the better.

Finally, I want to talk about the role of the "professional" in conferencing and
healing processes, because it too manifests fundamental elements of traditional
teachings.

Many aboriginal groups refer to Creation as the Great Mystery. It seems to me
that processes like conferencing start with the same kind of assumption, that the
relationships between all the parties, and out of which the problems have arisen,
are so numerous, so ever-changing, and so interconnected that it is folly to believe
that *outsiders to those relationships* could ever "know" them in a way that permits
either accurate prediction or predictable intervention. The only ones who might
have a chance at that are the parties themselves. For that reason, it is *they* who
must be the creators of change, not strangers. It is *they* who must pool their perceptions of the relationships, of the problems arising within them, then search together for ways in which each of them, according to their own skills and inclina-
tions, can make different and better contributions.

Western teachings, by contrast, suggest that solutions are best found by professional experts such as judges, lawyers, probation officers, psychiatrists, and so
forth, all of whom should come as "disinterested strangers" to each case. Collectively, they are expected to create and even *impose* their solutions, whether the
parties support them or not.

My Alice-in-Justiceland brain can't help but ask how forced reliance on professionals promotes either a sense of responsibility or the development of problem-
solving skills, but that's what we do.

In the relational vision, however, the role of the professional is paradigmatically
different. It involves creating and regulating respectful processes in which the
parties themselves can come together in open but nonblaming ways. It involves
helping them confront and discharge incapacitating emotions like alienation, grief,
anger, guilt, shame, and fear. And it involves guiding all of them into using their
newfound knowledge of the relational problems—and potentials!—that surround
them to propose workable changes in how they deal with each other. They thus
become the authors of their own recovery with respect to that particular problem,
and learn how to avoid, minimize, or respond effectively to any new problems that
come along.

And there it is, in capsule form: my outsider's glance at a different way of understanding the essence of Creation, as well as my outsider's sense of how that
understanding has shaped the problem-solving processes developed by aboriginal
peoples. It does not do justice to the sophistication of their vision, or to the power
of those processes. I wish that every reader could experience firsthand the power-

ful "feeling" sense of justice that emerges from relation-centered processes like conferencing; once felt, it can never be forgotten.

And to all those aboriginal people who stuffed my Indian Puzzles shelf so close to bursting, thank you for your patience, and for remaining so willing to share your gifts with the rest of us. We are honored.

2   Family Group Conferencing

Cultural Origins, Sharing, and Appropriation—A Maori Reflection

CATHERINE LOVE

Ko Taranaki te maunga	Taranaki is the mountain
Ko Tokomaru te waka	Tokomaru is the canoe
Ko Te Atiawa te iwi	Te Atiawa is the tribe
Ko Ngati Te Whiti te hapu	Ngati Te Whiti is the subtribe
Ko Te Whiti O Rongomai me	Te Whiti O Rongomai and
Tohu Kakahi nga poropiti	Tohu Kakahi are the prophets
Ko Te Tatau O Te Po te whare	Te Tatau O Te Po is the house

Any address by a Maori person begins with a pepeha or declaration of who one is in relation to one's canoe, mountain, tribe, subtribe, ancestors, and ancestral house. It may be considered to be at best irrelevant and, at worst in bad form, to introduce oneself as an individual. Thus, in introducing myself, I do not proclaim my individual name. Rather, I am known through my whakapapa/ancestry, whanau/family, hapu/subtribal, and iwi/tribal identity. In addition to pepeha, speakers in Maori contexts usually precede their core narratives with a mihi. The mihi is a greeting to and acknowledgment of the listeners present. It has the effect of providing explicit recognition of the respective positions of listeners. Thus, a statement made by a speaker in a Maori context is offered from an overtly subjective position and received by listeners from equally overtly subjective positions.

Different whanau, hapu, and iwi have different narratives; thus, there is recognition of the existence of multiple narratives, each being accorded a relative truth status. Through knowing who speakers are, in terms of where they come from and their history and philosophy associated with this, listeners may locate speakers' narratives within the wider context of their webs of meaning. This chapter is written from my perspective as a Maori woman, member of Te Atiawa tribe, Ngati Te Whiti subtribe, follower of the teachings of the prophets of Parihaka, psychologist, and family therapist.

INTRODUCTION

The Children, Young Persons and Their Families Act (CYP&F; 1989) heralded the widespread, formalized practice of "family group conferencing" and apparently signaled a radical shift in the way that child care and protection, and youth justice issues were to be approached in Aotearoa/New Zealand. The impetus for change was drawn most particularly from the Report of the Ministerial Advisory Committee on a Maori Perspective for the Department of Social Welfare, known as Puao-te-ata-tu (Ministerial Advisory Committee, 1986). This report, together with others [such as the report of the Royal Commission on Social Policy (1988) and the Report on Maori and the Criminal Justice System (Jackson, 1988)] high-lighted issues of racism and the effects of maintaining monocultural laws and poli-cies in child and family welfare and justice. The reports identified ways in which institutional racism and discriminatory practices operated to disadvantage Maori children and families. These reports gave voice to Maori perspectives, critiques, and aspirations as they related to social policy, justice, and child and family well-being. The legislation governing family group conferencing drew on Maori traditions of social and kin-based functioning, problem resolution, and on Maori models of "restorative justice."

This chapter will outline some elements of traditional Maori systems and mod-els, provide a history of Maori involvement with state welfare and justice institu-tions, and examine the current operations of family group conferences within state child and family, care and protection, and youth justice institutions.

A MAORI VIEW OF SELF, WHANAU, AND JUSTICE

Outlined below are some elements of Maori views of self, whanau (family) and justice as practiced within Maori social and ideological systems. These elements operate in relation to a complex system of cultural beliefs, values, and institu-tions. It is important to note that, although within Maori groups agreement exists on some tenets of Maori culture, there is also at least as much diversity of opin-ion and interpretation as there is within Western cultural groups. The views pre-sented below are my own, except where specifically attributed to another.

Whakapapa (Genealogy):   Whakapapa has traditionally provided the basis of identity, the cornerstone of social organization and the "glue" that holds Maori social units together. Maori whakapapa extends to the creator, Io Matua Kore, and to Papatuanuku (mother earth) and Ranginui (sky father). Indeed, whakapapa may be translated as "to be (one with) mother earth." Within our whakapapa is contained our spiritual essence, our place in the spiritual order of things, in the social world, and in relation to this land. Whakapapa to Maori is more than the recitation of lin-eage: it is the source of our spirituality, our identity, and our purpose in life. It also defines our selves in relation to others, and others in relation to our selves. We exist on this earth as an element of the ongoing linking of our whakapapa. Each baby born represents another link in the chain that binds us to our past and promises our future survival.

Whanau, hapu, iwi: The smallest unit in Maori society is the whanau. The whanau includes the nuclear family, and more extended kin such as grandparents, greataunts and greatuncles, aunts and uncles, cousins, and nieces and nephews. Individual identity exists within whanau and is indivisible from whanau. The word *whanau* is also used to refer to the process of birth. The next most basic unit in Maori society is the hapu, or subtribe, which is comprised of several whanau descended from a common ancestor. Whanau identity exists within hapu and is indivisible from the hapu. The word *hapu* also refers to pregnancy. The largest unit within Maori society is the iwi or tribe, comprised of a number of hapu who descend from a common eponymous ancestor. Hapu too exist within the auspices of the tribe and are indivisible from it. Sometimes the term *iwi* is used in reference to te iwi Maori or the Maori people. The word *iwi* literally means bones. Thus to be iwi is to share the same bones. Many Maori view the Treaty of Waitangi, signed in 1840, between hapu and iwi and the Crown in Aotearoa/New Zealand as cementing for hapu and iwi their status as independent and sovereign bodies within this land.

Whenua denotes land and also refers to the placenta that nourishes the baby in the womb. Following the birth of a baby, it is customary for the whenua (placenta) to be returned to the whenua (land) to which he/she belongs. This symbolically returns sustenance to the land that sustains us and affirms the link between the child and the land, cementing this as her/his turangawaewae (place to stand).

In times past whanau and hapu lived and worked together, providing a strong and cohesive social order and support system. Since the mid-nineteenth century, as a result of British colonization, Maori lands were increasingly alienated through confiscation, legislation, and purchase. Post–World War II government policies proved increasingly destructive to Maori family and social systems, resulting in (a) Maori being pushed off their remaining lands as building on, development, and utilization of communally owned lands was effectively prevented, and (b) the relocation of Maori through incentives designed to attract them to urban centers as unskilled and semiskilled labor; the traditional basis of whanau, hapu, and iwi functioning (that is, in part living and working together on ancestral land) has been eroded. However, as the roots of whanau, hapu, and iwi membership lie in whakapapa, displacement from ancestral lands, and disconnection from other whanau, hapu and iwi members, while often viewed as detrimental to health and wholeness, does not negate one's membership and belonging.

In the contemporary context, Metge (1995) sees urban Maori who have been separated from their ancestral land bases and tribal roots as developing "metaphorical whanau" systems. These operate in a manner akin to that of traditional whanau, hapu, and iwi. Although metaphorical whanau may lack the whakapapa (genealogical) links that underpin biological whanau, similar whanau roles, relationships, rights, and obligations are adopted. Membership of metaphorical whanau exists alongside membership of whakapapa based (biological) whanau, hapu, and iwi systems. The development of "metaphorical whanau" may be conceived of as a type of group "whangai" process.

Whangai: The institution of whangai is sometimes known as "Maori adoption" or foster care. In traditional Maori society, children represented valuable assets to be treasured and nurtured so as to maximize their future ability to contribute to the well-being of the group. Children were not considered to be the property of or owned by parents, but rather were seen as elements of whanau, hapu, and iwi with their own significant place in the whakapapa. Responsibility for the care of children was shared, with grandparents and other senior members of the whanau and hapu having primary decision-making responsibility on behalf of children and younger whanau members. Babies and children were sometimes given to whanau and hapu members, other than the parents, to raise. Sometimes they were also given to others, outside the whanau and hapu, to cement relationships between the whanau and hapu concerned. First-born children were often given to their grandparents.

The institution of whangai does not imply that children raised within other whanau lose their place in the biological whanau, nor does it entertain any thought of denying them knowledge of or access to their biological whanau and whakapapa. Whangai have a place within several whanau systems. This institution has come into conflict with Western adoption laws that effectively constitute a transfer of "ownership" of babies and children, and that have not recognized the primary rights of grandparents and other senior whanau members to care for and make decisions on behalf of their sons, daughters, and grandchildren.

Mokopuna: This term refers to grandchild or grandchildren. It is used in the specific sense to denote one's biological grandchildren, and in a more general sense to refer to any child or children of the grandchild generation, particularly those with whom one has a connection.

Rangatahi: Rangatahi are youths and young people. The term is sometimes used in a similar fashion to Western conceptions of youth. However it may extend in its application to people in their thirties, forties, and even fifties. Western laws provide "cutoff" ages, typically sixteen, eighteen, or twenty-one, at which youths become "adults." In Maori society, one's status as a youth may continue much longer and is related more to the adoption of full adult roles in Maori society, and in relation to other more senior relatives, than to age. Hence New Zealanders of Western origin are sometimes surprised to observe senior Maori colleagues, academics, or business people referred to by their elders as "boy" or "girl" and instructed to make cups of tea, sweep the floors, or take on a new job.

Maturity in Maori terms is measured by one's ability to work cooperatively as part of a group, to place the welfare of the group above one's own desires, and to convey appropriate humility and respect to others. This is in contrast to Western ideals, which emphasize independence, individuality, and autonomy as characteristics of maturity.

Matua: Matua are parents. The term is used more broadly than merely in reference to biological parents. Rather it may refer to all biological or metaphorical kin of one's parents' generation, who provide care for the younger generations.

Kaumatua: Kaumatua are the senior members of whanau, hapu, and iwi, consisting of kuia (female elders) and koroua (male elders). They provide sustenance for the people through their knowledge and wisdom. Important whanau, hapu, and iwi decisions are referred to them, and few significant actions are taken without their approval.

Tupuna: Tupuna are the ancestors. The term is also sometimes used to refer to very senior members of whanau, hapu, and iwi. The word tupuna describes an upstanding (continuous) spring. They are the source of those who follow, and the faces to which the mokopuna give life.

Rangatira: The term rangatira is sometimes translated as "chief" or "leader." However, these translations do not convey two of the essential qualities of rangatira. First, the ability to draw the people together in decision-making and action, and second, the spiritual origins and responsibilities of the position. Rangatira may operate at the level of whanau, hapu, and iwi decision-making. In the modern context, the words of rangatira are acknowledged and responded to with respect. Their opinions carry weight because their job is to consider the well-being of the unit as a whole, from a position of experienced service, and others may well defer to them in recognition of this.

In addition to these whanau roles there are a number of roles and relationships such as tuakana-teina (older and younger siblings and cousins), mana wahine and mana tane (the complementary and vital roles of men and women) that are relevant to whanau functioning.

MAORI MODELS OF HEALTH AND WELL-BEING

Maori models of health and well-being invariably include the whanau as a central element, reinforcing the indivisibility of whanau well-being from individual well-being. Along with this dimension, essential elements within Maori models of health and well-being include an emphasis on the spiritual dimension (seen as primary), the life force or essence, body, mind, heart, and ancestral teachings and traditions. These dimensions stand alongside the notion of mana, which may be interpreted as prestige, standing, and authority. Mana has a spiritual origin and provides strength, protection, and efficacy in the temporal and spiritual realms. These elements together form the basis of Maori models of health and well-being, and of conceptions of illness and dysfunction.

Any decisions relating to Maori whanau must take into account the complex webs of relationships, qualities, and needs outlined above. Prior to colonization in the nineteenth and twentieth centuries, Maori also had a full system of rules and regulatory systems that performed the functions of social control that legal and judicial systems perform for Western societies. Maori law was based in the social institutions and principles that governed Maori society as a whole, and hence was inextricably interwoven with the spiritual dimension. Tikanga is the central platform on which Maori systems of justice, regulation, and decision-making, are based.

TIKANGA AS THE BASIS OF MAORI LAW
AND DECISION-MAKING PROCESSES

The root of the word "tikanga" is "tika." Tika may be translated as "right, correct, true, and just." Maori law is based on consideration of what is right, correct, true, and just from a Maori perspective. Tikanga is the expression of this. Some principles and practices associated with tikanga, as they apply to the exercise of whanau decision-making and Maori law, are outlined below.

Mana: The maintenance of mana and a balance in mana relationships between groups provides the motivation for many Maori actions and decisions. Quantification and conceptualization of the seriousness of offenses and appropriate responses to these, are largely based on the effects of particular actions on the maintenance or diminution of mana. As previously noted, the mana of individuals is indivisible from the mana of the group (whanau, hapu, iwi) of which they are a part. Therefore an offense against one person is also considered to be an offense against his/her whanau. Similarly, responsibility for offending is carried by the whanau of the offender as much as by the individual offender.

Utu: Utu is the principle of reciprocity. This principle operates to provide balance in relationships and to maintain or increase the mana of participants in exchanges. The principle of utu is to bring closure and to restore harmony and balance, not to destroy it.

Muru: Muru is the practice of exacting compensation for wrongdoing.

Rangatiratanga: In this context, rangatiratanga may be described as the authority of the group (whanau, hapu, iwi) to make its own decisions, to enjoy relative autonomy in relation to its own processes, and to its own responsibility for its own members. This principle is sometimes seen to be in conflict with the right that the governance structures of the state claim to have, to control and make decisions on behalf of citizens.

WHANAU HUI AS THE MODEL
FOR FAMILY GROUP CONFERENCING

A hui is a gathering of people. Hui may be held for any number of reasons, however, the process of the hui and the principles by which it operates are consistent. Hui are an important part of the practice of tikanga and the maintenance of whanau, hapu, and iwi health, wholeness, and unity. For the purposes of this chapter, the emphasis will be on whanau hui, held to consider issues and make decisions on matters affecting whanau members.

Hui begin and end with karakia, which may incorporate Christian prayers, and which have the effect of ensuring that the hui process is enclosed in the wairuatanga or spiritual dimension. Whanau members, dead and alive, and their respective roles and contributions, are acknowledged. The group may join together in a waiata or song, to reinforce the words of the first speaker, who is usually a kaumatua or rangatira. Building on this important platform, discussion of the issue takes place. All members may express their thoughts and feelings, in a way that avoids putting down others. The ultimate aim of the hui is to rebuild the mana of the whanau, which may have been damaged by the actions of a member, or which may be under threat as a result of a crisis situation.

Caring for all members and helping to enhance their ability to contribute to the whanau and hapu is an essential ingredient of the rebuilding process. While anger, frustration, and pain may be expressed, it is the job of kaumatua and rangatira to ensure that these emotions do not become destructive to the group process. Songs, stories, wise sayings, and humor may supplement the talk. Once participants have expressed their respective positions and identified core issues, senior whanau members help to steer the discussion to consideration of possible solutions. These may involve a variety of actions; in the case of a young offender, some sacrifice may be required, and/or the whanau may wish to deliver to the offended parties an acknowledgment of wrong (akin to an apology). An offer of restitution may be made, but the onus is on the offended party to accept, reject, or identify the most appropriate compensation. In the case of offending, it is best for the offender and offended to have their own whanau hui to work through the issues and identify their own positions as whanau, prior to coming together. Sometimes senior whanau members will "prescribe" a means of resolution.

Following the discussion process, whanau members may be charged with the responsibility for performing particular tasks or functions. Resolutions will be aimed toward healing within and between affected whanau, in effect by restoring the balance in a particular direction. In the case of care and protection issues for children, the welfare of the child will be considered in relation to his/her place within the whanau, hapu, and iwi. It is very important to have senior whanau members present to monitor and guide the process. They have the authority to ensure that people are listening, respecting each other, and recognizing their obligations. The role of kaumatua cannot be overemphasized. Sometimes their day-to-day contact with the whanau is minimal, but the appropriate person can provide knowledge and perspectives to which younger or more involved members do not have access.

At the conclusion of the hui, a senior whanau member will summarize proceedings, acknowledge the participation of whanau members and the spiritual presence of the ancestors, and offer a karakia to close this particular piece of the process.

WESTERN CONCEPTIONS OF SELF, OTHER, AND LAW

It is clear that Maori conceptions of self, other, and justice are consistent with the models of self described by Sampson (1993) as "ensembled individualism." These conceptions of self exist in sociocentric cultures and typically include family, ancestors, and elements of the natural and supernatural world within the boundary of "self." Identity is constituted through roles and relationships, and responsibility and accountability is also defined through these. Locus of control and responsibility (Sue & Sue, 1990) thus tends to be external, rather than located within the individual. Duties and obligations to the larger unit have precedence over the notion of individual rights.

These sociocentric conceptions of self may be contrasted with the "self-contained individualism" (Sampson, 1993) that has underpinned Western systems of justice, welfare, and family law. Sampson proposes that the "self as container" metaphor is based on a number of culturally constituted "commonsense" Western assumptions about the nature of self, including the following:

1. The body is a container that houses the individual; thus the "essence" of a person, the physiological and psychological qualities, will, motivation, emotion, and soul are housed in the body.
2. All that is contained in the self is separate and distinct from that contained in other selves and other entities. Definitions of healthy selfhood, according to this conception of self, are those that have firm boundaries and function as independent self-contained units.

Sampson (ibid., p. 36) proposes that from this conception of self stems the notion that the boundaries of self are vital in the defense of the human core, and in sustaining the individual's integrity as a viable entity in the world. From this fundamental assumption, in turn, comes a conclusion that boundary maintenance and boundary defense are essential features of being a healthy and sovereign person.

Notions of individual pathology and family dysfunction are predicated on the above assumptions. Thus, for parents and other whanau members to lack clear boundaries between where they end and where their children begin, is seen as dysfunctional, as is the notion of a child living for his/her parents, whanau, or ancestors. Similarly a belief that one is "one with" or in communication with a tree, rock, or ancestor betrays a loss of boundaries synonymous with pathology.

A healthy self-contained individual, according to this conception of self, has firm boundaries between self and other, an independent existence, and an internal locus of control and responsibility (Sue & Sue, 1990). Within this conception of self and other, self is seen as primary, with relationships being derivative (that is; the self is seen as preexisting relationships) and relationships may be rejected if they do not meet the needs of self (Landrine, 1992). Notions such as self-esteem and the equation of independence and autonomy with maturity only make sense from this self-contained-individualist position. This position also forms the basis of laws that transfer the ownership of children through adoption, and that make sense of removing individual children from family systems as a means of providing them with opportunities for health and wholeness appear coherent.

HISTORY OF MAORI INVOLVEMENT WITH
STATE WELFARE SERVICES

The different conceptions of self outlined above lead to two contrasting philoso-
phies of good parenting, child rearing, and citizenship. Both have the potential to
contribute positively to the nation-state. However, problems arose because, in the
context of child welfare in Aotearoa/New Zealand, Western notions of individuo-
centrism became enshrined in legislation. With Western models of self, health,
and family seen as the only valid way to be, Maori conceptions became seen, by
default, as deficient or pathological. Coupled with this was the breakdown in Maori
society of the systems and institutions that traditionally supported whanau functioning. This led to a lack of resources in many Maori whanau with which to operate healthily within Maori systems as well as Pakeha (European) systems.

   In common with other indigenous peoples subject to colonization, Maori experiences of state welfare and justice systems have historically featured negative
interactions and negative outcomes. This is related to the imposition of an indi-
vidualistic philosophy, ideologies, and laws onto a sociocentric people.

PRINCIPLES UNDERPINNING TRADITIONAL
WESTERN WELFARE AND JUSTICE SYSTEMS

Since the advent of colonization, Aotearoa/New Zealand child and youth welfare
and justice institutions have operated according to a number of assumptions, related to the notion of self-contained individualism, located in Western cultures,
and in particular in postindustrial Western society. These assumptions include the
following:

1. *Parents possess rights of ownership of their children; these ownership
   rights are limited by the authority of the state over its citizens.* Associated
   with this assumption is a view that the "state" is the a priori parent of all
   citizens and its mechanisms and agents are ultimately responsible for the
   discipline, monitoring, and perhaps welfare, of its citizenry. If parents are
   seen to be not meeting their responsibilities for children, the state has the
   right to assume "ownership" and make decisions on behalf of the children
   and parents. This assumption negates the roles, rights, and responsibilities
   of whanau, hapu, and iwi and is contrary to the principle of the rangatiratanga (authority) of whanau, hapu, and iwi.
2. *The state is comprised of individual citizens who function as self-contained units of production.* In postindustrial Western society the individual
   is viewed as the fundamental unit of analysis. Individual dynamics are

seen as the source of all social, cultural, and economic dynamics. The role of the state is to develop citizens into productive units who contribute to the stability and profitability of the nation. This is carried out, in part, through a compulsory education system that delivers a national curriculum and through mechanisms of social control, including the justice and, some would argue, welfare arms of the state.

3. *Responsibility and accountability are located within individuals.* Systems of law and justice, mental health and illness, and other social systems and institutions are also based in individuocentric philosophy and ideology. For instance, responsibility and accountability for criminal acts are seen to be located in the individual perpetrator or perpetrators of the acts. Victims of crime are also conceived of in individual terms. Similarly, pathology while perhaps related to external conditions and relationships, is located primarily within individuals, and treatment for identified pathology or dysfunction is likewise limited to individuals, or perhaps to individual (nuclear) family units.

4. *Culture is a product of human learning and contained within individual selves.* Culture is seen as being learned and contained within individuals, who then negotiate shared meanings with other individuals who comprise the membership of their cultural groups. The rise of the culture concept and the demise of the construct of race was associated with an increasing tendency toward the "nurture" side of the "nature–nurture" debate. The assumption that "we are what we learn" is analogous to the idea that people are defined by what is "put into" their container selves. This is the basis of Western systems of adoption and of state-sponsored foster care.

These assumptions provided the basis for a raft of laws, institutions, policies, and practices that imposed a foreign and antithetical ethos on the indigenous Maori people. This imposition was not purely incidental, but was part of a planned process of assimilation of Maori into the Western culture and society of the colonizers. Children provided the most promising candidates for assimilation because their container selves were not yet full.

For Maori, the process amounted to a form of cultural genocide. Maori whanau were forced to send their children to schools where the speaking of Maori language was forbidden, the special and communal nature of Maori relationships with the whenua (land) was destroyed, and land passed from whanau, hapu, and iwi control to state and individual ownership. Maori were transported into the cities to work as unskilled and semiskilled labor in the factories and industries that grew in the post–World War II period and were housed according to a "pepper-potting" policy, which prevented them from living together in communities. Housing policies also mitigated against the maintenance of whanau support systems with three-bedroom state houses, which did not allow for extended family living without overcrowding.

By the late 1960s and early 1970s, most Maori had relocated from rural kin-based communities to towns and cities. Prior to this time, Maori rates of imprisonment and incarceration in psychiatric institutions were very low. As whanau struggled to maintain their mana and to survive in surroundings that were largely hostile to Maori traditions and values, and as many became increasingly disconnected from their cultural institutions and support systems, Maori began to figure in psychiatric, criminal conviction, and imprisonment rates. As the semi- and unskilled labor market dried up, Maori began featuring increasingly and disproportionately in the ranks of the unemployed; psychiatric institutionalization, criminal convictions, and imprisonment rates for Maori also climbed relentlessly.

Into this mix in the 1960s, 1970s, and 1980s, came the state guardians of social welfare. These were largely comprised of liberal Pakeha (white) social workers with good intentions and a commitment to contribute to the welfare of the nation and particularly to the welfare of "underprivileged" Maori children. Those who had university training had been introduced to the notion of "cultural deprivation" and the ideals of theorists such as Erikson, Kohlberg, and Maslow. They "knew" the importance and primacy of the mother-child relationship, the nuclear family unit, self-esteem, and self-actualization. In their efforts to divorce themselves from the horrors of race-related atrocities or any inkling of personal racism, these welfare workers also subscribed passionately to theories of individual human worth and the notion that, if the self-as-container had the "right" input from an early age, any one, even the most underprivileged child could succeed (that is, become "independent," "autonomous," "self-actualized," and filled with "self-esteem").

The social workers charged with caring for the welfare of the nation's children went forth into the community. Observation and anecdotal evidence indicates that very large numbers of Maori children were removed from the care of their whanau and placed under the guardianship of the director-general of Social Welfare. State foster-care homes were established, catering largely for Maori children, and numbers of liberal Pakeha couples opened their homes to Maori foster children and proceeded to provide them with the "right" values and motivation to aspire to the trappings of the Pakeha world. It became fashionable in 1970s and early 1980s Aotearoa/New Zealand to adopt or foster a Maori child.

In the meantime, thousands of Maori whanau, already struggling with cultural alienation and poverty, were demonized and instructed by well-meaning state welfare department workers about their inadequacies. Sometimes equally well-meaning psychologists provided technical names for these inadequacies. The Maori "welfare kids" of this era grew up to become the "social problems" of today. Often angry at their loss of identity, language, and mana, they provided clear evidence that the assimilation policy targeting Maori children and families and the dismemberment of Maori whanau structures had failed to achieve its goal. By the late 1980s a New Zealand Youth Court judge was openly describing the New Zealand Youth Court System as the "Maori Youth Court" (Ministerial Advisory Committee, 1986).

THE FAMILY GROUP CONFERENCE: THEORY AND PRACTICE

It was in this context that the reports outlined at the beginning of this chapter were written. The clear message has been threefold. First, colonial solutions for Maori problems, which had been created by colonialism in the first place, had failed. Second, the techniques for healing fractured Maori whanau, hapu, iwi, and society lay with Maori people, culture, values, and institutions. Third, the dismemberment of Maori whanau could only be repaired through strengthening and resourcing whanau, hapu, iwi, and Maori to address their own problems and manage their own return to wholeness.

The motivation for a system that had until that time been dismissive of Maori voices to introduce changes as apparently radical as the CYP&F Act (1989) probably lay in several threads that came together in the late 1980s. These included an increasing awareness of the existence and value of Maori culture, and a gradual acknowledgment that existing Western systems were not working for Maori. From the mid-1970s there was also increasing civil unrest among Maori. In addition, "Maori social problems," often involving the incarceration of youthful Maori in various institutions, was becoming very costly to the nation's coffers.

The family group conference was designed to be a key plank in the operation of the new legislation and philosophy adopted by child and family workers. Although modeled to some extent on the whanau hui, the conferences are designed to apply to all peoples. The Act features Maori terms and phrases, requires state representatives to consult with whanau and significant others, and aims to provide a more culturally sensitive, appropriate, and acceptable means of making decisions pertaining to children, young people, and families who have come to the attention of welfare and justice authorities. It is important to be clear, however, that the process of family group conferencing as described in the Act, *does not provide an open avenue for Maori control* of the processes and practices associated with the welfare and offending of their young. This has led to a perspective among some Maori that the radical changes heralded in the Act are more apparent than real.

Reports on the operation of family group conferencing in New Zealand are mixed. Many whanau, offenders, and victims who have experienced family group conferencing have found the process beneficial and preferable to the previous court-based system. There are, however, some concerns.

Underresourcing.   Underresourcing in terms of people, money, and time can result in key whanau members not attending family group conferences (particularly when travel from a distance is required), delays in conferences being convened, and too few opportunities for conferencing—particularly for monitoring, review, and reevaluation purposes. Underresourcing may also mean that whanau are not resourced to implement whanau plans, to provide the care, or to access the services that are needed.

Underresourcing: An Ideological Agenda?   There is suspicion in some quarters that efforts to return responsibility for young people who are in trouble, troubled, or in need to whanau, hapu, and iwi represent a step backward on the part of the state from accepting its responsibility for the creation of problems and for the resourcing of solutions. In some instances, whanau who are living in poverty, and struggling to survive after generations of systemic abuse themselves are expected to take on the responsibility of children and young people without resources being provided for counseling, specialized care, respite, and other needs.

The Involvement of Professionals in Family Group Conferences. If the model of whanau hui was to be followed, professionals and representatives of state agencies would not be present at family group conferences. Their presence can be intimidating and disempowering to whanau and can disrupt the process in a number of ways. Whanau, and particularly senior whanau members, may experience whakamaa (embarrassment and humiliation) or anger when their whanau processes are being observed by, or (as tends to be the case) led by Pakeha (European) professionals. This is particularly likely when young Pakeha people barely out of their teens feature in a role that may be perceived as arrogant, inappropriate and undermining to the mana and rangatiratanga of whanau and hapu.

Decision-making power: consultation vs. control. While agents of the state, such as police and departmental social workers, are required to consult with families about who should be invited to a family group conference, and where and when conferences should be held, the final decision is made by the state agents who convene the conference. This takes control out of the hands of whanau, and undermines the principle of rangatiratanga.

Decision-making power: leadership roles. The professionals who attend conferences are responsible for providing information and identifying options. This often leads them to take an "expert" position and assume a leadership role in the conference. This can disempower the whanau and obstruct the operation of whanau processes, roles and relationships. It may also undermine the roles of senior whanau members. In addition, the provision of information by professionals can be slanted to the perspective of the agencies they represent and to pathological models that feature in their training. This can create divisions within whanau, between those who adopt the perspective of the professionals and those who hold a different perspective. It also preempts the role of the whanau in defining and delineating the issues, once again undermining whanau, hapu and iwi rangatiratanga and mana. There may be an element of coercive pressure to adopt the "professional perspective"; not to do so may destroy any chance of retaining children and young people in the care of the whanau, and may risk making objectors themselves subject to pathologization or investigation.

Decision-making power: outcomes predetermined by professionals. Professionals, including police, social workers, and psychologists sometimes have a preferred outcome in mind. Some professionals have been known to inform whanau that their preferred choice is the only acceptable option and to threaten to veto any alternative proposed by the whanau. Once again, this serves to disempower whanau.

Adherence to a pathological perspective. While whanau may be privy to a holistic and historical perspective on the issues that have led to the family group conference, and may recognize strengths in the system as well as weaknesses, professional perspectives in family group conferences are too often entrenched in a focus on pathology. This can also serve to disempower whanau, obscure whanau strengths, and limit options.

Internalized oppression on the part of some whanau. Internalized oppression as a result of colonization, coupled with fear and distrust of representatives of "the system" can result in some whanau being scared to disagree with the position taken by professionals at conferences. whanau with a history of being pathologized and dismembered by "the system" and its representatives may give away what power they do have to the professionals who represent the system, and may become paralyzed by their fear of being reclaimed (or revictimized) by the system.

Underestimating the complexity of cultural knowledge and cultural systems. It is arrogant for Western professionals to assume that they can understand and achieve competency in Maori culture and systems through a series of modules in a study program, or through a series of formal and informal experiences and training. Western professionals typically undergo three to seven years training to achieve minimum competencies in their respective fields of study. In addition, they have had a lifetime of training in the core values, ideals and concepts of the Western culture on which their training and professions are based. Western professionals attending and facilitating family group conferences involving Maori whanau rarely possess a depth of Maori cultural knowledge or competence. Sometimes Maori colleagues are co-opted to ease the process, but co-opted cultural representatives do not typically have power in the system that controls the process. Additionally, their role may be to uphold the functioning of the system that employs them, rather than the mana of whanau, hapu, and iwi.

Appropriation and abuse of cultural processes. There is a fear that Western systems and their representatives may be engaged in a process of appropriating elements of Maori culture and using them to develop a more culturally sensitive tool of oppression. For instance, karakia may be used at the beginning and end of family group conferences, social workers and police officers may speak a few words in Maori (in fact they may be more proficient in Maori language than whanau members present), and conferences may be convened at marae. However, the power remains with the state representatives and the process is ultimately governed by state legislation.

Marae (communally owned and operated Maori houses and land that provide sites for the dissemination and performance of Maori forms and narratives) provide the primary haven for Maori authority and autonomy in this country. The practice of holding family group conferences on marae has had a mixed reception from Maori. Some believe that this practice increases the appropriateness, sensitivity and comfort of the process for Maori. However, others see this practice as an encroachment of the arm of the state into the last bastion of Maori authority. From this perspective, there is a very real possibility that the mana and relative rangatiratanga of Maori institutions, such as marae may be undermined by the introduction of family group conferences to such venues. In addition, the participation of state representatives in rituals that they do not fully understand or abide by can serve to devalue and corrupt the process itself.

SUMMARY

Family group conferences and the Aotearoa/New Zealand legislation that defines them, features some elements of a complex system of Maori cultural values, beliefs and practices. When well run and adequately resourced, conferences can be beneficial to children, young persons, their families, victims, and offenders. However, the danger from a Maori perspective is that the apparent state commitment to a culturally appropriate and empowering process is clearly limited. It may, in fact, serve only to provide a brown veneer for a white system that has historically contributed to state run programs of cultural genocide and whanau dismemberment. It may also serve to undermine Maori systems and institutions and to co-opt Maori people and cultural forms as agents in our own oppression.

For many Maori the legislative framework and operational practice of family group conferences do not go far enough. They do not provide whanau, hapu, and iwi with the power and the resources to resolve problems within whanau, hapu, and iwi. Maori lawyer Moana Jackson noted that: "Justice for Maori does not mean the grafting of Maori processes onto a system that retains the authority to determine the extent, applicability and validity of those processes" (1995, p. 34). For Maori who subscribe to the ideal of tino rangatiratanga (whanau, hapu, and iwi absolute sovereign authority) family group conferences represent another, insidious means of disempowering Maori whanau.

In some ways, family group conferences as practiced with Maori whanau represent an attempt to merge two systems of power relations, communications, and world views. The result is sometimes productive, but at least as often it results in a clash of the two systems, and the misappropriation and misinterpretation of Maori culture, systems, and values. While the attempt to reconcile or combine two different perspectives under one law is a worthy aim, the result has too often been a token acknowledgment of minority Maori culture, and the continued imposition of dominant Western perspectives. In effect, there is a danger that elements of the process represent a continuation of colonial processes, with the practice of oppression and cultural dismemberment overlaid with the rhetoric of caring and altruism.

Despite concerns and reservations about the formulation and operation of Family Group Conferences, it is undeniable they have stemmed the tide of lost children to some considerable extent. While the culture of colonialism is still evident in social services, there is also a growing climate of recognition of the important place of whanau, hapu, and iwi in the healthy development of children, young people, and communities. The family group conference serves as a starting point. However, it is not enough to hand back limited control, together with full responsibility, to families and communities that have been fractured and fragmented through colonization. There must be a parallel process of resourcing and healing in these communities. The best elements of the family group conferencing philosophy need to be broadened out to form widening circles that encompass meaningful hapu, iwi, and community participation in their own healing and wholeness.

REFERENCES

Jackson, M. (1995). Cultural justice: A colonial contradiction or a *rangatiratanga* reality? In F. McElrea (Ed.), *Rethinking criminal justice: Justice in the community* (Vol. 1). Auckland: Legal Research Foundation.

Jackson, M. (1988). *Maori and the criminal justice system: He Whaipaanga Hou: A new perspective* (Part 2). Wellington: Department of Justice.

Landrine, H. (1992). Clinical implications of cultural differences: The referential vs. the indexical self. *Clinical Psychology Review, 12,* 401–15.

Metge, J. (1995). *New Growth from Old: The Whanau in the Modern World.* Wellington: Victoria University Press.

Ministerial Advisory Committee (1986). *Puao-te-Atatu: The report of the Ministerial Advisory Committee on a Maori perspective for the Department of Social Welfare.* Wellington: Department of Social Welfare.

Royal Commission on Social Policy (1988). *The April Report, Future Directions.* Wellington: Government Print.

Sampson, E. E. (1993). *Celebrating the other: A dialogic account of human nature.* New York: Harvester-Wheatsheaf.

Sue, D. W., & Sue, D. (1990). *Counseling the culturally different: Theory and practice.* New York: Wiley.

3   Democracy, Community, and Problem Solving

JOHN BRAITHWAITE

In a historical period when representative democracy is sweeping away one dictatorship after another, democracy is becoming more shallow in its meaning for human lives. The lived experience of modern democracy is alienation. The feeling is that elites run things, that no one else has a say in any meaningful sense. It is certainly a poll-driven democracy, and polls are admittedly a kind of safeguard against the tyrannies the polls reveal as likely to reduce electoral support. However, a poll-driven democracy is also a tyranny of the unreflective median voter. We see this tyranny vividly with criminal justice. Crime is one of the insecurities of swing voters. In an unreflective democracy where the political imagination is limited to bigger doses of punishment as the cure for crime, the swing voters say they want longer sentences, and they defect from parties that come under attack in the mass media for being soft on crime. Such a democracy is impoverished. What our experience with restorative practices has taught us is that there is a rich diversity of things citizens want out of the justice process that they only come to grasp through serious deliberative engagement with it, by listening to the arguments and experiences of others and then reflecting on their needs and aspirations for decent outcomes.

But of course this malaise of democracy reduced to the politics of the opinion poll, television one-liners, and tabloid headlines is much wider. It results from the density of governmental decisions in complex societies and the number of people who would like to have a say. In such a world, to aspire to much more than the democracy of the ballot box seems romantic. There are just too many decisions and too many people for participatory democracy to be feasible. Besides, few of us want to spend our lives in the endless meetings it would require. The expanding impracticability of all affected citizens participating in important decisions that affect their lives has reinforced the dominant view that representative democracy is all that is feasible. At the same time, if Madison or Jefferson returned to America today they would be disappointed at how remote government is from the people and at how much power governments and, worse, democratically unaccountable corporations exercise in ways that educated citizens dimly understand. The utopianism of the participatory democracy they defeated has been used by generations of elected politicians to erode the sovereignty of the people in favor of the sovereignty of executive government. Roads and weapons systems are built by experts remote from elected officials, let alone from the citizens who travel by roads and are protected by the weapons. How could it be otherwise? Is it possible that we might save democracy from its own decay? Might it be that restorative practices could have a significant role in this rescue mission?

DEMOCRACY RENEWED

Progressively, the distancing of the people from the scale of modern state and corporate governance is producing a backlash. Contemporary Madisons and Jeffersons who see direct democracy as worse than an impossible dream nevertheless keep faith with the hope that a new amalgam of citizen participation can be forged. These are folk who participate in social movements like the social movement for restorative justice. My argument is that these citizens are indeed at the frontier of a new Madisonianism, a civic republicanism for a complex world.

Native American "republicanism" had an influence on American revolutionary republicanism. Regrettably, it had precious little in the two centuries after the revolution. The freedom of the Indian was part of the imagery of the Native American garb at the Boston tea party. Some of the framers of the U.S. constitution seem to have been admirers of the Iroquois confederacy, leading Iris Young (1997) to invoke Homi Bhabha's notion of hybridity to suggest that America may be a "hybrid democracy." We see the symbol of the Iroquois federalism, the eagle clasping bundled arrows, on the U.S. one dollar bill. What I see as the hybrid civic republicanism of the restorative justice movement equally draws upon the institutional wisdom of Native Americans and of Polynesian Americans, revealed through New Zealand Maori as well as Hawaiian experience. In the criminal justice system, Western alternative dispute resolution (ADR) models invented in the 1970s were going nowhere slowly during the 1980s until they incorporated three crucial lessons from indigenous practices in the 1990s:

First, dyadic mediation between a single victim and a single offender is an impoverished formula compared with bringing into a circle a multiplicity of people who are affected in different ways, but particularly people who love and want to support those directly affected. Western feminist critiques of power imbalance in mediation, for example, have more force when applied to a meeting of a man and a woman, a man and a child, or an adversarial encounter between a teenage rape victim and a cross-examining lawyer. They still have force, but less so, when applied to a healing circle where the affected parties are assured of support from both men and women, adults and children, who stand with them. Power imbalances can still be profound in a circle, but they are more cross-cutting than in one-on-one encounters.

The second lesson from indigenous practices was, in the words of Ada Melton (1995), that it is better to put the problem rather than the person in the center of the circle. There is a connection of the second insight with the first. This is the Maori view that it is barbaric to allow people to stand alone in the dock. While the shame of letting one's loved ones down can be healthy and readily transcended by love and forgiveness from them, the shame of exposure in the dock, individualized guilt, and stigma can eat away at a person's self.

The third crucial insight was that material reparation was less important than symbolic or emotional reparation (Retzinger & Scheff, 1996). Remorse and apology, as recent New Zealand evidence suggests, is more predictive of reduced reoffending following restorative conferences than material compensation (Maxwell & Morris, 1999). And symbolic reparation is often more important to victims (Sherman et al., 1998). In some contexts it can even make sense for the victim and the community to make a gift to the offender, as among the Crow people (Austin, 1984, p. 36). On Java I was told of a village where a boy was caught stealing and dealt with according to principles of *musyawarah*—decision by friendly cooperation and deliberation. The chief of the village summarized the feeling of the village meeting: "We should be ashamed because one from our village should be so poor as to steal. We should be ashamed as a village." Their solution was to give the offender a bag of rice.

To summarize so far, we have identified three crucial lessons for the West to learn from indigenous practices:

1. Widen the circle—democratize it, pluralize it.
2. Put the problem in the center, not the person.
3. Shift the emphasis from material to symbolic reparation—remorse, apology, love, even spiritual healing.

With this rediscovered institutional wisdom, the evidence is now strong that we can offer restorative rituals that, on average, citizens find more satisfying, fairer, and more respectful of rights than court. There are lively and important debates about differences between various kinds of conferences and circles that define a research agenda for evaluation scholars. However, I suspect there are more important things that are shared in common, and these include learning from the above three insights from indigenous practices. The more abstract lesson is that for most participants, circles and conferences are democratically satisfying. The practical lesson is that participants can be readily persuaded to attend so long as implementation failures are solved to make this convenient. It follows that conferences and circles can salvage some not insignificant participatory democracy in the twenty-first century. Moreover, we may be able to expand the application of conferences beyond criminal offending by juveniles and adults, beyond the care and protection of children, beyond bullying in schools, beyond business regulatory domains such as nursing home inspections (Braithwaite, 1999), to other problems that affect peoples' lives directly enough for them to want to participate. Candidates seem to me unemployment, homelessness, and truancy/dropout/educational failure.

Political scientists may say that such concerns do not go to the heartland of the democratic process. True. But how can citizens hack a path to the heartland of the democracy if the democracy has no strategy for teaching them how to be democratic citizens? Circles and conferences about matters ordinary people care about in their lived experience can teach them. If all students experience and witness serious acts of bullying at school and care about this, then before they reach adulthood all can have the experience of participation in circle solving of a difficult problem on which there are multiple perspectives. And democracy is something that must be taught. We are not born democratic. We are born demanding and inconsiderate, disgruntled whiners, rather than born listeners. We must learn to listen, to be free and caring through deliberation that sculpts responsible citizenship from common clay (Barber, 1992).

Punitive practices, like the accountability mechanisms of the contemporary state more generally, teach us not to be democratic, not to be citizens. This is because of their passive model of responsibility (Bovens, 1998). Passive responsibility occurs when we hold someone responsible for what they have done in the past. The president is censured for his sexual misconduct, the secretary of the treasury is fired for failing to prune the deficit, Colonel Ghadaffi's child is killed in a bombing raid on his home to teach the colonel that it is wrong to support terrorism. Circles and conferences, in contrast, teach active responsibility. Active responsibility means taking responsibility. In a healing circle, most citizens in the circle are not passively responsible for any wrongdoing; they are certainly not held responsible for criminal wrongdoing. Yet the hope so often realized is that they will take active responsibility for solving the problem. This is part of the ambition of putting the problem, rather than the person, in the center of the circle. In the most moving conferences, participants take active responsibility for confronting structural problems like racism in a community, sexual exploitation, domination of girls by boys in a school (Braithwaite & Daly, 1994), and even a prime minister taking responsibility for restructuring the regulation of the Australian insurance industry (Braithwaite, 1999). But mostly the active responsibility is more banal—the uncle who takes responsibility for ensuring that a car is left in the garage on Saturday nights to prevent a recurrence of drunk driving, the aunt who offers a home to a child abused by her parents, and the burglary victim who decides to install an alarm system.

The lesson that democracy requires active responsibility is being learned in the banal and personal cases just as it is in the less common cases that grapple with structural change. The outputs we hope for are not only solving the problem but also building community and building democracy, or at least the competence to be democratic. To rebuild a democracy of which Madison and Jefferson would be proud, we need to do more than motivate people to participate in circles that address problems of living that directly affect their personal relationships. The extra step to democratic citizenship is taken when the citizen moves from participating in restorative conferences to being active in some way in the social movement for restorative justice practices. It is taken when a citizen moves from supporting the residents of mom's nursing home in an exit conference following an inspection, to being an aged care advocate. It is taken when a young woman who learns in a school antibullying program how to confront bullying, and then applies those skills to confront corporate bullies who destroy forests on which our wildlife depends. It may be that much of the learning to be actively responsible has always arisen from restorative everyday practices in families, workplaces, and peer groups.

The approach to the revitalization of the civic republic I articulate has four components:

1. Institutionalize circles/conferences to enable all affected citizens to participate in solving problems that directly affect them in important ways (crime, the safety and well-being of children and of aged and infirm they love, unemployment, and homelessness).
2. Where appropriate, facilitate the personal becoming political in such cases. Bring in advocacy groups, such as feminist shelter workers, that can define options for structural change, possibilities for transforming personal troubles into public issues.
3. Foster social movement politics as vehicles for active responsibility in domains where we are not necessarily directly or personally affected. Abuse of power can be checked without everyone being actively responsible for every issue that concerns them. It requires that *some* citizens be actively responsible around every issue of central democratic concern. It helps when everyone is concerned about refugees in Kosovo or Ethiopia, but it helps more when a few have enough concern to be genuinely and effectively politically active on the issue.
4. In a civic republic where active responsibility is invigorated by the first three points, more of the most disenfranchised citizens might be motivated to take the responsibility to vote, thus revitalizing the representative democracy.

More briefly, this civic republican program is for restorative problem solving that teaches active responsibility, thereby motivating the making of the personal political, thereby motivating social movement politics and grassroots engagement with the representative democracy. For restorative justice to reach for these democratic ambitions, its advocates must advance certain values.

RESTORATIVE JUSTICE VALUES

If restorative justice means no more than a process for empowering through dialogue all the stakeholders affected by a problem, then it will be a rather limited force for reinvigorating democracy. It seems that the social movement for restorative justice needs to valorize active responsibility in civil society by pointing to the limitations of statist passive responsibility. It needs to valorize healing more than hurting following a wrong—restoration (especially of relationships) over ret-ribution. Most fundamentally, it should valorize democracy, especially core de-mocratic values such as all voices being heard and treated with equal respect. Yet if democracy is the most fundamental value, it brings a paradox. What if the re-sult of all voices being heard is that none of them want to take active responsi-bility, none want to heal, most want the state to invoke passive responsibility through brutal and exclusionary punishment? While this happens much less than we all expected, it does happen. When it does, if democracy is really our funda-mental value, then we will want the will of the circle to prevail and for the mat-ter to be handed back to the state. The paradox of democracy here is really a fa-miliar one: if the electorate votes in a government with an antidemocratic agenda, democrats who voted against them should not seek to overthrow them by unde-mocratic means.

Nevertheless, for the republican, majoritarian democracy is only the centrally sanctioned political process because it is a means to the end of a deeper value. This value is freedom as nondomination (Pettit, 1997) or nondomination (Braith-waite & Pettit, 1990), the freedom of not having your choices dominated by those with more power than you. For a start this means that we are not moved by the majoritarian will of the conference if the voices of deeply affected persons are dominated during the conference. But more fundamentally it implies a need to constrain majoritarian decision-making to protect against the tyranny of the ma-jority. Hence the will of the majority to flog a child should not be honored, be-cause this would be a tyrannous violation of fundamental human rights. A further paradox of democracy is that democracy is the only acceptable way to decide what are the tyrannies we should constrain majorities against imposing. The peo-ple should vote on a constitution that constrains them, constrains their legislature and judiciary from engaging in a variety of forms of domination. On the republi-can analysis, whose heritage includes Rome, Montesquieu, and Madison, free-dom as nondomination both motivates majority rule and is more fundamental than it. No one can enjoy freedom on this republican analysis in a society where majorities fail to legally tie their hands against trampling on the freedom as non-domination of those in the minority on a particular issue.

There is, therefore, a need for the justice of the law to constrain the justice of the people (especially through the institution of rights). Equally, however, there is a need to ensure that the justice of the people percolates up to influence the jus-tice of the law (Parker, 1999). A judicial system that is cut off from impulses bub-bled up from popular restorative justice will be an inferior one (Habermas, 1996). Equally, a restorative justice that is cut off from the filtering down of the justice of the courts will be inferior. This is a controversial claim in respect of indigenous justice. In a multicultural society, however, it would be intolerable to suggest that an indigenous girl who did not wish to submit to the justice of the elders should be denied protection that would be extended to her if she were nonindigenous. This is especially so if the girl contests her very membership in this indigenous group by dint of mixed birth, by attempting to leave the community, or perhaps even simply by asserting that she "doesn't want any of that Maori shit" (Maxwell & Morris, 1993).

Indeed it may be that just as Western justice has something to learn from indigenous restorative traditions, so indigenous justice has something to learn from the rights of liberal legalism. Today, many indigenous people themselves agree that fundamental legal protections against the tyranny of the majority should extend to all citizens regardless of ethnicity. That said, there are major dangers in reimporting restorative justice back into indigenous communities with added Western baggage. A good example is the accreditation of mediators. This kind of Western professionalizing project can disempower indigenous elders. While dialogue where indigenous elders and Western mediators/facilitators exchange the wisdom of their experience must be a good thing, policies that usurp respected elders for "better trained" nonelders are a threat to good governance (and are unjust). This follows from our republican analysis that active responsibility is the key to good governance. Indigenous peoples who have experienced Western occupation/domination have suffered loss of active responsibility to the most extreme degree. They have suffered most from the dead hand of passive responsibility of the Western state. Few acts of domination could therefore be worse than to seize back from them those manifestations of active responsibility that survive.

There will never be consensus on all the values that should inform restorative practices. Most restorative advocates think reintegration into communities, community development, holism, shared learning, repair of harms, restoration of relationships, forgiveness, and love are values that should centrally inform restorative processes. Many, especially indigenous elders, think spirituality is fundamental. All these values are contested to varying degrees within the movement, however. While dissensus and debate on most values is inevitable and desirable, it may be that there must be consensus on certain minimum values that allow the very possibility of a restorative space. My submission is that these values are democratic deliberation itself, equal respect for the voices of all stakeholders, a rule of law that secures freedom as nondomination and allows a space for those stakeholders to have a say.

CONCLUSION

This essay sought to understand how people in ordinary families and communities can have more of a say in a world dominated by big business, professional politicians, and technocrats. Democratic participation requires democratic competence that must be learned through the exercise of active responsibility. Restorative processes can be one crucial vehicle of empowerment where spaces are created for active responsibility in civil society to displace predominantly passive, statist responsibility. Representative democracy with a separation of powers is more sustainable than direct democracy. There are too many of us and the world is too complex for us to find time to participate in a direct democracy, even in endless citizen-initiated referenda. However, the conference-circle technology of democracy can give us an opportunity to directly participate in certain major decisions that impact our lives and those of our loved ones. Through this engagement with democratic participation in complex problem solving, citizens learn to be actively responsible. This is a deliberative theory's answer to a representative democracy that, by failing to cultivate relationships in a community, produces a people "characterized by selfishness, apathy, alienation, lack of knowledge and prejudice" (Warren, 1992, p. 11). Fishkin, Luskin, and Luskin (1999, p. 8) claim to observe among participants in their deliberative polling "a gain in empathy and mutual understanding." Restorative processes have produced more systematic evidence of such gains (Braithwaite, 1999).

Once citizens learn to be actively responsible, as opposed to learning to rely totally on protection by a state that enforces passive responsibility, they will become active in social movement politics. Nongovernmental organizations (NGOs) offer the second great avenue for revitalizing meaningful forms of citizen participation in a democracy. They can be as relevant to democratizing global institutions, such as the IMF, the World Bank, and the World Trade Organization (WTO), as they can be to redemocratizing the state (Braithwaite & Drahos, 2000). Nongovernmental organizations' influence can feed back into restorative justice conferences as advocacy of making the personal political, by invoking the possibility of agitating for structural change. The most important way this happens is when the justice of the people puts pressure on the justice of the law to change. This indeed is a shared project of the partnership restorative justice advocates seek to forge.

REFERENCES

Austin, W. (1984). Crow Indian justice: Strategies of informal social control. *Deviant Behavior, 5,* 31–46.

Barber, B. (1992). *An aristocracy of everyone: The politics of education and future of America.* New York: Oxford University Press.

Bovens, R. (1998). *The quest for responsibility.* Cambridge: Cambridge University Press.

Braithwaite, J. (1999). Restorative justice: Assessing optimistic and pessimistic accounts. In M. Tonry (Ed.), *Crime and justice: A review of research* (Vol. 25; pp. 241–369). Chicago: University of Chicago Press.

Braithwaite, J., & Daly, K. (1994). Masculinities, violence and communitarian control. In T. Newburn & E. Stanko (Eds.), *Just boys doing business.* London and New York: Routledge.

Braithwaite, J., & Drahos, P. (2000). *Global business regulation.* Cambridge: Cambridge University Press.

Braithwaite, J., & Pettit, P. (1990). *Not just deserts: A republican theory of criminal justice.* Oxford: Oxford University Press.

Fishkin, J., Luskin, J., & Luskin, R. (1999). *The quest for deliberative democracy.* Paper presented at European Consortium for Political Research, University of Mannheim, Bermand, March.

Habermas, J. (1996). *Between facts and norms: Contributions to a discourse of law and democracy.* London: Polity.

Maxwell, G., & Morris, A. (1993). *Family, victims and culture: Youth justice in New Zealand.* Wellington: Social Policy Agency and Institute of Criminology, Victoria University of Wellington.

Maxwell, G., & Morris, A. (1999). *Understanding reoffending.* Wellington: Institute of Criminology, Victoria University of Wellington.

Melton, A. P. (1995). Indigenous justice systems and tribal society. *Judicature, 79,* 126. Parker, C. (1999). *Just lawyers.* Oxford: Oxford University Press.

Pettit, P. (1997). *Republicanism.* Oxford: Clarendon.

Retzinger, S., & Scheff, T. (1996). Strategy for community conferences: Emotions and social bonds. In B. Galaway & J. Hudson (Eds.), *Restorative justice: International perspectives.* Monsey, NY: Criminal Justice Press.

Sherman, L., Strang, H., Barnes, G., Braithwaite, J., Inkpen, N., & The, M. (1998). *Experiments in restorative policing: A progress report.* Canberra: Law Program, RSSS, ANU.

Warren, M. (1992). Democratic theory and self-transformation. *American Political Science Review, 86,* 8–23.

Young, I. (1997). *Hybrid democracy: Iroquois federalism and the postcolonial project.* Paper presented at Conference on Indigenous Rights, Political Theory and the Reshaping of Institutions, Canberra, Australian National University, August.

4   Conferencing and the Community

KAY PRANIS

At the close of the twentieth century we face troubling questions about the impact of social services on community strength. Some argue that traditional social services have a weakening effect on communities and that services provided by professionals have displaced caring provided by communities. This view suggests that all of our interventions should be assessed, not just for their impact on individuals or families, but also for their aggregate impact on the community fabric. Family group conferencing offers an approach in which social service systems can partner with families and communities to produce outcomes that not only help the family but also build community cohesiveness and sense of efficacy. Conferencing holds enormous potential to strengthen communities through collective responsibility and collective accountability—in a caring context. Those characteristics of collective responsibility and collective accountability in a caring environment are also essential elements of healthy communities. Consequently, conferencing provides an opportunity to strengthen and reinforce key characteristics of strong, vibrant communities.

Relationships are the threads of a community and their interweaving is the fabric of it. Mutual responsibility is the loom on which the fabric of community is woven. Family conflicts or crises that result in the risk of children going to state care represent a failure of responsibility—often on many levels, individual, extended family, and community. Our response to these crises must strengthen or build relationships and emphasize and reestablish mutual responsibility on all levels—that is, spin new threads, add strands to old threads, and weave them together based on a pattern of answering to and for one another. Setting limits in a loving way, articulating norms of behavior, and reinforcing mutual responsibility are critical functions of healthy communities. Conferencing can contribute to the care and maintenance of those functions in community.

THE MEANING OF "COMMUNITY"

Much has been written about the meaning of "community" and lack of clarity is often cited as a problem, which must be solved before we can proceed to work with communities. Practical experience demonstrates otherwise. Communities themselves do not worry much about academic definitions. They soon define themselves based on the issue at hand. By community I mean a group of people with a shared interest and a sense of connection because of that shared interest.

Ronnie Earle, district attorney in Austin, Texas, defines community as "shared joy and pain." A planning group in St. Cloud, Minnesota, has defined community as "a group of people whose destinies are intertwined." With respect, I wish to modify the widely quoted assertion that "community is not a place." I would say community is not only a place, but that community of place matters for our long-term health as a society.

We all function in many different overlapping communities around different aspects of our lives—work, church, schools, neighborhood, family, hobbies, interests. Because we are a mobile society, many people deemphasize the community of place, which was the most common understanding of the term in earlier generations. Community of place, geographic community (neighborhoods, villages), is not the only form of community, but it is important around the issue of families in crisis for the following reasons:

1. Family conflict can affect those living in the surrounding geographic area, so there is a need to recognize harm in that community of place. Many people who are physically close to a family conflict are affected by it, even if they do not have a close relationship to the family. Generally, the geographic community around a family in crisis has a stake in peaceful resolution of the crisis.
2. Those families most impacted by family crisis do not have a lot of mobility. It is a luxury, related largely to income, to be able to choose your community in a variety of ways not related to the geography of where you live. So, in fact, community of place is still the primary form of community for many people, especially vulnerable people—those who are poor, young, or old.
3. The process of raising children is heavily influenced by the place in which they are raised. The creation of norms and expectations for children will be shaped by experience in the community of place even if there are strong nongeographic communities in the child's life. Families operate in the context of the place in which they live. Daily functions are shaped by the community of place. The degree to which parents can allow children to act independently, going out by themselves to school or to do an errand, depends upon the nature of the neighborhood. The degree to which children experience other adults interacting with them in a routine and informal way depends upon the neighborhood.
4. For most people, the sense of safety is related to place; therefore attempts to increase safety need to attend to place. One of the most important characteristics of safe places is community cohesion and sense of efficacy.
5. The immediacy of needs when families experience crisis requires resources and support that are available twenty-four hours a day and do not require a lot of time to access. In a crisis, neighbors can more readily provide that kind of immediate relief than friends who live across town.

It is important to draw on all forms of community that can contribute to supporting families in crisis, but it is also important to make sure that our resolutions work toward strengthening community of place as well as communities of interest. The future of the family will be affected by their geographic community.

CONFERENCING, VALUES, AND COMMUNITY

Conferencing has the potential to strengthen communities, but will not achieve that outcome unless we consciously build the practice toward that goal. The values underlying the practice, spoken or unspoken, will determine the quality of the outcomes of the process. Conferencing can be done in ways that weaken community. If the values guiding the process are not consistent with the values of a healthy community, then the process will undermine community. Communities are value-laden structures. Resilient, sustainable communities are built on respect, caring, taking responsibility, fulfilling obligations, and a sense of shared fate. If we want parents to be respectful with their children, they need to experience being respected. If we want parents to respond in a loving way when their children make mistakes, they need to experience a caring response when they make mistakes. If we want parents to take responsibility for the impact of their choices on their children, then we need to be responsible for the impact of our process on them. If we want parents to be committed to successful completion of their obligations, then they must have a voice in determining those commitments. If we want people to have a sense of responsibility for the fate of others, then we must have a sense of responsibility for their fate. If we want people to act in the best interest of children, then we have to act in their best interest.

At varying levels of intensity, community, that is connection to others, serves the needs and interests of its members. This is a reciprocal process. The values and expectations have to work in both directions. Every member both gives and receives. Clearly the existence of structures or processes that facilitate giving and receiving will increase the capacity of the community to meet the needs and interests of its members. Conferencing is a process that holds great promise for increasing community capacity for reciprocity among all of its members, but that promise will not be realized unless the process is guided by values that honor the dignity of every human being and the importance of caring relationships. This cannot be overemphasized. If the values of conferencing are not strong, healthy, and based on caring and respect for all participants, then the process will not be a community-building process. It will be a clever, new way to do the same old thing—disconnect, disempower, and label people.

Native people have much to teach us about keeping values at the center of human interactions. They have a way of describing these kinds of problem-solving processes that gives a helpful image. Ada Melton says that when native people come together in a circle to address behavior, they put the problem in the center—

not the family or individual. That makes a subtle but powerful shift in the nature of the process, in the attitude and relationships of the process. The image of the problem in the center helps to avoid creating an intrusive, negative focus on the family. If the problem is in the center, family members become an equal part of the group around the problem, contributing to the solutions—actors, not just recipients of anger, advice, or directives. If family members are symbolically in the center, there is a separation between them and others, but if the problem is in the center then family members are part of the *we* of all the others and together the *we* examines the problem and looks for solutions. In addition, putting the problem in the center places more focus on the children and their needs. When the parents are symbolically at the center, there is a tendency to focus primarily on them. While technique is helpful in doing effective conferences, values are more basic than technique. Participants can feel values in the attitude of how the conference is organized and conducted. Positive values reflected in respectful treatment and caring can overcome shortcomings in technique, but the experience of disrespect or indifference cannot be overcome by perfect technique.

Conferencing based on respect and caring can contribute to strong healthy communities in the following ways:

- demonstrate setting limits on behavior while loving and supporting those who have made mistakes;
- clearly articulate norms, expectations for parenting behavior for the entire community;
- reinforce a sense of mutual accountability, our responsibility to care about and take care of one another;
- practice a new form of democracy that gives all present an equal voice in decision-making.

Each of these has implications for effective practice that builds community while resolving individual cases.

Setting Limits on Behavior While Loving and Supporting

This is a critical skill for communities. Behavior in a community must be kept within certain bounds, even in the privacy of the home. The more community members can set those limits in constructive ways without recourse to fear, power, and outside enforcers, the stronger the community. Conferencing intertwines accountability and support. Answering to those you love and who love you, as well as those you hurt, is at the heart of conferencing. Knowing that you are loved and lovable, even if you have made a mistake, makes it possible to face the pain of full disclosure of the impact of your behavior. And those who love you know it is good for you to face yourself in a full understanding of what you did to others—but it would be harmful to you to do that without love and support. Accountability is a natural byproduct of appropriate caring. Loving comes first, accountability follows. If you love someone, you want them to be responsible. You do not want them to live in a way that hurts others, because you know that it will hurt them inside to do that. If you know you are loved, it will give you the courage and strength to acknowledge what you have done and to change for the future. The child protection system can exercise enormous power over the physical lives of family members, but it is relatively powerless in affecting their minds and hearts. The behavior change we want comes primarily from the heart and mind. Those who do have significant power to change the hearts and minds do that through caring and setting limits—in that order: caring, setting limits. But those who care about the family will not participate in a process that threatens the integrity of self or family members. If the process does not value family members, those with the most influence are not going to allow their influence to be used by the process.

Setting limits on behavior in an environment of caring has implications for the practice of conferencing:

1. Most members of the support group of the family must disapprove of the behavior and care deeply about the family. The process can accommodate some support people who do not disapprove of the behavior, if the support system overall is strong in its capacity to express disapproval.
2. Expressions of caring are encouraged and facilitated.
3. The larger the support system that cares and disapproves, the more reinforcement there is for the message of setting limits and caring. It is important to reach beyond nuclear family for supporters.
4. The support system is encouraged to take active steps in setting and enforcing limits in the future.
5. The process must clearly be respectful to engage the active participation of those who care about the family in disapproving the behavior.
6. The caring expressed for the adult family members is respected and reinforced by other participants.

Many child protection approaches attempt to enforce community standards (accountability) but lack any way for the community to reach out and weave the family back into the community fabric with the development of shared, voluntary commitments to community standards. Consequently, those strategies often create short-term relief, but do not change behavior in the long term. Those strategies also rely heavily on outside enforcers, the professional system, to solve the problem. No new skills are learned in the community to strengthen the community for managing this behavior in the future. When citizens participate in the process of disapproving the behavior, they strengthen the ability to set limits. When they treat the family respectfully and reach out to them, they demonstrate that caring and accountability go hand in hand. As they weave the family back into the community fabric, they reduce the isolation that contributes to and sustains the inappropriate behavior. Professionally driven processes allow the community to see the problem of the family conflict as belonging to the system. The community conferencing process sees the family crisis as belonging to the community and requiring a community solution.

By demonstrating an appropriate way to set limits while caring about someone who has made a mistake, conferencing teaches participants that it is possible to combine loving and accountability. Practice in the process over time can build the community's capacity to set limits in a caring way without the intervention of the formal child protection system. It is a primary responsibility of community to set limits without further damaging any community member. Conferencing provides a structure where community members can have a direct experience in successfully enforcing their standards without causing further harm to the family, while at the same time building their own capacity to solve problems, manage behavior, and reduce reliance on outside enforcers.

Articulating Norms and Expectations for Behavior for the Entire Community

Conferencing creates an opportunity to look beyond resolution of the specific incident to reinforce acceptable standards of behavior for the community as a whole. One of the prerequisites of community conformity to norms is a clear understanding of what behavior is and is not acceptable. We have very few processes in communities today in which community members discuss their expectations of one another. In contrast to earlier generations, children, adolescents, and adults get very little feedback about how their behavior is affecting others in the community or whether it meets community standards. Conferences focus on how behavior affects others and expectations for community behavior. The process reinforces those expectations, not just for the family, but for everyone sitting in the room. In its attention to the needs and interests of all participants, the conferencing process models an expectation that everyone will have an opportunity to tell their story and have a voice in determining what must be done. Through its process, conferencing establishes a norm that everyone will be treated with respect, listened to, and welcomed as participants in the resolution of a conflict.

Maximizing the potential for articulating and reinforcing community norms has implications for practice.

1. The more people participating in the process, the stronger the sense of the message about expectations as a broad-based message.
2. Involvement of community members who are not directly involved in the problem can strengthen the message of community expectations. A voice from outside the family that reinforces the message about appropriate be-

havior can have a very big impact. By establishing an expectation as that of the community, not just the system, a much stronger standard is set.

3. Reinforcement of community expectations for everyone will be stronger if the conference process does not focus just on the children but also emphasizes support and caring for all family members and a sense of collective problem solving.

4. Agreements that include contributions and obligations of others as well as the family will reinforce the understanding of broader community expectations of all members. The facilitator may ask supporters how each of them will help ensure fulfillment of the agreement.

Reestablishing Mutual Accountability and Collective Responsibility

Conferencing creates opportunities to strengthen the sense of mutual accountability and encourages collective responsibility for the welfare of all children and families. The intervention of the child protection system clearly communicates to families that they are accountable to others for their behavior even within their family. Conferencing provides the opportunity to affirm that the larger community has a stake in the quality of family life, particularly in regard to children. At the same time, conferencing should affirm that the larger community bears some responsibility for the quality of family life.

Over the past three decades community members have increasingly removed themselves from taking responsibility for the behavior of children and youth in public places. Adults often remain silent in the face of inappropriate behavior that thirty years ago would have elicited a clear response from the adult about standards of behavior. Nuclear families have been left to socialize their children to community standards without constant reinforcement by every adult in the community. That burden has created enormous stress for families. By involving extended family, neighbors, and other community members, conferences encourage sharing responsibility for the well-being of the children and family. Family conflict is not viewed as belonging to the family alone, but to everyone. Simply by participating, others acknowledge some level of responsibility. It becomes much easier for family members to take responsibility for mistakes if they feel they are not alone, that the responsibility is shared. Conferencing allows extended family members and supporters to be a part of determining the plan to resolve the problem, and consequently they have a stake in successful completion of the agreement. As participants in the decision-making, they become responsible for helping to make the agreement work. Instead of just the child protection worker checking to see if the parents are following the plan, an uncle or neighbor who was part of the conference may ask the parents whether they are attending parenting classes or practicing affirmations with the child. That is a far more personal prompt than one coming from the child protection worker.

Expressions of collective responsibility by extended family and supporters are very important to the community because once they acknowledge such responsibility, supporters are more likely to use their influence with the adult family members to inhibit inappropriate behavior in the future. Some agreements include ways in which other community members reach out to the family. Such actions powerfully reconnect the family in the community and reestablish a relationship of mutual responsibility and commitment to the welfare of all. Throughout the process the commitment of the community to the well-being of the family is reflected in statements of support and caring and in the creation of the process itself that allows full involvement by the family. Characteristics of practice will influence the degree to which collective accountability and mutual responsibility are achieved.

1. The wider the net of support for the family, including extended family, neighbors, and role models, the stronger the web of relationships available to give verbal and behavioral expression to a sense of collective accountability for past and future behavior. Typically, no single supporter can take this on alone, and therefore supporters may avoid commitments if they feel they will be stuck with all the responsibility. If the support system is large enough, then the small contributions of each supporter add up to a significant difference that is felt by all.
2. Collective accountability is unlikely to be expressed by family supporters if they feel the process is isolating and hurtful.
3. The tone of the session will significantly affect whether participants see themselves as having responsibility for one another beyond the resolution of the incident. If the conference is focused entirely on the birth parents, for example, others may have no sense of their own responsibility for a better future for all the participants.
4. Expressions of caring and support for the family reconnect them to the community and reinforce the community's stake in their welfare.

Practicing a New Form of Democracy

Conferencing gives the power to make a decision to those most affected by a decision. It provides disempowered families and their supporters with the opportunity to take control of a significant event in their lives. And it requires that the decisions made address the interests of all parties, because agreement requires everyone's approval. That is democracy in action—on a small scale—with enormous implications if practiced widely. In the conferencing process everyone has a chance to tell his or her story in relation to the issue. Every perspective is incorporated into the understanding of the situation that emerges from the process. The complexities and nuances of real life are allowed expression and consideration in reaching decisions. The information available to make decisions is not constrained by rules or structure.

This may ultimately be the most important contribution conferencing makes to building strong communities. Conferencing and the peacemaking circle process model democratic decision-making in communities in a new form that ensures that no one leaves the table with their interest ignored. Decisions in conferencing, as in circles, are based on consensus. Consensus decision-making requires all participants to pay attention to the needs and interests of every other participant so that an agreement might be reached. Decisions that include the interests of all participants seem to me to be more fundamentally democratic than decisions made by majority rule. The experience of finding consensus resolution around problems of crime, where there are very strong emotions, demonstrates that consensus decision-making is not an unrealistic possibility for groups of people around other issues as well.

Experience with both conferencing and circles teaches us that ordinary citizens do not need complex technical training to be able to sort through information from a variety of perspectives and pick out the most critical issues and craft ingenious solutions. Democracy is undermined by dependence upon professional classes to analyze and solve community problems. Conferencing moves responsibility and authority back to community members, including the family and their supporters. Having a say in those decisions that most affect your life is the essence of democracy. Conferencing and circles take the power of decision-making to the most fundamental level. This is grassroots democracy in a form that does not pit groups against one another, but through the consensus process builds a sense of shared commitment and collaboration. Majority rule democracy encourages competition and pursuit of self-interest or limited partnerships. Consensus building encourages cooperation with all other interests and pursuit of balanced interests for self and the larger community. These processes have the potential to transform our relationships with one another and our ways of working with one another at all levels—personally, in families, in the workplace, in community, and in government processes. But that will not happen unless we are clear about guiding values that emphasize respect and caring for everyone.

NOTE

This chapter is a revised version of a paper originally prepared for the First North American Conference on Conferencing, August, 1998, Minneapolis, Minnesota.

5   Guiding Principles of the Conferencing Process

DAVID MOORE and JOHN MCDONALD

INTRODUCTION

After a decade of debates, we believe a more general theoretical account of conferencing is emerging. So we begin this chapter with a simple claim and a matching definition. The claim: *the power of community conferencing is strongest when the process is understood as a mechanism for conflict transformation.* The definition: *community conferencing is a process for acknowledging and then transforming conflict within and between people.*

We use the phrase "community conferencing" to distinguish a generic version of the *process* from whatever *programs* are used to deliver it. This is an important distinction. Community conferencing can be adapted and modified for use in education, social work, criminal and civil law, human resource management, and a host of other areas. Programs in each of these areas will use language specific to the professional practice of their administrators. In our experience, however, legislators, administrators, and facilitators should clearly distinguish the language of these *programs* from the principles guiding the community conferencing *process.*

We believe the conferencing process can offer most to many areas of professional practice when it is understood in language derived from a range of disciplines. If the full reforming potential of community conferencing is to be realized, the process should be guided by principles derived not just from within a single field of professional practice. Rather, broader guiding principles for the conferencing process should derive from ground common to all conferencing programs. How we categorize strongly influences how we comprehend. If categories are derived only from programs, our comprehension of the process will be limited. We need to consider how conferencing programs have been categorized, and then consider the shortcomings of the categories.

EARLY GENEALOGY

The New Zealand National Parliament passed the Children, Young Persons and their Families Act in 1989. Any overview of conferencing recognizes this as a key moment. Then perspectives begin to diverge. Just what is the essential feature of conferencing? Is it that conferencing places the *family* in a central role in decision-making? Or does conferencing blur boundaries between family and community, extending and strengthening social networks, and so realizing a version of *communitarian* political philosophy? Is it that conferencing is similar to decision-making strategies used by *indigenous* peoples around the world? Or is it that the process can accommodate cosmopolitan cultural and ethnic *diversity,* since it seems adaptable to the protocols of many groups? Does conferencing realize a different philosophy of *justice*? Or are community conferencing and other *circle-based processes* examples of a more general mechanism of networked dialogue, a mechanism with benefits and applications that extend well beyond justice and welfare applications? Each of these questions merits examination.

Is the Essential Quality of Conferencing the Central Decision-Making Role It Gives to the *Family?*   As contributors to the current book agree, conferencing is consistent with a shift in the guiding metaphors of child welfare philosophy. The shift is from a metaphor of individual pathology to a metaphor of ecology. The ecological model supports a list of admirable values: is family-centered; aims to empower family members; emphasizes the importance of parent-child relationships; promotes a climate of safety; respects diversity; fosters parenting and other life skills. The model's optimism acts as a corrective to the pessimism of a model of individual pathology. But concern was raised early about the danger of overcorrecting with the optimism of the ecological model and the practice of conferencing. The question has frequently been asked: What if a family system really is weak or dysfunctional? Professionals are now looking for strengths in individuals, families, and communities that simply may not be there in some cases. Worse still, what if members of the nuclear family in question really are the primary problem, rather than part of the solution?

One obvious response to such concerns is to look outside or beyond that (nuclear) family system. In such cases, a measure of the success of an intervention could be whether it promotes greater collaboration with formal and informal resources in the broader community. The intervention could aim not just for an improvement and/or strengthening of existing relationships, but also for an extension of networks of relationships. In such cases, a community conference need not be seen as a discrete event. Rather, it can be seen as part of an ongoing process to improve relationships more generally. This approach is quite consistent with the ecological model, but it suggests that a focus on families may be too narrow.

Does Conferencing Blur Boundaries between Family and Community, Extending and Strengthening Social Networks? And Does It Thereby Realize a Version of *Communitarian* **Political Philosophy?**   The focus of an intervention may be extended beyond a family to the broader communities to which that family belongs. This broader focus seems consistent with "communitarianism," which is political philosophy's counterpart to the ecological model in social theory. Communitarian theory informs a social movement that is concerned to reclaim or rebuild communities. Since there are significant differences among self-styled communitarians on how best to achieve this goal, some theorists and practitioners prefer to bypass the communitarian debate. They speak instead of strategies to "increase social capital" (Putnam, 1993). And it seems that one way to increase social capital in a given neighborhood is to have many community conferences facilitated in that neighborhood. The cumulative increase in the number and strength of relationships in microcommunities can gradually strengthen the macrolevel communities of neighborhoods and beyond.

Again, concerns have been raised that communitarianism may be overcorrective. Seeking to remedy perceived weaknesses in liberal political theory, communitarian theory emphasizes the rights *and duties* of social individuals. The concern is that this corrective emphasis on duties to society might undermine individual rights if it allows an alliance between the state and an oppressive community. To avoid this danger, the role of the state must be very clear. The role of the state in a community conference should not be to impose an outcome; it should be to safeguard a process. And the process is designed to guard against inappropriate coercion by an oppressive community. To date, legislation for conferencing has tried to guard against inappropriate coercion primarily by setting parameters for conference outcomes. Outcome parameters may be necessary to avoid breaches of rights. But the emphasis, in the first instance, should be on the *process*. Facilitators should safeguard a process that is true to the principles of deliberative democracy, including nontyranny. This is the strongest safeguard against inappropriate coercion.

To determine who should attend, a conference facilitator seeks the advice of those most directly involved in the incident or issue. So what are the principles for deciding who should attend? In an adversarial system, people are gathered to support an attack on the arguments of the other side. In conferencing, people are gathered who support those most directly affected. But these supporters are there in their own right. They belong to the community of people affected. They are not to be used simply as a means to an end. People are asked to participate in an intervention using a process with which they may not be familiar. Referring in detail to the organizing principles of their particular community may be problematic when communities that organize themselves along different lines are involved in a conference. Favoring one community's organizing principles over another's will undermines the neutrality of the facilitator. In arranging the conditions for those most affected to reach an optimal outcome, a facilitator needs a minimalist set of principles that will be generally acceptable to all.

The ecological model seems a good candidate for those minimalist principles. It emphasizes relationships between people, their social environment, and the degree of social capital in that environment. But the ecological model does not indicate just what a facilitator should do when a family and other members of their community are brought together, sometimes with people from another community. To determine what a facilitator should do in these circumstances, we need both broad principles and more specific procedural guidelines consistent with these principles. In the absence of these guidelines, the default option has often been to follow "how it's traditionally done."

The Conferencing Process Is Similar to Decision-Making Strategies Used by *Indigenous* Peoples around the World.   The conferencing process is frequently compared with decision-making strategies used by *indigenous* peoples. But various circle-based processes are now being applied successfully with nonindigenous or mixed communities in parts of Canada and the United States, as well as in New Zealand and Australia. So it is appropriate and important to acknowledge the historical origins of New Zealand's pioneering legislation. And it is appropriate and important to acknowledge that similar processes have been retained in many indigenous cultures (Ross, 1996). But it may be less appropriate to suggest that, because circle-based processes have been retained in many indigenous cultures, these processes are therefore somehow *particularly suited* to people of recent indigenous heritage. This line of argument can lead to an ethnic essentialism that is certainly ahistorical and probably not politically helpful.

The line of argument that these processes are particularly suited to people of indigenous heritage is ahistorical because it overlooks the role of similar processes in earlier Western European systems of law and governance. Celtic, Germanic, and Roman systems all seem to have included similar processes for dealing with conflict among members of particular communities. When these proved incompatible with the authority of a centralizing state, the mechanisms of that central state eventually took precedence (Van Ness & Keetderks Strong, 1997). The issue is perhaps not so much whether people are of recent indigenous heritage, but whether or not their recent ancestors remembered and used some sort of conflict resolution processes that offered an alternative to the imposition of outcomes by state authorities.

To suggest that circle-based processes are particularly suited to people of recent indigenous heritage is politically unhelpful for several reasons. First, a common argument along these lines is that there is something more authentic, something deeper, about people of indigenous heritage and/or indigenous cultures. But this line of argument can prove divisive. It can create a sort of hierarchy of moral authority separating the authentic and deep from the—by implication—unauthentic and shallow. Perhaps more problematically, this line of argument can slow the pace of reform. It can also keep reforming processes marginalized. Conferencing reforms began at the margins of the youth justice system. Part of the reforming logic seems to have been an assumption that conferencing was essentially applicable to children. The logic that the process also applies particularly to people of indigenous heritage can carry worrying implications.

An alternative concern about the introduction of community conferencing in remote indigenous communities, particularly in Canada and Australia, has been that their communitarian element could actually diminish rights and protections. Concerns have been expressed in particular about potential outcomes of conferences to deal with undisputed harm, outcomes such as banishment, shaming, and payback. The point seems generally to be overlooked that harsh, punitive options in contemporary indigenous societies are perhaps best seen not as some "timeless" tradition, but as a symptom of people's understandable sense of anger and frustration about crime. They are thus much like calls for harsher penalties in any other cultural context. Calls for harsh punishment are common and understandable wherever there has been no attempt to address the conflict within and between people in the aftermath of the undisputed harm.

In general, it seems that circle-based processes, such as conferencing, are proving acceptable to many people of indigenous heritage not simply because the process seems familiar. They are proving acceptable because the benefits are particularly obvious. But it should be stressed that these benefits are available to any community. There is something universal about the ways in which a small community of people can acknowledge and then transform the conflict within and among themselves as they share perspectives, thoughts, and feelings, before seeking solutions to a shared problem. So if not from indigenous traditions, where does one seek broader principles and procedural guidelines?

The Conference Process Can Accommodate *Diversity* by Adapting to the Protocols of a Wide Variety of Cultural and Ethnic Groups. It seems that one reason why conferencing is proving acceptable to indigenous communities is that there is something universal about the dynamics of the process. Conferencing is being readily accepted by other minority groups for the same reason, particularly in the context of the multicultural settler societies of Oceania and North America. These societies have a pressing need for processes that can accommodate a *diversity* of ethnic and cultural values. Despite concerns, the involvement of people from different ethnic groups in community conferences has generally not proven problematic. Indeed, the process provides an opportunity for dialogue between groups that may not have communicated to any great degree. One persistent concern about conferences involving different ethnic groups is the issue of language and interpretation. For instance, interpretation can slow proceedings. To the extent that proceedings are slowed, our sense is that this is no bad thing. It emphasizes the power of affective communication as participants address the past and present before searching for a just outcome.

Do Conferencing and Other *Circle-Based Processes* Offer a Method of Communication with Benefits and Applications That Extend Well Beyond Justice and Welfare Applications? The short answer to that long question is yes. It has long been recognized that there is something qualitatively different about conversation that arises and agreements that are reached in the course of an open encounter among a group of people formally arranged in a circle. Dialogue can be differentiated from two other types of linguistic communication: debate and inquiry. Debate tends toward an either/or resolution of issues. It assumes win/lose outcomes on each disputed point and on the overall issue, so its emphasis is on *sending information*. Received information is judged primarily on its potential

value for repackaging and sending in pursuit of victory on the overall issue. Inquiry, conversely, emphasizes *receiving information*. But the general parameters
of that information are known in advance (McMaster, 1997).

Dialogue, in contrast to debate *and* inquiry, does not emphasize sending over
receiving, or vice versa. It does not specify in advance just what information is
sought. Rather it is a model of mutual creation, of "generative conversation," of
"connected intelligence" (de Kerckhove, 1997). Dialogue offers to create something new, something that emerges from the process of dialogue itself. An essential feature of this process is that it removes obstacles to communication.

A key obstacle to constructive communication is a state of conflict. A defining
feature of conflict is the absence of constructive communication. Another defining feature is that the most negative emotions are generated by the parties in conflict. So that cluster of negative emotions around anger, fear, and contempt fuel
and are fueled by conflict. By avoiding the conflict inherent in debate and inquiry,
dialogue seems to be the mode of constructive communication that offers a path
out of this impasse. And we suggest that the professions that have found a use for
community conferencing have this in common: they all seek to *address problems
caused by, and causing, conflict within people and between people*. It follows that
an interdisciplinary theory of conferencing should provide:

- an account of causes of conflict within and between people;
- a typology for different classes of *situation* marked by conflict;
- a typology for *processes* that respond to conflict;
- an analytical tool for determining the appropriate process for a given situation marked by conflict.

GUIDING PRINCIPLES OF THE CONFERENCING PROCESS

The general format of a community conference is that the facilitator:

- identifies sources of conflict in a system of relationships;
- brings the people in that system of relationships together in a circle;
- invites participants, in a scripted sequence, to respond to a series of open
  questions;
- begins with questions that help paint a picture of incidents and/or issues
  that have contributed to the conflict;
- then asks questions that foster acknowledgment and greater understanding
  of the conflict;
- safeguards the process as participants play out the transformation of conflict through all stages of the conference.

We believe that this process can only transform conflict among people if the
process does not itself become a source of significant dispute. It is not enough that

the formal outcome looks objectively fair on paper. The process itself must also be considered fair. The process must be governed by a set of rules that are acceptable to all participants, and these rules must include procedures to deal with any breach of the rules. Only then will participants believe that the intervention has been just. In short, justice requires fair rules, fair play, and fair outcomes. The achievement of all three is fundamental to the success of an intervention because justice is a universal human first principle. People have evolved an acute sensitivity to what psychologists call "social cheating" (Tooby et al., 1995). As we understand it, the rules for a community conference will only be perceived as fair if they are consistent with the precepts of small group or participatory democracy. To be fundamentally democratic, a conference must satisfy the precepts of participation, deliberation, equity, and nontyranny (Fishkin, 1995). Depending on the nature of the case and the supporting program, a facilitator may need lengthy preparation to determine who should attend and so satisfy the precept of *participation*.

The precepts of *equity* and *deliberation* are satisfied by having participants speak in an appropriate sequence, prompting them with open questions and allowing adequate time for them to speak and be heard. Finally, a facilitator may need to use subtle intervention techniques should one or more participants breach the precept of *nontyranny* by using position, personality, or political ideology to exercise excessive power over other participants. In short:

- everyone affected should be encouraged to attend;
- everyone in attendance should be given the opportunity to speak;
- each contribution should be listened to and given adequate consideration;
- no participant should be allowed to block the opportunity of another to attend, speak, be listened to, and have adequate consideration given to issues raised.

To achieve all of this is not easy. It is made more difficult by the tendency of institutions to focus excessively on *agency-specific procedures*. Unless their administrators are actively aware of the problem, agencies responsible for community conferencing programs will tend to emphasize midrange *agency-specific procedures* at the expense of (i) general *first principles* such as democracy, justice, principles of conflict, and an articulated theory of emotions, motivation, and interaction; and (ii) *widely applicable techniques* of conflict transformation in *personal* interactions.

Agency-specific procedures alone will not produce adequate, let alone good, community conference facilitation. Improved facilitation of conferences requires that facilitators be guided by *first principles* and skilled in *techniques* of conflict transformation. We have found three guiding principles particularly useful: transparency, clarity, and respect. By *transparency* we mean openness about all aspects of an intervention: openness about the guiding principles, openness about the process, and openness about the program under which the conference is occurring.

By *clarity* we mean methods of communicating that most effectively increase comprehension of workplace conferencing. To achieve clarity, facilitators should use and promote whatever words, analogies, metaphors, or images most effectively increase comprehension of conferencing principles, process, and program. *Respect* is a general stance that coordinators should cultivate toward all the people with whom they are working (Moore & McDonald, 2000).

SUMMARY AND CONCLUSIONS

A community conference is, in one sense, no more than a structured conversation. At the same time, it is a complex interaction that needs to be carefully and skillfully facilitated. In cases of conflict arising from an act of undisputed harm, a single conference (with a monitored agreement) may be a sufficient formal intervention. In more complex cases, such as care and protection matters or conflicted workplaces, a conference should not be seen as an "inoculation." Participants may require ongoing support in the form of conversations, visits, and referrals to professionals who can help them deal more effectively with their situation.

We have suggested that facilitators can best safeguard this complex structured conversation if they view the process as a mechanism for transforming conflict. The community conference provides a community of people with a formal style and system of communication. That style and system of communication enables them to shift away from conflict toward cooperation. To help them get there, the facilitator requires:

- the diagnostic tool of the distinction between disputes and conflict;
- the principles of justice and deliberative democracy; and,
- a theory of personality that explains the emotional transition at the heart of conflict transformation.

The facilitator needs a working theory of how communities move from the negative emotions associated with conflict to the positive emotions associated with cooperation.

REFERENCES

de Kerckhove, D. (1997). *Connected intelligence: The arrival of the web society.* London: Kogan Page.

Fishkin, J. (1995). *The voice of the people: Public opinion and democracy.* New Haven, CT: Yale University Press

Gilligan, C. (1982). *In a different voice: Psychological theory and women's development.* Cambridge, MA: Harvard University Press.

Hassall, I. (1996). Origin and development of family group conferences. In J. Hudson, A. Morris, G. Maxwell, & B. Galaway (Eds.), *Family group conferences: Perspectives on policy and practice.* Sydney: Federation.

Hudson, J., Morris, A., Maxwell, G., & Galaway, B. (Eds.) (1996). *Family group conferences: Perspectives on policy and practice.* Sydney: Federation.

Kohlberg, L. (1981) *Essays in moral development,* Vol. I, *The philosophy of moral development— Moral stages and the idea of justice.* New York: Harper & Row.

Kohlberg, L. (1984). *Essays in moral development,* Vol. II, *The psychology of moral development.* New York: Harper & Row.

McMaster, D. (1996). *The intelligence advantage: Organizing for complexity.* Newton, MA: Butterworth-Heinemann.

Moore, D., & Forsythe, L. (1995). *Family conferencing in Wagga Wagga: A report to the Criminology Research Council.* [Available online at the Australian Institute of Criminology Library: www.aic. gov.au/crc/oldreports/fulltext.html]

Moore, D., & McDonald, J. (2000). *Transforming conflict in workplaces and other communities.* Sydney: TJA.

McDonald, J., & Moore, D. (1998). *Community conference facilitator's kit.* Sydney: TJA.

McMaster, M. (1996). *The intelligence advantage: Organizing for complexity.* Boston: Butterworth-Heinemann. Putnam, R. (1993). *Making democracy work: Civic traditions in modern Italy.* Princeton, NJ: Princeton University Press.

Ross, R. (1996). *Returning to the teachings: Exploring Aboriginal justice.* Toronto: Penguin.

Tooby, J., Barkow, J., & Cosmides, L. (Eds.) (1995). *The adapted mind: Evolutionary psychology and the generation of culture.* Oxford: Oxford University Press.

Van Ness, D. (1990). Restorative justice. In B. Galaway & J. Hudson (Eds.), *Criminal justice: Restitution and reconciliation.* Monsey, NY: Willow Tree.

Van Ness, D., & Keetderks Strong, K. (1997). *Restoring justice.* Cincinnati, OH: Anderson.

Section II   Introduction: Practice Frameworks

JOE HUDSON and GALE BURFORD

Chapters in this section address principles, elements, and applications of conferencing, comparatively relating these to such child welfare interventions as in-home family support programming, social network theory and practice, permanency planning, wraparound programs. The first four chapters present frameworks within which to view conferencing, including a broad set of principles and values supporting and impacting on conferencing applications. Attention then shifts in the remaining chapters to viewing conferencing processes within the context of programming applications.

Anthony Maluccio and Judith Daly begin with a discussion of good child welfare practice principles, relating these to conferencing. The following chapter by Susan Kemp, James Whittaker, and Elizabeth Tracy elaborates on principles identified by Maluccio and Daly within the context of the Person-Environment Practice framework. In his chapter, Ted Wachtel, a practitioner with extensive experience using conferencing processes in a variety of program contexts, picks up on principles identified in the previous chapters, emphasizing the manner in which conferencing provides a way to work collaboratively with people, not doing to and for them. The critical matter of program implementation, where the slip between the cup and the lip so commonly occurs, is then addressed by Paul Nixon. Based on his extensive work with conferencing initiatives in the United Kingdom, Nixon draws implications for organizing and delivering conferencing programs.

The emphasis of the chapters then shifts from a focus on broad design and implementation principles to program applications, comparatively relating these to family group conferencing. Paul Adams describes the Patch approach and its relationship to conferencing, and Kay Pranis and Barry Stuart do the same for circle processes. Don Fuchs then describes social network theory and practice. John and Sara Burchard deal with wraparound programming, Jennifer Boland, Cynthia Collea, Judith Daly, Ruth Hale, and Thomas Hill describe the Making Action Plans program underway in Vermont, and Charles Waldegrave discusses Just Therapy in New Zealand. Joan Pennell and Gale Burford's chapter concludes this section, addressing the controversial topic of conferencing and family violence. All of these chapters consider conferencing principles and practices within a context of programs having the common aim of working with families and communities for the care and protection of children. Some of the major themes addressed in these chapters can be briefly noted.

Relationship of Formal and Informal Helping

A key question running through these chapters is the appropriate relationship between the formal helping systems of the state and informal mechanisms of care and control in families and communities. Paul Adams outlines these general approaches, calling one a neostatist position, emphasizing the central place of the state and its officials in dealing with child protection matters. As he notes, this position can often amount to discounting the importance of extended family, voluntary associations, schools, and neighborhoods. A contrasting position identified with family group conferences emphasizes working with families and communities to identify and build on their strengths. Neostatists are seen as arguing that conferencing processes and programs leave children vulnerable to the very families and communities that failed to provide for their care and protection in the first place. Chapters by Don Fuchs, and Susan Kemp, James Whittaker, and Elizabeth Tracy, directly address this issue by emphasizing the importance of identifying, building, and supporting the social support networks of families, not leaving them exposed and vulnerable.

Chapters by Ted Wachtel and Paul Nixon also address the proper place of formal and informal helping systems, viewing family group conferencing as a way to shift power relations from the state to individual citizens and offering a way to help families and communities. But these authors also describe the many difficulties associated with achieving such a power shift, specifically in getting professionals to share decision-making responsibility with families and communities. Nixon sees child protection systems being based on a culture of professionalism, in which agency norms, administrative procedures, and social work practices reflect values conflicting with conferencing principles, particularly in respect to the extent families are seen as able to take greater responsibility for making decisions affecting children.

Program Definition and Integrity

Several chapters discuss the tendency of professionals to adopt family group conferences in name, not substance, and in this way reduce conferencing to a tool, method, or label having little integrity to principles. Paul Adams illustrates this in his description of home visiting programs and the way these have been undermined and used as vehicles for enhancing the role of professionals. In a similar way, the values and principles of conferencing can be lost sight of, and the programs as practiced have little in common with what conferencing processes are all about. To help counter this, John and Sara Burchard emphasize the importance of program design specifications, using evaluation research to monitor the manner and extent programs are implemented according to design. Chapters in Part IV deal extensively with this point.

Conferencing Is Teamwork

These chapters emphasize a view of conferencing as a team-based approach amounting to the participation of a group of persons having complementary knowledge and skills coming together to plan, provide, and monitor services and supports for the care and protection of children. Interdependence, mutuality, and reciprocity are stressed as key features of conferencing. Planning for the care and protection of children is the driving force in the work of conferencing and teamwork seen as key to achieving this purpose. This means recognizing and respecting the validity of different kinds of knowledge and expertise held by different conference participants. Maluccio and Daly refer to this as respecting human diversity. No person in the conference group is assumed superior to others, and the power associated with formal authority roles is to be shared with conference participants so they come to see each other as essential to achieving the conference purpose. The aim is to promote a setting in which all participants feel welcome and their contributions valued.

Rationale for Conferencing

These chapters emphasize an ecological perspective and support conferencing principles fitting with the permanency planning movement, a competency orientation, and the ethical position of client self-determination. The ecological perspective underlying a conferencing approach is emphasized by Anthony Maluccio and Judith Daly; Susan Kemp, James Whittaker, and Elizabeth Tracy; and John and Sara Burchard. As these authors suggest, an ecological perspective views people and their environments dynamically interacting with primary sources of support coming from families, neighborhoods, and communities.

As Kemp, Whittaker, and Tracy note, a key premise of a competence or family-strengths perspective is one of identifying and building on the strengths of people to interact with their environments. A different perspective is offered by a deficit model based on assumptions of individual pathology, negative cultural stereotyping, and weaknesses of kin and community networks. A difference in these views for conferencing is seeing that people most directly involved in troubled and troubling relationships have abilities and motivations to make choices and share in responsibility for the helping work.

Anthony Maluccio and Judith Daly describe permanency planning as a process of ensuring that children grow up in a family setting, preferably their own, and in support of conferencing, several chapters cite research findings showing that children offered a family group conference are more likely to be placed with extended family, and the placements more likely to be stable, compared to usual case planning methods. Partnership and good outcomes appear related, and conferencing is seen to facilitate permanency planning by identifying problems, clarifying goals, and reaching agreement on services and supports to keep children and their families together and safe.

A major advantage seen for conferencing is that planning in isolation from young persons and their families can result in conflicts and that by bringing the significant persons together, the potential exists for differences to be identified and mutually negotiated plans prepared. A conferencing group composed of the significant persons in the life of the young person and family is seen to have a greater helping impact than would be the case if each person worked alone. Planning with people is respectful; not allowing opportunities for participating in decision-making clearly violates respect for self-determination and dignity.

Conferencing is seen as demanding active participation and creating a sense of empowerment in participants. Bringing together significant persons in the life of a family allows for responsibilities to be carried out by all participants to achieve conferencing goals. Conferencing is not an "easy way out" for families. They are encouraged and supported by the process to take responsibility.

Critical Assessments of Conferencing

A number of potential limitations and abuses of conferencing are identified in these chapters, including those relating to the power differentials of participants, dangers of using conferencing to further oppress or burden participants, and difficulties of achieving mutuality between professionals and family members. The unequal power base existing between families and child welfare workers is seen as potentially limiting family members in expressing different points of view, particularly when they conflict with those of statutory workers who hold formal authority over them. A different kind of power imbalance in conferencing is described by Joan Pennell and Gale Burford in respect to common fears felt by survivors of family abuse—fears of being attacked, shamed, and manipulated. They address these concerns, presenting principles to protect against them and offering research showing that violence did not occur at conferences, and abuse rates were lowered. While acknowledging perceptions of conferencing as involving power differentials, Paul Nixon and Paul Adams see the burden on professionals to ensure that conferencing principles are carried out and respect provided to families. As Paul Nixon notes, the alternative to a conferencing program where decision-making powers are shared is for state workers to operate out of a disabling approach of professional control and assessment.

The Work of Conference Coordinators

The critical role of the coordinator is discussed in these chapters, particularly in assembling the family group conference and inspiring the participants with a family-centered, strengths approach. The variety of tasks required of the coordinator are described, and Joan Pennell and Gale Burford illustrate the work of preparing participants for a conference dealing with family violence. Coordinators are responsible for identifying persons to be invited to a conference, discussing participation in light of the meeting purpose, and reaching agreement on the meeting date, time, and place. The importance of front loading information for family group conferencing is presented in these chapters. This can be time-consuming work and the larger the number of persons invited to a conference, the more time required for preparation. Getting birth family members to participate in conferences can be made more difficult if meetings are scheduled during normal workday hours convenient for professionals. Government times may not be convenient for others who have to take time off work and travel some distance to attend. But Paul Nixon notes UK experience showing that more difficulty is experienced getting professionals to attend conferences than family members. Meeting schedules likely account for this.

These chapters stress the importance of coordinators believing in the importance of inclusiveness and actively pursuing, encouraging, and supporting involvement. Initial coordinator contacts with family members are described as involving negotiations around such matters as the most convenient days, times, and locations for conference meetings, transportation arrangements, other difficulties that might constrain attendance at conferences, how these might be resolved, and obtaining the names and phone numbers of other family members who should be invited to attend. Obstacles to family participation need to be identified, alternative solutions considered, and solutions chosen.

The chapters also describe the preparation of family members for family group conferences as including telling family members how important their attendance is, openly discussing feelings of anger, sadness, and awkwardness that family members have about the difficulties being experienced, discussing family responsibility for participating, pointing out how young people may feel angry and insulted when their family does not participate, and clearly explaining who will be attending the meeting and how it will be run. As Joan Pennell and Gale Burford illustrate in their case example of conferencing with a family violence situation, family members must be assured that they will not be attacked by other participants, and their participation valued.

These chapters also emphasize the role of coordinators inviting and preparing professionals for family group conferences. To do this, coordinators contact those professionals important in the life of the children and families to: explain the purpose to be accomplished and process to be followed; explain who is expected to attend the meetings; and review the way the conference meeting is expected to be run. To balance what may well be a neostatist perspective held by officials, coordinators need to prepare professionals for the conference by reviewing such key expectations as nontolerance of inappropriate behaviors; respecting private family time; supporting plans established by the conference; maintaining confidentiality.

Another set of coordinator tasks discussed in these chapters has to do with holding family group conferences. Action steps to be carried out by the coordinator include: ensuring that all parties have an opportunity to introduce themselves and their role at the meeting; clarifying and reaching agreement on the purpose and process of the meeting and the agenda; reaching agreement on responsibilities for recording conference agreements; documenting the conference plan arrived at in terms of decisions made, and providing copies to all participants.

Nature of Family Group Conference Plans

A family group conference plan is seen in these chapters as amounting to a written, negotiated statement identifying the intervention strategies to be carried out, and objectives to be achieved within a designated time. Putting conferencing agreements in writing emphasizes their importance, improves clarity, reduces misunderstanding, and provides a basis for monitoring and reviewing progress. Characteristics of conferencing plans are seen as including clarity, flexibility, participatory, covering a specific time period. Family group conferences should be carried out and plans written in clear, simple language. Technical terms are to be avoided. The problems to be addressed, tasks or interventions to be carried out, and goals to be achieved should be stated precisely, free of ambiguity to reduce any confusion about who is expected to carry out what activities, to achieve what goals, and when. Conditions of the family group conference plans should be achievable, and if planned goals cannot be reasonably attained or the interventions practically carried out, plans amount to setups for failure and frustration on the part of participants. The total amount of work expected and the readiness of participants to take on particular kinds of activities should be considered. Priority matters should be addressed, recognizing that some problems and services should be deferred to another time. Flexibility is called for so that conferencing plans are seen as tools, not ends in themselves. They can and should be changed by bringing conference participants back together to discuss and make necessary modifications.

6 Family Group Conferences as "Good" Child Welfare Practice

ANTHONY N. MALUCCIO and JUDITH DALY

The philosophy and practice of family group conferences reflect basic principles of "good" child and family welfare practice. Following an illustrative case summary, selected principles common to both child and family welfare services and family group conferences are discussed, along with similarities with permanency planning and family preservation approaches.

CASE SUMMARY

The R. family, consisting of mother; father; another father in prison; Jane, age eleven; and two brothers, ages nine and fourteen, was referred in April 1998 by the state child welfare agency to a private child welfare agency for family group decision-making services. The referral summary indicated that Jane was residing in a state foster home and that two paternal aunts were interested in kinship care/adoption. Later, a maternal aunt and a maternal uncle also became interested in caring for her. Jane had been placed into state custody a year earlier as a result of sexual abuse by her stepfather, who was eventually convicted of the abuse. Recently he also abused the mother, who wavers in her relationship with him. At the time of the referral, there was a temporary restraining order on him, but he had skipped town.

According to the state worker, Jane was angry at her mother for not protecting her and for not "getting rid" of her husband. There were extended family on both sides who were involved with the child and whom she saw regularly. In particular, caring relationships existed with the two paternal aunts, the maternal grandparents, and a teenage cousin. Jane got along well with both of her brothers. They considered themselves close. The boys worried about her and wished that she was at home. She wanted to see more of them.

Following is a summary of the worker's report regarding the family group decision-making process with the R. family.

Initial Conference. *The initial conference was held in July 1998 to plan for Jane's needs, especially where she would live and how her family would maintain contact with her. Preparation for the conference followed the customary steps in the family group decision-making model (FGDM). I met with all the parties to prepare them prior to the meeting. The family was asked about location; they had no preference for the original meeting, so they asked me to arrange it, which I did at a local church. In addition to members of the immediate family and relatives, participants included Jane's current and previous foster mothers, the state agency worker, and the worker from the private agency. Some family members brought food, as did I, based on what they said they liked. Grandma baked a cake as it was near the child's twelfth birthday. During the family's private time, an aunt checked in with me several times, needing guidance. I was able to give her direction without going in and taking over. At the end, they did ask for help in going over the language of the plan to make sure it was worded well and was complete. I helped them with this, as by this time I had discovered that this was not an unusual request; families do not talk and think "plan language," and they know that they are trying to make this plan for the "system" and need some assistance with how to best express their ideas. The initial conference took six hours. The outcome was a plan to place Jane with relatives to be selected by the state agency. The agency soon placed her with her paternal aunt and uncle.*

Subsequent Reviews. The first review was held in September 1998 at another church, to which one of the aunts belonged. She suggested the location; it was OK with the family. The two other reviews in January 1999 and April 1999 were also held at this location. Again, various family members and I each brought snacks. The three reviews lasted less than two hours each. Most people came to all the meetings with some exceptions. I brought copies of the plan as well as the previous review, and stood with easel and markers going over the plan with them, celebrating the successes, and addressing what the family still wanted to accomplish.

Closing Summary (May 1999). This case proved to be quite successful. A broad section of people involved in Jane's life participated in this process. The result is that she has been successfully living with her aunt and uncle for almost a year now, and her mom and dad are willing to voluntarily relinquish parental rights for the adoption, which is what she wants. Jane has had to handle some profound disappointment that her mother did not get it together to be her full-time mom, but within the context of support that she has, she has been able to do this.

Events in the case also seem to have brought the family together in a way that is building on their ability to solve problems and learn to not make too much of a fuss over the little things. The extended family also appears to be trying to find ways to be involved with Jane's two brothers. While the FGDM process did not result in the mother becoming able to give Jane what she needs as a full-time parent, it did result in a viable, long-term permanent plan for the child, without a complicated court process. At this point, the case is closing, as all agree it is time. The group knows that the agency is available if they need our assistance in the future.

Follow-Up (August 1999). There has not been any official follow-up. However, we have informally learned that Jane is still doing well, the aunt and uncle are handling things satisfactorily, and they are working better with the mother on getting along. Mom is also being more consistent with visits and is, in general, doing better. The father is now out of jail and may be looking to petition for custody of the child.

SELECTED PRINCIPLES

Family group conferencing reflects a range of principles used to guide families through the process of making and implementing critical decisions affecting their children and other family members, as well as the functioning of the family unit as a whole. While these can be regarded as basic principles in child and family welfare services, their application indicates a coherent and distinctive approach that serves to promote family decision-making, case planning, and service delivery in a strengths-oriented fashion. The key principles used in family group conferencing are delineated in this section and illustrated through references to the preceding case example.

Self-Determination

The concept of self-determination implies that human beings have the right—within limits—to make choices and decisions for themselves. Accordingly, implicit in the conferencing model is the assumption that families, along with the partners they choose to participate with them, have the right, responsibility, and ability to determine the plan that is best for their children. Of course, as considered in a later section, the child's safety remains paramount. In the R. case, the worker met with the mother to have her identify who the participating parties should be. She also met with the child for the same purpose. The list of invitees was determined by the family. The family also added to the agenda of each session to meet their needs.

Family-Centered Orientation

Practice with vulnerable families and children at risk of out-of-home placement embodies as much as possible a conviction about the role of the birth family as the preferred child-rearing unit; recognition of the potential of most families to care for their children, with appropriate supports from formal and informal sources; and involvement—as appropriate—of any and all members of the kinship group or others who, while not legally related, are regarded by the child as "family" (Warsh, Maluccio, & Pine, 1994). In the R. family, various extended family members played a crucial role in the conferencing process as well as the planning for the child. In particular, the paternal aunt and uncle became the child's "permanent" parents, with support from family members and other members of the group.

Empowerment of Family Members

Social work practice with children and families is typically guided by an ecologically oriented, competence-centered perspective that emphasizes promoting family empowerment; building on the strengths and potentialities of parents, children, and other family members; involving members of the family unit and kin actively in the helping process; and providing them with needed services and supports as well as advocacy and social action. As with social work practice in general, empowerment is a key value in family group conferencing (Connolly & McKenzie, 1999). The model reflects a strengths-based perspective, which assumes that families have strengths or potentialities that can be brought to bear even in time of poor family functioning (Saleebey, 1997).

In line with this perspective, facilitators ask questions to get family members thinking about their own inherent strengths and capabilities and those of the rest of the group, as well as their suggestions about facilitating each meeting. There is emphasis on putting the family in the driver's seat of the process. The concept of conferencing recognizes that families are the ones who should be deciding the fate of the children, except where contraindicated in certain situations where a serious threat to the child's safety exists. In the R. case, the worker purposively engaged a range of family members and their extended and community networks. Extended family, friends, and informal helpers were substantially included. In particular, there was a strong showing of the extended family, who were looking for a way to have more voice in what happened to the child. Family members deliberated by themselves without the presence of the state agency worker, which was in itself empowering.

Safety of Children and Other Family Members

The safety of family members—particularly the child at risk—is paramount. Indeed, a core goal of child and family welfare services is keeping children safe from child abuse and neglect. In case situations in which there are issues of abuse and/or neglect, the risks are explicitly outlined, and corresponding state or court mandates are clearly identified with the family (Hardin, 1996). Safety is procured through helping the family members to identify who may pose a risk, and working with the facilitator to take safety measures. In addition, with the family's permission, the worker can involve friends, neighbors, and relatives in creating a supportive environment for everyone.

In the R. family, there was discussion as to whether the stepfather, who had sexually abused the child, should participate in the decision-making process. The family understandably decided that it was not appropriate for him to participate in any way.

Respect for Human Diversity

Another prominent value is respect for human diversity, such as culture, race, ethnicity, and sexual preference. Particular lifestyles and child-rearing methods should be respected in practice with people from diverse groups, as long as they promote a child's safety and development (Anderson, Ryan, & Leashore, 1997). In the R. case, the review meetings were held in the aunt's church, thus recognizing her ties to the church and helping the rest of the family feel comfortable.

Starting Where the Client Is

Starting where the client is—and *staying* with her or him—is another basic principle in social work practice. In conferencing, clients come to the meetings wherever they are in their development and thinking. In preparation, the worker helps them to share their perspectives and may ask questions that help them to articulate their views, while at the same time being respectful of their feelings, their decisions as to selection of participants in the decision-making process, and their conclusions and recommendations. In the R. family, the worker talked with the mother about what she saw as the issues, what she wanted, and what she thought might be best for the child. The worker did the same with the child. All the other invited participants were given the opportunity to discuss planning for the child from their perspectives.

Collaboration with Formal and Informal Resources

Promoting collaboration between the family and formal and informal resources is crucial. In many cases coming to the attention of child welfare agencies, much can be accomplished by helping parents and other family members identify and use actual or potential formal resources—such as other agencies—as well as informal resources—such as neighbors, friends, and volunteers. Implicit in the use of conferencing is the idea that natural helpers are very important players on the team, and families are encouraged to invite their participation. The R. family chose to involve the former and current foster parents and the child's court-appointed guardian. Also, letters from the child's therapist, school personnel, and two other maternal aunts were shared with the group in the various conferences. Utilizing space in the community to hold the conference also is a form of community collaboration, as it may link families with community resources. In this family, the initial meeting was held at a local church. This added to the feeling that their issues were being dealt with in a family/community way, not in the usual way at a typical agency office. Subsequent reviews were held at the aunt's church, as the family determined that they wanted to shift to a place directly connected to them.

COMPARISON WITH FAMILY PRESERVATION
AND PERMANENCY PLANNING

There are numerous similarities between conferencing and family preservation and permanency planning, including:

- viewing the family as the central unit of attention;
- focusing on strengths/potentialities of children and their families;
- teaching parents more effective coping and parenting patterns;
- mobilizing the extended family;
- helping families to empower themselves;
- emphasizing neighborhood or community-based services;
- developing partnerships among professional helpers, informal helpers, and family members;
- promoting continuity in family relationships in the lives of each child; and
- facilitating permanency planning for children at risk of out-of-home placement.

The philosophy and practice of permanency planning are especially congruent with family group conferencing. As delineated by Pecora and his associates (2000), permanency planning is the systematic process of carrying out, within proscribed time frames, a set of goal-directed activities designed to help children live in safe families that offer them a sense of belonging and legal, lifetime, family ties. Permanency planning thus refers to the process of taking prompt, decisive action to maintain children in their own homes or place them in legally permanent families. Above all, it addresses a single—but crucial—question: What will be this child's family when he or she grows up?

Permanency planning embodies a number of features that are quite consonant—if not identical—with the key characteristics of conferencing, including:

- a *philosophy* highlighting the importance of the biological family and the value of rearing children in a family setting;
- a *theoretical perspective* stressing not only that opportunities for stability and continuity of relationships should be thoroughly explored, but also that major changes in relationships and legal standing may be necessary to protect children;

- a *program* focusing on systematic planning within specified time frames for children who are in foster care or at risk of placement out of their home;
- a *case management method* emphasizing practice strategies such as case reviews, contracting and decision-making, along with participation of parents in the helping process; and
- *active collaboration* among various community agencies, child care personnel, lawyers, judges, and others working with children and their parents (Maluccio, Fein, & Olmstead, 1986, pp. 5–15).

CONCLUSION

The growing use of family group conferencing as a tool with certain families in diverse practice settings builds in basic child welfare principles and social work values. Through more extensive experience as well as ongoing evaluation of its effectiveness, family group conferencing can contribute to the further refinement of such principles and their coherent and systematic application in social work practice in general. In addition, the process of family group decision-making challenges the child welfare, legal, and court systems to become less adversarial in child protection cases.

REFERENCES

Anderson, G., Ryan, A., & Leashore, B. (1997). *The challenge of permanency planning in a multicultural society*. New York: Haworth.

Connolly, M., & McKenzie, M. (1999). *Effective participatory practice—Family group conferencing in child protection*. Hawthorne, NY: Aldine de Gruyter.

Hardin, M. (1996). *Family group conferences in child abuse and neglect cases: Learning from the experience of New Zealand*. Washington, DC: American Bar Association, Center on Children and the Law.

Maluccio, A., Fein, E., & Olmstead, K. (1986). *Permanency planning for children—Concepts and methods*. New York and London: Routledge, Chapman, and Hall.

Pecora, P., Whittaker, J., Maluccio, A., & Barth, R. (2000). *The child welfare challenge: Policy, practice and research* (Rev. ed.). Hawthorne, NY: Aldine de Gruyter.

Saleebey, D. (Ed.) (1997). *The strengths perspective in social work practice* (2nd ed.). New York: Longman.

Warsh, R., Maluccio, A., & Pine, B. (1994). *Family reunification: A sourcebook*. Washington, DC: Child Welfare League of America.

7   Family Group Conferencing as Person-Environment Practice

SUSAN P. KEMP, JAMES K. WHITTAKER, and ELIZABETH M. TRACY

Interest in family group conferencing has spread so rapidly in recent years that, as often happens in the human services, its proliferation as an innovative practice approach has leapt ahead of research on its effectiveness and related theory-building. If family group conferencing is to be more than just a currently fashionable but perhaps short-lived phenomenon, however, both evidence of its effectiveness and a more fully developed sense of its relationship to larger practice frameworks will be required. In this chapter we take up this latter task. Our focus is the linkages between family group conferencing and Person-Environment Practice (Kemp, Whittaker, & Tracy, 1997), an emergent practice approach that emphasizes the provision of social services within the natural ecology of consumers, with full participation by clients and communities, and with careful attention to using and building on local networks and resources.

Several reasons can be identified for taking the time to articulate the connections between family group conferencing and relevant practice theory. Robust connections between practice methods and larger conceptual frameworks allow for consistent and intentional use of strategies across practice settings and client populations, and reduce the difficulties that arise when interventions with proven efficacy in one context are replicated willy-nilly in others (Schorr, 1989). Furthermore, placement within a broader, clearly articulated practice approach reduces the likelihood that practice methods ("know-how") will become separated from the larger professional values and commitments ("know-why") that give them meaning and direction (Rein & White, 1981). By more fully specifying these connections, we aim to provide practitioners with a framework that allows them to use family group conferencing with greater precision and more clarity about its place in a larger set of practice commitments. We hope also to remind practitioners involved in family group conferencing that the important practice principles this intervention embodies have implications across all areas of their work.

In the first section of the chapter, we describe the major features of person-environment practice. The second section explores some specific principles of Person-Environment Practice, with particular attention to assessments and interventions directed to personal social networks. We conclude with comments and cautions on the challenges facing family group conferencing as it makes the transition from practice innovation to a more mature status among the array of strategies available for practice with vulnerable families.

WHAT IS PERSON-ENVIRONMENT PRACTICE?

Person-Environment Practice is an expanded approach to direct practice that makes strategic use of time to accomplish three things:

1. Improving a client's sense of mastery in dealing with stressful life situations, meeting environmental challenges, and making full use of environmental resources.
2. Achieving this end through active assessment, engagement, and intervention in the environment, considered multidimensionally, with particular emphasis on mobilization of the personal social network.
3. Linking individual concerns in ways that promote social empowerment through collective action (Kemp et al., 1997, p. 3).

Of central interest in this model are the links between people's current struggles and the mosaic of challenges and resources that exist in everyday life contexts. We assume that people's troubles and concerns typically have environmental as well as personal dimensions, and that engagement with contextual as well as personal factors is thus essential to effective helping. Hence, although Person-Environment Practice incorporates both personal/interpersonal and environmental change strategies, it places renewed emphasis on interventions that actively connect with and mobilize key factors in clients' environmental contexts.

In this direct practice mode, the unit of attention includes individuals, families, and their personal social networks *and* the community context in which these are embedded. Consistent with ideas that have long been at the core of social work theory and practice, we view social networks, neighborhoods, and community contexts as critical mediating structures (Berger & Neuhaus, 1977) that can buffer the force of personal and interpersonal difficulties. This uniquely social work focus provides the opportunity for practice that builds capacity in client systems at the same time as it is attentive to immediate needs and issues of concern.

In child welfare, for example, Person-Environment Practice involves sustained attention to the relationships between client families, their extended family and cultural contexts, key aspects of neighborhood and community environments, and the many formal and informal systems that may be involved in the effort to maintain family stability and keep children safe. In contrast to the categorical separation among domains that has traditionally prevailed in child welfare policy and practice, the practitioner's interest is children in the context of their families, and families in the context of their communities (Schorr, 1997). Within this holistic focus, practitioners will be committed to partnering with families and their networks, to mobilizing existing strengths and resources, and to building competencies (at different systems levels) that enable families to manage effectively in collaboration with the resources available in their local environment.

THE IMPORTANCE OF CONTEXT

In both assessment and intervention, Person-Environment Practice is centrally concerned with the relationships between people and their environmental contexts. In his classic work on the ecology of human development, Urie Bronfenbrenner described "the progressive, mutual accommodation between an active, growing, human being and the changing properties of the immediate settings in which this developing person lives, as this process is affected by relations between these settings, and by the larger context in which the settings are embedded" (1979, p. 2). For our purposes, three features of Bronfenbrenner's ecological perspective are particularly salient: (1) it brings into sharp focus the dynamic interactions between person and environment over time and across settings; (2) it makes clear that these interactions are reciprocal—that people both shape and are shaped by their environmental contexts; and (3) it reminds us that "the" environment is in fact a series of environments nested one within the other, from the intimate environments of home, family, and friends, to more distal environments such as social welfare institutions and political structures—and that each can and should be considered in the process of help.

In Person-Environment Practice, we view clients' networks, neighborhoods, and communities as primary sources of support, mutual aid, resources, and connection. Empirical support for this emphasis on person-environment relationships as a focus of intervention comes from a number of sources, including the growing body of research on resiliency in children and families who have experienced adversity, the well-established literature on social networks and social support, and the increasingly rich literature on the complex relationships between environmental factors and child and family well-being (for a full discussion of these empirical foundations, see Kemp et al., 1997, Chapter 3).

EMPOWERMENT-ORIENTED PRACTICE

A primary concern in Person-Environment Practice is the promotion of personal and social empowerment. Julian Rappaport (1990), one of the architects of empowerment practice, defined it as a commitment to "identify, facilitate, or create contexts in which heretofore silent and isolated people, those who are 'outsiders' in various settings, organizations and communities, gain understanding, voice, and influence over decisions that affect their lives" (quoted in Saleebey, 1992, p. 8). In Person-Environment Practice, this commitment involves sustained attention to issues of partnership, participation, and power, particularly as these are expressed in the relationships between client systems and professionals.

Partnership

The foundations of empowerment are laid in collaborative working alliances between professionals and clients. A growing body of research evidence suggests that inclusive relationships enhance clients' sense of control, investment in both the process and outcomes of help, and perception that interventions are appropriate to felt needs (Dunst, Trivette, Boyd, & Brookfield, 1994; Itzhaky & York, 1991). A commitment to partnership requires practitioners to recalibrate conventional, top-down understandings of professional roles and expertise. This does not mean, however, that workers are left with nothing to contribute. As we have noted elsewhere, "the professional skills and institutional resources available to social workers are both real and valuable" (Kemp, 1998, p. 221) and are essential to effective intervention. The challenge is to redefine the professional-client hierarchy, to recognize that the knowledge and expertise that clients bring with them is of equal, if different value to that of professionals, and to see workers and clients as having "equal moral agency" in the process of help (Simon, 1994).

Likewise, Person-Environment Practice is strongly invested in active *participation* by clients in decision-making and in the process of change. Through meaningful participation, clients gain a much needed voice in matters of central importance in their lives, and may in the process develop new perspectives of themselves and others. Opportunities for active involvement encourage clients to stretch beyond previous capacities and expectations and to experience themselves as having some ability to influence their immediate environments. Genuine (rather than token) participation thus feeds into and supports client empowerment, and vice versa (Lightburn & Kemp, 1994). Full use of the knowledge, skills, and resources in clients and their personal networks also enhances the ecological validity of both assessments and interventions. Furthermore, efforts to ensure client involvement in all aspects of assessment and intervention help to counteract the belief, common in clients, their surrounding systems, and the social institutions that serve them, that the solutions to client problems lie primarily outside themselves and their communities (Delgado, 1996; Simon, 1994).

The opportunity to participate does not, however, always translate directly into authentic participation (see, e.g., Lupton, 1998). Clients may lack the knowledge and skills to participate as full partners in complex proceedings that are still largely the domain of professionals. Nor do professionals always make room at the table for meaningful client participation, even when clients are nominally present. To be correlated with empowerment, participation must be associated with the belief that one can really influence decisions being made and have an influence in one's environment (Schulz, Israel, Zimmerman, & Checkoway, 1995). Rather than assuming that being present equates with participation, workers should consider the resources clients will need in order to be full participants, collaborate with clients to build relevant skills and knowledge, and provide opportunities for clients to participate in ways that are comfortable for them (Keenan & Pinkerton, 1991).

Power

"The goal of effective practice is not coping or adaptation but an increase in the actual power of the client or community so that action can be taken to change and prevent the problems clients are facing" (Gutierrez, DeLois, & GlenMaye, 1995, p. 249). Inherent in any focus on empowerment is the need for open acknowledgment of and attention to power differentials—between workers and clients; between clients and others in their social systems; and in the larger sociopolitical context in which clients and professionals are located. Particularly important is attention to the patterned inequalities experienced by clients of public social services, such as the marked overrepresentation of families of color among child welfare clients, or the multiple and overlapping oppressions (of race, class, and gender) experienced by a poor woman of color receiving public welfare. Such differentials translate into major inequalities in access to services and resources and also into an array of less obvious indignities and exclusions in the process of help. Sustained attention to issues of respect, inclusion, and access is thus as essential in the small but vital details of everyday helping relationships as it is in relation to larger questions of rights and opportunities.

STRENGTHS-BASED AND COMPETENCY-BUILDING PRACTICE

Beyond its attention to questions of power and empowerment, person-environment practice recognizes and values the resources and strengths (both actual and potential) in people and communities. As Weick and Saleebey (1995) have noted, "In a strengths approach we are obliged to make an accounting of what people know and what they can do. We are beholden to render a roster of resources that exist in and around individual, family, and community" (p. 4). In the assessment process, this dual focus on environmental as well as personal strengths is an important pathway to a more complex, contextualized, and complete view of client systems. At the point of intervention, not only are client system resources and strengths the foundation for change efforts, but understanding the environment as an ecology of opportunity as well as risk expands the potential number of resources available in the interventive process.

Key assumptions in this strengths-based approach (Sullivan, 1992) are that:

1. All persons and environments have strengths that can be harnessed to improve quality of life.
2. Client motivation and engagement are enhanced by a consistent emphasis on strengths, particularly as defined by the client and his or her communities of reference.
3. Discovering and building on strengths is best achieved through collaboration and partnership between client(s) and worker(s).

4. Cultural beliefs, customs, and practices are an important source of resilience and support.
5. All environments contain resources, actual and potential, which can be mobilized for change.

To focus on strengths and resources does not mean that attention should not also be given to the risks confronting client systems. Clearly, many persons who seek help from social service agencies are faced with overwhelming obstacles in their everyday environments. Reducing these risks, whether through strengthening community responsiveness to vulnerable families or by ensuring the safety of a child, is an essential element of the process of effective intervention. The literature on resiliency indicates, for example, that resiliency-enhancing interventions are most effective in moderate- rather than high-risk environments (Fraser, Richman, & Galinsky, 1999). The potential for effective practice thus lies, we suggest, in interventions that balance risk reduction with strategies that tap into and enhance the strengths and potentialities in clients and their communities.

Not all client system strengths are self-evident or fully developed. A focus on strengths thus requires a parallel commitment to the development of competence. Building on the work of Anthony Maluccio (1981), we define competence not as a personal construct but rather, in ecological terms, as a quality of person-environment transactions. Ecological competence, Maluccio suggests, is "the repertoire of skills, knowledge, and qualities that enable people to interact effectively with their environments" (p. ix). This transactional process has both personal and environmental dimensions: personal skills and capacities are elicited and supported by competence-enhancing qualities in the surrounding environment. Key among these environmental factors are opportunities (support, resources), respect by others, and power, which affords access to opportunities (Smith, 1968, cited in Maluccio, 1981). In other words, efforts to build personal and interpersonal competencies should go hand in hand with efforts to develop competency-supporting environments.

SOCIAL NETWORKS AND SOCIAL SUPPORT

Our interest in interventions that identify, mobilize, and strengthen personal social networks flows directly from our focus on supporting ecological competence in clients and communities. In social network interventions, the practitioner works through the client's personal social network and community systems to find social support in all its forms, to raise consciousness, and to promote solidarity for collective action. [By *social network*, we mean the structure and number of a person's social relationships. *Social support*, on the other hand, refers to exchanges within a network (emotional encouragement, concrete assistance or tangible aid, and advice and information) that are perceived as beneficial.]

In Person-Environment Practice, we emphasize two primary dimensions of social network interventions: network mapping, and network facilitation. Network mapping involves the identification of helping resources among network members as well as accurate assessment of areas of need. Network facilitation encompasses a range of interventions that focus on mobilizing and strengthening the social network as a resource and support. We discuss both dimensions of social network interventions in more detail below.

BUILDING BLOCKS OF PERSON-ENVIRONMENT PRACTICE

As shown in Figure 1, Person-Environment Practice is based on ten primary building blocks:

- **Partnership:**   Clients and professionals meet on common ground and work together as a unified team.
- **Mutuality:**   We create an atmosphere where clients and professionals communicate openly about their concerns in a relationship built on openness, trust, and mutual respect.
- **Reciprocity:**   We operate on what Reissman (1990) calls the helper principle, which recognizes the importance of help-giving and help-getting as a mutual process among clients, professionals, and members of their networks.
- **Social assets:**   In assessment and intervention we begin by looking at what is going right (strengths, resources, and potentialities) with clients rather than on what is going wrong.
- **Resilience:**   We are always alert for those protective factors and mechanisms that blunt and divert the effects of known risk factors and permit individuals, families, and groups to overcome very difficult life situations.
- **Optimization:**   Our goal is always to create conditions within which each individual, family, group, and neighborhood reaches the upper limit of its developmental potential.
- **Natural helping:**   Our search is for those approaches to change that draw fully on the ability of clients and communities to aid themselves (e.g., through mutual aid, ritual, spiritual practice, or reflection) and that make best use of local capacities and resources.
- **Social integration:**   We are interested in addressing critical social and contextual issues in the context of promoting individual and family change. The goal is to enhance the integration of families and communities—critical integrating function of connection between families and their neighborhoods and communities.
- **Coherence:**   We use this term in the sense intended by Antonovsky (1979, 1987) to describe the processes through which individuals, families, and communities discern a sense of meaning beyond the struggles of day-to-day existence.

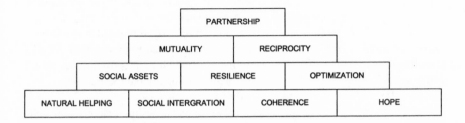

Figure 1. Ten primary buillding blocks of Person-Environment Practice.

- **Hope:** Ultimately, Person-Environment Practice is about fostering a sense of hope: hope that things can change for the better, that the power for change resides with in, that someone is listening . . . and cares.

ASSESSMENT IN PERSON-ENVIRONMENT PRACTICE

Not surprisingly, Person-Environment Practice emphasizes a contextual approach to assessment. Client issues are conceptualized as inextricably embedded in a social and environmental context and as needing to be understood and addressed from this perspective. This is particularly important given that the assessment process establishes the framework for intervention. Assessments that incorporate textured and multidimensional understandings of clients' social and physical environments make interventions at multiple systems levels more likely (Meyer, 1993). Similarly, assessments that pay attention to connections and personal networks provide an enriched understanding of who might be available to the process of change.

Priority is given to assessment methods that actively allow for client participation in the process of generating information. The goal is an engaged process in which clients and professionals develop shared understandings as a foundation for collaborative decision-making. Friends, extended family, and community members may also have important perspectives to offer or provide valuable resources for problem solving.

Both ecomaps and genograms (Hartman, 1978) generate useful information for person-environment assessments. Based on the earlier work of Tracy and Whittaker (1990), we also recommend consistent use of the Social Network Map, a versatile clinical assessment tool that helps both to identify network resources (both kin and nonkin) and to assess the client's perception of these resources. Often this process leads to the discovery of resources that are available but underutilized. [For an extended discussion of the use of the Social Network Map in assessment and intervention, see Tracy and Whittaker (1990) and Kemp et al. (1997, Chapters 4 and 5).] Used in combination these assessment tools help workers and clients to better understand not only who is in a client's personal social network but also the distribution of resources in the network and the surrounding environment. Such comprehensive assessments are particularly important in child welfare practice. They represent, however, an expanded paradigm for assessment that goes beyond prevailing risk assessment models, which focus primarily on actual and potential risks to the child and in general do not engage the family or community (Day, Robison, & Sheikh, 1998).

Careful assessment of clients' social networks is an essential element of accurate person-environment assessments. Social network assessment ensures that important social resources are identified, that gaps in resources are clarified, and that workers and clients are on the same page about who is available and how interactions with them are experienced. If social workers are to work with, and not against, a client's social network, accurate assessment of social network resources and competencies is a necessary first task. Social network mapping also provides access to important information on key factors such as clients' neighborhood and community connections, interactions with human service organizations, and perceptions and use of culturally relevant supports. This nuanced understanding of coping and social support strategies is essential to effective partnerships with client systems, particularly in communities of color (Green, 1995).

Social network assessments should be more than just an inventory of who is in a client's network. To this end the Social Network Map provides a multidimensional picture of social network resources that includes both their structural dimensions (network size, stability, and frequency of contact) and their subjective qualities (perceived availability, closeness, reciprocity, and direction of help). Network assessments should also involve critical analysis of the resources and challenges facing client systems in their everyday environments. The strengths and limitations of personal networks are inextricably shaped by larger social patterns of resources and constraints. Where both networks and the contexts in which they are located are depleted by the demands of chronic poverty and its related problems, for example, it is both unrealistic and ultimately destructive to look only to local resources as a source of change (Halpern, 1995). To accurately determine what external resources are needed and how these can be incorporated in ways that are a good fit with the needs and goals of the client system, network assessments must incorporate careful analysis of the relationships between a particular network and its larger social context.

INTERVENTION IN PERSON-ENVIRONMENT PRACTICE

As with assessment, the process of intervention should be consistent with a larger philosophy of practice. Lisbeth Schorr (1997) argues, furthermore, that effective interventions with vulnerable families and communities should reflect a "plausible theory of change" (p. 364). By this, she means that they should be based in a clear rationale that links activities and outcomes by way of a set of propositions about what is most likely to make a difference. In Person-Environment Practice, as we have described above, the guiding assumption is that activities that enhance connectedness to and efficacy within the environment (broadly defined) are central to improved outcomes for vulnerable individuals, groups, and communities.

We are fully aware that a range of interventions, from ongoing therapeutic services to crisis intervention, is required to meet the complex needs of vulnerable individuals and families. In child welfare practice, for example, families often need services that span the spectrum from mental health treatment to help with housing. In this brief overview, however, we have chosen to focus on social network interventions, which we see as a core component of practice that has as its goal enhanced person-environment relationships.

Network facilitation mobilizes the social network as a resource and support. It may focus on an existing network, or create a new one. It should be individually tailored, based on an identification of existing and potential network members and an assessment of the strengths and capabilities of the social network, including gaps in social support. Furthermore, network facilitation taps into the real power of natural helping, considering each involved person in terms of what they have to give as well as to receive (Swenson, 1981).

Network meetings are a key element of network facilitation. They are used both to solidify new linkages and to enhance the functioning of old ties. Family group conferences, for example, make creative use of network meetings for extended family decision-making. Meetings can also be useful in reconnecting past network members, so that through the renewal and regeneration of social ties networks are able to provide help more effectively.

Network skills training may be an important component of effective network facilitation, particularly since many clients have literally burned out their relationships with friends and family in the course of struggling with issues such as substance use or homelessness. Thompson's (1995) excellent review of the role of social support in child maltreatment makes clear, for example, that many parents who maltreat their children are embedded in social networks that are perceived as unsupportive, or where network members feel that they have little more to offer. Core network skills include the ability to identify network resources and to see them as useful, the ability to communicate needs and to listen to others, the ability to both give and receive help, and skills in engaging members of the network around specific needs (Swenson, 1981). Network members may also need to develop skills that relate to the actual tasks or roles that they agree to take on with each other, for example in providing assistance to a developmentally disabled child, or supporting a parent's abstinence.

A linked but different area of network facilitation focuses on developing the network's capacity for gaining access to and increasing its collective resources. Here attention shifts from the interpersonal dynamics of the network to its relationship to larger patterns of supports and opportunities. In most networks, the challenges facing one member probably are shared by many, even if they apparently are coping adequately. Particular challenges face networks in communities grappling with the multiple and interlocking demands of pervasive poverty, social exclusion, weak intracommunity ties, tenuous extracommunity linkages, and constricted access to resource-rich social networks. In child welfare practice, the needs of kinship caregivers provide a particularly good example. Very often, kinship caregivers are low-income families of color (Scannapieco, 1999). Research evidence suggests, furthermore, that there are significant differences in the resources and supports available to kinship foster parents compared with nonbiological foster families (ibid.). Unless such inequities are addressed—through capacity-building practice with the network itself *and* administrative and policy advocacy— network interventions will inevitably fall short of the principles of empowering practice to which they are often attached. In Person-Environment Practice, network development thus incorporates an additional dimension, directed to strengthening the associations between social networks and key sources of influence and opportunity.

PERSON-ENVIRONMENT PRACTICE AND FAMILY GROUP CONFERENCING: CONNECTIONS AND CAVEATS

As we have worked on this chapter, we have once again been struck by the degree of congruence between Person-Environment Practice and family group conferencing. The parallels are particularly evident in the growing body of work that builds outward from family group conferencing methods and findings toward more comprehensive principles for practice (see, for example, Connolly & McKenzie, 1998; Lupton & Nixon, 1999). In family group conferencing, the core commitments of Person-Environment Practice—to harnessing resources and strengths in the social ecology of clients, to collaboration and partnership, and to well-specified but flexible interventions that build efficacy and agency across client systems—come to life in practice.

At the same time, we are reinforced in our belief in the value of practice models that transcend any particular method or practice strategy. From this larger vantage point, we offer some observations that practitioners may wish to consider as family group conferencing makes the transition from practice innovation to a mature and tested practice method. For those who have hope, as we do, that family group conferencing will be a key leverage point for a larger paradigm shift in child welfare practice, these may be important to keep in mind.

Systematic assessment of both needs and resources is an essential component of effective Person-Environment Practice. In practice with personal social networks, for example, we encourage thorough and multidimensional assessments of network resources, competencies, and access to external supports. Ideally, such comprehensive and ecologically valid assessments will routinely be conducted across methods and practice settings. Day et al. (1998) point out, for example, that they are an essential foundation for community-based child protection practice. In family group conferencing, however, there is as yet little consistency in approaches to assessment, or indeed in the degree to which systematic assessments are seen as important.

In Person-Environment Practice, accurate, comprehensive, and participatory assessment opens the way for interventions designed to enhance core skills and competencies. Family group conferences likewise have the potential to be more than just vehicles for collaborative decision-making. Their contribution to capacity-building and empowerment in vulnerable client systems will not be fully realized, however, without consistent attention to the development of skills and competencies, both those required within personal social networks, and those that relate to the connections between social networks and larger opportunity structures. Research evidence on family group conferences suggests, for example, that practice in this area varies widely (see, for example, findings on the level of preparation of families for conferences), with mixed outcomes in terms of the ability of family networks to make agreements that they can fully carry out (Lupton, 1998).

Skills and competencies are only useful in the context of a responsive environment. To this end we also emphasize the importance of ensuring that client systems have access to needed resources and supports. Here too it seems that family group conferencing practice may be inconsistent. Despite the strong emphasis in family group conferencing on client system empowerment, several authors note that resources are not always available to fully support the decisions and investments of extended family networks (Connolly & McKenzie, 1998; Lupton, 1998). Taking this a step further, Lupton (1998) points out the potential for conferences to be co-opted by conservative views on responsibility and self-sufficiency. Halpern (1995) has similarly cautioned against overreliance on local initiatives where these place additional burdens and expectations on depleted networks without adequate investments of external resources and support. The challenge, as we see it, lies in accurately determining how best to supplement valuable informal resources and strengths (e.g., caregiving, mutual aid, cultural identity) with relevant external resources (e.g., financial supports, access to opportunity structures).

These analyses suggest the need, as family group conferencing models proliferate, for careful consideration of the extent to which they are connected to clearly articulated practice approaches that, in all their parts, support client participation and empowerment. The activities that proceed and follow family group conferences are doubtless as important to child and family outcomes as the conferences themselves. The extent to which the professionals involved are fully committed to participatory and ecological practice, not only in family group conferencing but across all of their practice activities, is probably also highly relevant. Is this the only domain in which parents and extended families will be involved as partners? Are the practice principles inherent in family group conferencing sustained in other areas of work with a family (e.g., in visitation practice, or in the reunification process)? Can practitioners identify the links between this potent but delimited strategy and a larger philosophy of practice? Such questions, and the answers to them, must be addressed as family group conferencing positions itself on the leading edge of a paradigm shift in child welfare practice with vulnerable families.

REFERENCES

Antonovsky, A. (1979). *Health, stress, and coping.* San Francisco: Jossey-Bass.
Antonovsky, A. (1987). *Unraveling the mystery of health: How people manage stress and stay well.* San Francisco: Jossey-Bass.
Berger, P., & Neuhaus, R. (1977). *To empower people: The role of mediating structures in public policy.* Washington, DC: American Enterprise Institute.
Bronfenbrenner, U. (1979). *The ecology of human development: Experiments by nature and design.* Cambridge, MA: Harvard University Press.
Connolly, M., & McKenzie, M. (1998). *Effective participatory practice: Family group conferencing in child protection.* Hawthorne, NY: Aldine de Gruyter.
Day, P., Robison, S., & Sheikh, S. (1998). *Ours to keep: A guide for building a community assessment strategy for child protection.* Washington, DC: CWLA.
Delgado, M. (1996). Community asset assessment by Latino youths. *Social Work in Education, 18,* 169–78.
Dunst, C., Trivette, C., Boyd, K., & Brookfield, J. (1994). Help-giving practices and the self-sufficiency appraisals of parents. In C. Dunst, C. Trivette, & A. Deal (Eds.), *Supporting and strengthening families,* Vol. I, *Methods, strategies and practices.* Cambridge, MA: Brookline.
Fraser, M., Richman, J., & Galinsky, M. (1999). Risk, protection, and resilience: Toward a conceptual framework for social work practice. *Social Work Research, 23,* 131– 43.
Green, J. W. (1995). *Cultural awareness in the human services: A multiethnic approach* (2nd ed.). Boston: Allyn & Bacon.
Gutierrez, L., DeLois, K., & GlenMaye, L. (1995). The organizational context of empowerment practice: Implications for social work administration. *Social Work, 40*(2), 49–58.
Halpern, R. (1995). *Rebuilding the inner city: A history of neighborhood initiatives to address poverty in the United States.* New York: Columbia University Press.
Hartman, A. (1978). Diagrammatic assessment of family relationships. *Social Casework, 8,* 467–74.
Itzhaky, H., & York, A. (1991). Client participation and the effectiveness of community social work intervention. *Research on Social Work Practice, 1,* 387–98.
Keenan, E., & Pinkerton, J. (1991). Some aspects of empowerment: A case study of work with disadvantaged youth. *Social Work with Groups, 14,* 109–24.
Kemp, S. P. (1998). Practice with communities. In M. Mattaini, C. Lowery, and C. Meyer (Eds.), *The foundations of social work practice: A graduate text* (2nd ed.; pp. 209–39). Washington DC: NASW Press.
Kemp, S., Whittaker, J., & Tracy, E. (1997). *Person-environment practice: The social ecology of interpersonal helping.* Hawthorne, NY: Aldine de Gruyter.
Lightburn, A., & Kemp. S. (1994). Family support programs: Opportunities for community-based practice. *Families in Society, 75,* 16–26.
Lupton, C. (1998). User empowerment or family self-reliance? The family group conference model. *British Journal of Social Work, 28,* 107–28.

Lupton, C., & Nixon, P. (1999). *Empowering practice? A critical appraisal of the Family Group Conference approach.* London: Policy.

Maluccio, A. (Ed.) (1981). *Promoting competence in clients: A new/old approach to social work practice.* New York: Free Press.

Meyer, C. (1993). *Assessment in social work practice.* New York: Columbia University Press.

Rappaport, J. (1990). Research methods and the empowerment agenda. In P. Tolan, C. Keys, F. Chertak, & L. Jason (Eds.), *Researching community psychology.* Washington, DC: American Psychological Association.

Rein, M., & White, S. (1981). Knowledge for practice. *Social Service Review, 55,* 1–41.

Reissman, F. (1990). Restructuring help: A human services paradigm for the 1990s. *American Journal of Community Psychology, 18*(2), 221–30.

Saleebey, D. (Ed.) (1992). *The strengths perspective in social work practice.* New York: Longman.

Scannapieco, M. (1999). Kinship care in the public child welfare system. In R. Hegar & M. Scannapieco (Eds.), *Kinship foster care: Policy, practice, and research* (pp. 141–54). New York: Oxford University Press.

Schorr, L. (1989). *Within our reach: Breaking the cycle of disadvantage.* New York: Anchor.

Schorr, L. (1997). *Common purpose: Strengthening families and neighborhoods to rebuild America.* New York: Anchor.

Schulz, A., Israel, B., Zimmerman, M., & Checkoway, B. (1995). Empowerment as a multilevel construct: Perceived control at the individual, organizational, and community level. *Health Education Research: Theory and Practice, 10,* 309–27.

Simon, B. (1994). *The empowerment tradition in American social work: A history.* New York: Columbia University Press.

Sullivan, W. (1992). Reconsidering the environment as a helping resource. In D. Saleebey (Ed.), *The strengths perspective in social work practice* (pp. 148–57). New York: Longman.

Swenson, C. (1981). Using natural helping networks to promote competence. In A. Maluccio (Ed.), *Promoting competence in clients: A new/old approach to social work practice* (pp. 125–51). New York: Free Press.

Thompson, R. (1995). *Preventing child maltreatment through social support: A critical analysis.* Thousand Oaks, CA: Sage.

Tracy, E., Whittaker, & Tracy & Whittaker, J. (1990). The Social Network Map: Assessing social support in clinical social work practice. *Families in Society, 71,* 461–70.

Weick, A., & Saleebey, D. (1995). *A postmodern approach to social work practice.* The 1995 Richard Lodge Memorial Lecture, Adelphi University School of Social Work, New York.

8   Restorative Practices with High-Risk Youth

TED WACHTEL

From its origins in New Zealand in 1989 to its more recent implementation in the United Kingdom, Canada, and the United States, the family group conference is influencing the way social workers do business. Bringing the extended family together to deal with child protection and child custody issues, and in some instances to deal with family violence, is a radical shift in practice. Decreasing the role of the professional and increasing the role of the family in dealing with significant decisions, the family group conference changes social welfare from something that agencies do unilaterally *to* or *for* people to something that agencies do collaboratively *with* people.

Because the New Zealand family group conference is used with both child welfare issues and juvenile offenses, it highlights the parallel development of processes in welfare and justice that reduce the power of the state in favor of the citizen. Our contemporary restorative processes involve ordinary people in decisions that were previously limited to professionals. As with the changes in social welfare, the conference process changes justice from something that courts do unilaterally *to* or *for* people to something that is done collaboratively *with* people.

Punishment in response to crime and other wrongdoing is the prevailing practice, not just in criminal justice systems, but in schools, families, and workplaces. Those who fail to punish are often labeled as "permissive." Given this perspective, the range of possible responses to wrongdoing is limited to a narrow punitive-permissive continuum (see Figure 1). But punishment does not work very well. In the United States, for instance, punishment by incarceration has not had a meaningful impact on crime. The prison population has grown to unprecedented numbers, yet crime rates, while they have declined modestly in recent years due to demographic shifts, are still unacceptably high. When the demographic trough we are now experiencing passes by, we will find crime rates climbing again, despite our aggressive use of punishment by incarceration.

Similarly, the increasingly common use of exclusionary punishments, like suspension and expulsion by public schools, has not stemmed the tide of outrageous behavior by the adolescent population of delinquent and high-risk youths. Rather, it has only served to push more youth out of the mainstream into negative subcultures, creating a burgeoning demand for special school and group home programs. Adults in contemporary families, schools, and communities seem increas-

Figure 1. Punitive-permissive continuum.

ingly frustrated by their inability to control the inappropriate behavior of young people.

Yet most people persist in equating punishment with accountability, which could hardly be farther from the truth. When we impose a punishment, the experience is largely passive for the offender. The young person is scolded and punished, with the penalty prescribed and imposed unilaterally by the authority figure. Usually the offender does not even have to talk. She does not have to come up with a plan for repairing the harm. She does not have to apologize. Instead she sits silently, wallowing in her resentment, seeing herself as the "victim." Focusing on herself, she completely ignores the feelings and needs of the real victims, those who were harmed or otherwise affected by her inappropriate behavior. By punishing young people and doing most of the talking for them, parents, educators, and other adults miss the opportunity to hold the offender truly accountable in ways that benefit the victims of the wrongdoing and foster responsibility and empathy in the wrongdoer.

If we move beyond the limited perceptions prescribed by the punitive-permissive continuum, we can begin to envision a more helpful way of seeing the situation. Rather than limit our thinking to a singular axis with punishment at one end and permissiveness at the other, we can try looking through a "social control window" based on two axes with "control" on the vertical axis (see Figure 2). This refers only to the control of wrongdoing, not the control of human beings in general. Our goal, in fact, is freedom from the kind of control that wrongdoers impose on others. On this axis we can move from the bottom toward the top, noting instances of increasingly stronger discipline or limit setting on the axis as we go upward. The horizontal axis is "support." On this second axis we can cite instances of greater encouragement or nurturing as we move from left to right.

When we respond to wrongdoing with a high level of control, but little or no support, we are being "punitive." When we are very understanding and nurturing

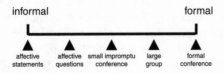

Figure 2. Social control window.

of the wrongdoer, but provide little in the way of control or limit setting, we are being "permissive." When we provide neither control nor support, we are being "neglectful." The "restorative" approach, the fourth possibility, combines both a high level of limit setting with a high level of support. One of the significant characteristics of the restorative approach is that we separate wrongdoing from wrongdoer. While holding wrongdoers accountable for their actions, we still value and support their inherent worth as human beings.

We can also use this social control window to represent parenting styles. The authoritarian parent metes out discipline but rarely provides nurturing, coinciding with the punitive corner of the window. The permissive parent always supports the child, but rarely sets appropriate limits. The neglectful parent is usually either absent or abusive. The restorative parent, who sets limits effectively but also offers substantial support and encouragement, is the very kind of "authoritative parent" whose approach to parenting seems to produce the best results.

We can summarize these four responses to wrongdoing with a few simple words—*not, for, to,* and *with.* When we are punitive toward children and youths, we are only doing something *to* them. When we are permissive, we are doing everything *for* them, but asking little in return. When we are neglectful, we simply are *not* doing. But when we are restorative, we are doing things *with* them and involving them, along with victims, family, and friends, directly in the process. The word *with* encapsulates the key distinguishing feature of a restorative process, the cooperative engagement of the individuals and families who have been directly affected.

The family group conference developed in New Zealand is built around a critical element called a "family caucus," that is, a period of time when the family members who have been gathered together have an opportunity to meet without any outsiders present, to develop a plan to deal with the needs of the child, or youth, or with what the young person has done. When it is a conference for a crime, not even the victim of the offense is permitted to attend the caucus, although the victim may be present before and after the caucus part of the conference. The original legislation intended to keep social workers and others from interfering with the deliberations of the family.

In 1991, about two years after conferencing commenced in New Zealand, an Australian police sergeant, Terry O'Connell, developed another version of conferencing specifically to respond to incidents of wrongdoing. In O'Connell's version of conferencing all of the offenders involved in an offense are dealt with simultaneously in one conference. The facilitator guides the conference by following a simple written script that prescribes a series of general questions that are open-ended in nature. Each person in the circle, without exception, gets an opportunity to speak. Although there is no separate family caucus, the script itself discourages the facilitator from interfering in the process. In addition to the offenders and their family members and friends, the victims and their family and friends are part of the process of deciding how the harm is to be repaired.

Conferences are emotional experiences. The questions in the conference script intentionally encourage people to express their feelings. Although many fear that bringing together victims, offenders, and their respective families and friends is potentially dangerous, even explosive, the expression of emotion is what makes conferences effective. The facilitator, having invited each person to attend, having politely answered questions, and patiently listened to concerns, has rapport with each individual, which ensures that the expression of negative emotion in the conference does not get out of hand. Usually the facilitator merely has to intervene lightly to calm a participant who is becoming abusive. It is not the facilitator's job to protect the offender from hearing strong feelings from victims and those who care about the victim, but to keep the expression of strong feelings from becoming verbal abuse. In fact, expressing emotions decreases their intensity. It is surprising how, if the offender takes appropriate responsibility, the anger of victims may subside, and they may be remarkably generous toward the young people who have committed crimes against them. For the youths, facing their victims is difficult, but it provides a valuable lesson in empathy.

However powerful the family group conference experience, it would be naive to suggest that a single restorative intervention can dramatically alter the behavioral patterns of delinquent and high-risk young people. Rather, these youths need to be exposed continuously to a restorative environment that confronts their inappropriate behavior while providing encouragement and nurturing. Terry O'Connell, upon visiting one of the schools operated by the Community Service Foundation (CSF), remarked, "You are running a conference all day long." In fact, CSF employs a variety of restorative interventions ranging from informal spontaneous interventions to the formal family group conference (see Figure 3).

The family group conference is the most formal of these interventions. It is more structured and less spontaneous, requires more preparation, takes more time to carry out, and involves more people. The payoff, however, is that it tends to be more complete and usually has more impact than less formal practices. Recently one of the CSF school counselors (CSF schools are licensed both as academic institutions and day treatment programs) convened a family group conference for "Jim," a boy who had been in a CSF program for a couple of years. Jim had become involved in assisting two girls who attended his school with a scheme to run away from their residential group homes. Living at home and having a car, Jim had offered to meet them at a convenience store and provide them with transportation.

Other students who heard about the plan told the school staff what was about to happen. That kind of involvement by other young people in the program is one of the positive outcomes of a program that engages students in the process, doing things *with* students, rather than doing things *to* or *for* them. Their decision to "tell on Jim" was done in a supportive way, out of concern for Jim and the girls who were running away. The informants were fond of Jim and regarded him highly, so their purpose was to protect him and the girls from doing something

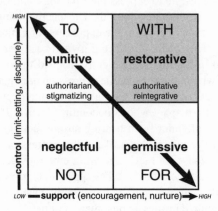

Figure 3. Restorative practices continuum.

foolish. Jim's longevity in the program made the counselor and other program staff feel especially upset with Jim's misdeed. They felt they had invested much time and energy in helping Jim and that he had made great progress in curbing his impulsive behavior. Because Jim had been through many groups, they felt he needed to experience a more formal event, one that might have greater impact on him.

In convening the conference the counselor asked Jim to nominate people, besides his mother, to support him in the conference. Among those he named were two boys who were relatively new to the program and viewed by some counselors as negative influences. Ironically, these two youths proved to be among the most powerful, positive influences in the conference. Although they often failed to curb their own negative behaviors and poor decisions, they were genuinely concerned for Jim and pointed out to him all the negative consequences that would have resulted from him helping the girls run away. Jim responded to the conference appropriately and seemed very sincere in his remorse. He readily agreed to do some community service as a tangible indication of his remorse. The conference was a far more useful intervention than the school merely imposing sanctions on Jim, without his, or his friends' and family's involvement, which is what typically happens in school settings.

In considering this example, it is useful to know that the average CSF student has been suspended from public schools many times. Punishment has not worked in getting them to change their behavior. Yet the use of restorative practices at CSF has created a school climate that is as good or better than what is found in most public schools. The restorative interventions to which these students respond are usually no more complicated than asking an offending student the same question that would be asked in a scripted formal conference: "What happened?"

"What were you thinking about at the time?" "Who do you think has been affected?" "How have they been affected?"

In a recent incident, a caseworker demonstrated the impact of making simple, affective statements. Her client was in trouble again and she was asked to take him home and tell his parents what he had done. He had boasted to friends that he had been using marijuana but had avoided getting discovered by urine tests because he was "cleaning out his system" by drinking mouthwash. He further claimed that he had laced brownies with acid and offered them to his teachers. Knowing how volatile the boy's father could be, the caseworker dreaded facing him. As expected, the father launched into his usual ranting and raving, verbally abusing the female caseworker and poking his finger angrily near the boy's face.

The caseworker cautiously withdrew from the home to the safety of her locked car. She seriously considered calling the police to protect both herself and the child, but decided instead to confront the father with her feelings. As he stood next to her car in the pouring rain, she talked to him through her slightly open car window, telling him how he had frightened her and how she was frightened for the safety of his son. Much to her surprise the father exhibited a complete reversal in his behavior. He apologized, told her that he did not realize how he had affected her, and assured her that he would not do it again. The restorative intervention, that is, simply telling the father how she was affected by his behavior, was a watershed in their relationship. He now talks about him and the caseworker "being on the same team" in trying to help his son and has not repeated the kind of angry and frightening behavior that occurred all too often in the past.

The power of affect is not to be underestimated. People who behave inappropriately rarely understand how their behavior affects others nor do they get that kind of feedback. All too often we take these insights for granted and miss the opportunity to provide important learning experiences for young people (and even adults) who lack empathy and insight into the implications of their own actions.

To change behavior, we must respond restoratively rather than with punishment strategies. Our restorative interventions must be designed to do the following:

1. *Foster awareness.* By expressing our own feelings, or getting others to express their feelings, or by asking the offender questions about how they think they have affected others, young people who rarely think about other people's feelings begin to gain insight and awareness. Awareness is the beginning of empathy.
2. *Avoid scolding or lecturing.* People react defensively when they are scolded or lectured. They figuratively or literally roll their eyes up and fail to see how they have affected others.
3. *Involve offenders actively.* Punishment is passive. Asking youth questions about how they think they have affected others or how they might repair the harm they have caused puts responsibility on them and engages them.

4. *Accept ambiguity.*   Sometimes several people have a piece in the problem. The intervention may still occur with people sharing how they were affected by what happened. The shared understanding of everyone's feelings is the primary goal, not the assignment of guilt.
5. *Separate the deed from the doer.*   Whenever possible we want to recognize the intrinsic worth of human beings and disapprove only of their behavior.
6. *See every instance of wrongdoing and conflict as an opportunity for learning.*   Social workers, teachers, and many professionals who come into contact with young people have opportunities to model and teach. We can turn negative incidents into constructive events, building empathy and reducing the likelihood of negative incidents in the future.

The systematic use of restorative practices will help delinquent and high-risk youth change their behavior far more effectively than the current system based on fear of punishment. Our experience indicates that restorative practices strengthen relationships, increase interconnectedness, and build community, outcomes that have the potential to reduce the fear, alienation, violence, and crime that plague our society.

9 Family Group Conference Connections

Shared Problems and Solutions

PAUL NIXON

This chapter traces some of the connections between the variety of interests that have impacted on the practice and development of family group conferences (FGCs) in the United Kingdom. In this context where the implementation of FGCs has been patchy, balancing the different and sometimes conflicting rights and responsibilities of families and the state has been an enduring theme in FGC development, in child care policy generally, and was a central concern of the 1989 Children Act (England and Wales). This act was inaugurated at the same time as New Zealand's Children, Young Persons and Their Families Act, 1989, and embodied very similar principles. Both sought to enable families to take up their responsibilities, while enhancing the participation of and protection for children and young people. Both envisaged that services would be delivered in partnership with families (Parton, 1991).

Social workers in the United Kingdom have struggled with the principles of participation, which being generally less explicit in child care legislation, have been slow to emerge in day-to-day practice. Family group conferences attracted interest, however, because they appeared to give meaning to those ideas but, paradoxically, could quickly be reduced by professionals to a method, "technique," or "gizmo" for agencies to *use on* families. Putting FGC principles into practice therefore should take account of the context within which they will operate. For different political groups, the concepts of responsibility and empowerment can have both liberatory and regulatory functions (Baistow, 1994/1995; Lupton, 1998; Lupton & Nixon, 1999). In a climate of resource cuts, FGCs can easily be transmuted to a procedure concerned with "gatekeeping" or social control, rather than embody a set of values that could shape all our work with families and the community.

VALUES AND DECISION-MAKING

Sharing decision-making responsibilities with families has not been at the forefront of orthodox social work practice in the United Kingdom, which appears to be predicated on a culture of professional expertise and control (Ryburn, 1991a). Consequently, greater importance is afforded to professional opinion about families than to the opinions of families about themselves. The working relationships between practitioners and families are operationalized through systems designed by the professionals and physically and conceptually dominated by them. These require that families "fit in" to professional interventions. Family group conferences by contrast provide a format for inclusion that means decisions made through family groups are more likely to reflect the culture, traditions and needs of that *particular* family (Marsh & Crow, 1998). Therefore FGCs tend to conflict with, rather than complement, usual decision-making processes.

Enhancing the participation of families does not necessarily mean that professionals hand over their *power*, but in spite of the opportunities FGCs provide for greater power sharing, there is still reluctance to embrace this approach. Professionals retain power through organizational structures and the control of resources that in many ways deny the full participation of families anyway. Even with the best intentions, the development of inclusive practices over decision-making will not, in itself, necessarily "empower" families. There are concerns in the United Kingdom that FGCs have often been interpreted by professionals as an intervention of last resort, used when all else has been tried, or employed to "rubber-stamp" professional ideas. Increasingly in the current political context, they appear to be seen as a method to squeeze resources out of the families. A great deal of debate and training is happening to try and move FGCs from this reactive or augmented role to one that is more central to practice and thinking. It is likely that most of the conflicts and disagreements about child care policy and planning can be reduced to differences in values of staff about the amount of responsibility that should be given to families in decision-making processes (Ryburn, 1997), and the introduction of FGCs has served to heighten these tensions.

In practice, when decision-making responsibilities have been given to families, there has been a high level of consensus over the decisions made, in both child welfare and youth justice settings (Lupton, Barnard, & Swall-Yarrington, 1995; Marsh & Crow, 1998; Jackson, 1998). This is perhaps because FGC decisions take more account of the whole family context, drawing upon the knowledge families have of their own systems, which can exceed that of the professionals. A key concern in introducing FGCs as a "good practice" construct (without legislation) was the way professional and family decision-making models would coexist. Early projects attempted this, but despite much training, research, and debate, use of conferences has remained marginal (Nixon, 1998a). Moreover the implementation of FGCs has been the domain of professionals who have designed the service, driven it, set the standards, and in doing so may have colonized and diluted the original spirit behind the approach. More work needs to be done to involve children, families and the community in shaping services, changing the practice culture in professional agencies and the systems in which they operate if FGC plans are to really reflect families' culture, values, and aspirations, and not just those of the agencies that should serve them.

KINSHIP TIES AND SOCIAL NETWORKS

The important day-to-day decisions about the care and protection of children take place most of the time in their families. In spite of this fact (or perhaps because of it) when problems emerge, professionals can quickly move in and take over, determining families as incapable of safe decisions. This is a "deficit-model," which focuses on the nuclear family and is built on assumptions of individual pathology, an inadequate knowledge base, and negative cultural stereotyping. By contrast the FGC seeks to engage the wider family and assumes a family strengths perspective.

One of the main blocks to the use of family group conferences relates to assumptions about the weakness of kin and community networks. This has been a major objection to the practical use of FGCs among professionals (Nixon, Taverner, & Wallace, 1996). Research into practice, however, highlighted that FGC coordinators generally had more difficulty getting professionals to FGCs than family members (Lupton et al., 1995). In the United Kingdom, national surveys into family life (Pulling & Summerfield, 1997) revealed that while family structures have changed markedly in recent years, family bonds have remained strong. The stereotyped family household, with married parents and children, is far from the reality for many of us and yet services are configured on this view. Moreover, when families do not fit the stereotype, they are often judged as developmentally disadvantaged from both professional and public groups alike (Fry & Addington, 1984). What research has shown us is that it is the *quality* of relationships, not family structures, that are key to the well-being of children. However, professionals can readily use assumptions and judgments that certain *ideal* family types are best for children, when there is no compelling evidence to support this (Schaffer, 1990).

FGCs begin with a broad definition of "family" and start from the assumption that this network has something integral and of value to offer in decision-making. A tangible level of commitment expressed within family groups is evident in the United Kingdom research, which demonstrates that families are more broadly involved than in any other type of social work meeting (Thomas, 1994; Lupton et al., 1995; Lupton & Stevens, 1997; Marsh & Crow, 1998; Smith & Hennessy, 1998) and express high levels of satisfaction with the FGC approach and plans.

The importance of kin has been highlighted in research elsewhere, while at the same time those networks are mostly overlooked or underused (Department of Health, 1991; Home Office, 1998). Research in the United Kingdom has frequently shown the value of kinship relationships favorably; for example, Berridge and Cleaver (1987) and Rowe and her associates (1984) found kinship care held qualitative advantages over "stranger care," particularly in the role grandparents play. In adoption placements the research evidence shows that where children retain links with their families of origin, the placements are less likely to disrupt and children are aided by having a clearer self concept (Ryburn 1995). While prevailing practice tends to overlook kinship ties, the introduction of FGCs has started to reassert the value of kin. One national study on FGCs in the United Kingdom showed that those children offered FGCs were more likely (than with orthodox methods) to be placed with extended family and that placement was more likely to be stable (Crow & Marsh, 1997, p. 18).

The idea of building on social support networks is not new. In the United Kingdom, community approaches have been strongly advocated in two national reports (Seebohm, 1968; Barclay Report, 1982). The increasing use of FGCs has increased the role of extended families who are more likely to get involved, offering help and support to their kin, than they are with traditional approaches. This was evident in a study that looked at eighty FGCs in the United Kingdom. In 94 percent of the sample, family members offered some level of support, and in 31 percent of these cases offered to look after the children for at least some period of time (Crow & Marsh, 1997).

PARTICIPATION AND PARTNERSHIP

The Children Act sought to "construct a new consensus" (Parton, 1991) on the role of families and the state in the care of children, and partnership with families was seen as the means by which, at a practice level, consensus could be built. "Partnership" therefore was a central theme in policy statements, but in practice, services have been slow to engage collaboratively with the kinship, social, and informal networks around children (Thoburn & associates, 1995; Cleaver & Freeman, 1995; Bell, 1996; Freeman & Hunt, 1999). A lack of involvement has left families feeling uncertain or uncommitted to plans imposed by social workers, which is often misinterpreted by the professionals as lack of family commitment to children (Rowe et al., 1984; Millham, Bullock, Hoise, & Hack, 1986). The net effect is to create a cycle of mistrust and misunderstanding that has a corrosive effect on relationships between families and professionals. Research in the United Kingdom into child protection practice showed how partnership and good outcomes were connected (Thoburn et al., 1995; Department of Health, 1995). In summarizing a series of child protection studies, the research concluded that the most important condition for success was found always to be the quality of the relationship between the child's family and responsible professional (Department of Health, 1995).

In contrast with current practice, FGCs attempt to create a different relationship between family and professionals based on developing consensus and collaboration. While this may not achieve an equal partnership, it certainly enhances the family's participation and influence on decisions. However, current organizational structures and culture in which families' voices are routinely marginalized mean that the terms and conditions of "partnerships" between families and professionals are often preset by the professional agenda (Braye & Preston-Shoot, 1995). This seems to be spilling over into FGC practice, so in the United Kingdom it may be useful to accept that there is a difference between true partnerships (which are rare) and participatory practices with FGCs. Social workers may need more flexibility from the constraints of agency protocols and procedure, if the space is to be provided for negotiation and common ground to be developed with families.

DEFINING PROBLEMS

In defining the problems of others, social workers are expected to identify the "right" solutions for "problem" families, which can quickly lead them into a culture of "us and them" (Croft & Beresford, 1988). The increasing emphasis on diagnostic roles, particularly with risk assessments, leaves practitioners with the quandary trying to predict the behavior of strangers through identifying individual pathologies. However, there are real doubts over how far a "disease model" approximates to the problems of child abuse (Parton, Thorpe, & Watham, 1997), how reliable the current knowledge base is (McDonald & Marks, 1991), and how well this in fact enables social workers to judge, with accuracy, levels of risk. Indeed, the way we understand and label problems tends to vary greatly according to class, culture, religion, ethnicity, and geography (Giovannoni & Becerra, 1979). Professionals therefore are likely to interpret the problems of others through the filters of their own values and beliefs, legitimate these perceptions, and call them assessment. This process takes up a great deal of social work time and could be described as *label intensive,* as it leaves little space for offering help and providing services.

As professionals and agencies are seen as the legitimate definers of the hierarchies of "need" and indeed are frequently the main providers for those needs, it may be self-evident that the way social workers view problems will also be profoundly influenced by their agency role (Ryburn, 1991b). Research in child protection, where perhaps the most structured decision-making takes place, offers little reassurance of a shared objectivity. The evidence suggests that there is little qualitative difference between those families processed through the child protection system and those dropped off at an earlier stage (Giller, Gasramley, & Willens, 1992). Child protection registers, which are the most standardized organizational measure available to social workers, reveal enormous variations in definition that cannot be accounted for solely by demography or social problems (Department of Health, 1995). Current obsessions with risk and risk assessment seem not entirely motivated by concerns about the safety and well-being of children; they are just as likely to be driven by the need to provide mechanisms to ration resources and/or allocate responsibility and subsequently blame (usually social workers) when things go wrong (Parton, 1997). Furthermore, assessment and investigation are dominating activities, with correspondingly few resources or services being provided; this when it is the arrangements for children and services provided that are most likely to help keep children safe.

Given the very real limitations to currently achieving a robust and well-informed objectivity, surely we should involve children and their kin more than we do, in defining their *own* problems and finding *solutions* to them. Services that focus on needs that are defined by children, families, and their community may be more accessible and more likely to be effective. In practice open, honest, and clear language is needed to create a dialogue, avoiding the tendency for social workers to use language that is full of bureaucratic terms and jargon. Family members will have information that professionals will not usually access and will be enabled to share this within the FGC approach and perhaps in particular within the private time with no professionals present. However, professionals can still dominate the decision-making by setting agendas and extensive "bottom-lines" so implementation programs need to consider how to help professionals fundamentally change their practice. In the study by Lupton and her associates (1995), 40 percent of professionals indicated to the family what they felt should be the outcome of the FGC at the start of the meeting, even when they had been trained not to do this!

LEGAL COLONIZATION AND
MANAGERIAL ANNEXATION OF SOCIAL CARE

There are inherent difficulties in providing sensitive and responsive services through complex bureaucratic structures. It is in this context that the proceduralization of social work has led to rigid, process-driven practice that has deskilled professionals and marginalized families. In particular, current concerns in child protection studies are that children and families are put through a process or procedure, in which social workers are losing sight of the children's *needs* (Audit Commission, 1994; Department of Health, 1995; Gibbons, Conroy, & Bell, 1995). In the United Kingdom in the 1970s and 1980s, a series of public inquiries into child abuse tragedies, chaired by lawyers, led to a plethora of legalistic and procedural responses to the problem of child abuse (Cooper, 1995). These procedures were developed on cases where things had, by definition, gone wrong. The consequence was that the procedures became defensive and reactive in nature (Parton, 1997).

Social work began to focus on procedure and became process rather than needs led, which meant that interventions were often perceived as harsh and bureaucratic. Quickly social workers found themselves caught on an intervention/non-intervention axis, with many families being investigated with little apparent benefit and many other families receiving no help at all (Department of Health, 1995). Consequently a wedge has been driven between the community and state agencies that has had a corrosive effect on relationships between families and professionals. In turn families are now even less likely to ask for help when they most need it. Research in the United Kingdom has shown that this approach is producing little benefit for most children. A set of studies for the Department of Health called Messages from Research (Department of Health, 1995) showed that social work had become forensic, focusing on *incidents and evidence*. However, the research also showed that serious harm to children rarely came from isolated incidents, but was more likely to come from living in an environment of *high criticism and low warmth*. Unfortunately this was the area in which the procedural child protection system was least effective (Jack, 1997).

The questions FGCs have made us ask are whether the protection of children could be better achieved by:

- better collaboration;
- more positive and inclusive services;
- addressing the child's context and environment;
- providing services that generally enhance children's welfare;
- focusing on problem solving and outcomes.

This is not minimizing risk but placing it in context. Research in the United Kingdom on FGCs has shown that children were considered to be *better* protected by FGC plans (none worse) and there are indications of reductions in reabuse rates compared to other approaches (Crow & Marsh, 1997, p. 20). This may be because the FGC breaks the power of secrecy and allows families to use their knowledge and networks for the protection of the child. More fundamentally, it may be a product of better working relationships between formal and informal networks, collaborating to keep children safe.

CHANGING ORGANIZATIONS AND SERVICES

In the United Kingdom there has been a strong push from research to move services away from the reactive, investigative models of intervention, to ones that are more proactive and supportive to families. This has been understood as *refocusing* services from child protection to family support and mirrors very similar debates throughout the world within children's services. However, refocusing services to family support has been a major challenge for service providers. Because of anxiety about the need for professional control, policymakers have sought to maintain existing models of intervention while developing parallel approaches that are supposed to represent the family support aspirations of the Children Act. This approach to refocusing services has left policymakers and practitioners with a type of *double vision*. A twin-track approach has proved too costly to implement and has given confusing and often contradictory messages to families and professionals. Deciding which family should be put into which system moreover has been more than a little problematic.

A key practice issue for FGCs in the United Kingdom has been the introduction of "independent" coordinators: facilitators outside the statutory agencies to run the conferences, based on the idea that as independent they will retain a neutral position and will not have an interest in influencing outcomes. In theory this will mean they are more likely to encourage each family to have more control over decision-making processes. The provision of coordinators has varied across the United Kingdom, some operating from within social work agencies but outside the direct line of decision-making, while others have worked completely outside any agency acting as independent community-based FGC workers (Marsh & Crow, 1998; Nixon, 1998b). Hampshire County Council in the United Kingdom has wanted to ensure that independence was as much a *state of mind* as *status,* so has drawn from a diffuse community, bringing in people with varying backgrounds such as marriage guidance counselor, artist, retired head teacher, typist, nurse, community worker, service user, biology professor. In this context coordinating FGCs could be understood perhaps better as *art* rather than *science.* Coordinators start with a blank sheet, rather than program or script, and work with families to enable them to fill the blank spaces, each family thereby shaping their FGC in their own way.

In developing the coordinator role, there are tensions between corporate standards and flexibility. The key skills of coordinating—respect, facilitation, negotiation, organization—are not exclusive to social work, so at present coordinators are coming from a range of backgrounds with no nationally accepted standards, training, or qualifications. Some projects have determined that there shall be no full- time coordinators, so that an institutionalized and expert-controlled culture does not develop around the work. This has been particularly noticeable in Sweden (Lilja, 1998). In the United Kingdom, practice is developing locally to respond to local need. Rather than procedures, mostly guidelines are being developed, which give coordinators far more flexibility and room for creative practice. The future location of FGC coordinators is open to much debate. A popular model has been to place coordinators in nongovernmental agencies but as the work grows and develops there will be the temptation to locate the coordinators more centrally within the bureaucracy of social services. This would seem undesirable given the constraints it would produce; however, while placing it outside the statutory agencies would keep it independent, it might maintain the problem of the marginalization of a service that is ultimately dependent on state referrals (Hudson, Galaway, Morris, & Maxwell, 1996).

Real power in organizations is often seen as placed in the hands of managers and resource providers who are removed from the domain of practice. If professionals are going to use FGC plans as the basis/focus of their work, agencies will need to reconfigure services to be more flexible and responsive. Ensuring that

FGC plans are implemented and service requests provided is a major challenge in this style of work (Lupton et al., 1995). If the organizational issues are not addressed, families may be placed in an invidious position of having decision-making responsibilities without the power to influence the resources, which the FGC approach needs to be effective. The role family and community representatives can have in shaping future child care policies and services is linked to the future development of FGC practice. If families are given a greater say at a service level, this should be matched with giving them more influence over the type of services agencies provide. This is likely to promote the development of more accessible family support services. Involving the community in decisions about service priorities will invariably lead to questions about assumed sanctity of certain budgets.

Social workers and agencies must continue to apply FGCs as an ongoing decision-making approach and not see the FGC as a "one off." This should increase the likelihood of plans being sustained and supported. Moreover, the systematic recording of FGC requests and nonavailable services should be mapped to create some kind of *wish list* defined by families that could help inform future services. Finally, if agencies are really committed to the FGC philosophy, they should restructure organizational hierarchies, moving away from "top-down" structures to ones that devolve powers and responsibilities to the frontline staff and those closest to the outcomes of decisions. This in turn should make agencies more accessible and accountable to the community. If managers are unwilling to let go of decision-making to their own staff, then it is unlikely they will be comfortable with enabling families to take up responsibilities for decision-making. Organizations should model the principles they espouse.

CONCLUSION: SHARED PROBLEMS AND SOLUTIONS

The Role of Children, Families, and the Community

To date, the development of FGCs has been predominantly professionally led. We must take steps to ensure that children, families, and the community are involved in the design and development of the FGC approach. This means providing wide-ranging representation on planning forums and careful consultation to ensure that communities have a voice. It also means giving communities and community groups more control over finances and resources to plan and provide services based upon these principles. Practice and policy developments must seek to develop partnerships that are local and owned by those involved. "Act small, think big" could be a statement that captures the local and grassroots nature of the work if it is to retain its integral principles.

The Role of Social Workers

FGC practice may go some way to reclaiming original social work values founded on principles of respect. Social workers may need time to rediscover old and develop new skills of facilitation, negotiation, and collaboration if FGC principles are to flourish into practice. More attention is needed on the role of social workers and what value they can bring to the FGC approach. Involving social workers in the planning and implementation of FGC work will give them an investment in projects and model FGC principles. Practitioners working in hierarchical and disabling structures will not find it easy to practice principles they do not experience themselves. There are still a number of key practice questions about the amount and type/quality of information presented at FGCs, about what conditions make FGC most effective, and where the approach can be further developed.

The Role of Organizations and the State

In order to hold on to the integrity of the FGC approach it is important that it is not simply assimilated into the current bureaucratic agency function/response. Placing coordinators outside the state bureaucracy could be a mechanism to ensure the integrity of the approach, but may further marginalize the work. More research is needed on what should be done to achieve the best outcomes from the perspective of children and families involved. Ensuring that children, families, and communities are more involved in planning services, defining good outcomes, shaping research, providing training, and developing advocacy should ensure that the spirit and ethos of FGC is retained. In the end, the extent to which good practice is attained will be contingent upon the extent to which families and communities have a real say over the way services are delivered.

REFERENCES

Audit Commission (1994). *Seen but not heard: Co-ordinating community health and social services for children in need*. London: HMSO.

Baistow, K. (1994/1995). Liberation or regulation? Some paradoxes of empowerment. *Critical Social Policy, 42*(14), 34–46.

Barclay Report (1982). *National Institute of Social Work—Social workers: Their role and tasks*. London: Bedford Square.

Bell, M. (1996). An account of the experience of 51 families involved in an initial child protection conference. *Child and Family Social Work, 1*(1), 43–56.

Berridge, D., & Cleaver, H. (1987). *Foster home breakdown*. Oxford: Blackwells.

Braye, S., & Preston-Shoot, M. (1995). *Empowering practice in social care*. Buckingham: Open University Press.

Cleaver, H., & Freeman, P. (1995). *Parental perspectives in cases of suspected child abuse*. London: HMSO.

Cooper, A. (1995). Scare in the community: Britain in a moral panic—Child abuse (Part 4). *Community Care* (August), 3 – 9. Croft, S., & Beresford, P. (1988). Time to build: Trust between them and us. *Social Work Today, 8*(September), 16–17.

Crow, G., & Marsh, P. (1997). *Family group conferences: Partnership and child welfare: A research report on four pilot projects in England and Wales.* Sheffield: University of Sheffield Press.

Department of Health (1991). *Patterns and outcomes on child placement.* London: HMSO.

Department of Health (1995). *Child protection: Messages from research.* London: HMSO.

Freeman, P., & Hunt, J. (1999). *Parental perspectives on care proceedings.* London: The Stationery Office.

Fry, P., & Addington, J. (1984). Professionals' negative expectations of boys from father-headed single-parent families: Implications for training of child care professionals. *British Journal of Developmental Psychology, 2,* 337–46.

Gibbons, J., Conroy, S., & Bell, C. (1995). *Operating the child protection system.* London: HMSO

Giller, H., Gasramley, C., & Willens, P. (1992). *The effectiveness of child protection procedures: An evaluation in four ACPC areas.* Cheshire: Social Information Systems.

Giovannoni, J., & Becerra, R. (1979). *Defining child abuse.* New York: Free Press. Home Office (1998). *Supporting families: A consultation document.* London: Stationery Office.

Hudson, J., Galaway, B., Morris, A., & Maxwell, G. (1996). *Family group conferences: Perspectives on policy and practice.* Annadale, NSW, Australia: Federation Press/Criminal Justice Press.

Jack, G. (1997). An ecological approach to social work with children and families. *Child and Family Social Work, 2,* 109–20.

Jackson, S. (1998). *Family justice? An evaluation of the Hampshire Youth Justice Family Group Conference Project.* Hampshire: University of Southampton Press.

Lilja, I. (1998). *Setting up an independent coordinators' service*: Svenska Kommunforbundent (Swedish Association of Local Authorities). Paper presented to Second International Forum on FGCs Breaking New Ground, Winchester, UK, September.

Lupton, C. (1998). User empowerment or family self-reliance? The family group conference model. *British Journal of Social Work, 28*(1), 107–28.

Lupton, C., Barnard, S., & Swall-Yarrington, M. (1995). *Family planning? An evaluation of the FGC model.* SSRIU Rep. No. 31, University of Portsmouth.

Lupton, C., & Nixon, P. (1999). *Empowering practice? A critical appraisal of the family group conference approach.* Bristol: Policy.

Lupton, C., & Stevens, M. (1997). *Family outcomes: Following through on family group conferences.* SSRIU Rep. No. 34, University of Portsmouth.

Marsh, P., & Crow, G. (1998). *Family group conferences in child welfare.* Oxford: Blackwells.

McDonald, T., & Marks, J. (1991). A review of risk factors assessed in child protective services. *Social Service Review* (March), 112–31.

Millham, S., Bullock, R., Hoise, K., & Hack, M. (1986). *Lost in care.* Aldershot: Gower.

Nixon, P. (1998a). Using family group conferences to re-focus to family support. Paper presented to the Second International Forum on Family Group Conferences, Winchester Guildhall, Hampshire, September.

Nixon, P. (1998b). Exchanging practice: Some comparisons, contrasts and lessons learned from the practice of family group conferences in Sweden and the UK. *Protecting Children, 14,* 13–18.

Nixon, P., & Taverner, P. (1993). Winchester project update. *Family Group Conferences National Newsletter* (Issue 2). London: Family Rights Group.

Nixon, P., Taverner, P., & Wallace, F. (1996). It gets you out and about or Family Group Conferences—The views of children and their families. In K. Morris & J. Tunnard (Eds.), *Family group conferences: Messages from UK practice and research.* London: Family Rights Group.

Parton, N. (1991). *Governing the family: Child care, child protection and the state.* London: Macmillan.

Parton, N. (Ed.) (1997). *Child protection and family support: Tensions, contradictions and possibilities*. London: Routledge.

Parton, N., Thorpe, D., & Watham, C. (1997). *Child protection: Risk and the moral order*. Basingstoke: Macmillan.

Pulling, J., & Summerfield, C. (1997). *Social focus on families*. London: Office for National Statistics.

Rowe, J., Cain, H., Hundleby, M., & Keane, A. (1984). *Long term foster care*. London: Batsford.

Ryburn, M. (1991a). The Children Act—Power and empowerment. *Adoption and Fostering, 15*(3), 10–15.

Ryburn, M. (1991b). The myth of assessment. *Adoption and Fostering, 15*(1), 20–27.

Ryburn, M. (1995). Adopted children's identity and information needs. *Children and Society, 9*(3), 41–64.

Ryburn, M. (1997). *Mobilizing the kinship network: Constraints and challenges*. Unpublished paper presented to Hampshire County Council Social Services Department.

Schaffer, H. (1990). *Making decisions about children—Psychological questions and answers*. Oxford: Blackwells.

Seebohm, F. (1968). *Report of the Committee on Local Authority and Allied Personal Social Services*. London: HMSO.

Smith, L., & Hennessy, J. (1998). *Making a difference: Essex family group conference project; research findings and practice issues*. Chelmsford: Essex County Council Social Services Department.

Thoburn, J., Lewis, A., & Shemmings, D. (1995). *Paternalism or partnership? Family involvement in the child protection process*. London: HMSO.

Thomas, N. (1994). *In the driving seat—A study of the Family Group Meetings Project in Hereford*. Swansea: Department of Social Policy and Applied Social Studies, University of Wales.

10   Bringing the Community Back In

Patch and Family Group Decision-Making

PAUL ADAMS

Perhaps the central question for all helping professions is the relation of formal to informal helping. In the case of child protection, what is the role of the state, with its bureaucratic-professional systems, in ensuring the safety of children, and how does that interact with the informal mechanisms of care and control in families and communities?

This chapter explores the relationship between two approaches to working with families and communities—*patch* and *family group decision-making* (FGDM)— which reflect a partnership- or empowerment-oriented answer to this question. It introduces this discussion by setting it in the context of another, increasingly influential kind of answer, one that seeks to strengthen the state and its coercive power vis-à-vis families and communities.

The task, in this latter view, is not to empower families and communities, but to restrict their authority over children (Bartholet, 1999; Costin, Karger, & Stoesz, 1996; Lindsey, 1994; Pelton, 1992). This perspective may be called neo-statist in that it gives central place to the relation of state and individual (child), discounting those structures of extended family, church, school, or neighborhood that mediate it. Programs that seek to work in partnership with families and communities, to identify and build on their strengths, fall under suspicion or open attack for failing to intervene coercively to protect children. These include family group decision-making (FGDM), family support and family preservation services, community partnerships, kinship care, and family-to-family programs. These approaches are seen as leaving children unprotected and vulnerable to the very families (and communities) that exposed them to violence or neglect. The problem is perceived as one of public safety, so that child maltreatment is criminalized and the state intervenes coercively. In short, families and communities need to be policed with a heavier hand in order to protect children. Some neostatists support universal monitoring programs like home visiting, but their general drift is in the direction of rescuing children from families where maltreatment has occurred and placing them, as rapidly and permanently as possible, with other families and in other communities.

Communities are not strengthened or made safer for children by this approach, however, so much as given up on. Paradoxically, the neostatists do not deny the link between poverty and child maltreatment. They acknowledge, and even emphasize the connection, seeing it as evidence of the futility of medical or psychological models of maltreatment. Even the most extreme and legalistic of the neo-statists, Elizabeth Bartholet (1999), in a final chapter entitled "Race, poverty, and historic injustice," admits the "strong connection between socioeconomic status and child maltreatment" (p. 233). "In the long term," she acknowledges, "the only good solution is the one that reduces the scope of the problem, that deals with the causes of substance abuse and child maltreatment" (p. 241).

In the shorter term, however, she argues for earlier coercive state intervention, earlier termination of parental rights, and an enormous expansion of adoption. Even efforts to maintain family or community continuity through permanent placement within the child's extended family or local community are to be rejected as preferred options, compared with adoption by more affluent people. Thus Bartholet (1999) quotes approvingly the position of Richard Barth, who argues for "productive development" rather than continuity in placing children. "These children often come from schools and neighborhoods that are almost unsalvageable. . . . Living in an advantaged neighborhood," on the other hand, "discourages teenagers from having children out of wedlock, encourages teenagers to finish high school, and increases teenagers' future earnings" (pp. 184–85). The narrowing of child protection services to a more coercive policing function, abstracted from any effort to strengthen families and communities, leaves neighborhoods that are experiencing the most severe poverty to function as departure stations for a new and larger orphan train.

Family preservation, especially in its form as a residual, crisis-oriented program, may have failed to reverse the impact on families of market-oriented economic and social policies that increased inequality and concentrated extreme poverty in certain neighborhoods (Fisher, 1995). Indeed, its staunchest proponents never claimed that it could, despite the unsupported charge that they advocated it as a "panacea." Some critics of family preservation (see, especially, Lindsey, 1994), who advocate making child protection primarily a police function, argue for a structural perspective that includes, but is not limited to, residual services. Lindsey's critique is of any residual approach to child welfare, whether oriented to family preservation or child removal, that does not address child poverty by including broader, more universal policies like family allowances and asset development accounts.

Too easily, however, and most notably in the hands of Bartholet (1999), this larger reform agenda becomes a parenthesis rather than a program. Acknowledging poverty and related neighborhood factors as key to the incidence of maltreatment, she offers not a panacea, but a counsel of despair. Since she believes that policies and programs to address the underlying issues of poverty and oppression will not be forthcoming in the foreseeable future, she seeks instead to strengthen the coercive apparatus of the state so as to evacuate individual children from their families and communities.

PROBLEMS

Such a strategy, however, will not interrupt the problem-perpetuating patterns in low-income neighborhoods, any more than a family preservation service approach that remains at the level of individual cases. It will not prevent the reproduction of abuse and neglect in the communities hardest hit by other economic and social policies, including a welfare "reform" that is increasing child poverty and reducing the capacity of many women to provide for their children (Sherman, Amey, Duffield, Ebb, & Weinstein, 1998; Sherman, 1999; Waldfogel, 1998).

The heavy reliance on policing and criminalization contrasts, too, with the growing awareness in criminal justice systems of the limitations of an adversarial relationship between state and community and the burgeoning of alternatives, including community policing and restorative justice approaches. The principles of community policing, for instance, reflect a realization that order and safety in a community cannot depend solely or mainly on the armed officers of the state. Instead, police, in this approach, recognize that they are but one element in the production of order in a community, and that they need to build partnerships with other formal and informal entities, sharing responsibility for finding solutions and coproducing order. Acting (and being perceived) as an occupying army is not only ineffective, it erodes the order-producing elements within communities. It undermines, as it substitutes for, community capacity.

A distanced, adversarial relationship of state agents to communities also restricts the information available to those wielding official power. They are unable to access local knowledge, wisdom, and resources, and their interventions tend to be blunt and heavy-handed because uninformed. In contrast, as several studies indicate, when professional agents of care and control work in partnership with each other or with informal community systems, social workers, police, and others intervene with a better knowledge and understanding of the situation and their interventions are less aggressive (Adams, Alter, Krauth, St. Andre, & Tracy, 1995; Waldfogel, 1998).

ALTERNATIVES

The neostatists, we have seen, give up on the most oppressed communities and seek to reform child protection systems so that they intervene more rapidly, coercively, and irreversibly, and with less or no regard to continuity of family, community, or culture. Their program has made considerable headway and is reflected in recent federal legislation, including the Multi-Ethnic Placement Act (1994) and Amendments (1996), and the Adoption and Safe Families Act (1997). Others, however, while recognizing the need for authoritative intervention in some cases, have argued for a more differentiated and holistic system of child protection. Such a system can intervene coercively or preventively, partnering with police, other agencies, schools, neighborhood, or advocacy organizations, according to the situation. Waldfogel (1998), who advocates this approach, draws on the experience of recent innovations in the United States, New Zealand, Britain, and elsewhere to show how a differentiated community-based system can act both authoritatively to protect children and empower families and communities.

Two important innovations in working with families and communities that Waldfogel (1998) discusses reflect this partnership perspective and have gained ground in recent years as approaches to child protection, youth justice, and other issues of social care and control (American Humane Association, 1997). The first, family group decision-making or conferencing, especially as it developed in New Zealand, but also in the form of the Family Unity Meeting that came out of Oregon, has had a wide and increasing influence in child welfare, and is the primary subject of this book. The other, the approach to locality-based, integrated social care and community-centered teamwork and partnership-building that developed in the United Kingdom as patch, but that also has a variety of forms and names and has undergone significant changes in Britain itself, is the focus of this chapter.

The two approaches developed largely independently, and patch remained a work of pioneers in pockets of innovation rather than the nationally and legally established practice that family group conferencing has become in New Zealand. Both, however, are expressions of the same paradigm shift and represent new ways of working with families, their cultures, and communities, and for the agencies with statutory responsibility for protecting children. Both reflect a fundamental rethinking of the relationship between state and community, and between professionals and families. Important principles of each are reflected in the major child welfare legislation of its country of origin, respectively, the Children, Young Persons, and Their Families Act (1989) in New Zealand, and the Children Act (1989) in the United Kingdom.

WHAT IS PATCH?

The term *patch* refers to a geographical area or neighborhood within which a social service team operates. Patch connotes too a way of integrating services through varying degrees of collaboration at administrative and case levels, and especially through locality-based teamwork. The term is also used to refer to a community-centered, strengths-oriented approach to social work practice that seeks to interweave formal and informal care and control (Bayley, Seyd, & Tennant, 1989; Smale, Tuson, Cooper, Wardle, & Crosbie, 1988).

As a model of service integration, patch involves the deployment of practitioners of varying levels and kinds of skill, often (but not necessarily) from different agencies, in neighborhood or local offices where they serve an area of about ten thousand residents. In the first effort to transfer this approach from the United Kingdom to an urban neighborhood in Cedar Rapids, Iowa, in the 1990s, the Patch Project integrated staff from five state and local agencies into a multiagency team. Included were four child protection social workers from the Iowa Department of Human Services (DHS), a county homemaker, a city housing inspector, a youth probation officer, a local community house worker, a resident and sometime service user, a social work graduate student, and a team coordinator. The composition has changed somewhat over time, but the public agencies, especially the one responsible for child welfare, have always been at the heart of the project. The DHS social workers were accountable for all the ongoing child welfare work in their patch. Patch teams have varied widely in composition and scope in the United States as they did in Britain. Basing themselves on a body of experience, developmental research, and core principles rather than a highly specified model, rural and urban communities in Iowa, Pennsylvania, Vermont, Colorado, Massachusetts, and elsewhere are reinventing patch in light of their own needs and conditions.

Localization of services, as illustrated by the movement of DHS workers in the Cedar Rapids example, from a central downtown building to a small neighborhood office, initially a church basement shared with a Head Start program, is an important and defining characteristic of the patch approach. As the evaluation of the Iowa Patch Project showed, localization made services more accessible, and workers more approachable and more knowledgeable about the local community and its formal and informal resources (Adams et al., 1995). Localization and collocation of services, however, do not necessarily result in a different experience of services for the local citizens and families who use them. Patch teams that have absorbed the principles of community-based practice engage in social work that seeks to be more proactive and preventive, and less reactive and crisis-oriented than traditional practices. They ask who else is involved in the problem and seek to build partnerships with them. They seek to share responsibility for solutions with families, social networks, and natural helpers, rather than seeing themselves as solely and entirely responsible for solving people's problems. They seek to offer services that are close to and guided by the community, tailoring resources to family needs and cultures (Hadley, Cooper, Dale, & Stacy, 1987).

PRINCIPLES OF COMMUNITY-BASED PRACTICE

Successful efforts to redesign human services so as to make them comprehensive, accessible, and less fragmented seem to share in common a more or less fundamental shift in relations between professionals and citizens. This new way of working recognizes the strengths and capacities of families, social networks, and communities, and seeks to work in partnership with them. Like family group conferencing, it sees solutions as arising out of the strengths and cultures, the wisdom, knowledge, and caring of the people involved with the problem.

This shift in focus, displacing the human services system from the center of the picture of which it is part, has profound consequences and is the core principle of patch, as of family group conferencing. It implies that professionals are not at the center of helping systems, but perform a small part of the work of care and control in communities. Formal human services represent, as Hadley et al. (1987) argue, "no more than a single strand in the complex web of relationships and services, formal and informal, statutory and nonstatutory, which together provide care and control in the community. The overall effectiveness of provision depends not on one part of this network alone but on how well the whole is woven together" (p. 95). From this perspective, the care and protection of children is a shared responsibility (Moroney, 1986), involving local communities as well as (extended) family and the state. Each of the partners has knowledge, resources, and skills to contribute to lasting solutions. This more modest view of the role of formal authorities and services does not imply a narrow targeting of intervention on the most critical situations. It should lead, instead, to a broader, more diversified conception of human services and state responsibility, as promoting and enhancing the development of families and communities, as well as responding to problems and deficits (Chapin Hall Center for Children, 1994). In such a conception, child welfare systems would not intervene only in the most severe and critical cases. They would also aim to provide a little help when needed, rather than insisting that a situation become critical before help could be provided. Sharing responsibility for solutions at multiple levels, from individual cases to issues of health and housing, economic and social development, they would work with formal and informal partners to build safe and healthy communities.

Decentering formal human services in this way implies a position of marginality for community-centered social workers (Adams & Nelson, 1997; Smale, 1995). Such practitioners cannot afford simply to adopt the appreciative stance of the anthropologist, though they need the ethnographic sensibility and respect for local cultures that this posture implies. Community-based practitioners seek to understand the patterns of interaction that generate or perpetuate problems that may involve multiple system levels (e.g., family, neighbors, school, and youth justice and social service systems). Failing to recognize these patterns may doom social workers and their agencies to become part of the problem-perpetuating pattern (Imber-Black, 1988; Holder & Wardle, 1981). It is often necessary to step back from the immediate situation, to go to a higher or metalevel, to see the larger patterns of which one may be part. One example is the work of GEARS, a community-based program in Portland, Oregon, that uses social workers and neighborhood "coaches" to work with local families and build community. When the GEARS team started to work with a housebound family, most of whose members had mental health diagnoses, the team noticed that many therapists from several agencies had worked with the family before they became involved, but to little effect. Indeed, the father had become expert in obtaining diagnoses for himself, his wife, and children as a route to services. Rather than offering more of the same and becoming part of this pattern of family-agency relations, the team cocreated with family members other options for meeting their needs, engaging them in work, school, and community activities outside the house (D. Gour, personal communication, November 8, 1999).

Decentering the professional-client relationship and recognizing the proper marginality of professionals imply the central importance of partnership. Community-based teams seek to build partnerships at every level, not only with other professionals, but also and more importantly with families and networks directly involved in the situation. Partnership is needed not only at the level of particular "cases"—the kind of partnership represented in a single family group conference—but also in the design, development, and oversight of services, programs, and projects in a community. In this sense, users of services are understood as contributors to the solution of their community's problems as well as their own.

From this perspective, people who use services are no longer seen as clients or objects of intervention. Nor are terms adequate that define people as users of services or consumers of resources. Recognition of the strengths, resources, and expertise that such "consumers" and their families and networks can bring to bear on their own situations is important, but not enough. A community-centered perspective points to the importance of recognizing the capacity of those involved with human services to contribute to the community (Adams & Nelson, 1997; Adams & Krauth, 1995; Checkoway & Finn, 1992; Checkoway, Finn, & Pothukuchi, 1995; Smale, 1995). Even social workers who see themselves as community-oriented and as having a rich involvement in their own communities may see their clients' relation to community in more impoverished terms, typically as a relationship of consumers to resources (Swenson, 1995). Or they may see community members as adjuncts who help the professionals carry out their tasks. A community-centered perspective, however, reverses this picture, showing it as the task of the professionals to join with the community and help it in carrying out its work of caring for and protecting its members (Smale, 1995).

Building effective partnerships with local people requires both teamwork and the devolution of decision-making as close as possible to those involved in the problem. Social workers and other professionals who enter into partnerships need to know the community with which they work and of which they become part. They need to understand the patterns of formal and informal care, and how they can effectively be interwoven. They need to be able to identify patterns in their collective caseloads and take initiatives and develop projects and programs in partnership with other agencies and organizations.

Teamwork makes these things possible. A team can share the knowledge and insights of its members, responding flexibly and quickly to needs and opportunities. Even workers with mandated responsibilities for child protection and youth justice can move in the direction of a shared workload within a team, as opposed to individual caseloads. Evaluation of the Patch Project in Iowa showed that even when individual cases remained the responsibility of a single team member, they were approached differently. The worker was able to bring to her work the shared knowledge of the community, the support of the team in identifying and building on family and community strengths, and the results of the team's prior work in the community. For example, the child protection workers, noting the number of isolated young mothers in their caseloads, were able to start a support group for them, which the mothers soon took over and ran themselves. A similar process led to the team working with city and school authorities to set up a summer recreation program for young children. The team's housing inspector, noting that a young mother new to the area had no furniture other than a sofa for herself and her two young children, brought her concerns to the team, though they were outside her individual professional responsibility. The team sent a social work student and DHS worker, who worked with the mother to contact local churches for furniture, to sign up her children for the Head Start program, and to include the mother in the new support group. All this happened without a formal case being opened. The team was able to provide what so many local parents said they wanted—a little help when they needed it. No one had to be "clientized" or diagnosed to get help, nor was it necessary for someone to harm a child or for a child to run away or commit a serious offense before help was forthcoming. In this case, the team's prior work in the community, building strong relations with local churches and with Head Start, enabled it to respond quickly and flexibly (Adams et al., 1995; Adams & Krauth, 1995).

A team has the capacity, which is beyond the knowledge or skills of any one practitioner in most circumstances, to intervene simultaneously and synergistically at multiple levels. It can work with individuals and families, groups and organizations. It can simultaneously respond to court-mandated individual cases and engage in community development. A community-centered social work team aims to share responsibility for addressing common concerns with others in the community. It is constantly engaged in negotiating care in the community, at the level of an individual family, or development of a new program, or improvement of relations among families, schools, and the child welfare system. All of these are part of the work of strengthening families and neighborhoods to keep children safe. The capacity of a team to engage in this kind of negotiation in good faith, and to do so without leaving a trail of cynicism and distrust in the community, depends upon the team having reasonable authority to use its judgment. If it cannot make agreements without being overruled by those higher up and further away from the situation, then negotiation with it will quickly be perceived as a waste of time (Smale & Tuson, 1993; Adams & Krauth, 1994).

Starting with the community rather than the bureaucratic, professional service system, we thus see a logically linked set of principles: decentering the professional-client relationship; marginality as the appropriate professional stance;

partnership; teamwork; and devolution of decision-making to those closest to the situation. In contrast, much child protection practice, and the thrust of the neo-statists, who call for narrowing of services and more coercive interventionism, moves in the opposite direction. That direction places the professional at the center of a rescue drama. It restricts the authority of families and communities rather than empowering or partnering with them. And it coerces social workers into a more rule- and procedure-bound practice, with less room for negotiation or the exercise of professional judgment.

CONFERENCING AND COMMUNI1TY

Behind the negotiation between social worker and family group that are part of the conferencing process, there also stands a negotiation between child welfare authorities and the social and cultural context in which the conferencing takes place. It is a dance, so to speak, of state and community. Pennell and Burford (1994, 1995, 1996) have shown the importance of this community development aspect of conferencing. They describe a lengthy metaprocess of community decision-making about the family group decision-making process, including dialogue among police, probation and parole services, policymakers, women's shelters, and advocates. It is a process whereby agents of the state (i.e., those with statutory authority and responsibility for the protection of children) work with community leaders to establish a culturally appropriate and locally acceptable form of conferencing. Community group conferencing may allow the experience of multiple family group conferences to be generalized to identify needs, resources, and opportunities for building a stronger community.

Conferencing is to that extent already part of a larger community-based approach to protecting children (and women where family violence is appropriately addressed) by strengthening families and neighborhoods. By widening the circle beyond the often isolated and secretive parent-child household, and beyond the exclusive professional-client relationship, family group conferencing is itself a form of community-based practice. It is not simply a technology available to or mandated for professionals. It is a strategy for changing the relations between families and authorities, a form of partnership or empowerment practice that shares responsibility between professionals and the family group at one level, and between state and community at another. Not only does family group conferencing return responsibility and accountability to the family for its children's safety, with support and resources from the state, it also, at least potentially and in some cases, returns to communities ownership of the process through negotiation and adaptation to the local culture. It has shown the capacity to engage the family group and community in taking responsibility for solutions to problems of abuse or neglect or violence against women in a process and plan that protect their most vulnerable members.

Conferencing arose in New Zealand out of a recognition that the state-centered, criminalizing approach to child protection and youth justice was especially counterproductive when Maori families were the targets of intervention. It drew instead on the traditions and wisdom of Maori culture itself, learning from it how to shape a more culturally appropriate practice that at the same time worked well with all sections of the population. This capacity to learn from cultures and communities previously seen as targets of state intervention, but not as sources of wisdom, especially from indigenous peoples with prestate traditions of community problem solving, healing, and restorative justice, has been a hallmark of conferencing in several countries. The Oregon Family Unity Model, growing out of an audit of the best practices of line workers in child protection, showed the capacity of those practitioners to step back from the impulse to control families, and to work with them and others in the community to cocreate solutions.

FAMILY GROUP CONFERENCING AND PATCH

Family group conferencing and patch have much in common and are highly compatible. Both have been implemented by public child welfare systems seeking to build partnerships with communities, including in the process all those who have information or resources to share, and those who care most about the children concerned. Both represent a new way of working with families, their cultures, and communities. They both seek to build a community of care to protect children, strengthening the capacity of the community to work together and protect its members. They work with the wisdom, solutions, and resources of families and their networks. The patch principles outlined above apply equally to family group decision-making: the conference process starts from the recognition that ensuring the safety of children is a shared responsibility, and professionals cannot substitute for a child's immediate and extended family, close friends, neighbors, church, community, and culture. In both cases, this redefinition of the professional role in relation to families and communities implies the need for partnership-building at multiple levels, including, for example, family group members, neighbors, congregations, schools, and advocacy groups. This in turn requires that the social worker(s) have the capacity to negotiate about and commit resources, which requires devolution of the authority to make such decisions as close as possible to those directly involved in the situation.

Both conferencing and patch represent a new paradigm in working with families and communities, including communities of interest and ethnic groups with distinct cultures as well as communities of place. They introduce second-order change, a change of the rules and new ways of doing business as opposed to or as well as change within the rules (Smale, 1998). They are subversive of established structures and practices at many levels, but at the same time both are subject to strong gravitational pulls to old practices shaped more by bureaucratic, professional, and funding imperatives than by community strengths, wisdom, and resources. Family group conferencing risks being reduced to another professional tool in a professional-dominated, disempowering system. In the United States, the policy context—the time limits, the ever-present threat of termination of parental rights, a lack of rights for extended family members, mandatory reporting, and a push to "free" children for adoption (none of which exists in New Zealand)—may undermine the integrity of conferencing. It could result in a tendency for overworked but powerful social workers to make and impose decisions for family groups in advance of meetings.

In the case of patch, as the Cedar Rapids experience showed, potential community partners, especially private providers, relying on a certain share of public child welfare moneys through purchase of service contracting, may at first see patch as another program or project in competition with other programs for limited resources. Or they may view the patch team as a virtual or real agency in competition with existing agencies (Adams et al., 1995). Patch team members and managers may see community building and preventive activities as an add-on to the preexisting, mandated parts of the job, rather than as a new way of carrying out their statutory responsibilities (Adams & Krauth, 1995). These are the kinds of challenges any innovation can expect to face if it represents the order of change involved in both family group conferencing and patch.

WHAT PATCH AND CONFERENCING OFFER EACH OTHER

One indicator of the compatibility of patch and conferencing is the enthusiasm with which patch team members in Iowa embraced Oregon's Family Unity Model of conferencing. This was part of the training of team members in the first few years of the project. The concepts, terminology, and approach became part of the team's way of thinking about its work. So great was the support for family group decision-making on the first Iowa patch team that when the members developed a document setting out requirements of a team member, they included a commitment to the use of family unity meetings. The commitment included: "acknowledging, emphasizing, and promoting the informal support networks of families [and] use of the strengths and resources of the community to assist families in generating possible solutions regarding concerns, with workers remaining peripheral" (Adams & Krauth, 1995, p. 106). Despite this enthusiasm and commitment, family unity meetings did not become part of the team's practice. The institutional supports were not in place and the Family Unity Model represented too large an additional innovation for a team of line workers to introduce in a system already adjusting with difficulty to the systemic impact the team itself was having. Instead, the approach, philosophy, and terminology of conferencing became part of the team's thinking about its work, encouraging and legitimating its innovative, family- and community-centered practice (Adams et al., 1995).

The family group conferencing approach to child protection planning has shown that it has much to offer a neighborhood-based integrated service team engaged in community-based practice. As a planning process, it offers extended family groups and their community supports an empowering way to work with mandated authorities to assure the protection of their vulnerable members. It offers community-based child welfare practitioners both an empowering way to approach their statutory responsibilities to plan for the safety and attachment needs of children who have suffered maltreatment, and a way of thinking about their work with families that extends beyond conferencing situations. It provides a way of working in partnership with families that is increasingly well understood and accepted as a "best practice" by courts and legislators.

Patch and related approaches to service integration and community-based practice for their part offer a way to enrich the community development aspects of conferencing. Patch brings public child welfare into neighborhoods, providing an approach to negotiating social care in communities that includes but extends beyond "cases." It counteracts the tendency to individualize social problems, shifting the focus from a worker who is situated at the center of a rescue drama to a team that shares responsibility and works in partnership with others involved in problematic social situations. The community-based team is concerned both with the resolution of individual situations involving child maltreatment (or other problems) and with strengthening the caring capacity of the community. This approach has shown the potential to reduce the statutory caseloads of workers substantially, while increasing their informal, preventive work (Hadley & McGrath, 1984). It involves partnership with local citizens, including service users, central helping figures (or "aunts" in some communities, who look out for children and to whom residents turn when they need help), and a range of informal and formal organizations (Collins & Pancoast, 1976).

Just as a social worker preparing for a family group conference works extensively with family members and others to identify strengths and resources that can resolve concerns, so the community-based team works with families and other formal and informal helpers in its patch. The work may, indeed, include preparation for a family group conference, but it also involves ongoing relationships that identify, draw on, and build community assets to strengthen communities and make them safe. The same team that organizes a family group conference to plan for a child in its care may also generalize from its experience. It may draw conclusions from several such cases about the need for a project, program, or community intervention that is not tied to a specific case at all, but might prevent families in need of help from becoming cases in the first place. It may identify and mobilize strengths within the community and also obtain and advocate for needed external resources. Such a team is able to bring a proactive, entrepreneurial approach to its work, empowering line workers to think and act strategically.

Patch, then, offers conferencing an hospitable and fertile ground. Allowing for a full range of options in a differentiated approach to child protection and sharing responsibility for solutions with those involved, it also offers an approach to preventive and proactive work with communities that extends teamwork and collaboration beyond individual cases. It enables frontline workers and managers to overcome the dichotomy between individual casework and community development. It enables social workers to work in partnership with others involved in problematic social situations at multiple levels, intervening to protect children without individualizing social problems or pathologizing those caught up in them.

CONCLUSION

This chapter has argued that family group decision-making and patch share common principles, are highly compatible, and are mutually enriching. Long-term solutions to poverty, inequality, and oppression in the United States, and the child maltreatment associated with them, lie beyond the capacity and cannot be the sole responsibility of human service professionals, however organized. They call for wider systemic changes that depend on larger economic, political, and social forces, and that address the fundamental problem of child poverty. Yet child protection strategies differ in terms of how far they support or undermine wider efforts to build healthy communities that are safe and nurturing for children. The perspective offered here, the new paradigm for working with families represented by family group conferencing and patch, involves social workers and other professionals learning from the cultures and building on the strengths of the communities with which they are engaged. It involves developing partnerships in which the wisdom, knowledge, skills, and resources available to professionals are joined with those of families and communities to protect children.

But can a community-based approach that joins the practices associated with conferencing and those associated with patch offer better hope of protecting children than the neostatist orphan train model? Can either be tested when coexisting as countervailing tendencies in the same internally contradictory child welfare system, which continues to be overwhelmed by the effects of economic policies and structures that generate and intensify inequality and child poverty? The research tasks implied by these questions are complex and formidable, both for the developmental research that refines and differentiates best practices and the summative evaluation research that informs choices among strategies and paradigms. The issues are both normative and empirical, reflecting differences about the value as well as the practicality and results of sharing responsibility for child safety among families, communities, and professionals representing the state. They touch on matters of principle as well as fact about the kind of society worth striving for and living in.

REFERENCES

Adams, P., Alter, C., Krauth, K., St. Andre, M., & Tracy, M. (1995). *Strengthening families and neigh-borhoods: A community-centered approach*. Final report on the Iowa Patch Project, University of Iowa School of Social Work, Iowa City.

Adams, P., & Krauth, K. (1994). Empowering workers for empowerment-based practice. In P. Nurius & L. Gutierrez (Eds.), *Education and research for empowerment practice*. Seattle: School of Social Work, University of Washington.

Adams, P., & Krauth, K. (1995). Working with families and communities: The patch approach. In P. Adams & K. Nelson (Eds.), *Reinventing human services: Community- and family-centered practice* (pp. 87–108). Hawthorne, NY: Aldine de Gruyter.

Adams, P., & Nelson, K. (1997). Reclaiming community: An integrative approach to human services. *Administration in Social Work, 21*(3/4), 67–81. Copublished simultaneously in M. J. Austin (Ed.), *Human services integration* (pp. 67–81). New York: Haworth.

American Humane Association (1997). *Innovations for children's services for the 21st century: Family group decision making and Patch*. Englewood, CO: Author.

Bartholet, E. (1999). *Nobody's children*. Boston, MA: Beacon.

Bayley, M., Seyd, R., & Tennant, A. (1989). *Local health and welfare*. Aldershot, UK: Gower.

Chapin Hall Center for Children (1994). *Children, families, and communities: A new approach to social services*. Chicago: Chapin Hall Center for Children at the University of Chicago.

Checkoway, B., & Finn, J. (1992). *Young people as community builders*. Ann Arbor, MI: Center for the Study of Youth Policy, School of Social Work, University of Michigan.

Checkoway, B., Finn, J., & Pothukuchi, K. (1995). Young people as community resources: New forms of participation. In P. Adams & K. Nelson (Eds.), *Reinventing human services: Community- and family-centered practice* (pp.189–202). Hawthorne, NY: Aldine de Gruyter.

Collins, A., & Pancoast, D. (1976). *Natural helping networks: A strategy for prevention*. Washington, DC: NASW Press.

Costin, L., Karger, H., & Stoesz, D. (1996). *The politics of child abuse in America*. New York: Oxford University Press.

Fisher, P. (1995). The economic context of community-centered practice: Markets, communities, and social policy. In P. Adams & K. Nelson (Eds.), *Reinventing human services: Community- and family-centered practice* (pp. 41–80). Hawthorne, NY: Aldine de Gruyter.

Hadley, R., Cooper, M., Dale, P., & Stacy, G. (1987). *A community social worker's handbook*. London: Tavistock.

Hadley, R., & McGrath, M. (1984). *When social services are local: The Normanton experiment*. London: Allen & Unwin.

Holder, D., & Wardle, M. (1981). *Teamwork and the development of a unitary approach*. London: Routledge & Kegan Paul.

Imber-Black, E. (1988). *Families and larger systems: A family therapist's guide through the labyrinth*. New York: Guilford.

Lindsey, D. (1994). *The welfare of children*. New York: Oxford University Press.

Moroney, R.M. (1986). *Shared responsibility: Families and social policy*. Hawthorne, NY: Aldine de Gruyter.

Pelton, L. (1992). A functional approach to reorganizing family and child welfare system. *Children and Youth Services Review, 14,* 298–303.

Pennell, J., & Burford, G. (1994). Widening the circle: Family group decision-making. *Journal of Child and Youth Care, 9*(1), 1–11.

Pennell, J., & Burford, G. (1995) *Family group decision making: New roles for "old" partners in resolving family violence*. Implementation report (Vol. 1–2). St. John's: Family Group Decision Making Project, School of Social Work, Memorial University of Newfoundland.

Pennell, J., & Burford, G. (1996). Attending to context: Family group decision making in Canada. In

J. Hudson, A. Morris, G. Maxwell, & B. Galaway (Eds.), *Family group conferences: Perspectives on policy and practice* (pp. 206–20). New York: Criminal Justice Press.

Sherman, A. (1999). Extreme child poverty rises sharply in 1997. Washington, DC: Children's Defense Fund.

Sherman, A., Amey, C., Duffield, B., Ebb, N., & Weinstein, D. (1998). *Welfare to what? Early findings on family hardship and well-being.* Washington, DC: Children's Defense Fund and National Coalition for the Homeless.

Smale, G. (1995). Integrating community and individual practice: A new paradigm for practice. In P. Adams & K. Nelson (Eds.), *Reinventing human services: Community- and family-centered practice* (pp. 59–80). Hawthorne, NY: Aldine de Gruyter.

Smale, G. (1998). *Managing change through innovation.* London: The Stationery Office.

Smale, G., & Tuson, G. (1993). *Empowerment, assessment, care management and the skilled worker.* London: Her Majesty's Stationery Office.

Smale, G., Tuson, G., Cooper, M., Wardle, M., & Crosbie, D. (1988). *Community social work: A paradigm for change.* London: National Institute for Social Work.

Swenson, C. (1995). Professional understandings of community: At a loss for words? In P. Adams & K. Nelson (Eds.), *Reinventing human services: Community- and family-centered practice* (pp. 223–43). Hawthorne, NY: Aldine de Gruyter.

Waldfogel, J. (1998). *The future of child protection.* Cambridge, MA: Harvard College Press.

11   Establishing Shared Responsibility for Child Welfare through Peacemaking Circles

KAY PRANIS and BARRY STUART

In the past twenty years, much blame has been heaped on families for their own problems and the problems of their children, including delinquency and school failure. Communities have failed families more than families have failed their children. A nuclear family cannot by itself socialize children to community norms and responsibilities. To understand their obligation to community, children must experience community. Families need the support and assistance of the whole community in caring for and setting limits for their children. At the same time, families must acknowledge that their actions have an impact on the community; consequently, what happens in the family that affects the community is the community's business.

Working out the relationship of family accountability to the community for what happens in the family, and community accountability to the family for how the community assists the family, is an ongoing process requiring respectful, reflective dialogue about family and community values and expectations. Families do their work embedded in the context of community. Families and communities have reciprocal obligations and responsibilities. Peacemaking circles provide a very effective forum for working out those reciprocal obligations. Deficiencies within communities call for courts to intervene, and once courts do, community dependence upon state service systems increase. Capacities within communities enable circles to intervene, and when they do, community self-reliance increases. One feeds on deficiencies and builds more dependence; the other feeds on capacity and builds more capacity.

Before sharing some thoughts on the use of peacemaking circles for child protection, we present a story about a child protection case that was processed through a peacemaking circle by a community just learning to use circles.

A FAMILY CRISIS: NINE-YEAR-OLD OUT OF CONTROL

Mark, nine years old, came to the attention of social services because he stole $140 from his grandmother, a cab driver, who had tip money around the house. In the two-month period after that referral Mark had thirteen new charges. His behavior had gone completely out of control. Mark's father has never been involved in his life. For the first three years of Mark's life, he lived with his mother, Colleen. During this time, Mark was physically and sexually abused by his mother's boyfriend. When child services moved toward putting him in placement, his maternal grandmother came from another state and took Mark, then age three, home to live with her and his sister, Mary, six years older. When Mark was seven, Colleen came to live with them. Colleen had very little patience and no parenting skills. Mark was looking for a mom, but she pushed him away. Grandmother remained in charge of the parenting process, but she also lacked parenting skills. Though Grandmother had lived in the neighborhood for many years, she and Colleen were quite isolated. They had no close contacts and rarely interacted socially with anyone in the community.

When asked whom he would want at the circle, Mark initially said he did not want his mom there: "She was mean." Before the first circle, he changed his mind and wanted her to be there. She agreed to attend. An initial circle of understanding was convened to support the family and seek understanding of the problems. Mark, Colleen, Grandmother, Mary, a family friend, a neighbor, mothers of two of Mark's friends, a community volunteer from a foster grandparent program, a county commissioner concerned about juvenile crime, a mental health therapist, YMCA youth staff, a community volunteer from the community safety net, and a community volunteer keeper attended. The mothers of Mark's friends were angry because they felt Mark was dragging their children into trouble. The neighbor was initially angry and afraid. She had turned Mark in for some of his behavior. In the circle the neighbor tearfully revealed that her own sons had been in trouble. Her husband had told her not to get involved, but she replied, "I can't stand by and watch this kid become like our boys."

In the circle, participants expressed their frustration with Mark, their fears about his future, their sense of helplessness, their concern about the family, and their desire to have Mark, the family, and the neighborhood safe. Mark was very responsive to the men in the circle. He sat slumped in his chair, avoiding eye contact, and constantly fidgeting. His actions depicted anger, frustration, and impatience. When the men in the circle spoke, he sat up, attentive, and made eye contact. After a few rounds of the feather, underlying problems and concerns were identified and proposals began to emerge. Colleen and Grandmother agreed to attend parenting classes. All family members agreed to participate in individual and family counseling. The county commissioner agreed to try to get Mark back in school. The foster grandfather agreed to spend time with Mark on leisure activities and help with homework. The YMCA staff agreed to find support for a family membership at the Y. The mother of one of his friends agreed to take Mark and her son rollerskating twice in the next month.

The circle ended with a number of commitments to begin addressing the issues identified. At the next circle a few weeks later, the circle discovered that Mary, fifteen, had a boyfriend living in the house with the approval of Colleen and

Grandmother. He was thirty-two years old. He had bruised Mark on several occasions by pinching him at sensitive pressure points to make him behave. Mary had a strong sense of responsibility for her brother, as if she were his mother. She struggled, but recognized that Mark's needs required the boyfriend to move out. The foster grandfather included Mary in some activities with Mark in which she could relate playfully to him as a brother. Mark loved dogs. The circle made arrangements for Mark to walk the dogs of several neighbors regularly. Mark's behavior improved and the family was cooperative with counseling and parenting classes, but Children and Family Services wanted to remove Mark from the home. They had concluded that despite some progress, the mother and grandmother did not have adequate skills to parent. A staffing meeting was held to discuss placement. The ten agencies involved with Mark were represented and three community people from the circle attended. The agency representatives consulted the files and began discussing the case. Circle members quickly realized that the professionals knew very little about Mark and his family and were proposing action that they believed would not help Mark. Circle members were torn about the issue. They recognized that Mark needed more than his family could provide, but they also knew that everyone in the family was working at better relationships and skills and they all were committed to each other. The circle asked the staffing group to allow them to develop a different approach.

Circle participants found a neighborhood foster home with a pair of very skilled foster parents. They convened the circle again, included the foster parents, and developed a plan that enabled Mark to live with his family, but go to the foster home twice a week to give his family respite and allow Mark to regularly experience a strong, nurturing environment. Grandmother and Colleen agreed to spend some time in the foster home with Mark to observe the foster parent interactions with Mark. Children and Family Services accepted the circle proposal and expressed amazement at the level of community support for this child. The agency representatives began to ask the circle, "What do you guys think we should do?" Over a period of many months the circle constructed a net of supportive relationships combined with skill-building activities for family members, community members, and social service agencies, resulting in a dramatically different environment for Mark and his family and a sense of hope in the neighborhood. Members of the circle committed to work with Mark and his family as long as needed.

What might have been the conclusion of the state agencies acting alone? Despite best efforts of state agencies and foster homes, many young children taken into state care end up before the courts or face years of difficulties as they work through the trauma of separation from their families. Many family circumstances are so dysfunctional that removing children is the only choice. Yet some dysfunctional families, with the help of resources from extended families, the community, and the state can offer a better environment than state care. How can all of these resources be marshaled to create options that the state alone cannot muster?

Not in all, but in many cases, peacemaking circles can create the environment necessary to develop the understanding and commitment necessary to make the impossible seem possible.

WHERE AND HOW CIRCLES ARE BEING USED

The first use of peacemaking circles for child welfare cases in the Yukon and in Minnesota emerged in the organic fashion that is a natural part of the circle process. They grew out of communities engaged in circle sentencing. In Minnesota, Brother Shane Price, a tireless community activist, attended a peacemaking circle training for a neighborhood project piloting circles with delinquent African-American juveniles with the hope that it would help heal his community. Believing that it takes a village to raise a child, Brother Shane had been puzzling over how to "call the village." After training in circles he was convinced that peacemaking circles are how we "call the village." Though the training focused on using circles for problems of crime, Shane, an employee of Children and Family Services, began to envision the process applied to families he worked with who were caught up in the child protection system. Inspired by a vision of a community-based response that wraps families in loving care, Shane enlisted the help of key resource people for planning, developed a proposal, and secured funding from a state fund designed to encourage innovative responses to child protection cases. At the first training for the child protection circle project, one of the community volunteers, Jessica Hughes, a lawyer who worked for the Office of Equal Opportunity at the University of Minnesota, immediately recognized the potential of the process. She began to use peacemaking circles to resolve complaints of discrimination in the workplace. Circles seed themselves in new places.

The contemporary use of peacemaking circles in public processes began in the Yukon with circles used in the criminal justice system to support victims, work with offenders, and determine sentences for offenders. The effectiveness of peacemaking circles in resolving conflict, revealing underlying causes, creating innovative solutions, and releasing emotions safely and constructively soon attracted the attention of people struggling with problems in other fields. Peacemaking circles have been used for problem solving, brainstorming, group decision-making, support, conflict resolution, mutual education, and sharing. They have been applied in criminal justice, social services, education, industry, churches, neighborhoods, and families. Educators began to use peacemaking circles to handle behavior problems in schools rather than simply suspending students. Educators also recognized that peacemaking circles could be used as a preventive measure by providing a place for students to identify emerging fears, tensions, or conflict before they escalate to destructive confrontation.

A transitional housing program for women uses peacemaking circles to explore the personal stories and pain of the women. A peacemaking circle in the Hmong community in St. Paul, Minnesota, provides a safe place for women to express their frustration at the role of women in traditional Hmong culture, while at the same time providing a place for traditional leaders to express their fear at the loss of their culture. In countless ways people are finding the peacemaking circles helpful in their daily lives.

CIRCLE PROCESS

Peacemaking circles provide a process for bringing people together as equals to talk about very difficult issues and painful experiences in an atmosphere of respect and concern for everyone. Peacemaking circles create a space in which all people, regardless of their role, can reach out to one another as equals and recognize their mutual interdependence in the struggle to live in a good way and to help one another through the difficult spots in life. Peacemaking circles are built on the tradition of talking circles, common among indigenous people of North America, in which a talking piece, passed from person to person consecutively around the circle, regulates the dialogue. The person holding the talking piece has the undivided attention of everyone else in the circle and can speak without interruption. The use of the talking piece allows for full expression of emotions, deeper listening, thoughtful reflection, and an unrushed pace. Additionally, the talking piece creates space for people who find it difficult to speak in a group. Drawing on both traditional wisdom and contemporary knowledge, the circle process also incorporates elements of modern peacemaking and consensus building processes.

Participants are seated in a circle of chairs with no tables. Sometimes objects with meaning to the group are placed in the center as a focal point to remind participants of shared values and common ground. The physical format of the circle symbolizes shared leadership, equality, connection, and inclusion. It also promotes focus, accountability, and participation from all. The circle process typically involves four stages:

- **Acceptance:**   The community and the immediately affected parties determine whether the circle process is appropriate for the situation.
- **Preparation:**   Separate circles for various interests (family, social workers) are held to explore issues and concerns and prepare all parties to participate effectively. Thorough preparation is critical to the overall effectiveness of the circle process. Preparation includes identifying possible supporters in the natural network of the family to participate in the process.
- **Gathering:**   All parties are brought together to express feelings and concerns and to develop mutually acceptable solutions to issues identified.
- **Follow-up:**   Regular communication and check-ins are used to assess progress and adjust agreements as conditions change.

At any stage multiple circles may be held to complete the tasks of that stage.

Circles are facilitated by keepers who are responsible for setting a tone of respect and hope that supports and honors every participant. All circles are guided by the following commitments participants make to one another:

- **What comes out in circle, stays in circle:**   Personal information shared in circle is kept confidential except when safety would be compromised.
- **Speak with respect:**   Speak only when you have the talking piece; speak in a good way about good and difficult feelings; leave time for others to speak.
- **Listen with respect:**   Actively listen with your heart and body.
- **Stay in circle:**   Respect for circle calls upon people to stay in the circle while the circle works to find resolution to issues raised.

Additional guidelines may be created by circle participants to meet the needs of that situation. Guidelines institute a covenant defining how people will interact and share space and time as a group.

Circles consciously engage all aspects of human experience—spiritual, emotional, physical, and mental. Ceremony and ritual are used in the opening and closing of a circle to mark the space of circle as a sacred space in which participants will be present with one another in a different way than in an ordinary meeting. While the design, procedures, and participants vary greatly from one circle to another, there are some fundamental principles common to all circles:

Participants:

1. Act on personal values
2. Direct participation
3. Voluntary involvement
4. Respect for all and all things
5. Self-design
6. Equal opportunity to participate
7. Shared vision

Process:

1. Inclusive of all interests
2. Easily accessible to all
3. Flexible to accomodate each case
4. Holistic approach
5. Spiritual experiences respected
6. Consensus outcomes
7. Accountability to others and to process

In the circle process, social institutions play important roles, but the process is centered on the community context of the situation. The circle throws a wide net to capture possible points of support or assistance and to gather all relevant knowledge. Potential contributions are expected even from those who are part of the problem. Multiple issues are dealt with at once. Circles recognize that the issues interact with one another and cannot be effectively dealt with in isolation. Circles promote mutual responsibility, the recognition that individual well-being depends upon the well-being of all.

DIFFERENCES BETWEEN CONFERENCES AND CIRCLES

Group conferences and peacemaking circles have both come from indigenous roots, but through quite different pathways. They share many characteristics, but have significant differences in their current forms. Some of those differences may be a product of the process of incorporation into modern society and may not be characteristic of their original form. Family group conferences stem from many of the same principles that shape circles. Conferences have been successfully used for child protection cases and many other kinds of conflict. Both have relevance for child protection cases, as do mediation and other emerging forms of alternative dispute resolution. Their differences, depending on the model of conferencing used, can be slight or significant. It is important to have some appreciation of their differences in order to consider the appropriateness of either to any specific case.

In the past, too much was invested in courts as the primary conflict option for dealing with child protection cases. While courts will continue to be best suited for some cases, investing in any one model of conflict resolution for child protection cases ignores the profound differences in each case and can squander the critical, often minimal prospects of serving the best interests of the child. For some cases, conferences will be more appropriate; for others, circles will be more appropriate. Knowing more about the dynamics of each process is crucial to maximizing the potential to realize durable, effective outcomes for children in need.

The Role of the Facilitator

In both processes the facilitator looks to participants to determine the outcome. However, the role of the facilitator in managing the process is different. In group conferencing the facilitator determines who will speak at any given point in the process. In peacemaking circles the use of the talking piece reduces reliance upon a facilitator, referred to as a "keeper," to direct or manage the dialogue. As the talking piece circulates around a circle every participant shares responsibility to move the process in a constructive direction because the keeper will not normally speak until the talking piece returns to the keeper.

Community Involvement

Group conferencing usually involves extended family and support people of the key parties involved in an issue, but does not typically involve other community members. Peacemaking circles include members of the community who are not directly involved in the issue that brought a conflict to a circle. The involvement of community members provides perspectives and resources that enrich the understanding of the problem and the range of possible solutions.

Addressing Community Problems

Group conferencing focuses on a plan to resolve the problems of the individual family. Peacemaking circles frequently begin to look at the larger community context in which the family is struggling and identify changes necessary in the community, not just in the family.

Community Development

Group conferencing is generally organized and facilitated by professionals. Peacemaking circles are often organized by community groups, dominated by citizens, and facilitated by community volunteers. Peacemaking circle projects usually begin with community organizing and cannot be effectively implemented until citizens are engaged. Group conferencing can be implemented without significant citizen involvement. The involvement of citizens in multiple peacemaking circles increases the opportunities for learning about the community as a whole, not just about individual families. Management of the process by the community clearly places primary responsibility for community health in the community, rather than in government services. Management of the process by the community also results in more significant power sharing by the system. Peacemaking circles provide a forum for a dialogue about personal and community values, about personal and community concerns and expectations. These dialogues, unlike discussions or debates, provide not only the basis for innovative solutions, but for generating better connections through mutual understanding and respect.

Focus on Healing, Not Shame

The development of theory about group conferencing has emphasized the role of shame in influencing behavior. Training, writing, and dialogue about peacemaking circles place no emphasis on shame. Healing is the primary conceptual construct of circles.

Incorporation of a Spiritual Dimension

Spirituality is probably an important component of both processes and is a factor in the success of both processes. However, group conferencing does not identify spirituality in its process or construct deliberate ways to call the spiritual dimension to presence. Peacemaking circles use ceremony and ritual in a very deliberate way to call participants to be present in all aspects—spiritual, emotional, physical and mental.

Support and Accountability

Conferences and circles depend upon a combination of support and accountability, but the order in which those occur seems to differ. In their application in Western culture, group conferences emphasize accountability in the context of a caring community—that is, accountability and then support. Circles emphasize the capacity of support to induce appropriate accountability—that is, support and then accountability.

Summary of Differences

Circles and conferences have significant overlap in function and process, but, in general, circles are more community directed and more comprehensive in the issues they reveal and address than conferences. The circle process typically is more involved and takes more time because circles may engage more interests and unravel more related concerns.

These are a few of the differences. There are many more. The significance of the differences in selecting the most appropriate process depends largely on how each process has been developed and used by the community in child protection cases. Both have enormous flexibility and lend themselves to being adapted by different communities to suit the particular circumstances and aspirations of the community. Ideally, both processes would be available in order to enrich the options in dealing with the wide range of circumstances in child protection cases.

CONSIDERATIONS IN USING CIRCLES

Relationships Between Family and Social Worker

Litigating child protection issues rarely enhances the relationship between a family and a social worker. In most cases, the litigation process, even before the hearing, deepens distrust and hard feelings, and by the end of the litigation, the capacity of a social worker to continue working with a family is difficult, if not impossible. In most child protection circumstances, regardless of the outcome, an ongoing relationship is a critical part of planning for the child's best interest. Circles, unlike courts, have a good chance of enhancing this relationship and of gaining a better appreciation by all parties of why an effective working relationship serves the best interests of the child, as well as the family and department. The circle, unlike the court, does not pit the department against the family, but calls upon a broad spectrum of people and resources to collectively, and in a collaborative manner, address the underlying issues that lead up to the need for the state to intervene.

Difficult to Share Responsibility

For many reasons, social workers may need to confront more pressures and hurdles in sharing responsibility with communities than any professional in the justice system. First, in child protection circles, the central focus is children—usually children of a tender age—living in circumstances that risk their well-being. The consequences of failure are much greater in child protection cases than in criminal cases. If a sentencing circle fails to rehabilitate an offender, the justice system will intervene again, much as it probably has in that offender's life many times before. If a family wellness circle fails to protect a child, the consequences are both less tolerable and less readily rectified. Second, in child protection matters, there is only one agency to carry the risk of failure. In sentencing circles, the police, prosecutor, probation, and defense counsel share the responsibility of a breakdown in the circle plan. The inclusion of a child advocate helps, but unlike criminal cases, in child protection cases, when something goes wrong all pointing fingers are targeted on the child protection agency. Accordingly, they are less likely to take risks. Some could argue that the courts afford child welfare agencies an opportunity to deposit any risk taking with the courts. If the courts return the child to the family and something goes tragically wrong, the judge—not the department—carries the blame.

Third, in most child protection cases, parents are struggling with substance abuse or psychological issues that call for significant treatment interventions. By the time the child protection cases reach court, especially applications for permanent care, the department has concluded that no one from the community is either interested or capable of making a difference. Further, the principles and practices of restorative justice, aptly suited for child protection cases, have not fully penetrated the community of professionals and broader communities engaged in child protection matters. Confidence in sharing responsibility and in collective action between professionals and communities is not as widely or as deeply known within child protection cases as it is within the criminal justice system. For all of these reasons, to generate a capacity to share responsibility, much more community development must take place to engage the state and communities in child protection circles than is required for sentencing circles.

CLOSING THOUGHTS

> Circles bring out more than you want to know.
> —Shane Price, Keeper, Community Child Protection Circle

Circles open the taps to pour out personal stories. Time must be dedicated to hear, respond, and work through difficult stories. The time and place for respecting personal stories can best be gained through a series of circles that build the support networks before all parties gather in a large circle.

> We can complain all we want about social workers. . . . It won't do any good. We need to learn to respect them, if we want them to respect us. Finding out about each other in a good way is the only way.
> —Jesse Scarff, Kwanlin Dun Elder

Sadly, perhaps unavoidably, due to the nature of responsibilities the state foists upon social workers, in matters of child protection they are often more feared than the police. Much work must be done for communities and families to understand and respect social workers, to see them as partners, not opponents or enemies. Communities must devote the time and patience to move past old attitudes about social workers and be open to gain new perspectives about how to work in partnership. Both have much to offer. Creating the ground for working together is a difficult, but essential step.

Commitments defined and enforced by the law can be important in carrying out measures to serve a child's best interests; so too are commitments defined and driven by values and moral obligations. External pressures drive legal commitments; internal pressures drive moral commitments. In carrying out plans to help families and children in need, both sources of commitment are needed. Circles create the basis for drawing on and making moral commitments. More important, circles blend together legal requirements and moral commitments from all participants, and in doing so increase the prospects of a durable, creative plan. Peacemaking circles allow others to be present for families in crisis in all dimensions of human experience, emotional, spiritual, mental, and physical—to be present in a complete and fully attentive way, wrapping those families in love and support.

12   Social Network Theory, Research, and Practice

Implications for Family Group Conferencing

DON FUCHS

Over the past two decades researchers and practitioners have become aware of the strength of neighborhood social network ties in preventing family violence. This chapter describes social network theory and examines applications and implications for family group conferencing. To be most effective, this chapter argues that family group conferencing interventions need to be developed in tandem with a more comprehensive social network intervention approach. Incorporating a social network approach in family group conferencing programs is necessary to fully understand the complex nature of the interrelated stress, support, and risk factors that exist in the family and their neighborhood social networks. This blending of approaches is essential to ensure that children and vulnerable adults are not maintained or replaced back in situations where they are at high risk of being reabused.

SOCIAL NETWORK/SUPPORT AND THE CONTEXT OF CHILD MALTREATMENT

The underlying assumption of the project developed in Winnipeg to implement a social network intervention process—the Neighborhood Parent Support Project—was that effective parenting required social support, and child maltreatment risk increased when parents did not have enough social support to offset the demands of parenting and other stressors in their life situation. The Neighborhood Parent Support Project conceptualized social support as existing in two spheres: (1) support for the parent as a person; (2) support for the parent in her/his parenting role (Lugtig & Fuchs, 1992). It focused on personal and neighborhood-wide social networks as the units of intervention. The project used social network intervention strategies to increase and strengthen social support for parenting, thereby reducing the level of child maltreatment risk, at both the neighborhood and personal network level of the parents. Garbarino and Sherman (1980) in their study of high-risk parents in high-risk neighborhoods, concluded that to effectively intervene in such neighborhoods to reduce the incidence of child maltreatment, traditional individual case approaches need to be reinforced by neighborhood-based approaches to social network intervention and consultation.

Garbarino and Kostelny (1993) indicate that the challenge of high-risk communities is to create formal support services and through informal neighborhood networking, an environment that helps maintain the integrity of the family and increases the level of personal and parent social support available at the neighborhood level. The negative physical and psychological consequences of living in high-risk neighborhoods are great for both parents and children. However, there are strategies that individual families, as well as communities, can utilize to cope with these problems and minimize the negative developmental consequences to children growing up in these high-risk areas. These include developing neighborhood parent support networks and meshing formal and informal support at the personal and neighborhood levels (Lugtig, Guberman, & Fuchs, 1999). Current interest in neighborhood social networks as abuse prevention avenues stems from a growing recognition that child maltreatment must be viewed within its broader social ecology (Belsky, 1984; Belsky & Vondra, 1989; Thompson, 1995). All of these ecological approaches are predicated on a thoughtful, systematic understanding of the social ecologies of families prone to abuse or neglect. In summary, much current research on social support/network intervention highlights the importance of a thorough understanding of the nature of social ties that constitute the social milieu in which families live, draw their support, and become at risk to abuse or abusing. An empirically grounded analysis of family social ties is essential in understanding the actual type of support, stress, and risk that flows over social network ties of each family.

THE SOCIAL NETWORK INTERVENTION STRATEGIES OF THE NEIGHBORHOOD PARENTING SUPPORT PROJECT

The Neighborhood Parent Support Project was a locality based social network intervention project aimed at increasing the amount of available levels of social support in a high-risk neighborhood in Winnipeg, Manitoba. The overall project goal was to reduce the risk of child maltreatment. The project implemented a social network intervention in five high-risk neighborhoods aimed at strengthening the personal parent social support networks and neighborhood-based support networks, and meshing the formal and informal helping networks at the neighborhood level. Based on the original Neighborhood Parenting Support Project, which operated in central Winnipeg from 1988 to 1992, the second phase of the project attempted to develop a community-based approach to strengthening families in the designated neighborhoods by employing a neighborhood Parenting Support Networker to assist the neighborhoods construct and maintain a neighborhood parent support network and assist individual parents improve their personal social network ties.

The project built on the research of Gottlieb (1986) and Wellman and Hall

(1985) defining a social network as a set of links between two or more persons or other social units. Social networks are seen as a determinant of the social support available and accessible to persons as individuals or in social units. The personal characteristics of individuals and those of others in a social network, the resources that they each have, and the characteristics of the relations these individuals have with each other all influence whether individuals actually do receive certain types of social support. Social support is defined as the verbal and nonverbal information, advice, tangible aid, effective response, and cognitive and behavioral feedback extended or received from others that has beneficial or other behavioral effects on the individual or social unit (Gottlieb, 1986).

The presence or absence of social support helps individuals know whether they have a sense of social identity and belonging and the information and resources for everyday life. In addition, an important aspect of a strong social support network is its reliability—having someone to turn to or count on when needed. Persons vary greatly in the amount and kinds of social support required. Also, life stages have different support needs and social network patterns. One of these major life roles requiring a large amount of various kinds of social support is *parenting*. The high social support demands of parenting depletes resources quickly. Thus, the parent constantly needs to receive emotional, mental, and social renewal. The tasks of parenting are so demanding that practical assistance is needed, such as child care on a regular and reliable basis to enable the parent to care for the child and to derive benefits from the other facets of their lives. Parents normally have a social support network of spouse, family, friends, neighbors, and coworkers to draw upon. Parents usually reciprocate with members of the support network in some fashion. Where parents do not have this supportive network readily available, parenting may be in serious jeopardy (Thompson, 1995; Warren, 1991). This is especially true when they are in a parenting situation of high demand, such as caring for a special needs child. Many occurrences of child maltreatment can be traced either directly or indirectly to lack of social support in the parent's environment (Lugtig & Fuchs, 1992)

Social network intervention in the Neighborhood Parenting Project attempted to assist parents to have more supportive networks for parenting purposes. It also assisted neighborhoods in being more supportive to parents.

The project found the following configurations of high-risk network patterns:

1. The parent is part of a negative network cluster alienated from the prosocial values of the larger society;
2. The parent is shunned by a positive or negative support network;
3. The parent is socially isolated by personal factors such as poor social skills or emotional and mental disturbance;
4. The parent does not get adequate support from the neighborhood for parenting because the neighborhood is either too transient or anomic to provide the kind of support required (Lugtig & Fuchs, 1992).

After identifying the high-risk network patterns, Project Networkers developed specific network interventions to increase or alter ties and enhance the quality of the social support that flowed over these network configurations.

THE SOCIAL WORK INTERVENTION STRATEGIES OF THE NEIGHBORHOOD PARENT SUPPORT NETWORK

The Neighborhood Parent Support Project built on Maguire's (1983) model and saw a network intervention as involving a three-phased process of identification, mapping, and linking steps. The first phase, identification, was viewed as a process in which the networker and the parents consult on the potential for networking in their social networks. This was an information-gathering phase in which the potential network members were named and their relationship to the parents identified. Their willingness to provide support was discussed, their resources and personal capabilities listed, and their willingness to provide help or support in different situations determined. Parents often identified child caring assistance as a priority need, but were not always aware of the importance of emotional support, feedback, or support reliability. The networker's efforts were aimed at increasing the parent's knowledge about their social network and the role it played in assisting the individual parent cope with the demands of parenting and the general day-to-day demands of living in a high-risk neighborhood. In addition, project networkers attempted to assess the level of support and its availability to the parents, both in the neighborhood and larger community.

Mapping is the second phase in the intervention process. Active and latent ties in the person's networks are mapped in terms of the strength of the ties, the frequency of contact, the basis of the relationship (whether spouse, family, extended family, friend, neighbor, or coworker), and the duration and intensity of the large number of interconnections (Tracy, 1990). Kemp, Whittaker, and Tracy (1997) indicate that if social workers are to work with, not against, social networks of clients, completing an accurate assessment of network resources is a necessary first task. This is especially true if a large percentage of helping exchanges occur within the informal helping network. Too often important social resources are not identified at all or identified too late to be of any help in implementing an effective intervention. Cultural differences between the client and the worker may exacerbate this difficulty in mapping ties. Green (1995) maintains that a social network perspective enables the worker to understand culturally specific patterns of giving and receiving. A culturally sensitive understanding of coping and social support strategies is essential for effective and early positive involvement of available resources.

Research indicates that a social network assessment assists in understanding, in an empirically grounded and highly individualized way, the actual nature of the social connections of individual and families at the local neighborhood and wider community level (Lugtig & Fuchs, 1992; Kemp et al., 1997). It helps understand the actual level of social support and nature of its flow over the social network ties, as well as the nature of the stress and risk that exists in an individual social network. This is an essential precursor to effective intervention. Network mapping is often seen as an essential component in preparation for partial network assemblies, such as family group conferences (Halevy-Martini et al., 1984; Trimble, 1980). By completing a network mapping instrument the networker and the focal individual or cluster may develop a specific networking plan. The plan outlines who should be involved in network changes and how they should be involved.

The third phase of the Neighborhood Parent Support Project linking began once the network was mapped, although occasionally it occurred during the identification and mapping stages as well. A determination was made about how networks can be changed or altered to provide different or better sources of social support. Ties may be strengthened through increasing the frequency and intensity of contact or by changing the kinds of support they carry. Ties may be weakened by gradual disuse resulting from the substitution of different or new ties for a particular type of support. The size of the active network could be increased to provide new sources of social support. In some situations of highly dense, ineffective, and destructive social networks, the size was decreased to make it more manageable by weakening and, in some cases, severing some network ties (Fuchs, 1993). The composition of the network could be changed to include a different balance of ties in such relationships as family, friends, neighbors, and coworkers. The size of a cluster could be increased by adding members, bringing different sources of information or new resources. The network itself or the clusters within it could be made more dense by increasing interconnectedness, thereby increasing opportunities for emotional belonging and esteem support.

Kemp et al. (1997) argue that linking and the related skills of brokerage involve at least three abilities. The first ability is to identify, engage, and assess resources. Second is to develop a plan and implement the steps required to make the linkage, whether the linkage is between two people, families, or a person and a community resource. The third ability is to monitor the linkage, addressing barriers and problems that arise and ensuring that the linkages remain over time. Family group conferencing may itself be seen as a form of linking, often referred to in the literature as partial or full-scale network assembly (Trimble, 1980). After the network members are identified and mapped, all or some of the segments are brought together to address an emergent or pressing situation that is having an impact on the whole network (Halevy-Martini et al., 1984). Thompson (1995) maintains that the meaning given to help depends on the nature of the linkage and the perceptions of the exchange between members of the social network. Thus, it is important that the family group conference practitioners effectively map the social networks before proceeding to convene or assemble the family group conference.

Lugtig and Fuchs (1999) found that in order to accomplish its overall goal of expanding and strengthening parenting support networks on both a personal and neighborhood level, the network interveners employed five intervention strategies found useful in other social network intervention efforts: *consulting, coaching, connecting, convening,* and *constructing.* While these strategies are discussed as being separate and distinct, in actual field situations they overlap and are often used in combination. The length of time it takes the neighborhood and the networker to proceed through these phases will vary. For example, in a highly transitory or anomic neighborhood it may take longer to assemble a core network of support persons than in a more stable neighborhood.

In the *connecting* phase, the neighborhood networker enters the neighborhood, connects with a wide spectrum of neighborhood members from the informal resident population and formal agency service representatives working in the neighborhood, explains and interprets the goals and objectives to the neighborhood members, secures tacit approval of the members for the work, and begins to identify and map the possible networks in the neighborhood. In the *consulting* phase, the networker seeks the opinions and views of neighborhood members about the existing and desired support for parents and children in the neighborhood. There are two aspects for the consulting strategy: first, consulting with the neighborhood residents to find out about their needs and concerns, identify natural neighbor helpers, and identify and map neighborhood networks; second, providing consultation to neighbor helpers and linkage persons, brokers, liaisons, boundary spanners, as well as central figures of neighborhood networks. In the *coaching* phase, the networker teaches and models networking at both the personal and neighborhood levels. The *convening* stage involves the networker assisting the neighborhood and individual parents to convene networks for purposes of network construction and parenting support. Finally, in the *constructing* phase the networker and neighborhood members begin the process of developing and strengthening the neighborhood parenting support network.

Each of these strategies is set out in logical order. First the networker connects with people in the neighborhood. Second, an elaboration of the connecting phase takes place. The networker's main task is consulting with neighborhood members. This deepens the personal linkage between the networker and neighborhood members and helps establish a relationship of trust. Once a relationship of trust is established, the networker proceeds to teach or coach neighborhood members on consciously constructing neighborhood parenting support networks and personal parenting support networks (Lugtig & Fuchs, 1992; Lugtig et al., 1999). At some point during this third phase, members consciously decide to follow up on these ideas and convene small meetings in order to strengthen support in the networks. Later in the convening stage, members assemble and consciously decide whether they wish to construct a neighborhood and/or personal parenting support network. When they decide to do this in the constructing stage, the members strengthen their ties, map the resources they can provide, and make themselves available to provide mutual support.

The intervention knowledge gained by the Neighborhood Parent Support Project can be useful for implementing family group conferences.

APPLICATIONS AND IMPLICATIONS FOR
FAMILY GROUP CONFERENCING

Pennell and Burford (1996) identify the importance of attending to the contextual considerations relating to family violence. The research of Halevy-Martini et al. (1984) and Trimble (1980) indicates that social network intervention, particularly the notions of connecting and convening, strengthens social ties and helps families prevent the risk of abuse. To participate effectively in conferences, families and communities must have the tools and supports available to them to work through and carry out decisions they come up with. Strategies for social network identification and mapping are useful tools in such efforts.

While family group conferencing highlights the importance of informal helping, it does not provide a great deal of attention to assisting in the assessment of the level of stress/support/risk that exists within the social networks of families at risk to child maltreatment. This may continue to leave individuals at risk to abuse from their immediate family or underestimate the support an individual will receive from formal and informal helpers. The Neighborhood Parent Support Project research suggests that family conference coordinators require skills to consult with local parents about the nature of parenting stress, supports, and risks at the local neighborhood level. The importance of social context, and consulting and convening strategies have been noted by Marsh and Crow (1998). They go on to note that a strategy for the implementation of conferencing works best if it includes a widespread package of family support measures. This is an important argument for the development of social network strategies at local neighborhood levels to increase the availability and actual supports for families at risk. The use of family group conferences is a local neighborhood strategy that could be used to reduce risk by increasing the level of available formal and informal support for at risk parents. The findings of the Neighborhood Parent Support Project indicate that not only can family group conferences give voice to concerns about abuse but combined with network intervention they empower persons experiencing abuse to bring about changes necessary to end abuse and strengthen families (Marsh & Crow, 1998; Lugtig et al., 1999).

SUMMARY

Results of the Neighborhood Parent Support Project indicate that for family group conferences to be effective in the prevention of family violence, they must be developed at the local neighborhood level in tandem with social network intervention strategies. The aim is to increase the parenting at both the personal and neighborhood network levels. Failure to assess and work with social support structures of the parent, family, and neighborhood often places children and families at great risk to child maltreatment and fails to use existing possible resources. The findings of the Neighborhood Parent Support network clearly demonstrate that social network interventions can assist both low- and high-risk parents to alter the size, composition, and supportive content of their parenting support networks and thus increase and enhance their levels of social support. In addition, the project demonstrates that informal network helping can be meshed with formal systems of help through the intermediary of parent support workers and neighborhood parent networks.

Major implications for family group conferencing are (1) informal helping and support can be strengthened by social network interventions; (2) the neighborhood formal helping network can be meshed effectively with personal and neighborhood informal helping structures; and (3) risk for child maltreatment in a community can be reduced by social network intervention. The project provides a promising model for strengthening community network ties to produce safer, healthier social contexts in combination with family group conferencing programs.

With growth in the number of family group conferencing programs, many families may be placed at risk of child maltreatment without a concomitant network intervention at the local neighborhood level aimed at increasing the amount of reliable social support for parents. Conferencing programs may become bureaucratized, emphasizing formal structures that do not mesh with informal neighborhood social support resources. The social network approach provides a means to assist neighborhood parents in high-risk areas to effectively participate in family group conferencing and obtain the support needed to continue to care for and protect their children. When incorporated into a family group conferencing program, social network intervention provides tremendous potential for the effective and efficient meshing of formal and informal helping resources to provide essential support for families at risk to maltreatment and family violence.

REFERENCES

Belsky, J. (1984). The determinants of parenting: A process model. *Child Development, 55,* 83–96.

Belsky, J., & Vondra, J. (1989). Lessons from child abuse: The determinants of parenting. In D. Cicchetti & V. Carlson (Eds.), *Child Maltreatment* (pp.153–202). Cambridge, UK: Cambridge University Press.

Fuchs, D. (1993). Building on strengths of family and neighborhood social network ties for the prevention of child maltreatment. In R. Rodway & B. Trute (Eds.), *The ecological perspective in family-centered therapy* (pp. 69–98). New York: Edwin Mellen.

Garbarino, J., & Kostelny, K. (1993). Neighborhood and community influences on parenting. In T. Luster & L. Okagaki (Eds.), *Parenting: An ecological perspective* (pp. 203–25). Hillsdale, NJ: Erlbaum Associates.

Garbarino, J., & Sherman, D. (1980) High risk neighborhoods and high risk families: The human ecology of child maltreatment. *Child Development, 51,* 188–98.

Gottlieb, B. (1986). Social support and the study of personal relationships. *Journal of Social and Personal Relationships, 2,* 351–75.

Green, J. (1995). *Cultural awareness in the human services: A multi- ethnic approach* (2nd ed.). Boston: Allyn and Bacon.

Halevy-Martini, J., et al. (1984). Process and strategy in network therapy. *Family Process, 23,* 521– 23.

Kemp, S., Whittaker, J., & Tracy, E. (1997). *Person-environment practice: The social ecology of interpersonal helping.* Hawthorne, NY: Aldine de Gruyter.

Lugtig, D., & Fuchs, D. (1992). *Building on the strengths of local neighborhood social networks for the prevention of child maltreatment.* Unpublished monograph, University of Manitoba, Winnipeg.

Lugtig, D., Guberman, I., & Fuchs, D. (1999).*The neighborhood parenting support network project: An interim report.* Unpublished monograph, University of Manitoba, Winnipeg.

Maguire, L. (1983). *Understanding social networks.* Beverly Hills, CA: Sage.

Marsh, P., & Crow, G. (1998). *Family group conferences in child welfare.* Cornwall: Blackwell Science.

Pennell, J., & Burford, G. (1996). Attending to context: Family group decision making in Canada. In J. Hudson, A. Morris, G. Maxwell, & B. Galaway (Eds.), *Family group conferences: Perspectives on policy and practice* (pp. 206–20). New York: Criminal Justice Press.

Thompson, R. (1995). *Preventing child maltreatment through social support.* Thousand Oaks, CA: Sage.

Tracy, E. (1990). Identifying social support resources of at-risk families. *Social Work, 35*(3), 252–58.

Trimble, D. (1980). A guide to the network therapies. *Connections, III*(2, summer).

Warren, D. (1991). *Neighborhood parenting support project: Preliminary comprehensive report on the findings derived from the community surveys.* Unpublished monograph, Faculty of Social Work, University of Manitoba, Winnipeg.

Wellman, B., & Hall, A. (1985). Social networks and social supports. In S. Cohen & L. Syme (Eds.), *Social support and health* (pp. 23–39). New York: Academic Press.

13   The Wraparound Process with Children and Families

JOHN D. BURCHARD and SARA N. BURCHARD

Wraparound is a relatively new approach to serving families and children experiencing significant psychosocial difficulties that has been growing throughout North America during the last ten to fifteen years. The wraparound approach has been variously described as a philosophy of service, a process for planning and providing services and supports, an intervention, and a treatment model. Basically it is a team-based approach to planning and providing services that is child and family centered, ecologically based, and addresses the needs of the child and family through the provision of services and supports that are individualized, strengths-based, flexible, and culturally sensitive.

Wraparound is not a program nor is it a specific, prescribed, or time-limited intervention, but an approach to providing supports in the family's community in order to improve the adjustment and functioning of the family system. Two of the originators of the approach, John VanDenBerg (VanDenBerg & Grealish, 1996) and Karl Dennis (personal communication, 1990) emphasize that wraparound is a zero reject model. The child and family cannot fail. The service plan must change to accommodate the current needs of the child. Hence the wraparound process is flexible and changes over time.

The purpose of this chapter is to describe wraparound and its relationship to family group decision-making. This will be done by describing the development of the approach, identifying the necessary elements and practice principles, illustrating its use through two case studies, summarizing developments in training and research, and identifying some of the similarities and differences with family group decision-making.

The basic philosophy that spawned the wraparound process is relatively simple: identify the community services and supports that a family needs and provide them as long as they are needed.

"Wrap" the services around the family in the community where they are, rather than remove the child, "fix" her or him, and then return the child to the same family and community context in which the difficulties originally developed. As one parent said, "This isn't rocket science, this is common sense."

It is a philosophy that developed in response to the realization that our traditional services for helping our most challenging citizens are not working. According to another parent, "It doesn't make much sense to ignore a family that has a child with severe emotional problems and then send the child away for expensive treatment that doesn't work."

While the initial philosophy behind the wraparound process intervention was relatively simple, the development and implementation of the process is complex. With the growing visibility and popularity of the wraparound model, the need to clearly articulate its principles, strategies, and essential practice elements has become evident. Practitioners sometimes apply the term "wraparound" to services that in fact may incorporate practices that are contrary to the philosophy and practice of wraparound.

Reflective of this transition to a more formalized intervention is the reference to wraparound as a process or approach rather than a service. The more ubiquitous label of a "wraparound service" has had a tendency to be interpreted as a specific service or an array of specific services that are available in a categorical sense to all clients who are eligible. For example, some agencies have declared that they had a wraparound service if they provided respite or individualized services, even though the parents were not involved in the decision-making process. Others felt they were doing wraparound because they utilized funding from two separate agencies, but all families received the same array of services. There has also been the misconception that wraparound can be administered outside the community in residential treatment centers or psychiatric hospitals. In a recent review of the comprehensive evaluation of a youth whose school was seeking his removal, the evaluation team recommended that this youth needed a "total wraparound" by being sent to a locked psychiatric residential facility for at least two years, contrary to the strongly expressed desire of the family, who wish to work with the youth in his home.

By 1990, the wraparound approach had been established as a viable alternative to residential treatment, with many advocates expressing the belief that it was more youth and family friendly, less costly, and more effective than traditional services. Since that time there has been a remarkable expansion in both the interest and the utilization of the wraparound approach. The results of a 1998 survey of the United States suggest that the current number of wraparound could be as high as two hundred thousand (Faw, 1999).

The rapid proliferation of wraparound has generated a need to answer two critical questions: Are there identifiable elements that must be in place in order for an intervention to be considered wraparound? And most importantly, is it possible to operationally define a wraparound intervention in such a way that it can be evaluated and replicated through controlled, empirically based research?

In the late spring of 1998, a focus group of nationally recognized wraparound leaders and family advocates met at Duke University to address these issues. The group identified a set of essential elements and requirements for practice that are necessary components of wraparound. These are listed below.

ESSENTIAL ELEMENTS OF THE WRAPAROUND PROCESS

1. Wraparound must be based in the community.
2. Services and supports must be individualized, built on strengths, and meet the needs of children and families across life domains to promote success, safety, and permanence in home, school and community.
3. The process must be culturally competent, building on the unique values, preferences, and strengths of children and families, and their communities.
4. Families must be full and active partners in every level of the wraparound process.
5. The wraparound approach must be a team-driven process involving the family, child, natural supports, agencies, and community services working together to develop, implement, and evaluate the individualized plan.
6. Wraparound child and family teams must have adequate, flexible approaches and flexible funding.
7. Wraparound plans must include a balance of formal services and informal community and family resources.
8. An unconditional commitment to serve children and their families is essential.
9. The plans should be developed and implemented based on an interagency, community-based collaborative process.
10. Outcomes must be determined and measured for the system, for the program, and for the individual child and family.

REQUIREMENTS FOR PRACTICE

1. The community collaborative structure, with broad representation, manages the overall wraparound process and establishes the vision and mission.
2. A lead organization is designated to function under the community collaborative structure and manage the implementation of the wraparound process.
3. A referral mechanism is established to determine the children and families to be included in the wraparound process.
4. Resource coordinators are hired as specialists to facilitate the wraparound process, conducting strengths/needs assessments; facilitating the team planning process; and managing the implementation of the services/support plan.
5. With the referred child and family, the resource coordinator conducts a strengths and needs assessment.
6. The resource coordinator works with the child and family to form a child and family team.

7. The child and family team functions as a team *with* the child and family engaged in an interactive process to develop a collective vision, elated goals, and an individualized plan that is family centered and team based.
8. A crisis plan is produced by the child and family team.
9. Within the service/support plan, each goal must have outcomes stated in measurable terms, and the progress on each monitored on a regular basis.
10. The community collaborative structure reviews the plans.

A more detailed account of the wraparound definition, values, essential elements, and requirements for practice is provided elsewhere (Burns & Goldman, 1999).

A CASE EXAMPLE: THE ROBINSON/JAMES FAMILY

The case of the Robinson/James family will help illustrate how the wraparound process intervention differs from other forms of intervention. The case is described in more detail in the wraparound Process Training Manual (VanDenBerg & Grealish, 1998).

The family was referred for wraparound services by a child welfare agency. At the time of referral the five children (ages 13, 11, 10, 5, and 3 years) were in the custody of the agency for various allegations of abuse and neglect. The four youngest children had been recently placed in emergency shelter care and the oldest, who was an alleged victim of sexual abuse, had been placed in a local psychiatric hospital for evaluation. The mother, who had a long history of marijuana and cocaine addiction, was the children's primary caregiver. Various fathers and boyfriends, most of whom were thought to be active in both addiction and criminal activity, were in and out of the children's lives on an irregular basis.

In this case, the social worker at the child welfare agency functioned as the resource coordinator. The resource coordinator conducted a thorough discovery of the family strengths, culture, and informal supports with the mother, providing a rich amount of information that was subsequently used for developing the wraparound plan. More than a hundred responses were obtained from such prompts as, "The things I like best about my children are . . . ", "My life would be better six months from now if . . . ," "The best times we have had as a family are . . . ," "My best qualities as a parent are . . . ," and "Our family traditions, cultural events, special beliefs are . . . "

Family goals were then established, based on a comprehensive assessment of the needs in each of a variety of life domain areas. The goals included achievement of sobriety for mother, reunification of the family into a safe community environment, sober friends for the mother, an appropriate education for the children, employment for mother, and a proactive crisis plan for the family.

More than forty different individualized supports and services were located and/or established to achieve the family goals. Some of the primary goals for the mother included short-term placement at a rehabilitation center, Narcotics Anonymous, a therapist, a consumer mentor, mentoring on safety and discipline practices, developing sober friends, constructing a family book, participating in service work while in recovery, recontacting her religious community, joining the Oprah Book Club, investigating the Community College for Medical Assistance Certification, and the provision of necessary child care and transportation.

For the children the supports and services included short-term foster care for the youngest and therapeutic foster care for the oldest, ensuring attendance in an appropriate school placement with tutoring if necessary, arranging for participation in positive community activities, and making a family history video. For the family the primary services focused on completing all the steps that were necessary for the family to relocate in a safe and supportive neighborhood.

Finally, a detailed crisis plan was established that identified the most predictable crises that might occur, specifying the options that might be taken to prevent them and specifying the services and supports that would be activated if they did occur. Some of the potential crises included the mother's relapse, neglect of the children due to the mother's stress or relapse, barriers to obtaining new housing, abuse/neglect of the children during home visits by the father, and self-injury by the oldest child.

As noted above, this is a brief example of the wraparound process that is described in more detail in the training manual. It should be reemphasized that it involves a family in the early stages of the process and that many of the specific supports and services that were identified will change over time, based on the outcomes that are achieved. It should also be noted that the initial team consisted primarily of the mother, the social worker (who also serves as the resource facilitator), the wraparound supervisor, and the foster parents. It is anticipated that team members will be added or subtracted as key people become more or less involved with the family. Those who are added might include the consumer/mentor who befriended the mother during an earlier placement in the rehabilitation center, a recovering roommate who might live with the family after their relocation into a new neighborhood, the oldest daughter who is recovering from being sexually abused, and a father or boyfriend. The most involved father/boyfriend was unwilling to participate at the beginning because of his active substance use and likely criminal activity.

The advocates of the wraparound approach believe it is this individualization of supports and services, flexibility, and utilization of informal as well as formal supports that focus on building strengths through normative activities of daily living that makes wraparound the most effective intervention for a given child and family. While this poses major challenges in terms of program development, training, and evaluation, there has been substantial progress in each of these areas.

TRAINING APPROACHES

In program development, the resource coordinator (case manager) plays a key role. This person is responsible for assembling the team, inspiring a family-centered, nonjudgmental approach, performing strengths discoveries, facilitating the development of the services and informal supports, evaluating progress, and preparing transition plans.

The diverse skills and functions that are required of the resource coordinator signify the importance of training. This is especially true given the limitations of most higher education training programs that stress values, skills, and attitudes that are inconsistent with those associated with the wraparound process. For example, most clinical training programs (e.g., counseling, psychology, psychiatry, social work, nursing) are based on curricula that are unidisciplinary and "guild-driven," focus on deficit discovery, and relate to family members as clients rather than partners.

In response to these limitations the proponents of the wraparound process are attempting to meet training needs in three general ways. The first is to establish formal training curricula. One highly developed curriculum is the PEN-PAL project at East Carolina University in North Carolina (Meyers, Kaufman, & Goldman, 1999). The training program, which is primarily focused on agency staff, is based on a comprehensive, seven-chapter manual that begins with an orientation and then guides the staff through the entire wraparound process. Similar wraparound training curricula are also being implemented in California, Illinois, and Florida (Burns & Goldman, 1999).

A second approach involves the creation of a new higher education training program that is based on the core competencies that are essential to the wraparound process. This approach is exemplified by the Program in Community Mental Health at Trinity College in Vermont. Essentially this is a distance learning, certification, and/or master's level training program that has been, or is being offered to more that two hundred students in Vermont, Connecticut, Pennsylvania, Wisconsin, Maryland, and Alaska (Meyers et al., 1999). The student population mostly consists of human service providers and administrators, family members, and consumers.

The most prevalent approach to training, according to a recent wraparound survey, is an expert-driven, train-the-trainer model. Eighty-six percent of the states that provide formal training report that they have relied on short training programs performed by a small group of wraparound experts. The people who are trained are then involved in training others, with additional consultation being provided as needed. As part of this effort there are now a comprehensive training manual and videotaped presentations on the essential elements of the wraparound process and the development and function of a child and family team (VanDenBerg & Grealish, 1998).

RESEARCH AND EVALUATION

Methods to monitor the quality of wraparound are being developed. In Florida and Illinois fidelity measures have been designed for the meeting process. In Vermont, a measure for evaluating the adherence to principles and practice elements is being field-tested.

The Florida fidelity form is administered to all team meeting participants immediately after each meeting (Burns & Goldman, 1999). The form consists of questions concerning who attended, the involvement of the youth, parents, school and community representatives, and other team members, and concludes with ratings of the extent to which some of the elements of the wraparound process were evident during the meeting. Thus far, there are no psychometric properties associated with this instrument.

In Illinois, a questionnaire has been developed that is completed by independent observers who have attended team meetings (Epstein et. al., 1998). The wraparound Observation Form has thirty-four questions that cover eight elements of the wraparound process. Although observer effects, having an observer present to score the instrument, may affect the validity of the measure for some elements, the instrument has been shown to have good reliability and is a promising tool for both training and research.

The third fidelity measure, which is currently being field-tested in Vermont, Kansas, and Baltimore, is a brief telephone assessment of nine wraparound process elements. Reports are obtained independently from the youth, parent(s), and service coordinators. This evaluation method is being compared to the results of a more rigorous on-site assessment of each wraparound case conducted by a nationally recognized authority to determine the validity of the short telephone assessments.

Does Wraparound Work?

In a recent review of the scientific literature fourteen studies were identified that address the effectiveness of wraparound (Burns, Goldman, Faw, & Burchard, 1999). The findings demonstrate the potential for wraparound to reduce institutional care and costs, to stabilize living situations in the community, and to provide benefits in the realms of behavioral, family, and school adjustment. There is, however, a critical need of further research involving larger samples, greater validation of the intervention as wraparound, more controlled comparisons with other interventions, and more standard sets of process and outcome measures. A brief summary of these studies follows.

The population targeted by these fourteen wraparound initiatives was either children who were at risk of out-of-home placement or children who were returning from some form of residential placement. Two studies used case study designs, ten studies used a quantitative, pre-post design, and two studies were randomized clinical trials.

The two case study designs examined programs developed by John VanDen-Berg and Karl Dennis, two of the pioneers of the wraparound approach. The first was an analysis of ten youth with primary diagnoses of schizophrenia (three), conduct disorder (five), and borderline personality (two), who received wraparound intervention through the Alaska Youth Initiative (Burchard, Burchard, Sewell, & VanDenBerg, 1993). One to two years after they began receiving the wraparound intervention, all the youth were still residing in the community after nine had been returned from unsuccessful institutional treatment. Five were no longer receiving services, four were still receiving services but their adjustment was relatively stable, and the adjustment of one youth was unstable.

The other set of case studies consisted of an analysis of eight child welfare families who had been receiving the wraparound intervention through the Kaleidoscope program in Chicago for an average of three years (Cumblad, 1996). These families entered wraparound with histories of abused and neglected children, poor parenting skills, substance abuse, depression, criminal activity, and unstable housing. During the three-year period when they received the wraparound intervention, there was no longer any evidence of abuse and neglect and none of the children were removed from their parents. At the time the study was conducted, all the children were in a more stable family environment and were no longer subject to the risk behaviors described above.

The primary purpose of these two studies was to provide detailed information on the wraparound process, particularly with respect to its use with very at-risk children and families. The studies provide rich qualitative information on how the child and family teams were assembled and how individualized service and support plans were developed and implemented. The studies also describe remarkable progress made by most of these children and families while they were receiving wraparound. However, the studies are not able to show that the outcomes achieved were due to the wraparound intervention.

Ten pre-post studies provide empirically based evidence suggesting that positive outcomes are associated with the wraparound intervention (Bruns, Burchard, & Yoe, 1995; Clarke, Schaefer, Burchard, & Welkowitz, 1992; Eber, 1994, 1996; Eber & Osuch, 1995; Hyde, Burchard, & Woodworth, 1996; Hyde, Woodworth, Jordan, & Burchard, 1995; Illback, Neill, Call, &, Andis, 1993; Kamradt, 1996; Yoe, Santarcangelo, Atkins, & Burchard, 1996). These studies provide more objective, quantitative data on a larger sample of children and families than the case studies and are prospective rather than retrospective. Approximately eight hundred children and families were involved in these ten studies. While there is variation across studies in terms of the age, gender, and previous agency involvement of the children, there is ample documentation that the vast majority of the children were experiencing severe emotional and behavioral problems and were at risk of residential placement.

The findings of these ten pre-post studies provide empirical evidence that the majority of the families who received the wraparound intervention showed significant improvement. The clearest evidence is that almost all of the children were living in the community months and sometimes years after they entered wraparound. This alone is a significant finding. Many children with severe emotional and behavioral problems who do not show progress are eventually placed in more restrictive programs outside their communities. This is evidenced by the findings of the National Adolescent and Child Treatment Study, in which 32 percent of the children and adolescents who returned from "successful" residential treatment were either readmitted or incarcerated in a correctional facility during the next twelve months (Greenbaum et al., 1996).

In addition, these studies demonstrate that the children not only remained in the community, but that there was an improvement in their adjustment. Although the studies employed different measures of child adjustment (Child Behavior Checklist, Teacher Report Form, Youth Self Report, Daily and Quarterly Adjustment Indicator Checklist, Child and Adolescent Functional Assessment Scale, etc.) each study reported multiple examples of pre-post improvement. On the other hand, there were no instances where the children (as a group) showed significant pre-post deterioration in their adjustment.

The two studies using random assignment provide some of the best evidence for the effectiveness of the wraparound. In the New York study (Evans, Armstrong, Kuppinger, Huz, & McNulty, 1998) children who were referred to out-of-home placements were assigned to either treatment in foster care ($n = 15$) or family-centered case management ($n = 27$). The latter condition employed most of the values and elements of the wraparound process, particularly at the family level, where case managers, parents, and parent advocates were all part of a treatment team that worked with a maximum of eight families at a time. However, there were no community- and state-level wraparound committees to support the child and family teams.

The results of the study showed more favorable outcomes for the children who received the wraparound intervention. There was a greater decline in behavioral symptoms (Client Description Form), lower overall impairment (Child and Adolescent Functional Assessment Scale), and fewer externalizing and social problems (Child Behavior Checklist). The children in the foster care condition did not show more positive outcomes than the wraparound children on any of the of the measures that were obtained.

In the Florida study (Clark et al., 1998) 131 youths in the foster care system were randomly assigned to either a wraparound foster care ($n = 54$) or standard foster care condition ($n = 77$). The wraparound foster care involved family-centered case managers who coordinated strengths-based assessment, life-domain planning, clinical case management, and follow-along supports and services. Each case manager eventually carried twelve active cases and up to ten maintenance-level cases that were monitored monthly and reactivated when necessary.

The major findings in this study were that the boys who received wraparound were more likely to show lower rates of delinquency and better externalizing adjustment than the boys in standard foster care. In addition, the older wraparound youths were more likely to achieve a permanent living arrangement with their parents, relatives, or adoptive parents, or be living on their own than the older youths receiving standard foster care.

More research that compares the effectiveness of wraparound to other interventions is needed. While the two random assignment studies, New York and Florida, described above provide a good start, their fidelity to wraparound was not clearly established. A broader assessment of the efficacy of this approach across a wider range of children and families is essential to its further development and effective application.

RELATIONSHIP TO FAMILY GROUP DECISION-MAKING

In general, the values that guide wraparound are very similar to those for family group decision-making. The aim of family group decision-making is to reduce family violence by strengthening partnerships among family, kin, friends, and community (Burford & Pennell, 1995). Instead of placing family members in residential facilities or shelters that are presumed to be safe, a group of committed kin and friends are brought together to help the family work out a plan to stop the abuse or neglect. The goal is to create a context in which family members are both safe and empowered to solve their own problems without the dislocation, isolation, and fragmentation that tends to be associated with the more conventional service delivery system.

These values—which highlight the importance of strengthening and empowering families, involving friends and relatives in the decision-making process, providing services and supports in the community, and preventing the placement of children into more restrictive forms of substitute care—are the same values that are basic to wraparound. Nevertheless, there are important differences between the two approaches.

First, it should be noted that the two approaches were designed for different purposes. Family group decision-making was developed within the child welfare system as an alternative method for developing a case plan in response to the substantiation of child abuse or neglect. Instead of relying almost exclusively on the caseworker and the casework supervisor, the plan is developed by the "family group" and submitted to the caseworker for approval. Wraparound grew out of the mental health system as a child- and family-focused, interagency approach to helping families with children and adolescents who are experiencing severe emotional or behavioral problems. Clearly there is considerable overlap with the two family populations that receive these interventions. There are children in child welfare families with severe emotional and behavioral problems and there are families within the mental health system who have been involved with the child welfare system because of child abuse or neglect. Nevertheless, the primary focus of the two approaches was different.

With respect to the intervention itself there are two important differences that pertain to the decision-making process. First, the family group that formulates the service and support plan in family group decision-making is comprised of family members, relatives, and friends of the family. As a plan is developed and agreed upon by the family group it is presented to the caseworker for approval. The caseworker is not part of the family group's formulation of the plan. With wraparound, the family members and their friends and advocates make up the core of the child and family team. However, relevant professionals (e.g., case manager, caseworker, teacher, therapist) also participate on the team. Although the role of the professional is that of a *partner* who is assisting the family, not that of an *expert* who is making decisions for the family, they participate in the decision-making process on an ongoing basis.

The professional-family partnership in the decision-making process is reflected in both of the wraparound cases described above. In both cases, however, it might have been beneficial had there been more nonprofessional representation (e.g., friends or relatives). The balance between professionals and nonprofessionals is an important element in wraparound. At times, however, it has been difficult to achieve. It would appear that wraparound could benefit from the more concerted effort that is made by family group decision-making to include friends and relatives in the process.

Second, with family group decision-making, once the plan is approved it is implemented by the family group under the supervision and assistance of the caseworker. In most instances, it appears the family group only meets once. With wraparound, the child and family team meets on an as-needed basis (usually at least once a week at the beginning of the process) until there is no longer a need for services. This is referred to as the unconditional care element in wraparound and is designed to counteract what Karl Dennis refers to as the "multiple placement disorder" (Karl Dennis, personal communication, 1992). In the traditional service delivery system if the child fails, he or she is sent to a new placement with new decision-makers. With wraparound there is a commitment on the part of the primary team members to stick with the child and family no matter how bad it gets.

With the two cases described above, the child and family teams had met on multiple occasions by the time the case studies were conducted and it is conceivable they are still functioning today (hopefully, on a much more limited basis, especially with respect to the involvement of the professionals).

Another important difference between the two approaches pertains to the intensity and probably the cost of the intervention. With wraparound, there is a resource coordinator (also referred to as a case manager or resource facilitator) who is responsible for helping the family create a child and family team, helping the team formulate an individualized service and support plan, facilitating the implementation of the plan, etc. A trained professional who works with four to six families at a time usually performs this role. With the Robinson/James family the role was performed by the child welfare caseworker (a situation that required a significant reduction in her caseload). The ideal situation is for the role to be performed by a family member (including the youth, depending on age and family circumstances). However, this is usually a goal that is only met through considerable training and support.

The need for the resource facilitator and the continuous involvement of the child and family team is influenced by the presence of a child or adolescent with severe emotional or behavioral problems. The families receiving family group decision-making may not have a child or adolescent with severe emotional or behavioral problems and even if they do, the family group may be able to implement a plan that meets everyone's needs. However, some of the follow-up data indicate that some of the plans were not implemented (Burford & Pennell, 1995). In those cases something more analogous to wraparound may have been beneficial.

In summary, wraparound and family group decision-making are based on a very similar set of values that are significantly different from the traditional, "remove it and fix it" orientation in child welfare and mental health systems. They both offer a promising alternative to the more medically based, rehabilitation models, which have not been shown to be effective. In addition to the need to further develop and evaluate these two approaches, it is important that the advocates collaborate with one another and learn from each other.

REFERENCES

Bruns, E. J., Burchard, J. D., & Yoe, J. T. (1995). Evaluating the Vermont system of care: outcomes associated with community-based wraparound services. *Journal of Child and Family Studies,* *4*(3), 321–39.

Burchard, J. D., Burchard, S. N., Sewell, R., & VanDenBerg, J. (1993). *One kid at a time: Evaluative case studies and description of the Alaska Youth Initiative Demonstration Project.* Juneau: State of Alaska Division of Mental Health and Mental Retardation.

Burford, G., & Pennell, J. (1995). *Family group decision making project: Implementation report summary.* St. John's, NF: Institute of Social and Economic Research, Memorial University of Newfoundland.

Burns, B. J., & Goldman, S. K. (1999). *Promising practices in wraparound for children with serious emotional disturbance and their families. Systems of care: Promising practices in children's mental health,* 1998 series, Vol. 4. Washington, DC: Center for Effective Collaboration and Practice, American Institutes for Research.

Burns, B. J., Goldman, S. K., Faw, L., & Burchard, J. D. (1999). The wraparound evidence base. In B. J. Burns & S. K. Goldman (Eds.), *Promising practices in wraparound for children with serious emotional disturbance and their families. Systems of care: Promising practices in children's mental health,* 1998 series, Vol. 4 (pp. 77–100). Washington, DC: Center for Effective Collaboration and Practice, American Institutes for Research.

Clark, H. B., Prange, M. E., Lee, B., Stewart, E. S., McDonald, B. A., & Boyd, L. A. (1998). An individualized wraparound process for children in foster care with emotional/behavioral disturbances: Follow-up findings and implications from a controlled study. In M. Epstein, K. Kutash, & A. Duchnowski (Eds.), *Outcomes for children and youth with behavioral and emotional disorders and their families: Programs and evaluation best practices* (pp. 513–42). Austin: Pro-Ed.

Clarke, R. T., Schaefer, M., Burchard, J. D., & Welkowitz, J. W. (1992). Wrapping community-based mental health services around children with a severe behavioral disorder: an evaluation of Project wraparound. *Journal of Child and Family Studies, 1(3)*, 241–61.

Cumblad, C. (1996). *The pathways children and families follow prior to, during, and after contact with an intensive, family-based, social service intervention in urban settings.* Unpublished doctoral dissertation, Department of Educational Psychology, Counseling, and Special Education, Northern Illinois University.

Eber, L. (1994). The wraparound approach. *Illinois School Research and Development Journal, 30(3)*, 17–21. Eber, L. (1996). Wraparound can enhance the development, application, and evaluation of effective behavior interventions. *Counterpoint, 17(2)*, 16–18.

Eber, L., & Osuch, R. (1995). Bringing the wraparound approach to school: A model for inclusion. In *The 7th Annual Research Conference Proceedings: A System of Care for Children's Mental Health: Expanding the research base.* Tampa: University of South Florida, Florida Mental Health Institute, Research and Training Center for Children's Mental Health.

Epstein, M., Jayanthi, M., McKelvey, J., Frankenberry, E., Hary, R., Potter, K., & Dennis, K. (1998). Reliability of the wraparound Observation Form: An instrument to measure the wraparound process. *Journal of Child and Family Studies, 7(2)*, 161–70.

Evans, M. E., Armstrong, M. I., Kuppinger, A. D., Huz, S., & Johnson, S. (1998). *A randomized trial of family-centered intensive case management and family-based treatment: Outcomes of two community-based programs for children with serious emotional disturbance.* Tampa, FL: College of Nursing.

Faw, L. (1999). The state wraparound survey. In B. J. Burns & S. K. Goldman (Eds.), *Promising practices in wraparound for children with serious emotional disturbance and their families. Systems of care: Promising practices in children's mental health,* 1998 series, Vol. 4 (pp. 61–66). Washington, DC: Center for Effective Collaboration and Practice, American Institutes for Research.

Greenbaum, P. E., Dedrick, R. F., Kutash, K., Brown, E. C., Larieri, S. P., & Pugh, A. M. (1996). National Adolescent and Child Treatment Study (NACTS): Outcomes for children with serious emotional and behavioral disturbance. *Journal of Emotional and Behavioral Disorders, 4,* 130–46.

Hyde, K. L., Burchard, J. D., & Woodworth, K. (1996). Wrapping services in an urban setting. *Journal of Child and Family Studies, 5(1)*, 67–82.

Hyde, K. L., Woodworth, K., Jordan, K., & Burchard, J. D. (1995). Wrapping services in an urban setting: outcomes of service reform in Baltimore. In C. Liberton, K. Kutash, & R. Friedman (Eds.), *The 7th Annual Research Conference Proceedings. A System for Care for Children's Mental Health: Expanding the Research Base* (pp. 255–60). Tampa: University of South Florida Press.

Illback, R. J., Neill, T. K., Call, J., & Andis, P. (1993). Description and formative evaluation of the Kentucky IMPACT Program for children with serious emotional disturbance. *Special Services in the Schools, 7(2)*, 87–109.

Kamradt, B. (1996). The 25 Kid Project: How Milwaukee utilized a pilot project to achieve buy-in among stakeholders in changing the system of care for children with severe emotional problems. Paper presented to the Washington Business Group on Health.

Meyers, J., Kaufman, M., & Goldman, S. (1999). Promising practices: Training strategies for serving children with serious emotional disturbance and their families in a system of care. In *Systems of Care: Promising Practices in Children's Mental Health, 1998 Series* (Vol. V). Washington DC: Center for Effective Collaboration and Practice, American Institutes for Research.

VanDenBerg, J. E., & Grealish, M. E. (1996). *The wraparound process training manual.* Unpublished. Available from M. Grealish, 204 E. Edgewood Drive, McMurray, Pennsylvania 15317.

Yoe, J. T., Santarcangelo, S., Atkins, M., & Burchard, J. D. (1996). Wraparound care in Vermont: Program development, implementation, and evaluation of a statewide system of individualized services. *Journal of Child and Family Studies, 5(1)*, 23–39.

14

"Just Therapy" with Families and Communities

CHARLES WALDEGRAVE

RATIONALE

"Just Therapy" was developed at the Family Centre in Wellington, New Zealand, to free both the practice and definition of therapy from its cultural, class, gender, and modernist constraints (Waldegrave, 1990; Waldegrave & Tamasese, 1993). The domain of therapy was pushed outside the traditional clinical setting to communities. The critical contexts for knowledge and healing, though embracing the social sciences, were taken beyond its traditions to those that primarily define meaning for people. These critical contexts are culture, gender, and socioeconomic status.

Just Therapy emerged in a reflective environment, where those who chose to respond to the needs of families and communities seeking help did so in a manner that addressed the fundamental issues that marginalize particular groups of people. These inequities have ensured that the same groups of people continue to be those most in need of the health and welfare resources from one generation to another. The issues in New Zealand are not that different from those in other countries, centering primarily around cultural, gender, and socioeconomic marginalization. The problem is that the therapeutic resources in most postindustrial societies were largely designed by middle-class intellectuals and practitioners. As such, they probably work well for people who have reasonable access to resources and place great stress on individual freedom. They have not been successful, however, in substantially transforming the lives of those who are marginalized, poor, and, until recently, women. As this practice has not substantially changed since the development of modern social work, psychology and other applied social sciences problems are passed on from one generation to another. Hosts of new middle-class intellectuals and practitioners are then paid to address the problems of the next generation of marginalized people.

The outcomes of this practice are quite inadequate. The inertia to change lies primarily in the powerful health and welfare structures that control massive budgets and efforts to define the social sciences as objective knowledge analogous to the physical sciences. Having taken this approach, other forms of meaning creation, such as gender, cultural, or class knowledge, are marginalized to an inferior anecdotal status.

Just Therapy was developed to value these other forms of knowledge and help put a stop to the repeated intergenerational failure of applied social science to those most in need of the health and welfare resources, enabling transformative change to emerge out of those communities on their own terms.

SOCIAL, CULTURAL, POLITICAL, AND ECONOMIC DETERMINANTS

The Just Therapy approach is termed "just" for two reasons. First, "just" refers to equity and justice. The work has grown up around the notion that many mental health and relationship problems are consequences of power difference and injustice. There is certainly a substantial body of literature that associates low-income households and inequality with physical and mental ill health (Benzeval, Judge, & Whitehead, 1995; Crampton & Howden-Chapman, 1996; Kawachi & Kennedy, 1997; Kawachi, Kennedy, Lochner, & Prothrow-Stith, 1997; National Health Committee, 1998). We also know that cultural marginalization is associated with ill health (Durie, 1994; Pomare, Keefe-Ormsby, & Ormsby, 1995; Bridgman, 1997; Tamasese, Peteru, & Waldegrave, 1997; Ministry of Maori Development, 1998), and that abuse, in all its forms, has long-term detrimental impacts on women and children (Walker, 1978; Elvidge, 1997; Luster & Small, 1997; Calam, Horne, Glasgow, & Cox, 1998; Gold, Lucenko, Elhai, Swingle, & Sellers, 1999).

Second, the "Just Therapy" approach attempts to identify the essence of therapeutic work. It is just (or simply) therapy, devoid of the commonly accepted excesses and limitations of some professional approaches. It is a demystifying approach that involves a wider range of practitioners, including those with skills and community experience or cultural knowledge. The term "Just Therapy" does not suggest a dilution of therapeutic knowledge and competence, but rather a distillation of therapeutic practices.

The approach was developed by a group of people at the Family Centre who wanted to address the profound experiences of social pain that were not being adequately responded to by caseworkers because of a narrow clinical focus. These were women and men, Maori, Samoan, and European. Some were highly educated and well qualified, while others had barely finished the compulsory requirements of the New Zealand education system. Some were community development workers, some were family therapists; most were both.

There were a plurality of starting points and a plurality of knowledge and experience drawn upon:

1. The vast body of social science knowledge.
2. No less important, the traditions of healing and the processes of healthy relationships in the three cultures: Maori, Samoan, and Pakeha (European).

3. Gendered experiences as women and men.
4. A shared commitment to social justice.
5. And a belief in a universal spirituality that acknowledges the sacredness of people's stories, particularly in their exposure of pain. A view of spirituality that is essentially about relationships in all cultures.

These five aspects were the pivotal points of collectivity in early reflections, sharing, and debate.

Many families who came to the Family Centre located the onset of their problem with events external to the family—events like unemployment, bad housing, homelessness, and racist, sexist, or heterosexist experiences. These were extremely depressing experiences that eventually led parents and children into a state of stress, opening them to physical and mental illnesses. At first we endeavored to treat the symptoms as though they were the result of internal family dysfunction. After years of listening attentively to the stories, however, we learned that, for many, their problems were actually symptoms of poverty, unjust economic planning, racism, sexism, and heterosexism.

We learned that when people came depressed and in bad housing, and we treated their symptoms, we were simply making them feel a little better in their poverty. We were able to help move them out of depression, but we then simply sent them back to the conditions that created the problems in the first place. Unintentionally, but nevertheless very effectively, we were adjusting people to poverty. Sadly, we realized that this is what most therapists and social workers do when working with poor or marginalized families. Furthermore, by implication we were encouraging the families in the belief that they, rather than the unjust structures, were the authors of their problems and failures.

LIBERATING MEANING

Psychology, social work, and the other helping professions have been taught within a largely positivist and modernist framework. The claims to a superior professional body of knowledge often center around social science claims to notions of independence, neutrality, objectivity, and verifiability. Medical metaphors with notions of diagnosis and cure, and biological metaphors with a systemic focus, are often used. The term *social science* is itself a metaphor modeled on the physical sciences. These all combine to create practitioners who search in varying degrees for objective diagnoses, objective causes, objective explanations, and objective cures.

These processes have built a status of superiority for the social sciences over other forms of knowledge, such as gender, cultural, and socioeconomic knowledge. Over time this has created many problems, because the social sciences have grown up in environments that involve a range of assumptions.

Prior to the last quarter century, white men devised most of the theory and taught most of the practice. Books written in Western Europe or North America by such people were sold throughout the world. Thus the cultural assumptions of a healthy family, for example, grew out of an environment where individual self-worth, choice, and secularism were seen as primary values. They were then picked up and taught in cultures whose primary values centered around communal identity, genealogical ties, and spirituality. To be professionally qualified, one had to adopt the dominant assumptions in training and practice. In Western Europe and North America, these assumptions are still dominant, and African-American, First Nations people, and Asian cultures in Europe are expected to absorb them as part of their professional growth and development.

Many people, however, remember a time when sexual abuse was regarded in clinical terms within the old medical, biological, and social science metaphors, characteristic of the more patriarchal assumptions of the times. Causes were sought and symptoms treated, but the abuse itself was often ignored or considered outside the clinical arena. Women politicized the issue, however, and clarified the meaning they gave such events (Bograd, 1984; Goldner, 1985; McKinnon & Miller, 1987; Kamsler, 1998). Professionals could no longer act as they did. Abuse and the meanings we give it have changed our practice, our explanations, and the law. The tired old positivist metaphors were simply inadequate to the task. In fact, they contributed to a lot of unethical behavior. It was the change of meaning to sociopolitical analysis that made the difference.

This was not discovered scientifically; it was the result of a political movement that created new awareness by drawing attention to the meanings given to events. In a critical postmodern sense, the old practice was deconstructed and its assumptions exposed. The chosen word "abuse" floated a new meaning that highlighted women's experience and placed responsibility on the perpetrators. None of this emerged out of the so-called objectivity of the social sciences. A political movement identified the injustice and insisted that the practice be changed.

This is an example of one of the dubious assumptions in the development of social science knowledge. There are many others. The Just Therapy approach questions assumptions that lock people into disadvantage or injustice. In that same critical postmodern sense, the meanings behind assumptions are sought, where appropriate they are exposed and new meanings created, which liberate and inspire resolution and hope.

Most psychological theories have been developed in Western Europe and white North America. In those cultures, as with Pakeha (European) New Zealand, individual self-worth is fundamentally important. Indeed, for practically all clinical psychological and psychotherapeutic theories, the primary goal of therapy is that of individual self-worth. That is because destiny, responsibility, legitimacy, and even human rights are seen to be essentially individual concepts. Concepts of self, individual assertiveness, and fulfillment are central to most of these therapies and theories.

If you come from a communal or extended family culture, however, questions of self-exposure and self-assertion are often confusing and even alienating. They crudely crash though the sensitivities in communally based and extended family cultures. Among individually based cultures, such questions can be quite appropriate. Outside these cultures, however, the questions are often experienced as intrusive and rude, because people in such cultures usually think of their identity in communal rather than individual terms. The questions can rupture cooperative sensitivities among people, and destroy the essential framework for meaning that should be drawn upon for healing.

Surely good social work and clinical practice should enhance people's sense of identity and belonging, but unfortunately the practices of applied social science have developed with Western cultural assumptions that so often render them ineffective with most nonwhite groups (Durie, 1986; Pere, 1988; Tamasese, Peteru, & Waldegrave, 1997; Waldegrave, 1998). This explains why so many marginalized cultural groups fail to communicate with the social professions paid to help them.

Spirituality offers another important aspect that stands out. Social scientists often boast that their discipline is a secular science. They are suspicious of anything otherworldly because they cannot measure or verify it. Families in non-Western cultures frequently associate healing with spiritual practices and traditions. At the Family Centre, Maori and Pacific Island people when working with people from their culture often share dreams, prayers, and numinous experiences that are important to the life of the family and the issues of health and wholeness. When violations are being talked about, there is often a need for spiritual rituals of protection. Those important aspects are considered sacred, and yet they are frequently disregarded by social workers and psychologists. As such, the social or clinical work is perceived as being culturally unsafe for the client family.

The mainstream assumptions, which are usually considered by their proponents to be somehow more professional and objective, are deconstructed in these examples. Tragically, they illustrate a colonial mentality that ensures that the health and welfare resources never reach the marginalized cultural groups on their own terms. It is little wonder these communities continue their disadvantaged profiles.

Effective social work and clinical practice needs to be developed by people from their cultures. All cultures have people who have the confidence of their community and know the emphases and meanings that enable health and well-being. In Just Therapy, resources are moved from ineffective mainstream outlets to cultural groups to develop their own paradigms that give dignity and add color and variety to the field. Furthermore, this process enhances employment opportunities in communities that often have higher unemployment rates.

JUST THERAPY PRACTICE AND FAMILY GROUP CONFERENCES

At the heart of the family group conference philosophy is the view that family relationships extend beyond the household or nuclear family unit. This was a major departure from mainstream theory and practice. It was an expression of Maori understanding of the nature of family rather than the standard view that owed its origins to the British heritage of the majority of the citizenry. Genealogical connections, extended family concepts, and communal processes were seen to offer greater safety for children than traditional mainstream approaches. Furthermore, the new philosophy of conferences involved a shift in power from professional decision-making and placement with or without family support, to extended family decision-making with the support of the authorities. The two groups were now required to work together for the greater good of the children involved. For Maori and Pacific Island families, this naturally involved the extended family of aunties, uncles, grandparents, and so on. Although there have been some exceptions due to underresourcing or family fragmentation, on the whole the young person or persons involved could be either placed and nurtured with close relatives or those relatives could support the immediate family to care for the young person's needs.

This change of practice has certainly led to significant improvements, but progress has been marred by a number of deficiencies in New Zealand, which relate to underresourcing over time, the variation in skills of FGC coordinators, an inadequate understanding of the vastly differing definitions of self, and the tendency of state officials to overinfluence and constrain family processes. Despite these problems, the FGC has greatly improved family participation in decision-making in contrast to other areas of health and welfare services. Many young people (though unfortunately not all), who previously would have become lost in a distant institutional or foster system, now remain part of their extended families.

The FGC is a developed model for extended families to significantly contribute to decision-making when their children are at risk and have come to the notice of the authorities. As such, it offers a process, with a reasonably coherent theoretical underpinning, for families and authorities when working with young people at risk.

Just Therapy, on the other hand, offers a comprehensive approach to the range of problems families experience. Whereas the FGC has developed a particular process for one applied area of social work, Just Therapy has developed a coherent theory that provides the tools of reflection, analysis, and action for all areas of applied social policy. The FGC, having drawn on Maori cultural practice, has opened the way for more innovative and respectful ways for dealing with families in their specific area of operation. Just Therapy calls for this type of innovation in all spheres of applied social policy that will enable the field to recognize gender, cultural, and socioeconomic knowledge.

This involves a fundamental shift in power and meaning. At the heart of the Just

Therapy approach is the recognition of women's knowledge and respect for their primary role in family life, recognition of the knowledge of marginalized cultures out of respect for their history and sense of belonging, and recognition of the knowledge of low-income households out of respect for their daily struggle to survive. The Just Therapy approach encourages an action/reflection methodology (Freire, 1972) whereby the cultural, gender, and socioeconomic contexts are addressed in every situation. We have learned that therapy is not something simply carried out with individuals, couples, or families, but must also involve communities, societies, and even countries.

With regard to culture, we are deeply committed to preserving the fundamental meanings, the modes of communication, and ways of nurture of our client groups. This has enabled us to develop approaches that are congruent with their way of life. Maori staff work with Maori clients, Pacific staff with Pacific clients, and Pakeha (European) with Pakeha people. Each cultural group has developed its own cultural approach to therapy and well-being, drawing deeply on cultural traditions of healing and those aspects of the social sciences that have proved useful.

This approach has had extraordinary impacts. Whereas Maori and Pacific families seldom voluntarily attended social work, therapeutic, or counseling services, we were not able to handle the response from these families once they knew wise people from their communities would work with them using their own processes. It was not simply the fact that these people came from their communities, but that a modern approach to work with their people was carefully devised by them, taken to their elders, critiqued by elders, and eventually launched with their blessing. In turn, this led to a process of accountability and partnership with the communities involved.

Before long we set up three cultural sections—Maori, Pacific Island, and Pakeha (European)—each staffed with workers from those cultures. Each cultural section works independently and interdependently. From these sections we have developed a leadership management team that has one coordinator from each. This replaced the previously staffed director position. Many staff members have been trained in the social sciences, but some have been employed simply because of their healing and nurturing skills, which have been recognized by their cultural communities. Our partnership with these communities has often led to their putting forward, and our agreeing to, the person or persons they want to see fill a vacant position.

We have also developed processes of cultural accountability both within and beyond the Family Centre. Each cultural section, including the Pakeha (European) one, has its own group of elders with whom it consults at critical times. The constitution of the organization was changed to ensure full representation of the three cultures on the Trust Board of the Family Centre. Staff members are closely involved in many of the community and organizational networks in their cultural groups, ensuring that they are continually in contact with current local and national issues that concern their people.

Within the Centre itself, we have developed accountability processes. These have become fairly well known through our publications (Tamasese & Waldegrave, 1993; Tamasese, Waldegrave, Tuhaka, & Campbell, 1998) and workshops. Essentially, they state that all work that involves Maori or Pacific people in any way is referred to their cultural sections and is always accountable to them. The Pakeha (European) section organizes its own affairs, but is accountable to the other two sections. Thus the Maori and Pacific Island sections carry out the role of guardians of cultural equity at the Family Centre. We often meet in cultural caucuses to work through an important issue separately, before discussing it together in the larger group.

These processes have been very important in developing a just integrity to our cultural work. They have been designed to ensure that the subtle modern processes of cultural dominance by one group do not continue to colonize. In doing so, they also ensure that the cultural communities involved are able to develop their own processes and draw upon their cultural knowledge for healing and wholeness. In the process, more of their people have been employed, more educational forums have been led by them, more papers have been written by them, more organizations have been inspired to develop similar processes, and so on.

This has led to a rich diversity of practice at the Family Centre that has enriched discussion and ways of working. As Maori and Pacific groups have drawn upon the social sciences in aspects of their work, so the Pakeha (European) section has drawn upon innovative aspects of the Maori and Pacific work, such as the use of metaphor in bringing about change and greater attention to notions of sacred events and processes in ordinary life.

These same principles have also been applied to our gender work. Using a feminist analysis in all our activities, we have endeavored to address the issues of gender justice. This is particularly important in work with families where women are so primary, when addressing abuse and the ongoing issue of the feminization of poverty, particularly for single-parent, women-led families. We have developed similar notions of accountability in the gender arena as we have in the cultural arena.

All gender work, including the running of men's groups, is accountable to the women in the agency. When making significant decisions in this area, we often first break into gender caucuses before discussing as a large group. Similar to the cultural approach, the men in the agency are accountable to the women. The women have been appointed the guardians of gender equity at the Family Centre. Those who have been unjustly treated in the broader society and those from marginalized cultures are considered to be the most informed about equity issues in these areas. In these ways, we endeavor to create a work environment that ensures that we reflect the values we wish to pass on to our various client groups.

We have also endeavored to address the socioeconomic contexts of those we relate to by expanding our understanding of social and casework. That work has on occasion led us into a range of community work initiatives. These include helping set up an unemployed workers union in our area, a national housing advocacy group, separate Maori, Pacific Island, and Pakeha (European) men for nonviolence groups, a street kids project, a Kaumatua group (Maori elders), and a Samoan Stop Abuse program.

We also lead a range of social policy research projects that provide solid data on the sorts of issues our client base experiences. These include the New Zealand Poverty Measurement Project along with two other collaborating organizations (Stephens, Waldegrave, & Frater, 1995; Waldegrave, Stuart, & Stephens, 1996), socioeconomic determinants of health work, Maori housing and Maori and income projects, and a Samoan mental health project. Thus, those who work with families also work in these other areas and are informed by the community and research work.

Some families we work with choose to participate in the community projects. Others simply know that we are as committed to the preventive work through community development projects, the research, and advocacy, as we are to the casework. We no longer address the symptoms of poverty and racism, for example, while ignoring the causes. We have developed a congruence between our casework and the rest of the work at the Centre. Each informs the other. For example, we can be much more helpful to families in assisting them with their housing needs when we work on housing projects and carry out research that highlights the levels of deprivation. We have a hands-on knowledge of life beyond the clinical room, which transforms both the conversations and processes of casework.

When working with families, we always try to honor the stories of survival of poor people that most other professional groups refer to as failures. Some families are referred to us in incredibly derogatory ways as "multiproblem families," for example. We often discover these people have suffered extreme disadvantage and developed many survival skills. Families who are forced to live in overcrowded houses, for example, often live under extreme stress. There is nothing more basic to a family and family health than a house. We endeavor to untangle the malign threads of meaning and weave new patterns of resolution and hope. We commend such people for surviving the housing crisis with their family still intact. We recognize their ability to survive the crisis as courageous, committed, and extraordinarily competent. We often add, quite truthfully, that if our families had to go through what they have been through, we are not sure we would have had the same courage and found ourselves in the same circumstances. In doing so, we are recognizing certain socioeconomic realities and encouraging the recognition of powerful inner strengths.

BELONGING, SACREDNESS, AND LIBERATION

We have learned to create our own metaphors better reflecting the warmth of our engagement with our community, than the cold social science ones. When describing case or therapeutic work, we often use the analogy of weaving. Although the symbolism of weaving is international, it is particularly appropriate in this context, because it evokes the activity of many women in the South Pacific Ocean. People come with problem-centered webs of meaning, and the task of the caseworker is to weave new threads of meaning and possibility that give new color and new textures. The weaving should loosen the tight and rigid problem-centered pattern, enabling resolution and hope.

Another metaphor we often use is that of spirituality. By spirituality, we are not referring to Christian institutionalism, but to something more akin to the sacredness of life or "soul" as in soul music. For us the therapeutic conversation is a sacred encounter, because people come in great pain and share their story. The story is like a gift, a very personal offering given in great vulnerability. It has a spiritual quality. It is not a scientific pathology that requires removal, nor is it an ill-informed understanding of the story that requires correction. It is rather a person's articulation of events, and the meaning given to those events, which have become problematic. The therapist honors and respects the story, and then in return gives a reflection that offers alternative liberating meanings that inspire resolution and hope.

Finally, we have chosen three primary concepts that characterize our Just Therapy approach. When assessing the quality of our work, we measure it against the interrelationship of these three concepts. The first is *belonging,* which refers to the essence of identity, to who we are, our cultured and gendered histories, and our ancestry. The second is *sacredness,* which refers to the deepest respect for humanity, its qualities, and the environment. The third is *liberation,* which refers to freedom, wholeness, and justice. We are interested in the interdependence of these concepts, not one without another. Not all stories of belonging are liberating, for example, and some experiences of liberation are not sacred. We are interested in the harmony between all three concepts as an expression of Just Therapy.

REFERENCES

Benzeval, M., Judge, K., & Whitehead, M. (Eds.) (1995). *Tackling inequalities in health: An agenda for action.* London: King's Fund.
Bograd, M. (1984). Family systems approach to wife battering: A feminist critique. *American Journal of Orthopsychiatry, 54*(4), 558–68.
Bridgman, G. (1997). Appendix 1, Mental health data presented to participants. In K. Tamasese, C. Peteru, & C. Waldegrave (Eds.), *Ole taeao afua, The new morning: A qualitative investigation into Samoan perspectives on mental health and culturally appropriate services* (pp. 77–92). Lower Hutt, Wellington: The Family Centre.
Calam, R., & Horne, L., Glasgow, D., & Cox, A. (1998). Psychological disturbance and child sexual abuse: A follow-up study. *Journal of Child Abuse and Neglect, 22,* 901–13.

Crampton, P., & Howden-Chapman, P. (Eds.) (1996). *Socioeconomic inequalities and health.* Victoria: Institute of Public Policy, University of Wellington.

Durie, M. (1986). *Maori health: Contemporary issues and responses.* Auckland: Mental Health Foundation of New Zealand.

Durie, M. (1994). *Whaiora: Maori health development.* Auckland: Oxford University Press.

Elvidge, P. (1997). *Health consequences of male partner violence facts sheets.* Auckland: Health Promotion Unit, Auckland Health Care.

Freire, P. (1972). *Pedagogy of the oppressed.* Harmondsworth, Penguin.

Gold, S., Lucenko, B., Elhai, J., Swingle, J., & Sellers, A. (1999). Comparison of psychological/psychiatric symptomatology of women and men sexually abused as children. *Journal of Child Abuse and Neglect, 23*(7), 683–92.

Goldner, V. (1985). Feminism and family therapy. *Family Process, 24,* 31–47.

Kamsler, A. (1998). Her story in the making: Therapy with women who were sexually abused in childhood. In C. White & D. Denborough (Eds.), *Introducing narrative therapy: A collection of practice book writings* (pp. 47–75). Adelaide: Dulwich Centre Publications.

Kawachi, I., & Kennedy, B. (1997). Health and social cohesion: Why care about income inequality? *British Medical Journal, 314,* 1037–40.

Kawachi, I., Kennedy, B., Lochner, K., & Prothrow-Stith, L. (1997). Social capital, income inequality, and mortality. *American Journal of Public Health, 87,* 1491–98.

Luster, T., & Small, S. (1997). Sexual abuse history and problems in adolescence: Exploring the effects of moderating variables. *Journal of Marriage and the Family, 59,*131–42.

McKinnon, L., & Miller, D. (1987). The new epistemology and the Milan approach: Feminist and socio-political considerations. *Journal of Marital and Family Therapy, 13*(2), 139–55.

Ministry of Maori Development (1998). *Progress towards closing the gaps between Maori and non-Maori: A report to the minister of Maori affairs.* Wellington: Te Puni Kokiri.

National Health Committee (1998). *The social, cultural and economic determinants of health: Action to improve health.* Wellington, NZ: National Advisory Committee on Health and Disability.

Pere, R. (1988). Te wheke: Whaia te maramatanga me te aroha. In S. Middleton (Ed.), *Women in education in Aotearoa.* Wellington, NZ: Allen Unwin/Port Nicholson.

Pomare, E., Keefe-Ormsby, V., & Ormsby, C. (1995). *Hauora: Maori Standards of Health. A Study of the Years 1970–1991.* Wellington, NZ: Te Ropu Rangahau Hauora a Eru Pomare.

Stephens, R., Waldegrave, C., & Frater, P. (1995). Measuring poverty in New Zealand. *Social Policy Journal of New Zealand, 5*(December), 88–112.

Tamasese, K., Peteru, C., & Waldegrave, C. (1997). *Ole Taeao Afua, The New Morning: A Qualitative Investigation into Samoan Perspectives on Mental Health and Culturally Appropriate Services.* Lower Hutt, Wellington, NZ: The Family Centre.

Tamasese, K., & Waldegrave, C. (1993). Cultural and gender accountability in the "Just Therapy" approach. *Journal of Feminist Family Therapy, 5*(2, Summer). Reprinted in *Dulwich Centre Newsletter, 2–3,* 29–45.

Tamasese, K., Waldegrave, C., Tuhaka, F., & Campbell C. (1998). Furthering conversations about partnerships of accountability: Talking about issues of leadership, ethics and care. *Dulwich Centre Journal, 4,* 50–62, Adelaide.

Waldegrave, C. (1990). Just Therapy. *Dulwich Centre Newsletter, 1,* 5–46.

Waldegrave, C. (1998). The challenges of culture to psychology and post modern thinking. In M. McGoldrick (Ed.), *Re-visioning Family Therapy: Race, Culture and Gender in Clinical Practice* (pp. 404–13). New York, Guilford.

Waldegrave, C., Stuart. S., & Stephens, R. (1996). Participation in poverty research: Drawing on the knowledge of low income householders to establish an appropriate measure for monitoring social policy impacts. *Social Policy Journal of New Zealand, 7*(December), 191–206.

Waldegrave, C., & Tamasese, K. (1993). Some central in the "Just Therapy" approach. *Australia & New Zealand Family Therapy Journal, 14*(1), 1–8.

Walker, L. (1978). Battered women and learned helplessness. *Victimology, 2/3/4,* 525–34.

15   Making Action Plans in Vermont

JENNIFER L. BOLAND, CYNTHIA M. COLLEA, JUDITH DALY,
RUTH HALE, and THOMAS E. HILL

In 1995, the Vermont Division of Casey Family Services began collaborating with the state Department of Social and Rehabilitation Services (SRS) and the University of Vermont in an initiative to provide family group decision-making (FGDM) to families in two regions of Vermont. Concurrently, a community collaborative introduced a planning activity (MAPS) to a region of the state as a tool to use in case planning for families involved within the system. Making Action Plans or the McGill Action Planning System (MAPS) had been created at McGill University in Canada (O'Brien, Forest, Snow, & Hasbury, 1989) to aid in the development of education plans for children in need of services. Social workers from the Casey Family Services Foster Care Division who were part of the FGDM initiative saw how MAPS could be used to organize a family meeting consistent with conferencing principles.

The MAPS process is a structured conversation consisting of a series of six steps, in which participants are asked to reflect on and answer questions about an individual or the entire family. The question categories are the family's or individual's *history* (a short description of the background, including important memories), *dreams* (a list of things they would like to see happening now and in their future), *fears* (a list of worries, concerns, challenges, or obstacles to achieving their dreams), *who* they are (a description of the family or individual's strengths, challenges, skills, likes, and favorite activities), *needs* (a list of things that need to happen to help make the dreams come true or avoid having their fears come true), and finally the creation of a *plan* (Furney, 1992).

The family and a team of people including extended family, friends, and professionals whom the family chooses, or they recognize as necessary for the process, come together to have a conversation around each of the steps. The information expressed through the process leads to a vision of what the youth and/or family hopes and dreams for, as well as ideas for ways to realize those dreams. The facilitator records the responses on large sheets of paper using bright colors and simple drawings, repeating aloud what is written down to verify the actual statement and the meaning. The papers are then displayed on the wall, providing an illustration of the team's efforts. The plan is developed from themes that emerge out of the process. After completing the MAP, the team follows additional steps to help ensure that the plan can be successful, including setting time for a review of the plan.

Between January 1996 and May 1999, Casey Family Services Vermont Division completed seventy MAPS with children and families. The three main referral sources were Vermont Child Protective Services [39 percent ($n = 27$)], internal referrals from the Casey Family Services Long Term Foster Care program [21 percent ($n = 15$)], and Mental Health [20 percent ($n = 14$)]. Other referrals came from Casey Family Services Post Adoption services [9 percent ($n = 6$)], families [7 percent ($n = 5$)], and schools [4 percent ($n = 3$)]. Slightly over half (56 percent) of the cases were involved with Vermont Child Protective Services for issues of abuse, neglect, or unmanageability.

As with the use of any new tool within a public system where professionals have historically been in control, the use of MAPS as a process for families takes some getting use to for all parties involved. Families and other service providers may have different expectations of the process and these could violate some underlying principles of the approach. For example, if a child welfare worker is mandated to create a service plan within a certain time frame, he or she may struggle to see the value of taking extra time to get extended family to the meeting.

PRELIMINARY PLANNING PHASE

The creation of the invitation list for the MAP is critical, as it affects the entire process. Great care is taken to assist the family in planning who they want invited to the MAP. Either the Casey social worker or the referral worker coordinates the invitation list with the family. This involves individual meetings or telephone calls with family members, extended family, friends, professionals, or other supports to explain what the MAP is and to encourage them to attend. Part of this preliminary planning can also involve addressing key family members about issues that need to be addressed, defining the focus of the MAP, as well as helping family members think about how to approach the meeting.

Of the seventy MAPS evaluated, Casey Family Services staff were the primary coordinators half the time. On two occasions the family chose to take on this role completely by themselves. For the other MAP meetings, the referral workers helped the family coordinate the invitation list. The family is encouraged to be as inclusive as possible when they think about whom to invite, and Casey Family Services social workers encourage families to look beyond immediate family. If a family does not want to be inclusive, their decision is respected.

Once coordinators establish the invitation list, they attempt to secure a convenient time and place for the meeting. Scheduling the MAP can be the most challenging part of the process. MAPS can be scheduled on weekends and evenings to accommodate families, but this does not always work for professionals. In this preliminary planning phase, the coordinator also works with the family to help decide on the focus of the MAP. For example, do they want the MAP focused on one child in the family, several of the children, or is it a family-focused MAP? For some families there are clear issues that help the family decide how the MAP should be focused; other times they need to think hard about what would be best for the family. This decision-making process helps the family see that issues they may have initially viewed as problems for one child may be better viewed as a larger family issue. Of the seventy MAPS evaluated in the Casey program, the focus was on one child in a family two-thirds of the time ($n = 47$), on the entire family one-fifth of the time ($n = 14$), on more than one child in a family 7 percent of the time ($n = 5$), and on one parent 6 percent of the time ($n = 4$)).

Research shows that the average of people attending a MAP is 7.8, ranging from 2 to 28. Most MAPS include children as part of the team, as the focus of the meeting, as part of the family, or as peer supports. Seventy children have attended MAPS meetings. In the MAPS focusing on children and families, the age of children attending ranged from 6 to 18 years, while the age of the children who did not attend ranged from 1 to 15 years. Of the 47 MAPS with a focus on a specific child, 38 of the children attended.

THE MAP MEETING

MAP meetings take time, ranging from two to six hours, with most taking four hours. There is the option of a MAP being completed in segments. Some workers have found that scheduling several shorter meetings has benefits, especially when family members have difficulty staying focused. Scheduling MAPS in segments occurred in approximately one-fifth of the cases.

The facilitator arrives early at the meeting to set up light refreshments and arrange the room so that people are able to see each other. Once everyone has arrived the facilitator makes introductions, welcomes them, and explains the purpose of the six steps. Everyone is then asked to introduce themselves and their relationship to the family or individual. Once introductions are completed, the facilitator reviews the ground rules. Examples of rules are:

* Take turns, avoid interrupting.
* Everyone's opinion counts.
* The child and the family will be given the first chance to respond.
* Make sure the recorder has written it correctly. If we get it wrong, tell us.
* You can "pass" if you choose.
* Try to state things in the positive.
* If you need a break, ask for it. If one person breaks, we all break.
* Don't get stuck on what can't happen! Be creative.

In advance of the meeting, each of the team members receives a packet of information explaining what a MAP is, the purpose of the MAP process, and an explanation of the six steps to be followed. Facilitators encourage team members to write down ideas before the meeting and bring them to the MAP. Also, a team member who is not able to make the meeting can submit his or her ideas to the facilitator in advance of the meeting. Throughout the planning and implementing of the MAP, the facilitator aims to respect and incorporate the cultural customs of the family.

Step 1: *History.*   In this step the facilitator asks the group to briefly describe the family or individual's history. The purpose is to help all team members develop a more complete picture of the events and people that have shaped the family. This is not meant to be a chronological accounting, but more a series of highlights to give a sense of the family or individual. This can be viewed as a warm-up step, allowing the family to discuss information about the past in ways they choose to share it. Depending on the family and the team this step can be very short or quite lengthy. Some workers find it valuable to spend a lot of time on history so that team members get a clearer picture of the family; whereas others feel that if the team spends too much time on history they lose energy for the steps to come. If people have a difficult time beginning this step, the facilitator may ask a few direct questions, opening possibilities for other information to be shared. A family may not want to discuss history at all and the facilitator may choose to move forward to dreams and give the family the opportunity to add things to history throughout the process. The newsprint is then taped to the wall with the assumption that it can be added to at any time.

Step 2: *Dreams.*   This is a time to be creative, to think big, as if money is not an object and anything is possible. This is often when the children get more involved in the process, as they usually understand the concept of dreaming. Families may begin with dreams or wishes for winning the lottery or their dream car and then move on to dreams for school, home, or relationships with people. This step can be very energizing and powerful for the family as they create dreams and see other people's dreams for them. Parents and children see this section as a time for hope. Dreams give direction, hope, and a possible route the MAP will follow as exploration continues.

Step 3: *Fears.*   Here, the family and team are asked to talk about their fears, especially those they see as barriers to realizing the family or individual dreams. This step can be uncomfortable and revealing, as well as a learning experience for team members, who often recognize the universality of fears people have for themselves and their children.

Step 4: *Who is . . .*   In this step the team is asked to describe the family or individual in as many ways as possible. The facilitator encourages team members to talk about strengths, challenges, skills, likes and dislikes, personal qualities, favorite activities, friends, and so on. This information helps team members learn more about the family members and invites the family and team to celebrate their accomplishments and gifts. This is often a lively step, inviting the participation of all team members. The positive comments that are often part of this step help to set the tone of the MAP as generally upbeat and create a positive image of the family or individual. Negative characteristics tend to be stated in a respectful, objective way. If the opposite occurs, the facilitator reminds the team of the ground rules and helps the team member rephrase statements.

Step 5: *Needs.* In the final step of the MAP, the facilitator asks the team to identify the key ideas from the previous steps. This helps the team to focus on the MAP's overall direction and vision as well as the important details. Once a list of needs is written the facilitator helps the team write a plan.

The Plan. To move to the plan, the team needs to organize and prioritize the information from the MAP. This can be done by identifying areas where there might be needs such as school, home, work, housing, employment, living situations, and then listing action steps for each category. The plan can identify tasks for any team member to complete. Following the MAP, the plan is typed and sent to all team members for review.

Reviews. The MAP is not intended to be a one-time fix and the process is to be ongoing. Families change. At the time of the MAP, the group decides when to schedule the review. The facilitator then sends review invitations to all team members several weeks before the review date has been scheduled. At the review, the Casey social worker brings the MAP that was created, tapes it on the wall, and begins a review of what has happened since the MAP. A revised plan is then developed. Of the 70 MAPS, 47 percent ($n = 33$) had no reviews, 31 percent ($n = 22$) had one review, and 22 percent ($n = 15$) had more than one review.

Theoretical Implications. The MAPS process tends to identify issues and externalize problems, rather than looking for pathology, blaming, stigmatizing, or diagnosing a person or family. The process of externalization creates a separation between persons and problems and opens space for new ways of relating to both. The MAP does this by framing problems as "obstacles" and "fears." This tends to free up everyone in the room, opening up space for conversation and possibilities and helps keep people from being defensive. Displaying the large colorful newsprint also helps children and adults to remain focused throughout the process.

The facilitator's and recorder's roles are not to evaluate, judge, or diagnose but to accurately reflect the stories by recording them on paper. They also ask questions and make observations to open possibilities, draw out people, and facilitate interactions in order to enrich the discussion and MAP process. The group can then see the themes, needs, and values in the conversations. The facilitator does not attempt to change what was said or put meaning into it. He or she aims to reflect exactly what was said. Unlike spoken words that can be lost, putting the MAP in writing preserves the words and stories told. The MAP essentially creates a shift from focusing on an individual's reality to a group or family reality.

Family-centered practice is as much an attitude and outlook as it is a particular method or approach. Ultimately, what is at the heart of this outlook is that families are the ones who know themselves best and need to be at the center of decision-making for their families and children. This means using an inclusive definition of family to include extended family members as well as the natural support system of friends, neighbors, and community resources.

REFERENCES

Furney, K. S. (1992). *Making dreams happen: How to facilitate the MAPS process.* Washington, DC: U.S. Department of Education, Office of Special Education Program under Federal Grant H 158A10001-92.

O'Brien, J., Forest, M., Snow, J., & Hasbury, C. (1989). Action for inclusion. Toronto: Frontier College Press.

16 Family Group Decision-Making and Family Violence

JOAN PENNELL and GALE BURFORD

Learning what is happening in situations of family violence is fraught with difficulties. Reports from perpetrators, survivors, witnesses, professionals, and researchers often differ on what happened and whether the situation can be defined as family violence (Johnson, 1996; Straus & Gelles, 1990). This variance in views adds to the debates on how to address family violence (Pennell, 1995; Stark & Flitcraft, 1996). The underlying fears are that the conflicting views will lead to family and community members' blaming survivors of family violence, exonerating the abusers, and becoming entangled in issues that they cannot resolve. Differences as to what had happened and would happen and what actions should be taken were evident in the case of family "F" referred to the Family Group Decision Making (FGDM) Project (Newfoundland and Labrador) for a conference.

INITIAL RESPONSES

Common fears of Family Group Conferencing (FGC):

- The survivors will be blamed.
- The abusers will be exonerated.
- The other participants will be overwhelmed.

FGC guiding principles:

- Mobilize key stakeholders to work on the issue.
- Prepare invitees to take part.
- Set in place mechanisms to protect participants.

At the time that the FGC coordinator received the referral from Correctional Services Canada, the father, George F., was in prison for violence against his wife, Sarah F. This violence had been witnessed by their two young sons, Kevin and Jason. The parole worker was under the impression that on release George and Sarah planned to reunite and, as a consequence, saw the need for a FGC to work out a plan to protect Sarah and the children. The referral, however, was nearly rescinded. As the FGC coordinator wrote in her reflective notes about the preparations for the conference:

Parole almost withdrew this referral because Sarah had indicated [later] to Parole . . . that she and George had agreed not to resume their relationship upon his release. Parole, therefore, did not see this as being high risk for further violence.

After meeting alone with Sarah, the FGC coordinator, who had extensive experience working with abused women, came to a quite different conclusion:

After my first meeting with Sarah, it was clear that this referral was very appropriate. Sarah expressed fear of George and was apprehensive about what would happen upon his release. She also clearly stated that her children were extremely frightened of this man.

For her part, Sarah also wanted the conference to take place:

Sarah was clear that it was her decision not to take George back and that although he was verbally going along with this, she knew he wanted to resume the relationship, and she had been feeling a great deal of pressure from his family to take him back. She also talked of the fact that she had taken George back so many times before and that she wasn't sure if she would be able to stick to her decision. She was able to say that she would need a great deal of support to do this. Her family were extremely angry with this man and were supportive of her, but . . . it was hard for her to talk to them about her feelings because they were so protective of her and negative toward him. She saw this Project as a way to get information to both sides of the family about her decisions and ask for their support. She also saw the Project as a way to get support for herself and particularly her older son (age 11) who had witnessed the most violence, had been a victim of emotional abuse by this man, and was experiencing the most fear.

Sarah's situation was like that of many abused women. In questioning her own resolve to remain separate from George, she recognized her difficulties in resisting the demands of his family to reunite when her own self-confidence had been undermined by years of abuse (cf. Hoff, 1990; Taylor, 1991). Her hope was that with support garnered through the conference she and her sons would be safeguarded from further violence. Recognizing that this process would be difficult, she selected a cousin to serve as a support person to stay by her during the conference and provide emotional support.

When invited to attend the conference, the relatives had mixed reactions. They were afraid about becoming reinvolved in a conflict-ridden situation but also were hopeful that the process might bring some resolution. On meeting with Sarah's family, the FGC coordinator learned that they had reason to personally fear George's violence:

Many of them had been victims of his violence, mostly through having their property damaged by him.

Such violence against family and friends of the abused wife is not uncommon (Pahl, 1985), and violence by the perpetrator is all the more likely to occur when he fears that she will separate from him (Mahoney, 1991; Wilson & Daly, 1994). Sarah's family needed the FGC coordinator to clarify that both sides of the family would be present and have the opportunity to express their views. Fearing that the conference would lapse into mutual recriminations and past hostilities, they were relieved to learn that:

the focus of the conference was . . . about ensuring the future safety of all family members—including ensuring that George [had] the best possible chance at rehabilitation.

With this information, Sarah's family agreed to take part.

George's family also required extensive preparations, in this instance, because of their own lengthy histories of family violence:

George's family was quite large (14 siblings). He grew up in a household where his father physically and emotionally abused him, his mother, and his siblings. His father [had] been a chronic alcoholic for 45 years.

The large and closed family profile, not an uncommon one for the intergenerational transmission of violence (cf. Burford & Pennell, 1995; Herrenkohl, Herrenkohl, & Toedter, 1983; Hodgson & "Phyllis," 1990), prompted the FGC coordinator to take special care in discussing their views in advance of the meeting. Her discussions with George's mother are particularly telling of the family dynamics and indicative of the likely ways in which his family would respond at the conference:

In meeting with George's mother, it was clear that she had the respect of all of her children. She admitted to me that she had been a victim of violence for the entire forty-five years she has been married to this man and discussed openly the impact the violence has had on her family. While she was supportive and protective of her son George, she also admitted that he is the sibling who most closely resembles his father in terms of his violent temper and his substance abuse. I was amazed at how candid she was with me, but I was also well aware that in public (i.e., at the FGC) she would defend him to the end.

To prepare George for the conference took extensive outreach on the part of the coordinator. Hurdles were imposed by the penal system and the correctional center for which FGC was a new approach. As the coordinator wrote:

One of the frustrations of the preparation process was my inability to adequately prepare George prior to the FGC because he was in a Federal Institution and I only had telephone contact with him. . . . [Being] unsure until four days before the conference whether he would be able to attend the FGC added to this frustration.

The confusion was compounded by the changeover in parole officer, who was responsible for escorting George to the conference and providing a report to the family group. In a follow-up interview, the parole officer had very clear memories of receiving this referral:

> It was a surprise to get the case just before the conference. This was a new area . . . , and all of the information that I had on the project was just a memo. I had only two-days notice. The other staff member had been reassigned to something else. . . . I wondered what I would get into at the conference since [there were] two families with a lot of members. I particularly wondered about the amount of work involved—would this mean a lot more time spent on one case, when I needed to budget my time? That worry was alleviated once the Coordinator came down and explained my role. [Afterwards] I felt a lot more comfortable.

In spite of these sudden personnel changes, the prison warden and correctional center authorities worked together to ensure that George could leave the penitentiary on a two-day temporary absence and reside during this period at the correctional community center.

Because of their previous involvement with the FGDM, other service providers readily responded to the request to take part. With parole on board, child welfare, which had already taken part in numerous conferences, lent support to moving forward with this referral and agreed to present a report at the conference and review the FGC plan in regard to safeguarding children. Likewise a worker at a local shelter for abused women and their children accepted the invitation to provide information at the conference on family violence and addictions. The worker was well informed about FGC because of prior consultations with women's groups on the model.

In addition to systemic hurdles, the coordinator found that George himself posed a challenge. His childhood exposure to family violence in all likelihood influenced his violent response to Sarah. As research has found, men who observed domestic violence as children are three times more likely as adults to abuse their partners (Statistics Canada, 1993). Moreover, as is characteristic of many men who batter their wives (Ptacek, 1988), George minimized his own violence and its effects:

> George is a man with little education who has limited ability to understand the full extent of the dynamics of abuse or the FGC model. He is a concrete thinker who had trouble seeing past the fact that he promised never to hit her again, that it didn't happen very often, that there were a lot of guys who are more violent than him, and that in time she would take him back. He was wary of the process at first—he pictured everyone ganging up on him and telling him what to do, and he felt everyone in the community would know his business and be gossiping about it.

As recounted below, probably the preparations that had the strongest impact later on the conference were with the elder son. As common among children who have witnessed domestic violence (Jaffe, Wolfe, & Wilson, 1990), Kevin was terrified of his father. The boy decided that he would not attend the conference but with the assistance of a John Howard Society worker, wrote out a statement to be read at the conference. Through this statement, Kevin was able to express the fear that his father would return home and continue the violence. Thus, even before the conference took place, Kevin (unlike his own father) made significant strides in moving away from identifying with an abusive father and in taking a stance in opposition to violence.

Thus, the various family group and professional participants arrived at the conference with quite diverse opinions on the family situation. Sarah's relatives blamed George for his violence while his family, ridden with violence for decades, defended George. Sarah, although wanting to remain separate from George, doubted her own resolve; he, in turn, took for granted that she would eventually relent and allow him to return; and their sons dreaded that George would be right. Not aware of all of these conflicts and uncertainties, parole initially presumed that if Sarah did not plan to reunite with George, then the matter required no further processing in the family group. This conclusion was countered by the coordinator, who identified Sarah's ambivalence and the children's fears. Mobilizing support for resolving the issues, she presented the conference as a potential forum for working through these divergent perspectives and reaching a collective plan to remedy the situation. Sharing her hopes, the family group members and service providers accepted the invitation to take part.

FORMING A COLLECTIVE RESPONSE

Common fears of FGC:

- Survivors will be coerced to forgive their abuser.
- Perpetrators will manipulate the family group.
- Survivors will be shamed and silenced.
- Abusers will react violently at the conference.
- Outraged relatives will attack the perpetrators.

FGC guiding principles:

- Provide sufficient information, supports, protections, and privacy for the family group to formulate a sound plan.
- Approve plans that promote safety and well-being of child and adult family members.
- Authorize needed resources to carry out the plan.

Bringing together the abuser, the survivor, and their families raises quite reasonable fears that the process will endanger participants during and after the meeting and yield unsafe plans. For just these reasons, many feminists and therapists have spoken out against the use of family and couples therapy in situations of domestic violence (Bograd, 1992; Hansen & Harway, 1993; Kaufman, 1992; Pressman, 1989). Likewise within the child welfare field, fears are expressed that family-centered approaches promote family unity at the expense of children's safety. These fears become all the more pronounced when envisioning a FGC meeting where adult abusers make decisions about children's lives without the presence of an advocate or lawyer present to safeguard the children's rights and interests (Bartholet, 1999; Shirk, 1999).

The critics raise concerns that need to be taken into account in envisioning and structuring FGC. Their criticisms would be justified if FGC were a treatment or planning process confined to a closed family unit. The vision, however, of FGC is about building "communities of concern" (Braithwaite & Daly, 1994, p. 192) and thus "widening the circle" of people to protect all family members (Pennell & Burford, 1994, 1997, 1999). The preparations, as described above for the F. family, are crucial for setting in place safety mechanisms for the conference (Burford, Pennell, & MacLeod, 1995; American Humane Association, 1997; Connolly & McKenzie, 1999). The structure of the conference itself is geared to promoting safe and effective participation within the culture of the family group (Burford & Pennell, 1996). Internationally, studies have found that violence does not occur at conferences (Marsh & Crow, 1998; Pennell & Burford, 1995) or occurs rarely (Paterson & Harvey, 1991), and in follow-up interviews shortly after and six months to two years following the conference, the Newfoundland and Labrador study did not find evidence that family members were subsequently abused because of the conference (Burford & Pennell, 1998; Pennell & Burford, 1995).

At the F. family's conference, the circle of concerned community members was widened by including family members from both sides of the family for a total of fifteen. Present from Sarah's family were Sarah herself as well as her mother, sister, aunt, and the cousin who was serving as Sarah's support person. Coming from a quite large family, George had more relatives with him at the conference: his mother, father, five sisters, a brother, and the boyfriend of one sister. The non-family group members present included the coordinator, researcher (who collected data on the conference), the parole officer, and the shelter worker. At the last moment, the child protection worker was unable to attend for reasons unrelated to the conference. Likewise, two relatives who had planned to take part sent their regrets. Family members assisted each other with rides to the community center where the conference was to be held. George was escorted by the parole officer, who observed that in the drive to the meeting:

"George was scared to death. He had no idea what this was all about."

Starting the conference at 9:15 A.M., the coordinator ensured that everyone was welcomed, seated, and introduced, and then she reviewed the conference's purpose, process, and ground rules. The last included maintaining confidentiality, listening, and remaining nonviolent. The family then heard a report from the parole officer about what had happened in the F. family, what concerns needed to be addressed in the plan, how parole operated, and what parole could offer in services. Later in an interview, the parole officer described their response to his half-hour presentation:

They were attentive: they hadn't heard a lot of this before, even though some had experience with parole before, usually they don't get this information.

After he completed his report, the shelter worker entered the room. Describing her presentation, the coordinator wrote:

[She] gave a fabulous presentation on the effects of violence and addictions on women and children in a way that was simple, clear, and respectful. This both gave a great deal of information and helped set the focus for the family (especially for the sisters of George who had up to now been pressuring Sarah to take him back). George's mother kept saying throughout the day, "If only something like this was on the go years ago." This was both positive in that she was praising the process, but also sad because it indicated that she believes it is too late for her.

The shelter worker's presentation was followed by an even more powerful statement. When the coordinator read aloud the letter from the older son, Kevin, George broke into tears and left the room. The parole officer explained that hearing Kevin's words "hurt" George but that "it was good for George to hear the effects of his behavior on others." Hearing the boy's words also affected George's family. They were able to acknowledge that no child should be so frightened and they stopped blaming Sarah for turning their brother over to the police. What amazed the parole officer was that George's father "showed up and stayed there most of the conference."

The group then adjourned for lunch at 12:15 P.M. Previously the coordinator had consulted with Sarah on the menu and then ordered the food brought in. The women in the family group dished out the food on plates, and everyone ate together. The parole officer noted that the informal discussions over the day helped to remove apprehensions about relating with the professionals. He observed that initially the family group members were "very leery" about speaking with him, but "with individual chats before the conference, during the breaks, and at lunch, some of them talked your ear off." This was particularly the case for George's sister, mother, and Sarah's cousin, and also for Sarah herself.

After a thirty-five-minute lunch, the family group moved into their private deliberations. The coordinator and parole officer, though, were available to be consulted at any time. As the parole officer recounted:

If they had questions on parole, they brought me in. . . . They had fears about "ratting" on George. I needed to educate them on ratting. I stressed that it was better to act right away. I think I got through on this. They put in the plan about reporting on George, and George agreed to it.

At the end of an hour and forty minutes, the family group invited the coordinator and parole officer back to the conference, and by 2:00 P.M. they had finalized the plan and concluded the conference. The coordinator remarked that this four-hour-and-forty-five-minute conference was her shortest one and the one with the least expression of emotion. She suspected that the shortness could be attributed to Sarah and her cousin being "really clear about what should be included in the plan" but also to George's family having "learned through years of abuse and hardship to shut down their emotions." She went on to comment:

The plan that resulted was a good one and was approved without hesitation by parole and [later] child protection. . . . Costs of [the] plan will be shared by parole and child protection.

As stated in the plan, the major issues addressed were:

violence and controlling behaviors of George toward Sarah, and the impact of this violence on the children in the home; and substance abuse of George.

It included specific steps for a "safety plan" for Sarah and the boys, visitation of George with the boys at the correctional center, counseling for Sarah and Kevin, and addictions counseling for George. Once George was discharged from prison, the plan specified steps for handling his making unexpected visits to Sarah and the children:

If George shows up at Sarah's house unannounced and/or uninvited, Sarah will call either his sisters or brother, who will assist her in making sure he leaves the premises. If he appears to be under the influence of alcohol or drugs parole will be notified immediately. George agreed to this since it was clearly stated at the meeting that he wants to deal with his addiction problem and family members would not be supporting him by covering for him.

The plan further specified that George's mother would "monitor" the implementation of the plan once he leaves prison by maintaining contact with family members and professionals. In addition, the plan included regular review meetings of the family group, child protection, and parole.

In interviews closely following the conference, the researcher found that George's mother and two sisters and Sarah and her cousin all expressed satisfaction about the conference. One of George's sisters stated that the conference "helped to unite the family to tackle the problems together"; and the other sister saw the plan as:

common-sense ideas which they had been discussing amongst themselves for some time, but had never seriously put forth [before] to George and Sarah.

Sarah's cousin likewise was "very pleased" with the conference but also "cautious." As she explained to the researcher:

She intends to watch things closely to ensure that the plan was carried out. She is aware of George's history and his ability to deceive people around him. Because of this, she plans to make sure that Sarah "keeps her guard up" and sticks with the plan. Her fear is that George will convince everyone that he is changed and reformed, and therefore the plan is not necessary.

For her part, Sarah said:

she was happy with the results of the conference and felt pleased with the plan. However, she is anxious for George to be released on parole so that the real work of putting the plan in action can begin. She also has concerns that George's mother assumed too much responsibility and may not follow through on it. But the cousin has reassured her that the plan will be carried out.

Reflecting on the postconference interviews, the researcher predicted that:

although the cousin is not the plan monitor, . . . she will actually fill this role.

Thus, despite their prior apprehensions and animosities, the family group members were able to come together without violence, to formulate a constructive plan, to reach agreement on the plan, and to have their plan affirmed by the service providers. Immediately afterward, the conference left them with a sense of satisfaction and cautious optimism.

FOLLOWING THROUGH ON THE PLAN

Common fears of FGC:

- The conference will provoke later retaliation.
- Families will be kept together at all cost.

FGC guiding principle:

- Work together to monitor and review the plan.
- Revise together the plan as needed.
- Carry through on resourcing of plans.

FGC plans are usually carried out in part but not in full; nevertheless, the large majority of family group participants see the family as better off because of the conference (Burford & Pennell, 1998). What appears to be important to family groups is not whether all items are carried out but rather whether key ones are (Marsh & Crow, 1998). Where family group or service providers fail to carry out significant action steps, then strong disgruntlement is voiced (Burford & Pennell, 1998).

Follow-up interviews in regard to the F. family found that only some of the plans were in effect because of a variety of changes in the family's situation. Two months after the conference, the parole officer reported that contrary to his and other's expectations at the time of the conference:

George was not granted parole by the Parole Board. He'll do two-thirds of his time and then one-third as parole. . . . Irregardless [*sic*]of the time frames, it was not wasted time. From an offender's point of view, it means a lot more people care about him, know what they will do to keep him from getting into a jam again. . . . The family members got a lot of education on safety and parole. . . . This could reduce return to institutions.

Fifteen months after the conference, George was still in prison but about to be released shortly when the child protection worker was interviewed. This worker, who had continued to follow Sarah and the children, noted:

During his incarceration, George had called Sarah and the children every Sunday. . . . The older child was no longer frightened by George; he has, however, displayed behaviors indicating a great concern for his mother should George return upon his release. . . . Sarah is somewhat concerned with what will happen when George is released from prison. Apparently she had no intention of getting back together with him, . . . but George has been sending a lot of letters and phoning regularly. In addition, [the prison authorities] phoned child protection to [report] that George was discussing with counselors his plan to return home.

Despite these uncertainties about George, the child protection worker noted that Sarah was following through on the plans for herself and making steady progress:

Sarah is back in school and doing quite well. She is seeing a counselor (specializing in abuse counseling) and seems to be full of self-confidence and appears empowered.

Reflecting on the children, the child protection worker observed:

In the past year there had been no child protection events [e.g., indications of child maltreatment], the children were doing well.

The interview a few weeks later with Sarah supported the child protection's observations about Sarah and the boys' progress:

Based on the information that she gave me for the children while filling out the Looking after Children [assessment of children's development instrument], all kids seem to be doing fairly well. . . . Sarah is doing quite well on her own. She has completed her [employment training] program and is currently on a job placement. . . . She seems to be displaying a great deal of confidence in her abilities and knowledge of where to go. . . . She is still in counseling [for abuse] and finds that it is very useful.

By this time George was released from prison. The interviewer learned from Sarah that he was visiting and that contrary to the plan he was arriving unannounced:

[George] is spending a fair deal of with her, although he is not living there yet. . . . He just comes over whenever and she's fine with that because she really isn't worried about him. She said that [the conference] was good since it got everything out into the open and it resulted in George and her getting along much better. . . . Sarah said that he has smartened-up quite a bit, is trying to get back in school, has managed to control his temper and overall is considerably more calm than before.

In addition, the interviewer learned:

Sarah is not in touch with any of George's family. Shortly after the conference there was a falling out (that apparently had nothing to do with the conference) that left both sides not talking. So, needless to say, little monitoring of the plan occurred and those who were expected to do things did very little.

With regard to George's unexpected visits, this meant that Sarah could not turn to his family to remove him from her home if he came by unannounced. Nor was she turning to parole because he was not arriving under the influence of alcohol or drugs.

Although over a year after the conference the FGC plans were only partially carried out, Sarah continued to be satisfied with the results. She was following through on her counseling and, as agreed, the service providers were providing the necessary funding. The same follow-through was not the case for George as well as his relatives, who by this time were not speaking with Sarah. This falling out between Sarah and George's family was worrisome in that she did not have their support in evicting George from her premises when he arrived unexpectedly. At the same time, she was no longer receiving direct pressure from them to reunite with George no matter how he behaved. Fitting the pattern of other mothers taking part in the FGC project, Sarah cut ties with some nonsupportive relatives while enhancing connections with some professionals (Burford & Pennell, 1998). The outcome study followed the F. family for a year and half after conferencing and for much of that time George was still in prison. Thus, unlike other participating families where the impact on abusers could be assessed, information is not available on whether or not over time George resumed his abusive behaviors. Because of the time lag in George's release, in all likelihood this family would have benefited from a second FGC to update the plan to meet the current situation. This could not occur because the project was no longer in effect. Nevertheless at the time of the final interview, Sarah had made progress through her counseling and employment efforts and had made strides in her self-confidence.

RESOLVING CHILD MALTREATMENT
AND DOMESTIC VIOLENCE

Common fears of FGC:

* Conferencing will decriminalize family violence.

FGC guiding principle:

* Sustain community and family partnerships that safeguard survivors.

The Family Group Decision Making Project tested FGC as a planning forum dedicated to stopping both child maltreatment and domestic violence rather than treating them in isolation from each other (cf. Carter & Schechter, 1997). The outcome study found that the thirty-two participating families showed an overall decline in indicators of child maltreatment and domestic violence while the reverse trend was apparent for a nonparticipating group of thirty-one families (Burford & Pennell, 1998; Pennell & Burford, (forthcoming)). These comparative findings came from analysis of child protection files one year before and one year after conferencing. The same pattern for the participating families was evident in police files and from private interviews with 115 family group participants. The convergence of findings from multiple sources supports the conclusion that FGC promotes safety for child and adult family members in a one- to two-year period postconferencing.

The F. family exemplifies a family violence situation in which the father's abuse of his partner and children was sustained by his family's norms on family violence and his intimidation of his wife's family, as well as by the lack of services for abused women and children. The incarceration of the father provided a limited period of protection for the mother and children, who all dreaded that on release he would return to their home. The mother was strongly pressured by her husband and his large family to accept him back. The FGC offered a forum in which the father's and mother's families came together to learn about the impact of family violence from the perspectives of protective authorities, women's advocates, and child and adult family members. The preparations in advance of the conference and the information given at the conference together assisted the family group to employ effectively their private time for deliberations. The family group generated a plan that parole and child welfare readily accepted and agreed to finance. The system of approval helped to ensure that the interests of child and adult survivors were addressed in the plan and also ensured needed financing of services requested. Because of the father's delayed discharge from prison, only parts of the plan could be put into effect right away and its impact on his long-term behavior cannot be evaluated. Using the plan well, the mother made significant strides in her confidence and employability, and the children progressed in a range of developmental areas.

Conferencing for the F. family and other participating families meant that they had existing legal measures to protect their safety (cf. MacLeod, 1990; Stark, 1996). For the F. family, participation did not shorten (or lengthen) the father's length of incarceration nor did it remove supervision by parole and child welfare. In addition to the extant provisions, conferencing meant that a safety plan was set in place for the mother and children with the input, approval, and resourcing of family, relatives, friends, and service providers. Because the plan was constructed by the family group, they could shape the action steps to fit their particular situation and culture and attend to needs of both child and adult family members. In so doing, conferencing helped to reduce the distance between the family and various service providers and promoted a greater sense of partnership to stop family violence.

NOTE

Gale Burford and Joan Pennell served as the principal investigators and project administrators for the Family Group Decision Making Project in Newfoundland and Labrador. The project and evaluation was made possible through funding from Health Canada (Family Violence Prevention Division), Human Resources Development Canada (Employability and Social Partnerships), Justice Canada (Discretionary Funds Section), and Solicitor General of Canada (Police Policy and Research). The Labrador Inuit Health Commission cosponsored the project in Nain.

REFERENCES

American Humane Association (1997). *Innovations for children's services for the 21st century: Family group decision making and Patch.* Englewood, CO: Author.

Bartholet, E. (1999). *Nobody's children: Abuse and neglect, foster drift, and the adoption alternative.* Boston: Beacon.

Bograd, M. (1992). Values in conflict: Challenges to family therapists' thinking. *Journal of Marital and Family Therapy, 18*(3), 245–56.

Braithwaite, J., & Daly, K. (1994). Masculinities, violence and communitarian control. In T. Newburn & E. Stanko (Eds.), *Just boys doing business? Men, masculinities and crime* (pp. 189–213). London: Routledge.

Burford, G., & Pennell, J. (1995). The family group decision making project: An innovation in child and family welfare. In B. Galaway & J. Hudson (Eds.), *Canadian child welfare: Research and policy implications* (pp. 140–53). Toronto, ON: Thompson Educational.

Burford, G., & Pennell, J. (1996). Family group decision making: Generating indigenous structures for resolving family violence. *Protecting Children, 12*(3), 17–21.

Burford, G., & Pennell, J. (1998). *Family group decision making: After the conference—progress in resolving violence and promoting well-being: Outcome Report* (vols. 1–2). St. John's: Memorial University of Newfoundland, School of Social Work.

Burford, G., Pennell, J., & MacLeod, S. (1995). *Manual for coordinators and communities: The organization and practice of family group decision making* (rev.). St. John's: Memorial University of Newfoundland, School of Social Work.

Carter, J., & Schechter, S. (1997). *Child abuse and domestic violence: Creating community partnerships for safe families: Suggested components of an effective child welfare response to domestic violence.* San Francisco: Family Violence Prevention Fund.

Connolly, M., & McKenzie, M. (1999). *Effective participatory practice: Family group conferencing in child protection.* Hawthorne, NY: Aldine de Gruyter.

Hansen, M., & Harway, M. (Eds.) (1993). *Battering and family therapy: A feminist perspective.* Newbury Park, CA: Sage.

Herrenkohl, E., Herrenkohl, R., & Toedter, L. (1983). Perspectives on the intergenerational transmission of abuse. In D. Finkelhor, R. Gelles, G. Hotaling, & M. Straus (Eds.), *The dark side of families: Current family violence research* (pp. 305–16). Beverly Hill, CA: Sage.

Hodgson, M., & Client: Phyllis. (1990). In T. Laidlaw, C. Malmo, & Associates, *Healing voices: Feminist approaches to therapy with women* (pp. 33–44). San Francisco: Jossey-Bass.

Hoff, L. (1990). *Battered women as survivors.* New York: Routledge.

Jaffe, P., Wolfe, D., & Wilson, S. (1990). *Children of battered women.* Newbury Park, CA: Sage.

Johnson, H. (1996). *Dangerous domains: Violence against women in Canada.* Toronto: Nelson Canada.

Kaufman, G. (1992). The mysterious disappearance of battered women in family therapists' offices: Male privilege colluding with male violence. *Journal of Marital and Family Therapy, 18*(3), 233–43.

MacLeod, L. (1990). *Sharing the responsibility for justice.* Speech presented at the Provincial Symposium on Woman Abuse and the Criminal Justice System, Moncton, New Brunswick.

Mahoney, M. (1991). Legal images of battered women: Redefining the issue of separation. *Michigan Law Review, 90*(1), 24–56.

Marsh, P., & Crow, G. (1998). *Family group conferences in child welfare.* Oxford: Blackwells. Pahl, J. (Ed.) (1985). *Private violence and public policy.* London: Routledge & Kegan.

Paterson, K., & Harvey, M. (1991). *An evaluation of the organization and operation of care and protection family group conferences.* Wellington, New Zealand: Department of Social Welfare.

Pennell, J. (1995). Encountering or countering women abuse. In P. Taylor & C. Daly (Eds.), *Gender dilemmas in social work: Issues affecting women in the profession* (pp. 89–105). Toronto: Canadian Scholars' Press.

Pennell, J., & Burford, G. (1994). Widening the circle: The family group decision making project. *Journal of Child and Youth Care, 9*(1), 1–12.

Pennell, J., & Burford, G. (1995). *Family group decision making: New roles for "old" partners in resolving family violence: Implementation Report* (vols. I–II). St. John's: Memorial University of Newfoundland, School of Social Work.

Pennell, J., & Burford, G. (1997). Communities of concern for resolving child and adult abuse: The family group decision making project. In G. Burford (Ed.), *Ties that bind: An anthology of readings on social work and social welfare in Newfoundland and Labrador* (pp. 280–89). St. John's, NF: Jesperson.

Pennell, J., & Burford, G. (1999). *Family group decision making: Communities stopping family violence: Questions and answers.* Monograph prepared for Health Canada, Family Violence Prevention Division. Hull, PQ: Minister of Public Works and Government Services.

Pennell, J., & Burford, G. (forthcoming). Family group decision making: Resolving child sexual abuse. In G. Burford (Ed.), *Broken icons: Essays on child sexual abuse.* St. John's, NF: Jesperson.

Pressman, B. (1989). Wife-abused couples: The need for comprehensive theoretical perspectives and integrated treatment models. *Journal of Feminist Family Therapy, 1*(1), 23–43.

Ptacek, J. (1988). Why do men batter their wives? In K. Yllö & M. Bograd (Eds.), *Feminist perspectives on wife abuse* (pp. 133–57). Newbury Park, CA: Sage.

Shirk, M. (1999). New Zealand social work tactic hits shore, makes waves: Is family group an exciting tool for abused kids and juvenile offenders, or an expensive fad? *Youth Today* (October), 1.

Stark, E. (1996). Mandatory arrest of batterers: A reply to critics. In E. Buzawa & C. Buzawa (Eds.), *Do arrests and restraining orders work?* (pp. 115–19). Thousand Oaks, CA: Sage.

Stark, E., & Flitcraft, A. (1996). *Women at risk: Domestic violence and women's health.* Thousand Oaks, CA: Sage.

Statistics Canada (1993). The violence against women survey. *The Daily*, November 18.

Straus, M., & Gelles, R. (1990). *Physical violence in American families: Risk factors and adaptations to violence in 8,145 families.* New Brunswick, NJ: Transaction.

Taylor, I. (1991). For better or for worse: Caring and the abused wife. In C. Baines, P. Evans, & S. Neysmith (Eds.), *Women's caring: Feminist perspectives on social welfare* (pp. 204–233). Toronto: Oxford University Press.

Toronto: McClelland & Stewart. Wilson, M., & Daly, M. (1994). Spousal homicide. *Juristat Service Bulletin, 14*(8), Statistics.

Section III   Introduction: Comparative
Practices

JOE HUDSON and GALE BURFORD

Chapters in this section describe the implementation of family group conference programs in several countries and states. Coming out of these experiences, program design and implementation issues are described and assessed, along with questions about the manner and extent to which conferencing principles are actually reflected in practice. Chapter authors have all been closely involved with conferencing programs, serving as researchers, program consultants, trainers, and staff persons, and the observations made are often supported by evaluation research findings.

Most fittingly, Mike Doolan and Pam Phillips begin this section with a description of the New Zealand FGC development and implementation experience. Knut Sundell follows with a description of Swedish experiences, along with evaluation research findings on the first three years of practice. Peter Marsh and Gill Crow then describe legislation, policy, and research frameworks influential in conferencing developments in England and Wales, along with major policy and practice issues. Linda Crozier follows with a description of the evolution of conferencing in Northern Ireland within the context of the civil strife that country has undergone. Conferencing implementation in the United States is then described by Lisa Merkel-Holguin, followed by Paul Ban's description and assessment of conferencing initiatives in four Australian states. Judy Cashmore and Patricia Kiely then complement Ban's discussion by describing the New South Wales experience at implementing and evaluating conferences. The final chapters by Joan Pennell and Marie Weil; Paul Sivak, Nathaniel Green, and Teri Kook; and Ted Keys and Anna Rockhill describe North Carolina, California, and Oregon experiences of implementing conferencing programs, respectively.

PROGRAM DESIGN ISSUES

Key design issues addressed in these chapters include the process followed in designing programs, mandating conferencing programs through legislation or the use of guidelines, contracting out, referral population, and timing.

Processes Followed in Designing Programs
An important question addressed in these chapters is the extent to which the actual design and implementation of conferencing programs mirrors principles of teamwork, inclusiveness, and partnership. For example, chapters by Peter Marsh

and Gill Crow; Joan Pennell and Marie Weil; and Paul Sivak, Nathaniel Green, and Teri Kook address this topic, emphasizing the importance of practicing such conferencing principles as inclusiveness and partnership when designing and implementing programs. These authors argue for involving a variety of persons in planning work to ensure that a range of perspectives and interests is considered. Included should be state agency officials, including managers and line-level practitioners, as well as private agency representatives, family members, and cultural groups. The point is that if the work of designing conferencing programs and planning for their implementation fails to demonstrate key conferencing principles, the results of the work are not likely to resemble what conferencing is intended to be about and instead look like old-line state practices with a new label.

Mandating Programs

The issue addressed here is the extent to which a mandated or discretionary approach should be followed to establish conferencing programs. Based on her review of American conferencing practice, Lisa Merkel-Holguin suggests that mandating conferencing practices in legislation may result in poor programming, particularly when insufficient funding is provided. Oregon legislation, as described by Ted Keys and Anna Rockhill, seems to support this point. The key may well be adequacy of resourcing, not whether conferencing is mandated in legislation. Besides the question of mandating conferencing practices in legislation, these chapters address the related question as to whether conferencing programs should be a required practice or at the discretion of child protection workers. South Australia, Oregon, and New Zealand mandate conferencing, while England and Wales, North Carolina, New South Wales, and Sweden are among the countries and states described where child protection workers have discretion to refer to a family group conference. The main problem with this type of discretionary decision-making is that relying on child protection workers to refer to conferences will likely mean little use of conferencing programs. Peter Marsh and Gill Crow, for example, note that in England and Wales a large proportion of child protection workers do not refer to conferences, and Knut Sundell reports similar practices in Sweden. These authors argue for mandatory referrals of eligible families to family group conferences, leading to greater use of conferencing and then, given reasonable funding and support, conferencing processes are more likely to become the accepted way of doing child protection work.

Organizational Capacity

The question here for the design of conferencing programs is whether they should be operated by a state agency or contracted to local private agencies. Peter Marsh and Gill Crow deal thoughtfully with this issue and identify advantages and disadvantages of contracting for family group conferences, as compared to a state agency retaining responsibility for local conference programs. Among the advantages of contracting are that the roles of coordinators and referral workers will be more distinct, with less likelihood of coordinators maintaining a neutral position and being co-opted by state workers. Arguments against contracting conferencing projects include difficulties of integrating the local project into mainstream practices and reduced sense of ownership by state officials, with increased vulnerability of the project to state agency budget cuts.

Referral Population and Timing

What should be the target population for a conferencing program? Should a program be targeted at high-need and high-risk families and their children or serve a broad spectrum of families? An important consideration here is the cost of conferencing programs. Also, the population of families to be served relates directly to the decision point in the child protection system at which referrals are made to conferences. A conferencing program could accept referrals early in the child welfare system, but these families may not have such severe needs as other families with children likely to be placed in out-of-home living arrangements. The objectives to be met by the program—whether as a child protection service for all families seen to be at risk as in New Zealand, or as an alternative service to conventional practices for families with children likely to be placed in out-of-home living arrangements—should ultimately dictate answers to this question. But without clear specification of the target populations to be served, conferencing programs pose challenges for implementation and evaluation.

IMPLEMENTATION ISSUES

A number of implementation issues are raised in these chapters. Their number and variety attests to the critical place of policy and program implementation. The extensive body of research reported on program implementation underscores the point that implementation is a lot more than the time between an idea for a program and convening the first conference. In her chapter, Lisa Merkel-Holguin refers to "model drift" in describing the way operating programs are implemented to fit with local circumstances, while contradicting the theoretical and philosophical spirit and intent of conferencing. Paul Sivak and his colleagues illustrate how family group conferences can easily get converted into poor child protection practice, with a decline in adherence to basic principles and return to familiar practices. Paul Ban also gives support for this concern when reporting that in Western Australia, only one of four family group conference pilot projects remained loyal to design. Ban also makes the important point that without careful specification of the steps to be carried out to plan and hold conferences, little change is likely to occur in conventional case-planning practices. This detailed specification should be in legislation according to Ban, while Lisa Merkel-Holguin argues for guide-lines to set the practice standards to be met. All chapters in this section can be read as implementation case studies, pointing to the many issues that arise during implementation and having substantial implications for the extent to which the operational program resembles the program as designed.

Funding Adequacy

A number of implementation issues relating to resourcing conferencing programs are covered in these chapters. One is the adequacy of funding for the position of family group conference coordinator. The number and complexity of coordinator tasks were described in the previous section, and chapters here underscore the point that without adequate resourcing, the coordinator's work will not get done. In her assessment of American conferencing developments, Lisa Merkel-Holguin observes that many conferencing programs have not adequately funded the coor-dinator position, while Paul Ban questions the extent to which Tasmania's legisla-tion providing for the use of independent coordinators will be adequately funded.

A related resource issue addressed in these chapters concerns statutory work-ers responsible for conference referrals. In their assessment of the Oregon expe-rience, Ted Keys and Anna Rockhill note that funding constraints posed the biggest implementation challenge, particularly the lack of resources allocated to state child welfare workers for carrying out the extra work seen as involved with conferencing. Since these workers were often responsible for referring to confer-ences as well as serving as conference coordinators, the issue of inadequate re-sources gets magnified, and large caseloads allow little time to adequately plan and hold conferences. Knut Sundell supports this point in his report that a large proportion of surveyed statutory workers in Sweden saw conferencing programs as requiring added work for them, while additional resources were not provided. Joan Pennell and Marie Weil see resourcing as the biggest challenge to imple-menting conferencing programs and as a consequence of limited conferencing funding, see child welfare workers closing cases prematurely before conferenc-ing plans have been completed. Caseloads simply do not allow for seeing plans through to completion so that family crises are addressed and temporarily re-solved, but no resources are allowed for continuing services and supports. The next crisis then calls and Band-aid solutions get applied again. Fueling this kind of practice-by-crisis and exaggerating the problem of inadequate resources is a lack of proper orientation and training provided to statutory workers about the purpose and process of conferencing programs. The importance of ongoing ori-entation and training, not one-shot efforts, is dramatically illustrated by Knut Sundell in his report of the Swedish experience, where almost half the social workers turned over during the two-year family group conference implementation period, with new workers having no training in the conferencing initiative. The poor practices likely to result may then be attributed to the faulty concept of family group conferencing, rather than to poor implementation.

In summary, these authors are consistent in their views about the importance of adequately resourcing conferencing programs. Practically, this means adequately funding and supporting the work of coordinators, providing for the reasonable support of services called for by conference plans, reducing caseloads of state child protection workers so they can reasonably prepare and participate in conferences, and providing funds to orient and train coordinators and referring workers.

Locating Coordinators and Defining Their Roles

Addressed in these chapters are questions about where conference coordinators are located and, specifically, whether they should be placed in the same agency as child protection workers who refer to conferences. A related issue is the extent to which the duties of coordinators are distinct from the responsibilities of statutory workers. Where coordinators are located is likely to directly affect the extent to which they are seen as neutral and independent. Lisa Merkel-Holguin, for example, emphasizes the importance of separating the role of coordinator from statutory workers responsible for referring to conferences, providing information, and assisting in the resourcing of plans. Ted Keys and Anna Rockhill support this point in describing Oregon practices under state Family Group Decision Meeting legislation in which referral workers may also serve as coordinators. These authors observe that this has led to family members being afraid to share information at conferences for fear of its being used against them. This contrasts with the New Zealand experience described by Mike Doolan and Pam Phillips as well as the state of South Australia described by Paul Ban, in which coordinators and child protection workers are located in different state agencies with distinct sets of responsibilities. Judy Cashmore and Patricia Kiely note that locating coordinators and child protection workers in different departments or agencies fosters perceptions of coordinator independence. A slightly different approach is taken in the Australian states of Victoria and Western Australia, where coordinators are employed by the statutory child welfare authority, but located in administrative units separate from child protection staff. However, the extent to which this type of firewall arrangement counters perceptions of coordinator bias is at least questionable. On the one hand, family members are not likely to appreciate the subtle significance of coordinators and child protection workers operating out of separate administrative units in the same department and more likely to see them as working for the same agency. On the other hand, the point could be made that it is not so much where the coordinator is located that makes a difference to families, as it is a matter of clearly specifying the tasks to be carried out and providing enough resources to reasonably carry out the work in line with conferencing principles.

Preparing, Holding, and Following Up Conferences

Several chapters emphasize the importance of properly planning, holding, and following up on family group conferences. For example, Lisa Merkel-Holguin emphasizes the importance of proper conference planning and preparation, estimating twenty-two to thirty-five hours required for each conference, and Judy Cashmore and Patricia Kiely report similar findings from the New South Wales project. Ted Keys and Anna Rockhill support the importance of conference planning, seeing this as a major deficiency of Oregon conferencing practice. As these authors report, conference preparation in Oregon often amounted to little more than a recorded set of instructions left on the phone with the family by child protection workers.

Several of these chapters report that a major problem in holding conferences is a failure to provide for private family time. Ted Keys and Anna Rockhill describe Oregon research showing that families are not given an opportunity to have private family time during conferences. Lisa Merkel-Holguin observes that failing to allow for private family time makes conferencing look like traditional case planning practices with professionals talking to themselves in front of families, making decisions affecting family members. Failing to provide for private family time is one way to control a conference. Other methods of professional control include withholding information, failing to adequately prepare families for conferences, unilateral decision-making, dictating conferencing plans, as well as setting unreasonable and nonnegotiable bottom lines or conditions to be met by conferencing plans.

Not dealt with very extensively in these chapters is the importance of holding review meetings and following up on original family group conference plans. This raises a question about how plausible it is to expect that a single conference can have significant long-term outcomes with families having long-standing and serious difficulties in living. Might it not be more realistic to plan for a series of conferences, each building on and supporting the incremental gains from earlier meetings? Judy Cashmore and Patricia Kiely refer to this when they describe the main problem with the conferencing project in New South Wales as being the lack of follow-through on conferencing commitments by family members and child protection workers. These authors note that putting a review process in place midway through the project proved helpful to families in completing their plans.

17   Conferencing in New Zealand

Child Protection

MIKE DOOLAN and PAM PHILLIPS

The family group conference as a legal process for resolving issues of child abuse and neglect outside formal court proceedings began in New Zealand on November 1, 1989, when the Children, Young Persons and Their Families (CYP&F) Act 1989 came into effect. While the family group conference is one of the better known aspects of this law, a number of other provisions support new ways of working with families having abuse and neglect issues.

New Zealand's radical new child protection laws, as embodied in the CYP&F Act, grew out of and were influenced by three key social and professional debates taking place at that time. These debates centered around the economic reforms introduced by the newly elected Labour Government, which raised the issue of the role of the state in the lives of ordinary citizens. Also important was the changing community perception of the role of professionals, as the new political and economic climate forced people and groups to use their own resources to meet social needs. As reliance on the "experts" decreased, communities called for greater professional accountability to individual clients and client groups. Running through and reinforcing these discussions were those relating to the indigenous people of New Zealand who were making new and more determined efforts to secure self-determination in a monocultural legal system that had traditionally placed little value on Maori customs, values, and beliefs.

To provide some perspective on New Zealand developments, two core systems can be seen as providing frameworks within which child protection services are carried out: the medicolegal and the ecological approaches. The medicolegal system is characterized by:

- A child-focused practice paradigm with attention centered on the child, with parents and extended family having less importance in decision-making processes.
- Investigative/forensic practice with social services largely provided by agencies other than state child protection services.
- Mandatory reporting of child abuse with sanctions for failure to report.
- Child abuse registers for recording details of children at risk.
- Resolution processes dominated by professional and/or court decision-making, with strong reliance on court-dominated outcomes and resolution processes.

- Court processes that ensure social workers are held accountable for their decisions and through which families can seek redress.

The alternative and quite different ecological system, which New Zealand is attempting to consolidate, is characterized by:

- A child-focused, family-centered practice paradigm. Emphasis is given to the child or young person staying within his or her family or family group and family decision-making is strongly supported.
- An initial inquiry followed by an assessment of need and either the direct provision or coordination of services by social workers.
- Voluntary reporting supported by community and professional education on child abuse and neglect.
- Public awareness programs focused on enhancing the recognition of abuse and neglect and how to respond when this occurs.
- Information sharing by means of joint working arrangements with other groups or agencies, such as the police, and through case conferencing and other similar processes that gather community expertise.
- Non–court-based resolution wherever possible.
- Non–court-based accountability mechanisms.

The initial draft of the CYP&F Act put heavy emphasis on the interests of the child as the first and paramount importance in any consideration of the child's welfare. This emphasis prompted an extensive public debate that eventually led to careful wording in the Act to balance both the interests of the child and the importance of family. In practice, however, it has at times been difficult to balance the fine line between the interests of the child and the importance of family. A 1994 amendment to the legislation strengthened the "paramountcy of the child principle," whereby the care and protection provisions of the Act should ensure that "the welfare and interests of the child or young person shall be the first and paramount consideration" (Children, Young Persons, and Their Families Amendment Act 1994, section 3). The family group perspective means that social workers, as agents of the state, will work in partnership with families and family groups to help them provide safe and nurturing environments for their children.

THE FAMILY GROUP CONFERENCE

The family group conference is the statutory process that is central to the CYP&F Act. It is a legal construct with entitlements, processes, and obligations clearly spelled out. The decision-making processes are governed by the principles of the Act. They are the linchpin of the legislation, providing the context for all procedures and giving guidance to those using the Act. These principles are:

- Participative decision-making. The family group should participate in decisions affecting their children [CYP&F Act, section 5(a)].
- Strengthening of familial relations. Wherever possible, the relationship between the child and his or her family should be maintained and strengthened [CYP&F Act, section 5(b)].
- Consideration of the child's welfare and stability of the extended family. Consideration must be given to how a decision concerning a child will affect welfare and the stability of his or her family [CYP&F Act, section 5(c)].
- Consideration of the child's wishes. Ascertaining the wishes of the child and giving appropriate weight to these, having regard to the age, maturity, and culture of the child [CYP&F Act, section 5(d)].
- Obtaining the child's and the caregiver's support. Effort should always be made to obtain the support of the child and his or her parents, guardians, and caregivers when taking action under the Act [CYP&F Act, section 5(e)].
- Deciding and implementing decisions within a time frame appropriate to the child. Decisions affecting a child should be made and implemented within time frames appropriate to the child's sense of time [CYP&F Act, section 5(f); Trapski's Family Law, 1998].

Under the Act, statutory officials called Care and Protection Coordinators were introduced. Their primary role is convening and facilitating the family group conference. Coordinators receive referrals from social workers after an investigation and assessment. It is not the role of the conference to investigate whether there is a care and protection concern. Rather, the role of the conference is to consider such matters relating to the care and protection of the child or young person, and this includes reaching agreement on whether the child is in need of care or protection. Unless there is an urgent safety issue, a social worker cannot make an application to court for a declaration that a child or young person is in need of care and protection unless a coordinator has convened a family group conference.

The role of the statutory social worker changed with the introduction of the Act. Where previously the social worker had been the key decision-maker following the outcome of an investigation, he or she now must work within the principles of the Act to ensure the safety and well-being of the child or young person by:

- assessing immediate risk to the child and establishing appropriate response times;
- conducting a thorough investigation;
- identifying and understanding the care or protection issues;
- referring the matter to a coordinator, if the social worker believes statutory intervention is required;
- explaining his or her actions and concerns to the family group conference;

- being satisfied that the decisions, recommendations, and plans of the family group conference address the care or protection issues.

The family group conference is made up of three phases: setting-up, private deliberations, and reaching agreement. Decisions that need to be made in the setting-up phase are:

- **Who should attend the conference.** The legislation identifies a number of people who are entitled to attend and be party to decision-making. This entitlement to attend includes the child or young person, any member of the child or young person's family group, the coordinator, the social worker, counsel for child, and any other person the family wish to have attend. Decisions for the coordinator at this stage include deciding on the makeup of the family group and whether any persons should be excluded from the conference.
- **Where and when to hold the conference.** The legislation requires the coordinator to consult widely with the family group to determine the time, date, venue, and procedure for the conference. The procedure identified for the conference is most often based on the cultural protocols of the child or young persons' family group.
- **What information the conference will need to make an informed decision.** This may include information to enable the conference participants to determine whether the child is in need of care and protection as well as information on services available to address issues identified.

The setting-up phase is also helpful in alerting coordinators to potential difficulties that may arise at the conference. By identifying issues at this stage, such as relationship issues between family members, the coordinator has the opportunity to work out strategies to deal with areas of dissension.

The conference begins when the entitled members come together at the agreed time, date, and place. The initial gathering of the family group, along with others involved, is often a critical point as the members of the conference may not know each other and may also bring with them conflicts and distrust. At this time it is important that the coordinator negotiates some ground rules, and takes time to explain procedures and the role of all members for the conference. All entitled members of the conference must agree that the child is in need of care or protection before proceeding to make plans, and also agree with the decisions, recommendations, and plans made. At any time during the conference the family group may deliberate in private. The proceedings of the conference are held to be privileged and confidential.

Following a welcoming statement, introductions and setting of ground rules, the coordinator invites the social worker to present information and the basis of concerns for the care and protection of the child. The aim of this stage of the conference is to ensure that the participants receive all of the information they require to make a responsible decision. The social worker must clearly state to all present that they believe the child is in need of care or protection and the reasons for this belief. Others may also be asked to present and discuss their information.

Following the information-sharing phase, it is usual for the family group to deliberate in private. They must decide whether they believe that their child is in need of care and protection and begin to make plans to remedy the situation. When the family completes their private deliberations they are joined by other members of the conference to complete a plan that will ensure the safety and well-being of the child or young person. The coordinator's responsibility at this stage is to guide the conference to develop a plan that is comprehensive, addresses the child's need for care and protection, and is in accordance with the principles of the Act. A good plan fits the age of the child or young person and the circumstances requiring intervention. Each factor that has been identified as placing the child or young person at risk should be addressed in the plan.

A change of caregiver is the most significant outcome of a family group conference. In line with the principles of the Act, a child is only removed from the family group if there is serious risk. The first consideration must always be a safe placement within the family group. All of the entitled members must agree with the decisions of the conference and their time frames for completion of tasks and review dates. The coordinator makes a written record of the decisions, recommendations, and plans, and distributes them to persons entitled to receive them.

REFERENCE

Trapski's Family Law (1998). Children, Young Persons, and Their Families Act, *Introduction to care and protection of children* (NT.3.03). New Zealand.

Family Group Conferences
in Sweden

KNUT SUNDELL

If one country were to be singled out that in practice resembles the modern welfare state, postwar Sweden would definitely be a top contender. The Swedish child
welfare system emphasizes a family service orientation that gives children and
parents the right to receive support if needed, stressing partnership with the family. This attitude is exemplified by the Social Services Act, 1980, regulating social support and interventions such as financial assistance, preschool childcare,
care of the elderly and handicapped, and care of substance abusers. A second act,
the Care of Young Persons Act, 1980, provides the authority to take individuals
under the age of twenty into care without the parent's or the individual's consent.
Swedish child welfare legislation makes no strict distinction between child protection and youth justice.

Although theoretically the Swedish child welfare system emphasizes family services and partnership with families, practice differs somewhat. Three of four investigations are initiated because a report has been made, and only one of four investigations is started because of an application from the parents or the child. As
in other countries, the Swedish child protection system is characterized by such
problems as a high rate of underreporting suspicions of child abuse and neglect to
the social services, many reports not substantiated, and a high recurrence rate.

IMPLEMENTATION AND EVALUATION

The implementation of family group conferencing (FGC) in Sweden was launched
and run by the Swedish Association of Local Authorities (SALA) with the aid of
a grant from the Swedish Ministry of Health and Social Affairs. The National
Swedish Board of Health and Welfare and Center for Evaluation of Social Sciences funded the evaluation. When preparing for implementation, representatives
of SALA contacted professionals in the United Kingdom that had already implemented FGCs. This initial contact eventually was extended to include the use of
British social workers as teachers in training Swedish social workers about FGC
procedures. Consequently, the FGC model implemented in Sweden closely parallels the model used in the United Kingdom in respect to social workers referring families to a FGC and the use of "nonprofessional" coordinators.

From twenty-three local authorities that applied to participate in conferencing
implementation, SALA selected ten representing different regions of Sweden.

The local authorities represented metropolitan areas, industrial towns, and rural districts. To participate, each local authority had to meet two vital criteria: there had to be social workers in favor of using FGCs and local political support. These criteria were not always met. In each local authority at least one project leader was appointed. The only financial support given local authorities was training for coordinators and social workers. The local authorities were chosen at the end of 1995, training of social workers and coordinators initiated early in 1996, and the first FGCs held in May 1996. By October 1996, all ten local authorities had held at least one FGC.

This chapter describes the implementation process from May 1996 until May 1998, focusing on all FGCs held between November 1996 and October 1997. A total of 74 FGCs involving 111 children were organized and carried out during this period. The 111 children in these FGCs were compared with a random sample of 183 children (controls) that were not referred to a FGC during the same period. Each of the FGC and control children was followed up twelve months after the close of the investigation.

THE FAMILY REFERRALS

The FGCs were compared with a random sample of traditional child protection investigations in order to obtain a fuller understanding of the referral process. Results disclosed, somewhat surprisingly, that the social workers provided only one-third (35 percent) of the investigated families with an offer to set up a FGC. Half of the offers from the social workers occurred within the first two months of the investigation. However, there are cases of the family being offered a FGC after more than one year had elapsed. There was wide variation between the ten participants: In two local authorities, less than 20 percent of the families were afforded a FGC; in three local authorities about 40 percent of the families were furnished with a FGC; in four local authorities approximately half of the families were offered a FGC; and in one local authority two thirds were provided with a FGC.

The families offered an opportunity for a FGC differed in two respects from those not offered FGCs. First, the social workers of the former group generally had a more positive attitude toward the FGC model. Second, the social workers of families offered a FGC claimed that these families were less willing to collaborate during the child protection investigation. In all other aspects, the two groups were comparable.

Of the families offered a FGC, only about one-quarter accepted. Those families accepting FGCs differed significantly in several respects from those declining. The families accepting the offer were more frequently in contact with the social services, and their children had more experience in out-of-home care. The social workers also judged the families accepting a FGC as having somewhat more serious problems than those families declining the offer. Thus, the selection process is partly based on the nature of the problem, with more difficult problems given priority. Because of the serious nature of their problems, parents who were in favor of a FGC were perhaps more willing to try new alternatives to solve problems. Alternatively, it could be that these parents did not wish to challenge the local authority's FGC offer, fearing that this would lead to an out-of-home placement.

Of the invited extended family members, three-quarters were found to attend the FGCs. The average number of participating family members, excluding children, siblings, and parents, was six; the mean average increases to 9.5 when parents and children are also included. The majority of children (67 percent) involved were seen to have participated. Almost all (95 percent) of the children over nine years of age participated in the FGC program.

The families were generally allowed to discuss their problems without the professionals. In a minority of the FGCs (9 percent), a professional, though not a social worker, participated during the private sessions. The reason why the professionals attended the private meetings is unclear, and it is uncertain whether the family invited them for additional support. The presence of a professional was not a factor in the family's satisfaction. Family sessions held in complete privacy were considered just as satisfying by family members as those sessions in which a professional participated.

All families were able to agree on a plan to solve their problems. Of the seventy-four plans that were included in the study, seventy-two (97 percent) were accepted by the social services. Of the two unacceptable plans, one was accepted by the social services at a later date.

EMPOWERED FAMILIES

The FGCs seem to have empowered the families. The extended families spent, on average, 160 minutes in private family time. Such an extended period suggests that the family members were supportive and determined to solve the problems effectively.

Furthermore, in five of six plans (86 percent) the extended family members volunteered to assist the child and parents. The normal support procedure involved having the extended family and the social services or other organizations act jointly in assisting the child and parents. Although 42 percent of the resources contained in the FGC plan were to be provided by the extended family, this still left a great deal to be delivered by social services (35 percent) and other organizations, such as the school (25 percent). Family support was also extensive, including accommodation of the child, and sometimes intrusive (e.g., informing the social services if the parent reverted to former drug use).

The plans also demonstrated that the families frequently addressed the questions that social services asked them to address (e.g., where the child should live). Of the 158 questions asked by social services, 109 (69 percent) were dealt with in the plans. Besides the forty-nine questions not dealt with in the plans, a further seventy-seven areas not specifically addressed by the social services were covered in the plans. One example is that twice as many plans dealt with drug abuse by the parents or young persons, as were identified as problems to be addressed by the social workers (twenty-eight vs. fourteen). Another example is that educational support to the child was present in almost twice as many plans (thirty-one vs. seventeen) as questions social workers wanted addressed.

Immediately following the FGC, each participant was asked to answer a short series of questions. The majority (81 percent) of the 460 extended family participants reported that they were adequately informed about how a FGC works, over four-fifths (86 percent) believed that all the important persons attended the meeting, and almost nine out of ten (89 percent) stated that the social workers had presented adequate information about the problem to be solved. Over three-quarters (76 percent) of the FGC participants indicated that there was sufficient opportunity to express their views during private time and that others (71 percent) respected their convictions. Most (85 percent) were satisfied with the plan, and more than half (54 percent) mentioned spontaneously that they felt empowered to provide help directly after the FGC.

In contrast to traditional child protection investigations, the FGC children and their parents more frequently received some kind of support from social services. Sixty-one percent of the FGC families and almost half (48 percent) of the non-FGC families received support. This finding does not concur with certain Swedish skeptics who feared that FGCs would serve as a method for the local authority to save money.

About one-third of the 111 FGC-associated children changed their living style as a consequence of the FGC. Only one of these children was placed in a residential center. The most frequent alternatives were that the child moved from one parent to the other ($n = 13$), moved to a relative ($n = 8$), and moved from a foster care center to the parents or started their own household (both $ns = 6$). Of the FGC children for whom a placement was required, over two-thirds (70 percent) remained within the extended family but changed their place of residence. The corresponding figure for non-FGC children was just over one-tenth (12 percent).

FOLLOW-UP

The Swedish FGC study evaluated the child's situation twelve months after the child protection investigation was terminated. The results indicate few differences between FGC families and those investigated more traditionally. Irrespective of FGC, three-quarters (75 percent) of the children continued to receive support from social services and one-fifth (22 percent) had been referred a second time. However, only four of 293 children were referred again because of suspected sexual or physical abuse. The rate of re-referral is within the limits of other studies (Farmer & Owen, 1995; Fluke, Yuan, & Edwards, 1999).

Although the situation in general did not reveal any differences between FGCs and traditional cases, one striking difference did emerge. Of those nineteen children that moved to kinship foster homes, seventeen had been from the FGC group and only two from the comparison group. Of all the children, three-quarters (77 percent) of the FGC children and two-thirds (60 percent) of the other children continued to be placed twelve months after the initial child investigation was terminated. This difference is in accordance with findings showing that kinship foster care tends to be both more stable and longer lasting.

IMPLEMENTATION PROBLEMS

The total number of FGCs held was quite small, indicating a serious problem. Of all the investigations that occurred during the study, only 10 percent resulted in a FGC. The number of referred cases varied considerably between local authorities, and the distribution of FGCs over time indicates a decreased use of the model. Approximately half of the local authorities continued to use FGCs two years after the start of the implementation, though on a less frequent basis. This decrease suggests that the social workers became increasingly disappointed with the FGC model over time.

Attitudes among the Social Workers

The main reason for the low rate of FGCs was that the social workers only offered every third parent an opportunity to participate. After two years, less than half (41 percent) of the social workers had referred a family to a FGC. Of these, two-thirds (67 percent) were referred to only one FGCs. These results conflict with the generally positive attitudes reported by the social workers toward FGC. Of the 123 social workers who were involved in the implementation, over three-quarters (76 percent) were positive and very few (2 percent) were negative; the remaining one-fifth (22 percent) were uncertain.

Interviewing nineteen social workers can, at most, provide only tentative explanations to account for the low number of FGCs held. Of the social workers interviewed, fourteen expressed doubt about the FGC, either because of distrust in the use of the extended family or because of fear of losing control. More than one-third of the social workers also reported negative experiences with the FGCs. For instance, several pointed out that they were criticized by the extended family for poor performances in previous investigations. Six of the nineteen social workers claimed that FGCs meant an increased workload.

High Staff Turnover

During the first two years of FGC implementation, over two-fifths (42 percent) of the social workers changed jobs. This high staff turnover might have affected referring to FGCs in two ways. First, the new employees lacked training in and knowledge of the FGC model. Of those social workers employed at the start of the implementation, nine of ten received training. Of those employed after the first FGC was held, only half received some form of training. The latter group felt less informed about the FGC model, and only one-fifth (22 percent) referred a family to at least one FGC, compared with over half (53 percent) of the social workers employed from the beginning of the implementation who referred to FGCs. A second consequence of the high staff turnover is that new employees need time to adjust and raise their level of confidence in order to undertake something "new." No newly hired social worker referred to a FGC until at least a half year had passed on their new work site.

Parents Decline the Offer

Another reason why so few FGCs were held is that three-quarters (75 percent) of the families declined the offer. Some tentative explanations can be offered to account for this high rate of refusal. Based on eighteen interviews with families not participating in FGC: (1) there were no extended family members available to participate; (2) the parents did not have faith in the extended family; (3) the parents did not want to reveal their problems to the extended family; or (4) the parents knew exactly what they wanted and thus were not interested in alternatives such as the offered FGC. These reasons for refusal are consistent with earlier findings (Lupton, Barnard, & Swall-Yarrington, 1995; Trotter, Sheehan, Liddell, Strong, & Laragy, 1999).

Although a parent's refusal is one important explanation for the overall low rate of FGCs, other explanations are warranted. The fact that in some local authorities more than half of the families accepted FGCs supports this contention. Another contributing factor for the low rate of FGCs is that some social workers presented FGCs to parents in a negative light.

Local Implementation

Support for implementing FGCs in the ten Swedish local authorities was generally poor. Implementation was primarily characterized by a top-down perspective with a short preparation time before the first FGC was held, no extra resources to employ a project leader, and restricting participating agencies to those responsible for investigating child abuse and neglect. The importance of project leaders is evidenced by the fact that the three local authorities that increased their number of referred cases during the last six months of the study had employed a project leader. Those local authorities having a project leader specifically employed to run the implementation locally and having well-trained staff had the highest number of FGC referrals. This is consistent with the findings of Marsh and Crow (1998).

Fewer Participants from the Father's Extended Family

In Sweden the parent taking part in child protection investigations has traditionally been the mother. In this study, the mothers were present in almost all the investigations (95 and 88 percent in the FGC and traditional investigation, respectively). Of the fathers, 70 percent participated in the FGC and 60 percent in the traditional investigation. Furthermore, the extended family participated in 45 percent of the investigations involving FGCs and in 33 percent of the traditional investigations. Although the extended families were more often present in the FGC, the results demonstrate that the kin and friends of the father were more often missing compared with the kin and friends of the mother. This was particularly apparent when the mother was the single custodian. In one-third of the FGCs no representative of the father was present while this figure was only 3 percent for the mothers.

Fulfillment of Plans

Another problem related to the extended family was failure to fulfill obligations according to the plan. Of thirty-six parents who were interviewed seventeen months after the FGC was held, slightly less than half (44 percent) reported that extended family members did not satisfy their part of the agreement.

THE FUTURE OF CONFERENCES IN SWEDISH CHILD WELFARE

Today, three years after the first FGC was held in Sweden, more than fifty Swedish local authorities, equaling approximately one-sixth of all local authorities in Sweden, have trained their social workers using the FGC model. This extensive interest is accompanied by 1998 legislation calling for social workers in cases of placement to examine alternative solutions within the extended family. Earlier legislation merely recommended, but did not require child welfare officials to seek this alternative. Thus, the future of the FGC model in Sweden looks promising. Some of the initial early problems with the Swedish FGC model also seem to have been solved. Today, it is understood that one FGC does not bring about instant change, but that a series of FGCs are needed where a succession of problems are dealt with, and the extended family is motivated to continue to support the child and parents.

REFERENCES

Farmer, E., & Owen, M. (1995). *Child protection practice: Private risks and public remedies*. London: HMSO.

Fluke, J., Yuan, Y., & Edwards, M. (1999). Recurrence of maltreatment: An application of the national child abuse and neglect data system (NCANDS). *Child Abuse and Neglect, 23,* 633–50.

Lupton, C., Barnard, S., & Swall-Yarrington, M. (1995). *Family planning? An evaluation of the family group conference model* (Rep. No. 31). University of Portsmouth: Social Services Research and Information Unit.

Marsh, P., & Crow, G. (1998). *Family group conferences in child welfare*. Oxford: Blackwell Science.

Trotter, C., Sheehan, R., Liddell, M., Strong, D., & Laragy, C. (1999). *Evaluation of the statewide implementation of family group conferencing*. Victoria: Government of Victoria, Department of Human Services.

19   Conferencing in England and Wales

PETER MARSH and GILL CROW

This chapter outlines Family Group Conference (FGC) use in England and Wales, in terms of the legislative policy and research frameworks influential in their development. Major policy and practice debates underway are examined, concluding with key questions that will need answering over the coming years if FGCs are to grow and flourish.

LEGISLATION

In England and Wales, FGCs have almost universally developed in the child welfare field, within the context of the overarching legislation covering all child welfare matters, the Children Act 1989. While there is no mention of FGCs in the Act, nonetheless in terms of services, requirements on social services for children, and overall philosophy, the legislation is very much in tune with the conference approach. The Act is firmly based on research stressing the importance of family contact, involvement and participation of service users, and the flexible use of care and other services to support families (Department of Health and Social Security, 1985; Packman & Jordan, 1991). The Act provides a framework for services relevant and supportive to FGCs, but in common with most English and Welsh legislation it has little detail about what form of practice should enact the legal detail. The Act does, however, include requirements that are very relevant to FGCs. For example, it promotes an overall philosophy promoting the idea of partnership between professionals and service users as the practice frame within which work should be undertaken (Marsh, 1990, 1993).

However, like all legislation, there are gaps between the law and policy and practice. Practice differs from the spirit of the Act and its accompanying policy in varying ways. The Act was implemented in a relatively hostile political climate (Frost, 1992) and it has in some ways never been able to show its full potential. It has become clear, for example, that joint work between social services and other agencies, and even within the different parts of social services, has been slow to develop and sometimes completely absent (Audit Commission, 1994), and the development of partnership approaches with service users has been mixed, not least in the face of continuing perceived pressures for child protection.

It is important to bear in mind the dominant role of Council-run social service departments in England and Wales in providing child welfare services to higher risk families. These are by far the majority providers; there are not large numbers of private agency providers. The Council-run social services have been relatively slow in developing innovative approaches to enact the philosophy of the Children Act. Nonetheless the Act is a major opportunity for FGCs, promoting many of the core values explicit or implicit in the model (Lupton & Nixon, 1999, pp. 31–52; Marsh & Crow, 1998, pp. 1–20).

POLICY

The ten years of development under the Children Act show the difficulty of moving services to more family support models. The continued domination of investigative processes to assess risk in the child protection area has been one key factor that has made progress slow on family support and family work. Research has indicated that there should be a move away from the dominant forensic investigation model to a wider enquiry into a need approach (Department of Health, 1995), but the child protection work is still dominant. The more communitarian family support side of the work (Jordan, 1997) is weak. While the Labour Government has attempted to tackle some of the issues (Department of Health—Social Care Group, 1999), it is not clear how far this new program will promote FGCs. In the short term the advantage may be that there will be more money in the system and a greater incentive for new ideas, but there will also be a diversion of management and staff time to cope with the new initiative. In the medium term it may make a more professional and less proceduralistic approach to child welfare work, which could encourage more radical models like FGC. But given that the program does not place much emphasis on family decision-making or family involvement, it may be that there will be little encouragement for FGCs. Other changes now under way in England that could affect the development of FGCs include a new draft framework for the assessment of children. This may help provide families with good information for planning, but emphasis seems to be on the use of assessment information by professionals. Draft guidance for child protection does mention FGCs, but continues to promote very firmly a child protection planning model based on the professional case conference with parents present. Again it is likely that the way these are used by managers and practitioners will dictate whether they provide support or hindrance to the development of FGCs.

RESEARCH

Research in FGCs has been well disseminated, appears influential in the work of FGCs in England and Wales, and well connected to practice. The general climate for the use of research is becoming more positive with the growth of practice and policy interest in "evidence-based decision-making" and the accompanying development work of organizations linking research and services (Research in Practice, 1999). The current English and Welsh review of FGC research (Marsh & Crow, 1999) has been widely disseminated throughout the country. It provides a summary of the main questions that practitioners and policymakers have been asking, and the research addressing these questions. These are summarized here.

Can You Do It?

Initially there were doubts as to whether the extended family still existed as a useful entity for children in Britain's current social culture and, if it did exist, would the extended family members be willing and able to offer support. Experience has shown that where families are contacted and invited, significant family members can nearly always be identified to participate in FGCs. Of these, on average, six to eight attend FCC meetings and, in almost all cases, produce an acceptable plan to meet the identified needs, often to the surprise of the referrer. It has been the complexity of implementing the model in statutory state services that has, if anything, limited the development of the model, so that small-scale projects are still the norm.

Is It Popular?

Feedback from family members has indicated that many are pleased to be given the opportunity to offer support and would recommend the process to others facing difficulties. Satisfaction with the plans among both family and professional participants is high, with the professionals involved reporting positive opinions of the model. However, issues of power and anxieties around accountability in child protection cases have led a proportion of practitioners to avoid referring to FGC projects.

What Does It Do for Children?

Children referred with child protection concerns (up to 65 percent of all referrals in projects in England and Wales) are thought by practitioners to be as well protected or better protected in the great majority of cases through the use of FGCs. The number of children being removed from the child protection register subsequent to the FGC is higher than would be expected in other circumstances, and re-referral rates have been comparatively low, except for long-standing abuse cases. In addition, children have been enabled to maintain contact with their family networks, both through family members becoming carers where public care might otherwise have been needed, and through the facilitation of communication between family members. Placement decisions made at FGCs have been found to be relatively robust, with children experiencing fewer care moves, including fewer moves in and out of state care than would otherwise be expected.

Can You Reduce School Exclusions and Crime?

To date, there are very few English or Welsh projects using FGCs in education or in youth justice, so local research data are scarce, or available only on small numbers of young people. Youth justice workers are increasingly aware of the model and of the international research that is beginning to indicate that FGCs do play a role in reducing offending. In England, FGC instead of a first court appearance seems favored by families and agencies. In education, early work suggests that the model can be used to address education-based problems, and the plans made can lead to the involvement of new forms of help and support from family members and the education system.

Can You Say the Model Is Cost Effective?

Family group conferences are not a cheap option due to the costs of the coordinators' time, venue hire, and other conference facilities. Financial data and analysis are not, in common with other child welfare areas, easily available. As projects in England and Wales have not been on a scale to measure whole population changes, savings estimates rely on the opinion of referring agencies. For this reason researchers have tended to argue only that the FGC model is, overall, cost neutral.

THE CURRENT STATE OF PRACTICE

Legislation, policy, and research on FGCs in England and Wales has supported the development of the model, from both management and practice perspectives. However, practice implementation is still patchy. Although about half of local authority social services have some FGC development, only a few have invested substantially in FGCs, generally in child welfare areas. Perhaps 10 of the 150 or so authorities have made this major commitment, with another thirty running some FGCs, and a further thirty doing the planning work with a low level of current use. Enthusiasm for the model from some staff within one social services department is often offset by suspicion or disinterest from others in the same department. The mainstream work culture is based on very different assumptions from the FGC model regarding, for example, the value of extended family and the role of family decision-making in planning. Many practitioners and policymakers are still involved in debating the principles of the model and the challenges it brings in practice, despite agreement that it accords with government policy and guidance, and despite evidence from practice and research over the past six years that it can be used successfully in England and Wales.

POLICY AND PRACTICE DEBATES

Developing FGC projects is a complex task, with a number of key implementation decisions to be made. The policy and practice issues at the center of these decisions in FGC work have recently been explored with additional interviews with project managers and coordinators in eight of the most well established and substantial projects in England and Wales. The issues investigated provide some insight into the process of running FGCs in England and Wales, and the way the current systems may or may not be able to support this way of working. They relate to the fact that the English and Welsh FGC projects focused on child welfare within social services departments. A brief discussion of these policy and practice issues bearing on FGCs follows.

Steering Groups

The way that FGC projects have most successfully managed to become established and subsequently expand has been through having an influential steering group. Experience has shown that the steering group needs to have representatives from all the agencies potentially involved or affected by the FGC work at a senior management level, and input from those who will be the referrers or champions of the model at the practice level. Both groups need to have time to assimilate the principles behind the model and the implications for their service. If senior managers are not involved, a small project may manage to continue successfully, but without funding or recognition and with no chance of becoming mainstream, it is likely to flounder. If, on the other hand, the senior managers are involved but the practitioners are not included, a project may be ready to go in terms of systems and guidelines, but receive no referrals. There have been examples of both cases in England and Wales over the past six years. Widely based steering groups seem very important for the successful development of the model.

Contracting and Financing

The process of setting a contract with a voluntary organization is complicated. Contracts are relatively inflexible to changes in local conditions and changing them can be time consuming. However, contracts made with organizations outside the local authority are seen as a way of setting standards, which can more easily be maintained. On the other hand, there are concerns that if the local authority accepts a low bid from a voluntary organization, there will be pressure on the project management to cut corners, for instance, by encouraging coordinators to communicate with family members by mail rather than by visiting, or by reducing expectations on family members to travel distances to attend. While contracting out does give clear financial parameters, which allow for realistic planning, critics maintain that it may not allow the flexibility to respond to individual family needs. It may also require more professional time diverted to financial procedures.

Executive and Multiagency Support

Contracting project management to a voluntary organization brings the advantage that the project is perceived as being more "neutral," which may enable partnership with other agencies to be negotiated more smoothly. For instance, the voluntary organization may be able to gather a more influential steering group, and reach agreement on principles and procedures more easily. The local authority then has responsibility for monitoring the contract and will need to liaise closely with the project manager to incorporate the learning points from the project into mainstream practice. This may be difficult as the project manager does not necessarily have access to local authority meetings, and the local authority will not necessarily have any influence over project management once the contract is set. There is the further difficulty that once contracted out, the FGC model will be less high profile within the local authority. As well, there is a danger that commitment to the model and sense of ownership of the work will diminish and the contract may then become vulnerable to cuts. Identified channels of communication between the project manager and named local authority managers are therefore seen to be important, with the local authority managers being of sufficient seniority and influence to support the project in financial and practice matters.

Staff Support and Creativity

The most commonly identified advantage for contracting out project management relates to the issue of staff support and clarity of roles. With coordinators being managed, supervised, and supported by the voluntary organization, the different roles of the coordinator and the social worker are likely to be more widely appreciated. The local authority is then able to focus more on the needs of social workers, which have often been neglected when coordinators are being managed in house. At the same time, the coordinators can more easily maintain their neutrality and resist pressures to fit into or acquiesce to the system's status quo. They may therefore be able to be more creative in meeting the needs of the family.

Compulsion vs. Voluntariness in the Referral Process

One of the recurring difficulties in projects in England and Wales has been practitioner resistance to the model. Research has consistently found that where referral of families for an FGC is left up to the assigned social worker, about a third
of them do not refer families (Marsh & Crow, 1998, pp. 181–82). This, even
though the great majority say they agree with the principles of the model. For
many social workers the model is all right, it just does not seem appropriate for
"their" families. This has led to a debate about the referral process and how it
might address the unequal access to FGCs that results from social workers acting
as gatekeepers. While some projects have continued with voluntary referral, others have set clear criteria for referral that all practitioners are expected to follow.
Comparing data on referral from both types of referral processes, it is clear that
set criteria and accompanying compulsory referral does increase the proportion
of social workers referring families from about 60 to 80 percent (Crow & Marsh,
1998). While this suggests that there is still a small proportion of practitioners
who are avoiding engaging with the model by ignoring, circumventing, or undermining the referral process, it does indicate that families are being offered the opportunity to have an FGC on a more equitable basis.

Social workers in those areas with compulsory referral did not usually like the
imposition of referral routes, but were more willing to accept them if they or their
colleagues had been involved in the development and introduction of the model.
They felt that using set referral criteria had led to the involvement of some "un-
suitable" families in the process, but also included families they would not have
thought of as suitable but who managed the process well. It does appear that social workers often underestimate the ability of families to meet without violence
and make good plans in the best interests of their children.

While compulsory referral increases the number of social workers referring
families and gives more families the opportunity to show that they can work constructively with the model, it also increases the number of referrals that do not result in an FGC. The proportion of "non-FGCs," as we have called them, appears
to rise from 20 to about 50 percent with compulsory referral (Crow & Marsh,
1998). This means that coordinators are being allocated to families and beginning
the process of convening a meeting at some cost to the agency, without the meeting taking place. At first sight this might seem a costly way of offering the model
more equitably. However, when the outcomes of the non-FGC referrals are stud-
ied, it becomes clear that a considerable proportion of the families have managed
to resolve their difficulties themselves without recourse to the FGC. Family resolution occurs in about half of all non-FGCs and seems to be particularly likely
where families have requested that their child be taken into care. Of course, the
ability of the family to resolve the crisis cannot be directly, causally linked to their
introduction to the FGC process via the coordinator, but anecdotal evidence from
coordinators and social workers suggests that initiating the process can be instru-
mental in bringing the family together.

The evidence on compulsory and voluntary referral systems suggests that set referral criteria can be helpful both to the agency and to the family. However, in England and Wales there is no agreement on the issue of compulsory or voluntary referral, with some projects moving from the compulsory use of set referral criteria to a more voluntary referral system, and others moving in the opposite direction. In the light of the evidence and the practice, it may be that compulsory *consideration* of the model, rather than compulsory *referral,* would be the best option for FGC projects.

Targeting Types of Cases

Most projects have found that whatever the agreed upon referral criteria, social workers can identify families on their case load whom they think would be helped by the FGC model, and many want to access the service for these cases. Projects have therefore generally been flexible over the range of referrals accepted, whether in addition to set referral criteria or not. This raises the question as to which types of referrals are best to target, and at what stage of the service provision process, in order to use the model most effectively. Generally speaking, research in England and Wales has failed to provide any clear answers to this question, as successful conferences have been held with almost every type of case at a number of stages of case management in different projects across the country.

Initially, pilot projects targeted cases carrying less risk, such as accommodation requests. Outcomes for this group of cases have been good, with the great majority remaining within their family group after the FGC, and two-thirds maintaining stable placements over at least a year (Marsh & Crow, 1998, pp. 159–60). Where referral has been voluntary, cases of neglect are more often referred, but where referral has been compulsory, cases have been fairly evenly distributed across the other categories of abuse—physical and emotional abuse and neglect. Sexual abuse cases have generally been avoided, both through agreed upon project procedures and by social worker choice, but there have been a number of successful FGCs for sexual abuse cases, demonstrating that there is no reason to rule them out of referral processes completely. The case for maintaining access to the FGC process for a wide range of cases is strong as there is no clear evidence that outcomes differ between types of case. Families almost always make an agreed upon and acceptable plan, which often leads to a reduction in concerns and to comparatively stable living arrangements for the child. The issue is therefore more one of targeting cases that are identified as in need and at relatively high risk, given the additional costs of this approach. Then it will be necessary to provide the service as equitably as possible to those cases.

Regarding the timing of the referral, practitioners report that they would prefer to use the FGC early on in case management as a preventive measure, as they see it as a way of reducing demands on their time. Family members also often say that they wish the FGC had been held sooner, both to reduce distress and to enable the extended family to be involved more effectively. However, there are drawbacks to using a rather costly and difficult process in situations that have not yet been identified as those most in need, and there can also be difficulties in gathering the wider network together when there is not yet a feeling of crisis within the family. Timing of the referral is also a matter of balancing risks. Holding an FGC after the usual procedures have been followed clearly removes a lot of anxiety about risk, but means that the model is seen as an extra. In projects where this has been the referral process agreed upon, there has been some confusion around what the referral is for, because the outcome of standard procedures (for example, a child protection conference) is usually a set of decisions. The FGC may therefore seem superfluous to the family and to the professionals.

Referral for an FGC before, or instead of, the normal practice procedure can be seen to be more obviously productive for the family, but entails perceived risks for the practitioner. If the situation is at crisis point, very short time scales for action may be required and practitioners may feel they have to follow the usual processes to "cover their backs." Whatever the referral route there is therefore a need for considerable multidisciplinary negotiation at a senior management level to ensure that the procedures are fully agreed upon. Practitioners need to know that they will be supported in their work with FGCs and feel confident in using them to the benefit of children even where there are elements of risk. Targeting relatively high-risk cases, with strategic local use for specific groups of children, is probably the best model, with referral for FGC at a point when the family still have space for genuine decision-making.

Effect of Using the Model on Work Practice

The negotiation of agreed upon policies and practice for implementing FGCs at a local level often raises a number of issues for the agencies involved. This seems to be because the FGC model sparks vigorous debate about the principles of child welfare work, and it demands clear procedures that are understood and accepted across a range of professional agencies. The process of implementation therefore tends to show up a lack of clarity in other parts of the organization. For instance, it may show up the inconsistencies in case management, or the unclear professional roles in other decision-making processes. While the reexamination of current policy and practice that this initiates can be seen as a good thing, it does make the FGC implementation process more difficult and stressful at an organizational level.

This sometimes painful process of examining current practice also happens at the practitioner level. Implementing the model often appears to question the values and assumptions at the heart of practice and requires a lengthy process of debate. Implementation is inevitably a "hearts and minds" process. Those engaging in this debate, and then experiencing partnership with families through using FGCs, learn new skills and begin to question their standard practice. Social workers have thus reported changing their own ways of working, and team leaders have confirmed that practitioners working with FGCs tend to develop a more collaborative and respectful approach to families. However, social workers also report experiencing the discomfort of the dissonance between FGC practice and other practice within the same agency. Reports so far are of a beneficial effect on the organization. FGCs have been a change of approach that has sometimes been reflected at a strategic level, with increased weight being given to user views and to consulting community groups as the ethos of collaboration becomes more pervasive.

Coordinator Skills and Employment

Coordinators need to be independent. At the same time, they need to have the confidence and trust of all the parties. Indications so far are that the formal training of the coordinator is less important than interpersonal skills and a commitment to the model (Marsh & Crow, 1998, pp. 83–85), but that the role is complex and demanding (ibid., pp. 122–38). The recruitment of coordinators therefore needs to balance the demand for flexible, creative, and skillful workers with the need for people who have the respect of practitioners as well as family members. Respect comes not only with perceived status but also with the quality of service delivered, which is a concern to those commissioning and managing FGCs. Here again, there may be tension between the need for coordinators to be creative and flexible, and demands for meeting overdetailed standards. There is a real concern in England and Wales, as elsewhere, that the pressure to proceduralize the coordinators' work will diminish their effectiveness. Currently in England and Wales, those employed as coordinators have been genuinely enthusiastic about, and committed to, the model and there has been widespread praise for their skills. Proceduralization is likely to be resisted by these coordinators and could lead to their leaving the work and to a change in the nature of the people recruited to the role.

Costs

Not surprisingly in the current local and international climate of needing to prove the effectiveness of interventions and provide "best value," the cost of FGCs is an issue for policymakers and practitioners. It is therefore important to consider whether the English and Welsh cost of around five hundred pounds per conference provides good value. Unfortunately, it is difficult to judge their value relative to other decision-making processes, as little work has been done on costing, nor has work been done on documenting the medium- or longer-term outcomes for children in terms of a specific decision-making process. Contrary to early managerial expectations, the model has not been found to increase demands on social service departments once it has been introduced and implemented. Overall, managers do not feel that there are more demands on social work time than would normally be the case, and the resources requested by families are thought to be reasonable. In addition, they note the research indications of a slightly reduced need for statutory procedures, legal proceedings, and costly services over the long term, such as state care. Perceived advantages for the organization include an improved public or user image and increased practice in working with other professionals and with families. These advantages also reflect positively on practitioners, who often feel stimulated and motivated by the practice model and appreciate having a way of moving difficult cases on. On the other hand, practitioners also experience some stress in using the model at first, particularly as it is perceived as reducing their power, and they may later feel tension between their new skills of working in partnership with families and the demands of other procedures.

THE NEXT STAGE

The development of FGCs in England and Wales has been an extraordinary success story even without legislative backing, in the face of a relatively unsupportive professional climate and with minimal financial resources. There is no doubt that the work will continue, but whether it will continue to grow and how far it will keep to quality standards are more uncertain questions. Radical proposals within bureaucratic cultures will inevitably struggle. There may be outright objections to such departures from the status quo, and there may be gradual co-option. It is probably the latter that is most damaging to the overall development of FGCs, as it will begin to water down key elements of the model and take away the factors that are associated with its value stance and successful outcomes. The difficulties may be compounded by a confusion of the model's emphasis on minimizing intrusion into family processes, with a desire of service managers to minimize service provision. This is a low-intrusion model, not a low-service model; it is about aspects of self-help, but most situations will need some form of service support to get that help going or to maintain it. Pressures such as these accompanied by misunderstandings and distrust around partnership approaches, with oversimplification and tokenism being two of the main problems, will make the task of increasing the number of high-quality FGCs quite difficult.

It is vital that corners not be cut, and that the principles and values lying behind FGCs be respected. The families who have been helped so far have had this commitment, and the families who could be helped in the future need and deserve it just as much.

REFERENCES

Audit Commission (1994). *Seen but not heard—Co-ordinating community health and social services for children in need.* London: HMSO.

Crow, G., & Marsh, P. (1998). Family group conferences in Haringey. *C&FW Findings Series, 4,* Sheffield: University of Sheffield.

Department of Health (1995). *Child protection—Messages from research.* London: HMSO.

Department of Health—Social Care Group (1999). *Quality protects programme.* London: Department of Health.

Department of Health and Social Security (1985). *Social work decisions in child care.* London: HMSO.

Frost, N. (1992). Implementing the Children Act 1989 in a hostile climate. In P. Carter, T. Jeffs, & M. Smith (Eds.), *Changing social work and welfare.* Buckingham: Open University Press.

Jordan, B. (1997). Partnership with service users in child protection and family support. In N. Parton (Ed.), *Child protection and family support: Tensions, contradictions and possibilities* (pp. 212–22). London: Routledge.

Lupton, C., & Nixon, P. (1999). *Empowering practice? A critical appraisal of the family group conference approach.* Bristol: Policy.

Marsh, P. (1990). Changing practice in child care—the Children Act 1989. *Adoption and Fostering, 14*(4), 27–30.

Marsh, P. (1993). Family preservation and reunification—The need for partnership between professionals and users. In P. Marsh & J. Triseliotis (Eds.), *Prevention and reunification in child care* (pp. 39–53). London: Batsford.

Marsh, P., & Crow, G. (1998). *Family group conferences in child welfare.* Oxford: Blackwell Science.

Marsh, P., & Crow, G. (1999). Family group conferences. *Highlights, 169,* London: National Children's Bureau/Barnardos.

Packman, J., & Jordan, B. (1991). The Children Act: Looking forward, looking back. *British Journal of Social Work, 21*(4), 315–27.

Research in Practice (1999). *Quarterly briefing: Programme 1999/2000.* Dartington and Sheffield: Dartington Social Research Unit/University of Sheffield.

20 The Evolution of Conferencing within Child Welfare in Northern Ireland

LINDA CROZIER

This chapter examines the development throughout Northern Ireland of Family Group Conferences (FGCs) within the welfare field. The legislative background that allowed for the possibility of FGCs, the involvement of the voluntary and statutory sectors, and the importance of the role of the coordinator are reviewed. Northern Ireland has been in the grip of violence for over thirty years. Families have had to cope with the fear of bombs and bullets and few families do not know someone who has been maimed or killed. Those things that the majority of the British Isles take for granted like shopping, travel, and schooling have not gone smoothly in Northern Ireland. At our worst moments, surviving was the priority. Working out other family difficulties never made the priority list at all. Time moves on, however, and we need to be conscious that we are dealing with damaged souls. There are parents who have come together, raised their children, and are looking at grandchildren, all during this thirty-year period; peace is a hope for the future. They know no other life—this is what we work with and this is where we need to begin. Family group conferences can be a part of this process.

Northern Ireland, with a population of approximately 1.6 million, is currently divided into four Health and Social Services Boards (HSSB)—Northern, Southern, Western, and Eastern. Each of the boards has within it trusts. The health boards are purchasers of services while the trusts are providers of the services required by the health boards. Along with colleagues in Juvenile Justice, each of these agencies has been involved in the birth of FGCs in Northern Ireland. The gestation period has been lengthy but necessary, producing offspring that are similar but different, taking on their own personalities and developing at their own rate within their own specific family.

LEGISLATIVE BACKGROUND

The Children and Young Persons Act 1968 lasted within the province until the Children (Northern Ireland) Order 1995 was implemented in November 1996. In the rest of the United Kingdom, legislation had been regularly changing usually as a result of various inquiries, however in Northern Ireland we had other problems that got in the way, namely, "the troubles." Our legislation therefore lasted twenty-seven years without change. The old legislation was primarily focused on child protection. Families were included in child care reviews and in the early years were invited to attend case conferences to present their concerns and hopes and to hear the decisions made by others around the table. As years passed, the families were invited to stay longer and the table disappeared in an effort to make the professionals appear more approachable and the proceedings seem less formal. Other professionals came to accept that openness between the family and them was to be the norm rather than the exception but the process was still heavily weighted against the family. It was always on the professional's premises, at times best suited to their needs and in particular the needs of the GPs, who, it must be said, rarely attended. The new legislation recognizes the need for child protection while at the same time guiding workers into looking at how they can support families who need services, preventing them from entering the child protection system. The new legislation has five guiding principles known as the 5 Ps: paramountcy (the welfare of the child is paramount), parental responsibility, partnership, prevention, and protection.

In the year preceding implementation, training took place provincewide to introduce staff to the legislation. The first year of the Children Order was not only difficult and anxiety provoking, but very much a letdown. There was a concentration on forms, regulations and guidance documents, and policies and procedures. The result was that the philosophy and practice issues of the order were largely overlooked. Social workers felt more like bureaucrats and data collectors and their previous feelings of being deskilled were compounded by all the paperwork.

THE VOLUNTARY SECTOR

In October 1996, Jane Wiffin from the Family Rights Group in England was speaking to a group of Post Qualifying students at Queen's University Belfast. A field social worker, Jim McGrath, sat in her audience and saw how this model embraced partnership and empowerment. When he returned to his agency, he tried to introduce it. The agency gave permission to run a FGC but was unenthusiastic.

In May 1997, a half-day conference was held that sparked interest in conferencing. One outcome was the formation of an Interest Group, including Jim McGrath. He was now working in a family center belonging to the private agency, Barnardos, in Moy, a town forty miles southwest of Belfast. Barnardos was keen to promote FGCs and the family center in Moy was to spearhead this within its organization. Time was spent promoting the model throughout the local trust of Armagh and Dungannon. This raised the profile but not enough to generate referrals.

Still keen and very much a believer in FGCs, Jim McGrath and his line manager agreed to offer this way of working to families who were already attending the family center. Moy saw its first FGC take place with ten family members, neighbors, and a community worker. It was a success, with some of the outcomes being that the family became more involved in protecting the children, there was more awareness of community responsibility, and it brought the managers on board.

Two more FGCs followed, one centered on domestic violence, the other with obsessive/compulsive behavior at its core. The word spread within the trust, social workers began to see the value of FGCs, pressing their managers for more. The local Area Child Protection Committee was provided with awareness training, and in March 1999 the board agreed to pilot FGCs in partnership with Barnardos with some funding released. From 1997 to the present, Barnardos has provided the service to ten family groups. The momentum has gained speed and the agency plans to have a manager, two FGC coordinators, and six sessional workers in the near future. Barnardos sees the capacity growing from forty FGCs in the first year to eighty in each of the following two years.

THE STATUTORY SECTOR

The first statutory agency to grasp the nettle was Homefirst Health and Social Services Trust. In February 1996, a two-day FGC workshop was organized by their Area Child Protection Committee (ACPC) within the northern board. Workshop participants were enthused and resolved to share their experience with other colleagues in their work settings. Eventually it was decided to run a few conferences. In May 1997, they received their first referral and, following a number of referrals that did not proceed to conference, convened their first FGC in August 1997.

This situation involved a teenage boy living in residential care and referred by his review panel. They were concerned that a situation of his drifting in care was evolving. After two conferences, his family proposed a plan to rehabilitate him with them. The plan was accepted by the professionals involved and successfully implemented. Sam and his coworker, Catherine McCambridge, presented this case and their other experiences of working as coordinators to the Regional Interest Group, later formalized as the NI Family Group Conference Forum.

The Ulster Community and Hospitals Trust (UCHT) covers North Down on the eastern side of the province. The FGC had its birth following the May 1997 conference. News was brought back to the trust about this new way of working and the Programme Head for Family and Child Care was furnished with reading material. He was vital in the introduction of conferencing into the Family and Child Care Programme. In February 1998, he led a group to a conference in Essex. This group had staff representing every level within the Programme. The conference opened up the world of FGCs and allowed exploration of issues that the group had identified as needing clarification. Discussions took place as to the best way forward, agreement was reached, and a lunchtime seminar took place. This was followed by a full day of awareness raising and most importantly gaining commitment to this way of working. Crucially, monies were obtained to enable a pilot to proceed.

A Steering Group was established chaired by the Programme Head and included a cross section of staff. This met monthly. It was decided early on that staff needed to be kept informed and therefore it was agreed they would be circulated with copies of the Steering Group minutes. A simple referral form was developed and a system put in place. Despite the initial enthusiasm, many people did not refer. This meant going out again to repeat the message. Staff often ruled out families because they could not see them buying into the process but were not giving families a chance to make that decision for themselves. Therefore the message had to be repeated many times. The Programme Head, recognizing fears and apprehensions that can block introducing FGCs to an organization, cited three key players as having their own fears and apprehensions about conferencing.

Managers:

- Is it going to make more demands on them personally?
- Is it going to make more demands on resources?
- Are they opening a Pandora's box?
- Will they end up with egg on their faces?

Practitioners:

- Will their practice be exposed?
- Where do they stand in terms of participation and partnership?

Families:

- Is partnership real or lip service?
- Information is a powerful weapon; the professionals hold these weapons; they need to be decommissioned!

The pilot project in UCHT eventually got under way during July and August 1998. Coordinators were selected and the first families were contacted in October, having first had the process explained to them by their social workers. Difficulties arose within the staff group. Three points were identified as being of importance: suitability of the family; the "bottom line;" working outside hours. Referrals were still slow to come, but as referrals have grown and success stories have spread, there has been steady growth.

ROLE OF THE COORDINATOR

Child Protection Case Conferences are a key decision-making forum and formal mechanism for the professional and family systems to interact. Families who attended have indicated that they were essentially professional-led meetings. The attendance was overwhelmingly professional, the venue was usually in a professional place, and the timing of meetings was arranged to suit professionals. They found them to be a problem-focused process in which the professionals were seen to be the experts. The professionals can have private time, control the information that is shared, make decisions, and draw up plans. The process was not child friendly. Family group conferencing is a radical restructuring of the decision-making process. It is family led, attendance is overwhelmingly family, the venue is neutral, and the timing suits family members. The families are viewed as their own experts. Information is provided by professionals and considered by the family. The family has private time. The family makes decisions and plans for the consideration of professionals. The process is child friendly and many children see it as their conference. The coordinator's task is to manage the process in a way that creates the maximum potential in each case.

The first contact with potential participants is crucial as it is an opportunity to shape perceptions and expectations. The coordinator is responsible to ensure that professionals and family members understand the reasons for a conference and the importance and value of their involvement. The first meeting with potential participants is also an opportunity to explain how the process will work. Direct, personal contact is vital. People are more likely to discuss their anxieties on a face-to-face basis and more likely to respond to encouragement. Meeting them is respectful and an indication of the importance of their contribution. Coordinators need to be dedicated and tenacious in obtaining face-to-face contact. They also must be enthusiastic about the model, having some positive experiences to draw upon that can be transmitted to potential participants. Parents often say they do not know what the professionals' concerns are, while professionals say that parents fail to take their concerns seriously. Coordinators can reframe these positions and offer conferencing as a way in which the professionals will be encouraged to be clear and precise about their concerns, and the family will be given the opportunity to address the concerns. Extended family members may say that they do not feel that the professionals are doing enough. Again, this can be presented as an opportunity for them to explore what it is that the professionals have to offer.

It may well be that in some situations the outcomes are not significantly different than would be achieved through the existing decision-making models. However, we believe that our experience illustrates that the process of decision-making and planning is so qualitatively different for all concerned that eventually this will become the preferred way of making decisions and plans for children and families.

THE FUTURE

As in other parts of the world the growth rate in Northern Ireland has been slow but steady. Learning is going on and the strength lies in sharing knowledge and contacts. Mistakes have been made and adjustments developed. Conferencing within Northern Ireland's child welfare system may be in its infancy but it is a growing practice. This is particularly dramatic in light of the fact that for over thirty years people have lived in a war zone. Families faced outside dangers alongside difficulties of their own family cultures. Partnership as we see it developing in the conferencing movement would not have flourished but instead would have fallen on stony ground withering before it had the chance to see the light of day. Our history will not go away and it invades all our lives here, but we all have the power to effect change. FGCs may be a small part of that.

21   Diversions and Departures in the Implementation of Family Group Conferencing in the United States

LISA MERKEL-HOLGUIN

What New Zealand mandated by legislation in 1989—the use of family group conferences (FGCs) when children were abused or neglected—numerous countries have since voluntarily imported to resolve similar concerns. While family group conferencing has evolved to such diverse countries as Australia, Canada, England, Sweden, South Africa, and the United States, the phenomena instigating the initiation of this process are commonplace. International data provide a troubling snapshot of worldwide trends, including an increase in the number of children in out-of-home care; a growing, disproportionate number of minority children represented in the child welfare system; an escalation in the number of placements and the length of time children spend living in foster care; and a recognition that current services are not having an overall dramatic improvement on child and family well-being. At the same time, internationally supported practice and policy shifts support family group conferencing as a process. Family group conferencing embodies family-centered, strengths-based, and solution-focused theories that are increasingly guiding child welfare reform throughout the world. As part of this reform movement, child welfare systems are being redesigned to be community-based, where both responsibility and authority are shared by child protection agencies, communities, and families.

Family group conferencing is supported and reinforced in the United States by federal and state policy, practice, and law, which emphasize the significant role kin can play in providing care for, and supporting, their children. With a recent U.S. federal law—the Adoption and Safe Families Act of 1997 (PL 105-89), which reemphasizes child safety, promotes adoption and other permanent homes for children, and supports families—family group conferencing is being used as a process to expedite permanency for children. The shift in the underlying core values and beliefs about families, supported by legislative processes and mandates within the last decade, are converging to produce worldwide momentum to devise family group conferencing initiatives. The 1990s has seen an exponential growth in community-based family group conferencing initiatives. For example, in the United States, what started out as an innovative practice to resolve concerns of abuse and neglect in approximately five U.S. communities in 1995 has been expanded to over one hundred communities in 1999.

QUESTIONS OF IMPLEMENTATION

While adaptations to family group conferencing are important to respect the cultural diversity within each community, it also creates "model drift." This affects the integrity of the process and, ultimately, leaves families vulnerable to the same interventions that have led to their dependency and failed attempts at permanency. At this stage in the evolution of FGC, there are no established international practice standards. Without universally established standards, the quality of the process is sacrificed and the ability to consistently evaluate the outcomes of the approach is increasingly difficult. In addition, practice standards would increase the public's awareness and understanding of FGC, and help community decision-makers decide about the viability of this approach from political, economical, and organizational standpoints. While the lack of standards is not diminishing community interest in this approach, it is creating variability in implementation practices and policies. Some of these practice diversions contradict the theoretical and philosophical spirit and intent of FGC; others compromise the safety and ultimately the well-being of children and family members. This chapter explores some of the core principles that challenge communities to implement quality and integrity-loaded FGC processes.

Exclusion of Cases

New Zealand's legislation supports the notion that FGC has universal applicability to all cases of child abuse and neglect. This results from the philosophy that all families, defined to be inclusive of the extended family, social, and community networks, have strengths, abilities, and resources to develop plans that protect and care for children. With that as the underlying premise, why is it then that communities in the United States and other countries strive to exclude certain types of cases from FGC processes?

The two most common candidates excluded from FGC processes are those involving domestic violence and child sexual abuse. Opponents concerned about domestic violence suggest that batterers would dominate the decision-making process, severely diminishing the ability of the adult woman victim to provide for her safety as well as the children's. Others argue that the dynamics of child sexual abuse, which sometimes can be unintentionally supported by multigenerational family member denial or can be culturally accepted, severely curtails the efficacy of this approach. While the inclusion of these types of cases is controversial, current research and a decade of practice experience suggests that, with careful preparation and skillful coordination, FGC can be used to generate plans that safeguard children even in the most difficult circumstances (Pennell & Burford, 1997).

Preparation

Research demonstrates that both the coordinator's ability and the quality of preparation and planning correlate to the overall success of the conference (Merkel-Holguin & Ribich, in press; Paterson & Harvey, 1991; Maxwell & Morris, 1993). While the amount of time it takes to adequately prepare a family, professionals, and community members varies based on case- and family-specific circumstances, data from communities worldwide suggest that an average of twenty-two to thirty-five hours per family group conference is necessary to ensure comprehensive preparation and planning (Gunderson, 1998; Pennell & Burford, 1995; Crow & Marsh, 1999). Without intensive, careful preparation, FGC more closely mirrors traditional case planning methods. Why then, with the international evidence and practice wisdom clearly pointing in one direction, are numerous U.S. communities departing from this accepted standard, shortchanging the preparation activities?

Another factor that reduces quality relates to the staffing of the coordinator position. New Zealand's legislation created a framework for implementation that adequately funded the coordinator position within government. The roles and responsibilities of the coordinator are clearly defined. Many U.S. communities have not properly resourced the coordinator position, whether it is located in the public child welfare or a community-based agency. In one state that conducts thousands of family meetings yearly, Rodgers and Rockhill (in press) explain that either the referring public agency worker or the appointed facilitator for the family meeting can conduct the preparation activities. This lack of role definition, coupled with placing additional responsibilities on professionals who already have heavy workloads, is likely to contribute to a minimal emphasis on preparation. An analysis of practices suggests that preparation activities are negated when the coordinator position is insufficiently resourced. The multiple responsibilities of the coordinator role have been documented (Pennell & Burford, 1995; American Humane Association, 1997). Minimal preparation may result in fewer family and community members understanding the purpose of and attending a FGC. It may also mean that the family does not have the opportunity to build a trusting relationship with the coordinator, who will not likely have spent time learning about the family and its history.

The location of coordinators raises questions of professional neutrality. If the coordinator's responsibility is to encourage the family to question the information presented during the FGC, how likely is it that a professional who conducted an abuse and neglect investigation would support family members and others to challenge their analysis and decision-making authority? The only roles that referring social workers should play during an FGC are to provide relevant case facts—not their opinions or resource suggestions—during the information-sharing stage, and assist the family group with detailing the plan during the decision stage to ensure that resources are sufficient and that all safety and care concerns are adequately addressed.

Opponents of FGC claim that it creates additional safety concerns and emotional vulnerability for children and other family victims. This is likely a fair criticism when conference preparation work is inadequate. The preparation phase centers around learning and understanding a family's dynamics to better facilitate the FGC. When coordinators have not interacted with family members, learned their patterns of communication, helped family to put aside longstanding differences not relevant to the FGC, they are at a significant disadvantage of ensuring safety for the participants at the conference and afterward. When coordinators have a keen understanding of family dynamics, they are in a better position to identify support persons for adult and child victims and offenders. The use of support persons is one mechanism to lessen legitimate safety concerns for those attendees who are emotionally and physically vulnerable as well as those with violent tendencies. These support people can represent the voices of children who may be disempowered, can help to neutralize anger of victims or offenders, and can provide a physical and emotional shield for attendees. When Bartholet (1999) suggested that children are unrepresented in FGC processes, she conveniently overlooked the critical role of the support person for a child and inaccurately portrayed the legal representation of children to be nonexistent. Lawyers, guardian ad litems, and court appointed special advocates can play an important role during a FGC, as demonstrated in New Zealand and some U.S. communities. This does not necessarily reflect an adversarial, legalistic process because FGC is about blending accountability, responsibility, and healing through building of partnerships. Children are represented, if in a different way.

When FGC preparation processes do not construct the essential safety net, there is a greater likelihood of revictimization. It is the coordinator's responsibility, in partnership with the family and community members, to promote safe and healthy participation of all those attending the FGC. This can only be accomplished when the coordinator has adequate time and resources to concentrate on the up-front preparation activities.

The Conference

As developed and legislated in New Zealand, the FGC is a process with distinct stages, based on a family-centered and strengths-based philosophy. While many countries throughout the world have modified the actual FGC to fit with community and political cultures, adaptations should be undertaken cautiously and reflectively. What should remain intact is not the prescribed FGC stages as in New Zealand, but the philosophy that underpins the approach. There are some examples in the United States of community practices that contradict the philosophy of the model, including professional control and lack of private family time in a conference.

During the information-sharing stage of the conference, the social worker, who conducted the abuse and neglect investigation, along with other professionals who have been engaged with the family present relevant case facts from which the family is to craft their plan. While in most U.S. communities, this is probably carried out with families in a strengths-based manner, there are other examples of practices that propel information givers into a role that disempowers family members and negatively impacts their decision-making. This reexertion of control occurs in subtle, but significant ways. First, when information providers knowingly withhold facts, they corrupt the process. Families are set up to construct plans with insufficient facts, undermining the redistribution of power concept inherent in FGC processes. Second, some U.S. communities implementing family group conferencing believe that the professionals' presentations should include their plan recommendations and opinions, including available resources and services. The expansion of the information giver role beyond its original purpose has also been documented by Hassall and Maxwell (1991) and Lupton and Stevens (1997). While professionals presenting their recommendations seems like an insignificant practice, it gives credence to the authorities' opinions, suggests them to be the experts, and stunts family creativity, revokes the opportunity for family to question the information presented, and decreases the mobilization of the informal support network. These practices are more likely to occur when professionals believe the FGC process challenges their competency, threatens their professionalism, and invalidates what should be their decision-making authority.

Another practice diversion from New Zealand's family group conferencing approach is the debate in some U.S. communities over the importance and need for private family time as an element of the process. However, some progressive communities and states have labeled private family time as nonnegotiable. They recognize that without this essential element and the up-front preparation activities, the FGC process reflects more of a traditional case planning approach—one that is professionally dominated by external experts to the family. New Zealand developers incorporated private family time into the family group conferencing process for significant philosophical reasons. First, families are not typically as willing to divulge family circumstances, secrets, or history when professionals whom they do not trust are present. In the end, when information is not shared freely, the plan is compromised. Second, when professionals are involved, there is a greater likelihood that they facilitate or dominate the process. Third, private family time symbolically represents a trusting of the family, further encouraging families to rely on their own internal network of capability and expertise.

With such a rationale for private family time, it is hard to understand why this is such a stumbling block for many U.S. professionals interested in implementing family group conferencing. While multiple reasons abound—from professional distrust of family decision-making abilities to concerns that children and adult victims would be scapegoated, revictimized, or physically unsafe—another factor is a misunderstanding of the interconnection between private family time and the decision-making stage of the family group conferencing process. For example, some critics (Bartholet, 1999) have mischaracterized family group conferencing as an abdication of state responsibility, reducing governmental power to, and community ownership in, the protection of children. However, FGCs set up a structure to *share* decision-making responsibility and authority between the broadly defined family and professionals. Private family time gives the family network the first opportunity to develop a care and protection plan. The decision stage, where the family presents its plan to child welfare authorities, community representatives, and other nonfamily support people, provides those with legal responsibility for the protection of children to further construct the plan to ensure child well-being and safety.

During the decision stage, everyone involved in the family conference reviews the initial plan presented by the family. Specific activities, responsibilities, time frames, resource availability, and accountability and monitoring methods are outlined. The intended outcome is to have the family and professionals agree to a workable plan that maximizes child safety and well-being. Even in participatory decision-making that involves open give and take between the engaged parties, sometimes consensus cannot be reached. Professionals, in these cases, should respectfully present their concerns to the family and provide them with another opportunity to dialogue in private to resolve the issues. While research shows that those with veto power judiciously exercise this option, when plans do not protect the child it is the responsibility of the legal authorities to reject them. In balance, family group conferencing does not delegate authority to the family, but meaningfully and respectfully shares it with them.

Prescribing Outcomes

While family group conferencing provides families of origin and communities with a process to share decision-making authority with formal child welfare systems, it does not prescribe an outcome. In the United States, a troubling phenomenon is occurring in an increasing number of communities that, to receive much needed political support to initiate family group conferencing, are casting this approach as a cost-savings or containment mechanism, or one that results in certain outcomes. When this occurs, the intent of family conferencing is lost.

Family group conferencing may result in earlier and more appropriate decisions being made on behalf of at-risk children, the achievement of permanency for children more quickly, or more children may remain with their extended family circle or within their culture of origin (Merkel-Holguin, 1996). However, when family group conferencing processes direct families to craft a certain plan (e.g., kinship care, adoption, guardianship), they counter the intent of this innovative approach. Instead, it becomes a superficial process that stifles family creativity and originality, dismisses family knowledge and strengths, and counters the philosophy of shared decision-making.

Family group conferencing should not only mobilize the wider family and community network to share decision-making, it should also create a community environment and openness to recraft services based on family recommendations and needs. If communities are implementing family group conferencing with cost containment as the backdrop, then it is likely that the family does not have the latitude to devise a plan. The flexibility of services to resource a family's plan is also questionable. The achievement of one of the by-products of this approach—that family members become the drivers of community-based services—will not be realized unless communities implementing family group conferencing understand its philosophical underpinnings.

Sustainability

Family group conferencing within a legislative framework is the way child abuse and neglect concerns are resolved in New Zealand. There is growing debate in various countries as to whether a legislative framework would hinder or help the advancement of family group conferencing. New Zealand's law establishes the family group conferencing process, outlines the structure for its conduct, clarifies jurisdictional authority, defines practice standards, provides policy directions, and endows resources to the implementing agencies. Yet, shepherding legislative change at the federal or state level can be a risky endeavor—one where key decisions can be made with or without the expertise and knowledge of those who fully understand the intent of the proposed legislation. Enabling legislation might produce more harm than good. Making FGCs a right, without establishing standards and resources to appropriately support the time- and labor-intensive parts of the practice, could result in poor practices. Indeed, without legislation, some creative U.S. communities have ensured that state confidentiality statutes and other policies are not used as a mechanism to limit the attendance of extended family members at an FGC. These communities embrace the philosophy that the child belongs to the family and community, not solely to the parent. Local policies have been reconfigured and resources dedicated to maximizing the inclusion of family in the process.

CONCLUSION

Practice guidelines and standards, supported by formal or legislated policy, are needed to ensure the efficacy of family group conferencing. The flexibility with which communities are experimentally implementing FGCs is creating many poor practices that contradict the approach and its founding philosophy. Numerous U.S. communities embark on implementing family group conferencing without fully comprehending its radically transformative practices. Communities too often see conferencing as a quick fix to resolve child abuse and neglect concerns. FGCs become a perfunctory process to get limited family buy-in to already agency-developed solutions. If family group conferencing continues evolving in wayward directions, both supporters and critics will have legitimate concerns about an innovative, nontraditional practice that has provided evidence of improving the lives of children and families.

REFERENCES

American Humane Association (1997). *Innovations for children's services for the 21st century: Family group decision making.* Englewood, CO: Author.

Bartholet, E. (1999). New programs promote traditional ideas. *Nobody's children: Abuse and neglect, foster drift, and the adoption alternative.* Boston: Beacon.

Crow, G., & Marsh, P. (1999). *The Swindon and Wiltshire family group conference project evaluation report.* Sheffield: University of Sheffield.

Gunderson, K. (1998). Pre-conference preparation: An investment in success. *Protecting Children, 14*(4), 11–12.

Hassall, I., & Maxwell, G. (1991). The family group conference. *An appraisal of the first year of the Children, Young Persons and Their Families Act 1989.* Wellington, NZ: Commissioner of Children.

Lupton, C., & Stevens, M. (1997). *Family outcomes: Following through on family group conferences* (Report No. 34). Portsmouth, UK: University of Portsmouth Press.

Maxwell, G., & Morris, A. (1993). Family group conferences: Key elements. Paper presented at the Mission of St. James and St. John, Melbourne, Australia.

Merkel-Holguin, L. (1996). Putting families back into the child protection partnership: Family group decision making. *Protecting Children, 12*(3), 4–7.

Merkel-Holguin, L., & Ribich, K. (in press). Family group conferencing: An "extended family" process to safeguard children and strengthen family well-being. In E. Walton, P. Sandau-Beckler, & M. Mannes (Eds.), *Family-centered services and child well-being: Exploring issues in policy, practice, theory, and research.* New York: Columbia University Press.

Paterson, K., & Harvey, M. (1991). *An evaluation of the organization and operation of care and protection family group conferences.* Wellington, NZ: Evaluation Unit, Department of Social Welfare.

Pennell, J., & Burford, G. (1995). *Family group decision making implementation report.* St. John's, NF: Memorial University.

Pennell, J., & Burford, G. (1997). *Family group decision making: After the Conference—Progress in resolving violence and promoting well being.* St. Johns, NF: Memorial University.

Rodgers, A., & Rockhill, A. (in press). Research on family unity meetings in Oregon: Report of key findings and the challenges of applying them to a large state child welfare agency. *1999 National Roundtable on Family Group Decision Making: Summary of Proceedings.* Englewood, CO: American Humane Association.

22 Family Group Conferences in Four Australian States

PAUL BAN

Australia has a population of nineteen million people living in a country of three million square miles, and is divided into six states and two territories. The bulk of the population lives along the coastline of two states, New South Wales and Victoria. This chapter outlines the development of family group conferencing in child protection during the 1990s in four of the six states, with the most populous state—New South Wales—covered in a separate chapter. The four states covered here are Victoria, Tasmania, South Australia, and Western Australia. Each utilizes family group conferencing as a planning strategy based on the New Zealand model. They all use a preparation stage prior to the three-stage conference, consisting of an information stage, private time, and discussion of family plans.

Comparisons are made here between the four states on four key sets of conferencing matters. First, the use of pilot projects for the implementation of conferencing is considered. A second matter discussed is whether the states have incorporated family group conferencing in child welfare legislation. The location of conference coordinators and their perceived independence is a related matter and, finally, the role of evaluations to assist the implementation process is considered in the four states.

VICTORIA

Victoria is a geographically small state at the bottom of the east coast of Australia with most of its population of 4.7 million people living in the multicultural city of Melbourne.

Pilot Project

The initial pilot project for family group conferencing in Australia was carried out in Victoria over the two-year period, 1992–1994, on the basis of funding provided by a philanthropic trust. The project steering committee included statutory authority staff sympathetic to the family group conference (FGC) model and in a position to integrate conferences into mainstream work with families if the pilot was successful.

Based on the success of the pilot project, government funding was provided to test the early findings over a larger number of families. While still considered to be in a pilot phase, the statutory child welfare authority took over funding responsibility from the philanthropic trust. The main advantage to having the pilot project carried out by a nongovernment agency with private funding was in getting the project started. At the time, the Victoria government showed no interest in trying conferencing, believing that the principles behind FGCs were already being practiced in mainstream services. A purpose of the pilot was to demonstrate to the statutory authority the benefits of conferencing. The main disadvantage of the pilot was that as the initiative did not come from within the statutory authority, momentum to implement the process subsequently varied throughout the state, never becoming government priority.

Legislation in Victoria

The Children and Young Person's Act, 1989, was passed in Victoria the same year as the New Zealand Act. While aware of New Zealand developments, government officials in Victoria did not specify that family group conferences be included in their legislation. Instead, the Victoria legislation provided for a case plan to be established with the family within six weeks after an order was made by the Children's Court. The principles behind case planning were outlined in the legislation, with emphasis on engaging the family in a participatory manner. These principles were intended to be the basis by which all planning with the child and family occurs. The Victoria government chose to ensure in legislation that a plan with reviews occurred once the statutory authority had a legal role in the life of the family. This contrasted with the statutory provision in New Zealand to hold the key planning meeting (family group conference) twenty-eight days after involvement with the family and prior to court action. The Victoria legislation does not describe how the planning meeting is to occur, as compared to the detailed outline of the process to be followed by family group conferences in New Zealand legislation. Drafters of the Victoria legislation decided that principles of case planning should determine practice, not legislation stipulating practice.

Independence of the Facilitator

The pilot project in Victoria was facilitated by two employees of the private family and child welfare agency receiving philanthropic trust funding. The facilitators were independent of the statutory child protection service. The evaluation of the pilot project highlighted the positive views of families about the neutrality of the person coordinating their meetings. Professionals involved in the pilot conferences as information givers also stated their support for the independence of the facilitators.

Based upon evaluation results showing that existing case planning meetings organized by the statutory authority lacked true family participation, a decision was made by government to incorporate the principles of family group conferencing into the planning meetings. The most effective way seen to incorporate the principles was to have the statutory authority employ facilitators on a salaried basis and locate them in the same premises as child protection workers. The pilot project had shown that the facilitators experienced difficulties receiving adequate numbers of conferencing referrals, and it was thought that referrals would be more forthcoming if the facilitators were visible and in regular contact with the child protection workers. Consequently, the Victoria model of "independence" is for the facilitator to be part of the child protection system, but not responsible for regular child protection duties. In addition, some limited use has been made of private agency facilitators.

Evaluations

The initial pilot evaluation in Victoria was privately funded, with an evaluator and evaluation committee independent of the statutory child welfare authority. The evaluation showed consistently high numbers of family participants and a high level of family satisfaction with family group conferences. It confirmed that families preferred to be treated according to the principles underlying family group conferencing, and would rather participate in a family group conference when holding planning meetings with professionals.

The second Victoria evaluation was conducted by the statutory child welfare authority and limited to interviewing authority staff. The purpose was to determine child protection staff satisfaction with FGCs. The pilot evaluation had interviewed child protection workers and other professionals, finding higher satisfaction levels for FGCs than for other planning meetings. The second evaluation confirmed this initial finding and recommended the authority incorporate the principles behind family group conferencing more proactively into all work areas. It also recommended that family group conferences play an ongoing role in child protection services.

The third evaluation was commissioned by the statutory child welfare authority twelve months after the authority had established a family group conference facilitator in each of the nine regions of the state. Conducted by an independent body, the aims were to examine the implementation of FGCs according to their initial principles, regional variations, and the extent FGCs had worked in partnership with families. Overall, the evaluation found that there was some variation in the use of conferences, with the family's private time sometimes not occurring, meetings taking variable time, and differing use of FGC follow-up reviews. Greatest variation was found in the use of the process, with some regional staff making a large number of referrals while others made few. The role of management in the regions was found to be critical to successful use of FGCs. In regions where managers were committed to family group conferences and the values underlying them, frontline staff were more likely to make referrals to the facilitator. Consequently, some regions gained extra funding for more facilitators while others either transferred the position to take over other functions, with effectively no family group conferencing service, or used the service infrequently.

SOUTH AUSTRALIA

This state is approximately one-seventh the size of Australia and predominantly rural, with desert areas in the north. Most of the population of 1.5 million live in the capital, Adelaide, which is on the southern coast. In the early 1990s the South Australian government developed new legislation in the juvenile justice area, which included family group conferencing. Because juvenile justice and child protection were together in the old legislation, there was a need to establish new child protection legislation. Since the South Australian government was already interested in the New Zealand model of family group conferences in juvenile justice, it decided to incorporate "family care meetings" into its new legislation.

Pilot Project

South Australia did not trial a pilot service, because a decision was made by senior government staff (including a new appointee from New Zealand) that the practice would be incorporated into legislation and be mandatory for all families where it was likely a child would be removed from the family's care. The belief was that New Zealand had already piloted and established family group conferences in legislation, with the initial evaluation and anecdotal evidence from New Zealand highlighting the benefits for families and children.

Legislation

The South Australian Child Protection Act, 1993, outlined in some detail the purpose and procedures for a family care meeting. To underline the significance of the family care meeting, the legislation states that the statutory child welfare authority cannot apply to the court for an order to remove the child from the family network, with minor exceptions, unless the meeting takes place. South Australia had the benefit of New Zealand experience before passing its legislation four years later, whereas Victoria developed a legislative model for working in partnership with families at the same time that New Zealand developed family group conferences. South Australia had a tradition of advocacy for children in statutory authority planning meetings, with a body representing children established under the old child welfare legislation. Considerable debate occurred in developing the 1993 legislation over the rights of children versus the rights of families. Supporters of the child advocacy service were concerned that the voice of children would not be heard, as there was no provision in the new legislation for the advocacy service and there was a belief that families would not take into proper account the welfare of children. The purpose for a family care meeting under the legislation was for the child's family, in conjunction with the facilitator, "to make informal decisions as to the arrangements for best securing the care and protection of the child, and to review those arrangements from time to time." At the same time, the statutory child welfare authority was still to provide its own planning and review service in partnership with families.

Independence of the Facilitator

Debate developed over the location of the service to facilitate the family care meetings. Based on the early findings from New Zealand that families preferred the facilitator to be independent of the child protection service, a decision was made to develop the new service under the auspice of the Children's Court. Opponents believed this showed a lack of faith in the ability of the statutory child welfare authority to identify and empower extended family networks. Supporters believed a service totally separate from the child protection system better reflected the impartiality of the facilitator.

Families understand that facilitators are attached to the court process and are independent of child protection investigations and applications to remove children from families. South Australian facilitators have their responsibilities outlined in legislation and are required to conduct family care meetings within the spirit of empowering families along the lines of the New Zealand family group conference process. Although the statutory child welfare authority is required to develop plans for the safety of children in partnership with families, there is no expectation of holding a family group conference. While it is possible for statutory authority staff to use family group conferences as part of their own case planning with families, the belief is that family group conferences are only to be facilitated by court-appointed and trained independent professionals.

Evaluations

While statistics have been maintained on the annual number of family care meetings held, attendance, length of meetings, and decision outcomes, there has been no evaluation of family care meetings from the perspective of families or statutory child protection workers.

WESTERN AUSTRALIA

This state occupies a third of the continent, with most of the land consisting of desert. Most of the 1.8 million people live in the southwest corner, including the capital city, Perth. Family group conferencing was initially implemented in juvenile justice under the Youth Offenders Act, 1994. Interest in using the technique was based on the successful use of family group conferences with Maori and Pacific Island young offenders in New Zealand. The state has a high proportion of young aboriginal offenders, and the initial application was considered appropriate for this group, who are overrepresented within the justice system. When the minister responsible for juvenile justice changed portfolios to take responsibility for family and child welfare services, she developed a project to prevent children from entering the justice or child protection systems.

Pilot Project

The West Australian government piloted family group conferences as a preventative service for families with children under ten years of age. Funding was provided for the two-year pilot to be implemented in four regions, with the facilitators employed by the statutory child welfare authority. The pilot was established to test the application of conferencing in service areas the politician responsible thought were in greatest need. Funding was assigned to establish and evaluate the pilot, with government employees responsible for administering the two-year service.

Legislation

While practice guidelines incorporate case planning with families, no legislation directly referring to family group conferencing has been passed.

Independence of Facilitator

The West Australian pilot used salaried facilitators employed by a family support section of the statutory child welfare authority. The facilitators were employed on a full-time basis, but were not responsible for dealing with child protection matters, other than coordinating conferences. They were identified as working within the preventative/supportive section of the agency, rather than the mandatory investigation and legal intervention section.

Evaluations

An internal evaluation of the pilot program for children under ten years of age was conducted. The purpose of the evaluation was to determine whether the pilot should be expanded throughout the state. While the evaluation found that only one of the four pilot projects had remained loyal to the family group conference process, it also found that the principles of encouraging and supporting families to make decisions about themselves reflected good practice. The evaluation recommended that expansion of the pilot occur, viewing implementation problems as largely related to organizational issues rather than concerns about the conferencing process itself.

TASMANIA

Tasmania is a small island state at the southern end of Australia, with a population of half a million people. The Tasmanian government passed the Children, Young Persons and Their Families Act and the Youth Justice Act, both in 1997. Both pieces of legislation explicitly include family group conferencing for involving families and community members in planning and decision-making. The developers of the legislation stated they had explored best practice models and were influenced by legislative provisions for conferencing in South Australia and New Zealand.

Pilot Project

A pilot was undertaken by the statutory child welfare authority in preparation for the new child protection legislation. The pilot conferences were facilitated by independent professionals with the government monitoring practice. As there was a commitment from within government to incorporate family group conferences into mainstream work with families, the pilot was more a trial run of the practice before it became part of the legislation.

Legislation

Tasmania had the advantage of drawing on the experience of both New Zealand and South Australia before passing their Children, Young Persons and Their Families Act in 1997. The Tasmanian legislation outlines the purpose and process of conferencing in some detail, making reference to extended family participation, the three stages of the meeting, and the need for a review of the arrangements planned by the family.

The legislation specifies that conferences may be held at the discretion of the statutory child welfare authority or if ordered by a magistrate; it does not specify a particular stage in the court or case management process where it is compulsory. The legislation has a section on the role of the facilitator. The principles and objectives behind the Tasmanian legislation reflect the belief that children should be kept safe, preferably in the context of their family, culture, and community. Due to an economic downturn in Tasmania, the legislation passed in 1997 has not yet been implemented. The Tasmanian government has not been able to resource the new act and, in the meantime, family group conferences continue with minimal resourcing.

Independence of the Facilitator

The Tasmanian legislation provides for establishing a register of independent facilitators. The responsibilities of facilitators in conducting a family group conference are outlined in legislation in a similar manner to South Australia and New Zealand. While waiting for the legislation to be enacted, a small number of family group conferences have been carried out using independent facilitators from nongovernment agencies paid on a contract basis per family group conference. In addition, some experienced statutory authority staff have considered taking on the role of facilitator. It remains to be seen whether the government will use their own salaried staff as facilitators rather than pay for contracted facilitators. Regardless of the intention of the legislation to ensure that families receive independent facilitators, economic considerations may redefine "independence" similar to the development in Victoria.

Evaluations

While Tasmania has held approximately twenty pilot family group conferences over a two-year period, apart from a published article discussing the process by one of the independent convenors, there has been no formal evaluation.

ISSUES FOR IMPLEMENTATION

Promotion of the Principles of Empowering Practice

The development of an effective family group conference service will be limited if the professional practice environment of the statutory child welfare authority is controlling and disempowering toward families. Ideally family group conferences should be a natural development arising from professional practice, which actively engages family networks by treating them with respect and adequately informs them about choices and resources they can use to improve their situation. The use of strengths-based interventions assumes that the affected parties seek to maximize opportunities to overcome obstacles. This means working in partnership with families.

The position taken by the statutory authority in Victoria is that the principles of empowerment should inform all child protection practice rather than be restricted to family group conferencing. Consequently, the statutory authority has promoted statewide projects, using family group conference pilots as the early pacesetters for empowering values. The West Australian statutory authority has actively promoted strengths-based practice in child protection work over the past four years, embracing family group conferences into their philosophy of working with families. South Australia and Tasmania have new child protection legislation that promotes family group conferencing and endorses the principles behind the process. However, the practice of statutory authority child protection workers does not always reflect the stated direction of policy and legislation. The belief of engaging family networks to plan for the safety of their children and acknowledging their capacity to do so is unfortunately not yet the dominant practice paradigm in Australia. While the promotion of empowerment in policy will reinforce the practice of some statutory authority workers, others may see the approach as only applicable on a discretionary basis.

Discretion and Timing in Using Conferences

If it is accepted that family group conferences should be an integral part of a statutory child welfare practice, a key issue is when conferences should take place. It is tempting to support the flexible use of the process through both pre– and post–court-mandated involvement with families, as experience has shown that conferences can be held at a number of points in case processing. However, if family group conferences are totally discretionary, they may be hardly used.

The Tasmanian legislation provides for conferences to occur at the discretion of either the statutory child welfare authority or the court. A result of this flexibility could be the belief that only "suitable" families or situations will benefit. In Victoria, the discretionary nature of FGC use has led to widening discrepancies between the regions. Over three years some regions rarely used family group conferences, while others have expanded the service and promote it as representing a key strategy in working in partnership with families for the welfare of children. The alternative to the optional and discretionary approach, whether through policy in Victoria or legislation in Tasmania, is to have family group conferences occur on a nondiscretionary basis. The main issue is when to hold the nondiscretionary conference after professional child protection intervention into the lives of families.

South Australia has legislated that family group conferences take place on a compulsory basis if the statutory child welfare authority is considering a court order to remove a child from his or her family network. Despite the initial tensions over the service being based at the court rather than administered by the statutory authority, all matters involving the removal of children must be considered for a family group conference. The majority of cases reach an agreement through the family owning the plan, with the minority decided by the court process. This model successfully ensures a consistent service for all families, and the process occurs at the most critical point of child protection intervention, when the removal of children from their families is considered. The key is that the nondiscretionary use of family group conferences ensures a consistency of practice to families at a particular stage of their involvement with statutory child welfare authorities.

All four states promote the values of working in partnership with families; however, South Australia has a nonnegotiable process ensuring full family participation at the time of greatest crisis. This approach has shown that most families do participate and develop their own protective plans, rather than some families in special circumstances as has been the case in Victoria and Tasmania. South Australia has chosen to legislate for the specific timing of family group conferences. Victoria and Tasmania could make a policy decision that family group conferences must take place at the time removal of children from their family is being considered. This decision would not exclude the use of family group conferences at other points in the process, but would ensure they always take place at a particular stage.

23 Implementing and Evaluating Family Group Conferences

The New South Wales Experience

JUDY CASHMORE and PATRICIA KIELY

The Australian state of New South Wales (NSW) has now initiated several family group conference or, as they are more formally called, family decision-making projects in different areas of the state. The project, which is the focus of this chapter, was established by Burnside, the welfare arm of the Uniting Church, in conjunction with the Department of Community Services, which jointly funded the implementation and the evaluation. The program is based in Western Sydney in an area that contains one of the highest number of children in the state below one year of age, an ethnically diverse population, high unemployment, and a large number of single-parent families.

The pressures providing the impetus for the family decision-making initiatives in NSW were similar to those affecting the care and protection systems for children in other jurisdictions in Western countries, including an increase in the number of children being referred to the statutory authority for suspected child abuse and neglect or incapacity of their parents to cope, increasing pressure on the capacity of the child protection and substitute care system to meet the demand, and identified gaps in service provision. At the same time, there was a growing understanding of the importance of parental responsibility and involvement, and an increased awareness of the problems of public care.

DEVELOPING THE PROJECT

The values underpinning family decision-making fit with Burnside's plan to develop programs involving greater accountability of professionals, increased transparency in procedures, and consumer participation in collaborative decision-making. Before referrals began, considerable work was undertaken training Department of Community Service staff about the program so they could understand what it offered and refer appropriate families. Like the introduction of the program in other jurisdictions, referrals were slow to come. Regular visits to the department's Community Service Centres by the coordinator of the program helped establish contact with the staff and inform them about progress to engender interest in referring families. As the process has no legislative base in New South

Wales, success rested on the workers in the statutory service, the Department of Community Services (DoCS), being willing to refer families and support the family's action plans. A great deal of effort went into establishing protocols and procedures to foster an effective partnership between DoCS and Burnside.

The pilot started in March 1996 with the guidance and support of several groups. One was an operational group composed of the project coordinator and staff from the department to guide the day-to-day work of the pilot and encourage DoCS staff to participate and refer families to the program. An interagency steering committee was also established to oversee the project and inform its practice. This committee consisted of managers from the two agencies (DoCS and Burnside), the health department, relevant academics, and two solicitors working in Children's Courts.

Criteria for the referral of cases to the family decision-making project were jointly prepared by Burnside and the DoCS. The two primary criteria were the family's willingness to participate and the need for some decisions to be made about the care and support for children when there were serious concerns about their safety, welfare, and well-being. Workers were also encouraged to start with the question: Why is this case *not* suitable for family decision-making? rather than, Is it suitable for family decision-making?

PREPARING AND ORGANIZING CONFERENCES

Responsibility for organizing family decision-making conferences and doing most of the preparation work lies with the Burnside Family Decision-Making Facilitator. This includes liaising with the departmental worker to obtain background information and establish the department's "bottom line," contacting agencies that may be able to offer services to the family, and tracing and contacting family members and informing them about the family decision-making process. It also includes discussing with family members whom they would like invited to the family decision-making meeting, what their level of contact with and significance to the child is, what areas of conflict there may be among family members and between the family and the department, and whether they are aware of past abuse issues within the family or any other problems or dynamics that may have an impact on the family's ability to devise a workable plan for the child. This is a time-consuming, sensitive process and generally takes considerably longer than the conference itself.

Other practical aspects involved in the preparation include exploring any cultural issues, and consulting with the family to organize the location for the conference, travel, childcare, and culturally appropriate food and refreshments. These costs are paid by the program to ensure that no one is excluded because of financial means. This also sends a signal to family members about the importance of the meeting and the value placed on their attendance.

The "Bottom Line"

Set by the department or the Children's Court, the "bottom line" specifies the nonnegotiable aspects of any plan to meet the department's protective concerns and ensure the safety and welfare of the children. It includes decisions already made by the authorities based on information from the confirmed notifications. The "bottom line" may be, for example, that the child cannot live at home with the parents while their drug use results in neglectful conditions for the children. Beyond or above the "bottom line," the family is encouraged to make their own decisions. To assist in developing their plan, questions are formulated by the co-ordinator in consultation with key family members and departmental staff to guide the family's discussion. The result of this is the development of the family's action plan.

The district officer retains responsibility for the care and protection of the child and continues to work with the family in the usual manner. This may involve supervision of the family, arranging contact between the child and family if the child is in care, and providing any other requirements the child may have.

Who Is Invited?

The consent of both parents is obtained whenever possible before members of the extended family and service providers are invited. Where some family members strongly resist the inclusion of others who could provide support or assist the child, the facilitator discusses this openly with the family and tries to encourage them to focus on the benefits for the child of wider family participation in the planning process. In the end, however, the family's decision is respected; the concern is that to do otherwise may undermine the family decision-making meeting and any plans arising from it.

Children are usually invited to participate in the conference from the age of ten years and are prepared for this by being informed about what is likely to happen at the meeting, what the consequences of various outcome options are likely to be, and being asked what they would like to happen. They may also nominate an advocate or support person to attend and participate in the conference. Other family members may also choose to have family friends, family support workers, or other welfare professionals act as advocates. This has been important for some family members who have a mental illness, developmental delay, or fear being overwhelmed by power imbalances within the family.

The Structure of the Conference

The stages of the pilot family group conferences have followed the original New Zealand model and the practice of other states of Australia and the United Kingdom:

- **Information sharing** by professionals with the family about assessments and about possible services to the family to help in the formulation and support of their plan. Guidelines were developed to assist professionals prepare their presentation after finding that some focused on the family's problems rather than their strengths and used inaccessible jargon.
- **Private family time,** where the family is left alone to discuss the information and decide on a plan; the facilitator or statutory worker is available, however, to assist the family on request.
- **Ratification,** where professionals rejoin the family to reach agreement, endorse the plan if it is seen to ensure the safety and well-being of the children, and discuss issues and resources for implementation.

The plan outlines in some detail the part that various agencies and members of the family and friends will play, with timelines specified. In the latter part of the pilot this also included a timetable for review meetings to monitor the progress of the plan. In the pilot, departmental workers are responsible for the implementation of the plans, but the Burnside facilitators have convened a number of review meetings. These meetings are usually much shorter and do not require the attendance of as many family members or professionals as the initial conference. The aim of these meetings is to monitor the outcome of the plan and make any necessary adjustments to it.

THE EVALUATION

The pilot study included twenty families who participated in the project between June 1996 and June 1998. Information was obtained from various sources: from key family members ($n = 48$), including the children when they participated in the conference and were willing to be interviewed; the departmental officer who referred the family to the project and attended the conference (twenty questionnaires from seventeen different workers); the case worker responsible for case management and for implementing the plan (twenty interviews with sixteen different workers); the Burnside facilitator (twenty interviews with six facilitators); and by observing most of the twenty conferences and some of the review meetings. The interviews with key family members and case workers were conducted by telephone six months to one year after the conference and taped with consent of the participants for later transcription.

The Families and Reasons for Referral

Thirty-one children (fourteen boys and seventeen girls) between the ages of eight months and fifteen years were referred for conferences. For eleven families, the referrals included all the children or the only child in the family. For the remaining nine families, only one ($n = 6$) or two ($n = 3$) children in the family were referred. The most common reason for referral to the project was to determine the most appropriate form of placement for the referred children (nine families), or to support their current or planned return home after living in foster care or with relatives (six families). In the other cases, the main issue was providing support for the parent and child or to plan and support contact between the child and the parents and other family members (five families). Alcohol or other drug use and domestic violence were common problems in these families (thirteen and ten families, respectively, and both in eight families). Other background issues included the mother's mental illness (two families), the child's developmental disability or problems (three families), and parental imprisonment (two families). The child's behavior or unwillingness to live at home was an issue in five families, with juvenile justice involvement in four cases.

Preparation and Process

The amount of time spent preparing for the conferences was considerable, ranging from five to forty hours for the facilitator (mean = 20.6 hours), and an additional one to eleven hours (mean = 4.8 hours) for the project coordinator. This included an average of about four home visits per conference. The project coordinator supervised and advised the facilitator and attended each conference to provide support. The departmental workers recognized and appreciated the work done by the facilitator in arranging and preparing the participants for the conference, indicating that they did not have the time or resources to do this work. Most (79 percent) family members indicated they felt adequately prepared for the conference. Their main concerns before the conference related to the tension or conflict between particular members of the family, their lack of confidence in the capacity of the process to bring about change, and their distrust of departmental staff and their intentions. In several cases, a telephone conference link was used to allow fathers to participate in the conference without being present in the same room as their ex-partners.

Participants' Views on the Conferences

A total of 135 family participants and 142 professionals attended the twenty conferences. This included both mothers and fathers in sixteen families and at least one grandparent or aunt or uncle in all but three. One mother and one father in different families declined to attend, and two fathers who had not been involved in their children's lives were not invited. Two parents had died. In seven of the conferences, eight children aged eleven to fifteen years participated, but the parents of one other child over ten did not consent to the child's involvement, a decision that the facilitator regretted but accepted.

The average length of the conferences was just over four hours. The shortest (and smallest) was just over two hours and the longest, six hours. Just over half the family members said they found it too long. Some said it could have been kept on track more, but others, some of whom still thought it was too long, were unsure how it could have been any shorter to cover the areas and "discuss what needed to be discussed."

Most family members were positive about the information they received in the first stage of the conference, saying they learned much more about the services available to them, and in some cases that they understood much better the problems or concerns in relation to the children. They were also generally positive about the private time, because it allowed family members to discuss issues quite frankly in a way they had not done before. Almost three quarters (70 percent) of the family members said they felt able to say what they wanted during the conference, but about a quarter, including two of the children, felt constrained by the presence of so many people or felt excluded by the domination of particular family members. About two-thirds said they were not sure what they would have done if they had been unhappy with the plan. An unexpected but valuable aspect of the conferences was the opportunity provided for the workers and service providers to develop relationships and networks with others in their area and become more aware of the type and extent of the services provided by other agencies.

The Plans

In all except one case, families were able to decide upon a plan, which was then ratified by the departmental officer. In the one case, family members were unable to agree because of the considerable hostility between the two "sides" of the family, and so the department determined the placement of the children. In another case, some family members were unhappy with the outcome but a plan was finally decided upon. Family members were generally positive about the plan and, in some cases, were explicit about the value of seeing the commitments from family members and from the services, especially the statutory service.

Most plans included a combination of services and family involvement that focused jointly on the needs of the family, the parents, and the children. In some cases, the family's commitments included the care of the children in the short or longer term, and in others, respite care and supervision of the parents' contact with the children, transport, and general support. The support provided by services included accommodation and care for some children, assistance with housing or relocation, medical and professional assessment and treatment for developmental and behavioral problems, financial assistance for child care and preschool for younger children, and tutoring and support for older children to attend school or special school programs.

Seven plans included assessment and management of parents' drug and alcohol problems, with parents due to undergo detoxification and rehabilitation programs or monitoring in relation to their drug use. This was, however, one of the least successful aspects of the plans with only one parent successfully managing his drug use on a methadone program. Several parents denied accusations that they were not trying to carry out their part of the plan, saying they had not been able to gain access to an appropriate service in their area; several were transient and therefore not able to remain with the one service.

Implementation of the Plans

While most family members and workers responsible for the plans were satisfied with them, both groups indicated that most plans were only partially carried out (fifteen of the twenty plans). A minority was seen to have been carried out in full (five as judged by family members and three in the judgment of workers) and only one was not implemented at all (in the judgment of the worker but not the family). In most cases, the workers were in agreement with the families about the main reasons for the plans only partially being carried out. These were the failure by some family members (most often the parents) to follow through on their commitments (particularly in relation to drug and alcohol problems), a change in circumstances, and the department's slowness or inability to follow through. In several cases, the failure to follow the plan was attributed to the level of conflict between the parents or other family members (with neither side accepting responsibility) or to one family member withdrawing. In half the families, some family members were critical of the lack of support they received, not only from other family members, but also from the department. Their complaints about the department concerned the lack of continuity of workers and their failure to return their calls or to hear their calls for help and meet their commitments. In four of these cases, the departmental worker admitted there had been problems or delays in the management and monitoring of the plan.

Follow-Up

Six to twelve months after the conference, nearly two-thirds of the thirty-one referred children were living at home (eleven children in six families) or within their family group (eight children in six families). One was in stable out-of-home care. Three children had entered out-of-home care (from two families) and orders were being sought for the placement of another four children (in two other families) because the arrangements within their families as specified in the plan had broken down. Three children (three different families) had also changed their placements in out-of-home care.

Overall, the workers believed the risk to the children had been addressed and reduced as a result of the plan. Their reasons were that the family shared a greater awareness of the department's protective concerns, that the family had access to some additional support and resources, and that there were changes in the family relationships that were likely to afford increased contact for the children with other family members and increased monitoring of their safety and welfare within the family. The workers were, however, not at all confident about the future stability of five children (in three families) who were living within the family group and three (in two families) in out-of-home care. The parents had continuing problems with alcohol and other drugs in four of these five families.

In judging the success of the outcomes, it should be noted that most of the families that were referred to this pilot program were at the "hard end" and family decision-making was seen by some of the departmental workers as a last resort. Most of these families had long histories of family dysfunction and unresolved family issues, including drug and alcohol problems and domestic violence. Family decision-making in these circumstances was not an early intervention strategy, and one of the comments made by the facilitators and some family members was that such a process would have been helpful and may have been more successful if it had been used earlier.

Effects on Relationships

Another significant effect of the family decision-making process was its effect on family members' relationships with each other and with the department. Family members were fairly evenly split between those who said that their family relationships had improved since the conference and those who said they had not. A few said that some relationships within the family were worse than before; this was generally between the relative who was caring for the children and the parent who was seen as not having made any commitment to change. A quite common positive change within some families, however, was a shift in the interaction between family members "for the sake of the children." This was particularly apparent in several cases between maternal and paternal grandparents, and in one case between the two parents.

Family members and departmental workers were also asked whether there had been any change in their relationship since the conference. While both family members and workers were fairly evenly split between those who said there had been a change in their relationship with the department and those who said there had not, the direction of the disagreement was different. Only about a quarter of the departmental workers said there had been a worsening or continuation of a poor relationship, but family members were about as likely to say the relationship had worsened or remained poor as they were to say it had improved or remained good. The main reason for this difference was that positive perceived changes were directly attributed to the family decision-making process, but perceived negative effects were more often attributed to other factors such as a change in the family's circumstances, or a change in worker, or to the lack of contact or follow-through on commitments, predominantly by departmental workers.

Overall Perceptions

While generally seen as positive, the main problem with the family decision-making process for both family members and departmental workers was the lack of follow-through on commitments by family members or by departmental workers and, as a result, the failure to secure a long-term positive outcome for some children. The positive aspects family members commented on were the benefits of "clearing the air" in relation to conflict within the family, being open about the problems the parents were facing, and finding out about available services. In a number of cases, they indicated that they would have preferred to have had this information earlier and to have had access to such a process before departmental intervention had become necessary.

Most family members (nearly 90 percent) and at least one in nearly every family said they would recommend family decision-making to other families in similar circumstances, but a fairly common comment was that it should happen earlier and only if people were prepared to follow through on their commitments. All the facilitators and most of the departmental workers were supportive of the broader application and extension of family decision-making in child protection work, although some had reservations about the time required to work with families in this way and the timing of the process.

IMPLEMENTATION AND PRACTICE ISSUES

Independence of the Facilitator

There was very strong support among family members (81 percent) and especially among departmental staff (100 percent) for the facilitator being independent of the statutory service. Family members' comments focused on their distrust of the department based on its previous failure to listen to them or act constructively. Departmental workers saw a number of advantages for the family, for the likely success of the process, and for the department in having an independent facilitator. In addition to seeing the family as being more likely to trust the process and be more at ease with a neutral facilitator, some departmental workers saw significant value in being able to be seen as "one of a group of professionals" and as a service provider rather than being in control and in opposition to the family.

The issue of power and control was a critical part of the process for many departmental workers, with a number commenting that the family decision-making process allowed them to be seen as more human and helpful once the "bottom line" concerns were settled. Although some family members did comment on their increased appreciation of the work that departmental workers had to do, the more significant issue for many family members, and one that was acknowledged by some departmental workers, was the need for the department and family members to follow through on their commitments.

Children's Participation

Despite the attempts that were made to involve children and young people in the process by preparing them for what might happen, encouraging them to participate, and allowing them to have an advocate at the conference, it is not clear that this process is much better than other adult-oriented forums at allowing them to really "have a say." They were generally seen as not being very interested in the whole process, and several expressed some reservations about needing to be there or being able to say what they wanted. One option would be for children to be present for part of the meeting with an advocate who understood and was prepared to represent their views staying for the whole meeting, informing them what was being discussed, and consulting with them at various stages. Departmental workers and family members were fairly evenly split about the need for an advocate, with some saying that others already involved could play that role. Others believed that it was necessary for someone to ensure a focus on the child's needs and to assist the child to understand the process and the outcome. What is clear, however, is that more work needs to be done and the processes further developed to allow children to feel comfortable and secure in participating in what is still an adult forum.

Need to Monitor the Implementation of Plans

Part way through the pilot study, a decision was made to include a schedule for review meetings to monitor the plan and the outcomes for children. Given the concern among family members about the failure of other family members and departmental workers to follow through on their commitments, this was a sensible and necessary amendment to the process. Having a review process in place is likely to have been one of the factors that contributed to the positive outcomes and full implementation of several of the plans in the second half of the pilot. It is particularly important that there is a review process and, perhaps, a further conference where the family circumstances change following the conference, or where there is a change of worker, or a transfer of the case from one area to another. The need for reviews is also consistent with the experience from other evaluations in Britain (Marsh & Crow, 1998) and in Victoria (Trotter, Sheehan, Liddell, Strong, & Laragy, 1999).

REFERENCES

Marsh, P., & Crow, G. (1998). *Family group conferences in child welfare*. Oxford: Blackwell Science.
Trotter, C., Sheehan, R., Liddell, M., Strong, D., & Laragy, C. (1999). *Evaluation of the statewide implementation of family group conferencing*. Melbourne: Victorian Human Services.

24   Initiating Conferencing

Community Practice Issues

JOAN PENNELL and MARIE WEIL

Community development has historically emphasized the participation of citizens in identifying issues and their engagement in mutual processes of community problem solving (Gamble & Weil, 1995; Rubin & Rubin, 1992; Ross and Lappin, 1967). These basic community practice tenets build on a shared vision and commitment to action. The principle of mutuality underlies and sustains partnerships for resolving community-identified issues. Families and communities in crisis, nevertheless, need resources and protections from public agencies and other services. Thus, a collaborative approach is required that remains guided by shared concerns and brings together the assets of a full range of stakeholders (Wilder Research Center, 1992). Collaboration is particularly necessary in child and family services because of the vulnerability of children and their wide range of needs. Tensions exist, however, because child protective services must make decisions on the basis of risk and endangerment of children, whereas families, communities, and community-based agencies attend to a broader range of concerns (Waldfogel 1998b; Weil, in press).

Our work in North Carolina has highlighted the importance of concern as a guiding focus to bring together diverse groups to conceptualize, initiate, implement, and evaluate the model of family group conferencing (FGC). Guided by a shared concern and utilizing community development principles, groups are more likely to resist systemic pressures and prevent model drift (Gamble & Weil, 1995; Rubin & Rubin, 1992). Our understanding of concern has been informed by social work values about the worth and interdependence of people. As the social work historian Barbara Simon (1994, p. 35) has demonstrated, these values are based on empowerment traditions in social work, including the democratization premises of the Society of Friends (Quakers). Concern has served as a guide to social reform efforts of Quakers. In community development practice, a shared concern leads to a shared commitment to action. In the Quaker tradition, the process may begin with an individual or individuals prepared to hear the concern (Hutchinson, 1961/1964); they then convince others to join in carrying out this responsibility. How the concern is to be acted upon becomes clearer as the group enlarges. Within this greater assembly, the wisdom and strength to resolve the concern emerges (Brinton, 1964). This Quaker experiential framework of concern can help to illuminate the ways in which agencies can engage with families and communities.

In this chapter, the notion of concern is used to conceptualize the process of initiating family group conferences in North Carolina. The difficulties in mainstreaming family group conferencing are considered, and a partnership approach is proposed for respecting the integrity of FGC philosophy and practice. Building and sustaining partnerships is emphasized across all phases from initiating the model to implementation through to evaluation. Reflections are offered on how the concept of concern can offer a simplifying starting point for alternative approaches to child welfare reform.

FAMILY GROUP CONFERENCING

In situations of family violence, FGC is about building partnerships within and around families to protect child and adult family members and advance their well-being (Pennell & Burford, 1994). This means that protective authorities work in a mutual way with families and that the involved agencies and community groups collaborate around particular family issues. Central to the model is that the family and their relatives and other close supports are given the privacy to cooperatively develop a plan for resolving the concerns. Before the plan goes into effect, the mandated authorities must approve it. This allows for a safety check of the plan and ensures that the public agencies provide necessary resources for its implementation. Once the approval is granted, the various partners work together in carrying out the plan and reconvene as necessary to review developments and plan further action steps.

The FGC process is designed to create a forum in which protective service families can have a meaningful voice over their affairs (Pennell & Burford, 1999). Thus, emphasis is given to preparing family group members and professionals, weighting conference participation toward the family, respecting the culture of the family, and ensuring timely approval and implementation of plans (Burford & Pennell, 1996; Connolly & McKenzie, 1999; Gunderson, 1998). Over a three- to four-week period, a FGC coordinator works with the family to organize their conference: identifying who is in the family group, strategizing on how to keep the process safe, and making practical arrangements for holding the conference (Burford, Pennell, & MacLeod, 1995). Likewise, the service providers require preparation around how to take part in the conference in a respectful and helpful manner. The invitations are purposely skewed toward family group members to reflect the many sides of the family and to ensure that family and supportive friends far outnumber the professionals. If necessary, the services of an interpreter are secured so that the conference can be held in the language of the family group.

The structure of the conference places the family group at the center of planning (Pennell & Burford, 1995). The opening emphasizes the family's culture, possibly through a prayer, a statement from a senior family member, or simply seating themselves in a circle. After the FGC coordinator reviews the process and introductions are completed, the group turns to the concerns to be addressed. Rather than placing the onus on survivors to disclose their maltreatment, the involved protective authorities such as child welfare, correctional services, and police report on what has happened and what issues need to be addressed in the plan. So that the family group has sufficient knowledge for planning, other information providers may present on relevant topics such as substance abuse and domestic violence as well as the services available.

Once the family group is clear about the areas of concern from the perspective of the service providers and informed about the relevant resources, all of the professionals, including the conference coordinator, leave the room. This private time provides the opportunity for the family group to develop their sense of concern and to formulate their own plan for resolving the concerns. Notably, the Newfoundland & Labrador Study (Pennell & Burford, 1995) found that the main way in which family groups reached their decisions was through consensus by a process of building a common understanding and reaching a collectively agreed upon plan (Barber, 1984). On completing this task, the family group invites the coordinator back into the room to review the plan and to ensure that it includes clear steps and a system of monitoring and evaluating the implementation of the plan. Then the involved mandated authorities are asked to approve the plan, preferably at the conclusion of the conference or shortly thereafter.

While the plan is being carried out, the protective services remain responsible for monitoring the safety of family members. With the plan in place, the family group and involved community organizations work with the authorities to protect and assist family members. If the plan becomes unfeasible or unhelpful or the family's situation changes dramatically, an FGC can be reconvened.

Fairly comprehensive evaluations of the FGC process have been carried out. They show that conferencing can be carried out without violence, that family groups usually come up with plans, and that the authorities typically approve their plans (Paterson & Harvey, 1991; Pennell & Burford, 1995). Far less is known about child welfare outcomes when FGC has been used (Robertson, 1996). The limited studies available, nevertheless, suggest that conferencing reduces child maltreatment (Lupton & Stevens, 1997; Marsh & Crow, 1998) and domestic violence (Pennell & Burford, 2000), decreases the disproportionate number of children of color in care (Crampton, 1998), and promotes the well-being of children and other family members (Burford & Pennell, 1998).

MAINSTREAMING THE MODEL

In the early 1990s when the Newfoundland & Labrador Project was initiated, little research on the process of conferencing was available. Common questions raised by agency workers about FGCs included:

- Will families show up at conferences?
- If they attend, will they break out into fights?
- Aren't our families too dysfunctional to make sound decisions?
- Won't the perpetrators manipulate the conference?
- Will the plans endanger the survivors?

Behind these questions was a profound ambivalence on the part of professionals about letting go of control that could only be resolved through seeing how conferencing actually worked.

Today, in setting up the North Carolina Family Group Conferencing Project or in speaking about the model with others, we hear the same questions repeated. The difference now is that the questioners are aware that FGC is considered by many a "best practice." Sometimes the objections are reframed as: That might work elsewhere, but our families have too many drug problems or they don't have any family and friends. Increasingly, however, we are hearing questions not about the families but about systems: Will our agency let us spend the time needed for preparations?

- Since families usually want to meet in the evenings and on weekends, can we get compensation for taking part in conferences?
- How much confidential information can be shared at a conference, especially on addictions?
- Won't defense lawyers block their clients from taking part?
- Is there sufficient time before a court hearing to hold a conference?
- Will FGC duplicate other services?

Underlying these questions are staff's fears of more work and more conflicts among professionals, but also a fear that agency policies, procedures, and structures will undermine FGC initiatives.

A prime example is the initial response by child welfare workers to our use of the language of concerns. In speaking of the areas to address in a plan, we employ the term *concerns* rather than risks, problems, or harms. The main message that we wish to convey is a commitment to taking action, a message that can be lost through starting with terms that highlight individual vulnerabilities, deficiencies, or injuries. Usually in our workshops, training participants welcome beginning with a strengths- and solutions-focused approach (Saleebey, 1997); at the same time, the child welfare staff identify how the language of concern can contravene their agency mandate.

Under U.S. laws, child welfare workers are expected to protect children from "substantial risk" of abuse, neglect, or dependency (lack of care) (Wells, 1995). The term *concern* encompasses far more than the officially required minimum levels of care and protection. Family groups, however, think broadly about their relatives, as evident in their plans (Pennell & Burford, 1995). For example, family groups include in plans expected items such as addictions treatment but also less expected items such as funding for family outings (ibid.). For their part, the child welfare workers recognize that plans such as outings help to strengthen family bonds, but they are also aware that keeping a case open in order to fund such an activity could be viewed as widening the child protection net and jeopardize the state review of their agency. However, as soon as they come to see the FGC as a partnership framework, child welfare workers are able to create solutions to overcome systemic hurdles.

Funding constraints may pose the greatest challenge to implementing FGCs. The outcome study of the Newfoundland & Labrador Project found that families felt betrayed when child welfare workers closed their cases once the crises were over but before all plans were completed (Burford & Pennell, 1998). For instance, when serious risks were no longer evident, the social service agency decided on its own to close a case even though all of the conditions of the plan to which the agency had agreed were not carried out in their entirety. Unilateral decisions by the agency contravened the FGC philosophy of families having a say over their affairs and limited the potential of conferencing to safeguard children and other family members in the long run.

BUILDING PARTNERSHIPS

Too often, we have found that agencies view FGC as another tool in their tool kit, an addition to what they are already doing. Such a view leads to a procedural view of conferencing in which workers can be quickly trained to facilitate FGCs. This assumption disregards the core principles of FGC, that is, enhancing family responsibility, advancing children's rights, respecting cultural diversity, and building partnerships. All of these principles require a rethinking of the roles of agencies and a reshaping of how they work with families, community groups, and other services. We recommend the following partnership-building steps for initiating and sustaining a FGC program:

1. **Involve diverse groups in planning for the program:**   Gather a group of concerned individuals to serve as planners, ensuring that a range of perspectives are included. This allows for the perspectives of different family members (e.g., women, children, grandparents), cultural groups, and service providers.
2. **Formulate a guiding philosophy:**   Early in the planning develop a guiding statement of philosophy or framework for the program. This serves to make explicit the concern that is guiding the planning group as it identifies its assumptions and objectives for FGC and identifies the model's core processes. With this agreement in place, the group is then better able to

develop program policies and procedures and evaluative criteria in line with its philosophy.

3. **Offer inclusive training:**   Invite representatives from a wide range of organizations and groups to participate in the training. This will help build communitywide understanding of the model and support for its enactment.

4. **Adapt policy:**   Examine how state and agency policies and procedures may or may not support FGC. Work out agency adaptations as needed for sustaining this model.

5. **Establish advisory committees:**   A statewide advisory committee with representation from different groups can provide ongoing oversight to the program and foster a broad set of connections and resourcing for the program. Local advisory committees serve the same function at the community or county level.

6. **Develop a local plan:**   Work out with the planning group and/or local advisory committee a plan for ensuring local ownership of the program, collaboration by key stakeholders, and adequate resourcing of conferencing.

7. **Secure local coordinators:**   It is important to recruit coordinators who are attuned to the local culture and committed to working in a respectful and effective manner with the different family members and workers involved.

8. **Evaluate the program:**   Guided by the statement of philosophy, an implementation evaluation can identify if core processes are being carried out. The outcome evaluation can assess the extent to which the program objectives are realized. This information can be used by advisory committees, staff, and others to reflect upon and reconfigure the program as needed.

STARTING WITH CONCERN

The series of recommended steps is a way of acting collaboratively upon a concern to safeguard children and other family members. This process for mainstreaming an FGC program is congruent with conferencing principles and can better offer a sustaining milieu for family groups to resolve concerns. Emphasis should be placed on diversity in participants, preparation for taking part, dialogue to reach an agreement on concerns and means for resolving them, cooperative enactment of a collectively owned plan of action, and reshaping the actions on the basis of reflective evaluation.

Once a group reaches a shared sense of responsibility to resolve a specific issue, or what Friends refer to as a concern, they have a richness of insights for developing a plan and greater strength for achieving a resolution. As the Quaker Thomas Kelly ([1941] 1984) experienced, the guidance of a concern serves to simplify the work at hand: it focuses the group's strength rather than dissipating energy across numerous endeavors. By coming together around one program or around one family, the partners can undertake a responsibility that is within their reach.

A range of efforts to reform the child welfare system seeks to improve practice and outcomes in protective services and to strengthen the support side of the service continuum (Weil, in press). Family group conferencing works to strengthen families, assure safety for all members, and promote family-centered practice and community-based partnership building. The paradigm for the child and family service system is shifting to more shared responsibility among public agencies, nonprofits, community groups and organizations, and families (Waldfogel, 1998b; McCroskey & Meezan, 1998; Burford & Pennell, 1998). How to build extended community responsibility for the welfare of children and families and how to maximize child safety with family, extended family, or community are central questions in this important arena of service (Courtney, 1998; Schene, 1998; Waldfogel, 1998a; Weil, in press). The family-centered, partnership-building framework of FGC offers one means of making the service system more responsive to family and community concerns. Perhaps the concepts of shared concern and commitment to action can be used with principles of simplicity and partnership to offer new possibilities for family problem resolution and community-based means to protect, nurture, and safeguard children and other family members.

NOTE

Joan Pennell wishes to acknowledge the guidance of her father, Dr. T. Noel Stern, on the meaning of "concern" within the Society of Friends. She (Pennell, 1999) presented an earlier version of this chapter at the Building Strong Partnerships for Restorative Practices Conference, Burlington, Vermont. The North Carolina Family Group Conferencing Project is funded through North Carolina Division of Social Services.

REFERENCES

Barber, B. (1984). *Strong democracy: Participatory politics for a new age.* Berkeley: University of California Press.

Brinton, H. (1964). *Friends for 300 years: The history and beliefs of the Society of Friends since George Fox started the Quaker movement.* Wallingford, PA: Pendel Hill and Philadelphia Yearly Meeting of the Religious Society of Friends.

Burford, G., & Pennell, J. (1996). Family group decision making: Generating indigenous structures for resolving family violence. *Protecting Children, 12*(3), 17–21.

Burford, G., & Pennell, J. (1998). *Family group decision making: After the conference—progress in resolving violence and promoting well-being: Outcome Report* (Vol. 1). St. Johns: Memorial University of Newfoundland, School of Social Work.

Burford, G., Pennell, J., & MacLeod, S. (1995). *Manual for coordinators and communities: The organization and practice of family group decision making* (rev.). St. John's: Memorial University of Newfoundland, School of Social Work.

Connolly, M., & McKenzie, M. (1999). *Effective participatory practice: Family group conferencing in child protection*. Hawthorne, NY: Aldine de Gruyter.

Courtney, M. E. (1998). The costs of child protection in the context of welfare reform. *Future of Children, 8*(1), 88–103.

Crampton, D. (1998). Kent county families for kids initiative evaluation project. In L. Merkel-Holguin, J. Alsop, & C. Race (Eds.), *National roundtable series on family group decision making: Summary of proceedings, assessing the promise and implementing the practice* (pp. 59–65). Englewood, CO: American Humane Association.

Gamble, D., & Weil, M. (1995). Citizen participation. In R. Edwards (Ed.), *Encyclopedia of social work* (19th ed.; pp. 483–94). Washington, DC: NASW Press.

Gunderson, K. (1998). Pre-conference preparation: An investment in success. *Protecting Children, 14*(4), 11–12.

Hutchinson, D. (1961/1964). The spiritual basis of Quaker social concerns. In *Faith and practice of New England yearly meeting of friends* (pp. 179–80). Cambridge, MA: New England Yearly Meeting of Friends.

Kelly, T. R. ([1941] 1984). Testament of devotion. In D. Steere (Ed.), *Quaker spirituality: Selected writings* (pp. 290–305). New York: Paulist.

Lupton, C., & Stevens, M. (1997). *Family outcomes: Following through on family group conferences* (Report No. 34). Social Services Research and Information Unit, University of Portsmouth.

Marsh, P., & Crow, G. (1998). *Family group conferences in child welfare*. Oxford: Blackwells.

McCroskey, J., & Meezan, W. (1998). Family-centered services: Approaches and effectiveness. *Protecting children from abuse and neglect. The future of children, 8*(1, Spring), 54–71.

Paterson, K., & Harvey, M. (1991). *An evaluation of the organization and operation of care and protection family group conferences*. Wellington, New Zealand: Department of Social Welfare.

Pennell, J. (1999). Mainstreaming family group conferencing. In *Building Strong Partnerships for Restorative Practices* (pp. 72–82), Proceedings of the conference sponsored by Department of Social Work, University of Vermont; State of Vermont Department of Social and Rehabilitation Services and the Department of Corrections; and Real Justice. Bethlehem, PA: Real Justice.

Pennell, J., & Burford, G. (1994). Widening the circle: The family group decision making project. *Journal of Child & Youth Care, 9*(1), 1–12.

Pennell, J., & Burford, G. (1995). *Family group decision making: New roles for "old" partners in resolving family violence: Implementation report* (Vol. I). St. John's: Memorial University of Newfoundland, School of Social Work.

Pennell, J., & Burford, G. (1999). *Family group decision making: Communities stopping family violence: Questions and answers*. Monograph prepared for Health Canada, Family Violence Prevention Division. Hull, Québec: Minister of Public Works and Government Services.

Pennell, J., & Burford, G. (2000). Family group decision making: Protecting children and women. *Child Welfare, 79*(2), 131–58.

Robertson, J. (1996). Research on family group conferences in child welfare in New Zealand. In J. Hudson, A. Morris, G. Maxwell, & B. Galaway (Eds.), *Family group conferences: Perspectives on policy and practice* (pp. 49–64). Monsey, NY: Willow Tree.

Rubin, H. J., & Rubin, I. (1992). Being a conscience and a carpenter: Interpretations of the community-based development model. *Journal of Community Practice, 4*(1), 57–90.

Ross, M., & Lappin, B. (1967). *Community organization: Theory, principles and practice* (2nd ed). New York: Harper and Row.

Saleebey, D. (Ed.) (1997). *The strengths perspective in social work practice*. New York: Longman.

Schene, P. (1998). Past, present, and future roles of child protective services. *Protecting children from abuse and neglect. The future of children, 8*(1, Spring), 23–38.

Simon, B. (1994). *The empowerment tradition in American social work: A history.* New York: Columbia University Press.

Waldfogel, J. (1998a). *The future of child protection.* Cambridge, MA: Harvard University Press

Waldfogel, J. (1998b). Rethinking the paradigm for child protection. *Protecting children from abuse and neglect. The future of children, 8*(1, Spring), 104–19.

Wells, S. (1995). Child abuse and neglect overview. In R. Edwards (Ed.), *Encyclopedia of Social Work* (19th ed.; pp. 346–53). Washington, DC: NASW Press.

Weil, M. (in press). Services for families and children: The changing context and new challenges. In C. Garvin & P. Allen-Meares (Eds.), *The handbook of direct social work practice.* Thousand Oaks, CA: Sage.

Weil, M., & Gamble, D. (1995). Community practice models. In R. Edwards (Ed.), *Encyclopedia of social work* (19th ed.; pp. 577–94). Washington, DC: NASW Press.

Wilder Research Center, Amherst H. Wilder Foundation (1992). *Collaboration: What makes it work? A review of research literature on factors influencing successful collaboration.* St. Paul, MN: Author.

25 Family Decision Process

Healing the Fractured Relationship

PAUL M. SIVAK, REVEREND NATHANIEL GREEN, and TERI KOOK

In 1995 a group from New Zealand presented information on family group conferencing and in the audience were two members of the social work faculty from California State University (CSU) at Stanislaus, and key managers from the Child Welfare Section of the Stanislaus County Community Services Agency. While the conferencing approach to families made sense for child welfare work, it was clear that there were broader and more dramatic implications for our communities. During the last four years, organizations ranging from child welfare to grass roots community groups have been experimenting with this change in practice and the vision that it proclaims. This range of expression has produced a model that is fundamentally a community-building empowerment approach for working to address many social/human issues.

In order to implement this new approach with families, an intensive training and community involvement effort was launched through collaboration between county child welfare and the university. A trainer was brought in from Oregon to present basic information about both family unity and family group conferencing. Every social service agency in Stanislaus County and some adjacent counties were invited and over two hundred service providers received information on family-involved practice. After this initial training round, faculty from the university agreed to conduct a series of training/program development meetings. A procedure manual and all the initial forms for beginning the new family decision practice were prepared for implementation. For a host of reasons the development meetings were ended prematurely, and over time, practices fell into old patterns. During the first year that a family decision process was implemented there was a slow decline in adherence to the basic principles and a return to familiar patterns, including inadequate premeeting preparation and underrepresentation of extended family at meetings. There often was little connection between the family's plan and the operating case plan, and in some cases the meeting was used as a vehicle for workers to get the family to agree to already existing plans. In spite of this, there were enough well-run meetings to produce a first glimpse into the power of the model. Families demonstrated support for their plans, meetings produced significant changes in the worker-family relationship, and the number of kin placements increased well above state and regional rates. During the last year under new leadership, child welfare has been moving aggressively to regain lost ground and devote itself to applying conferencing principles.

At the same time family group conferencing was developing in public child welfare, work began in a local grassroots community organization, the West Modesto King Kennedy Neighborhood Collaborative. The effort in this community focused on a partnership between the collaborative and local schools, initially on introducing a family decision process in one elementary school. The collaborative had been organizing in its neighborhoods for many years. A partnership between the social work program at CSU, Stanislaus, and the community collaborative was created to focus on implementation and training. The first step was to meet with the neighborhood leadership and present conferencing concepts. They immediately saw the value of this way of working with families and approved moving to the next steps of meeting with each cultural/language group.

Presentation/discussion groups, employing interpreters respected and trusted by their communities, were established to allow a full explanation of the family decision process and to allow any questions to be answered directly. After conducting five separate meetings with people speaking Hmong, Laotian, Cambodian, Spanish, and English, a combined community discussion was scheduled. During this community meeting the entire membership voted to support moving forward. The process took several months but it ensured that the people who live in this community both understood and supported what had begun with the schools. The plan became theirs, in many ways paralleling the process of the family decision process itself. The collaborative applied for and received funding for a coordinator and operating expenses for a planning period of eighteen months. A community activist and member of the faith community was hired as family group conference coordinator.

The principal of the local school was contacted and meetings held. Being clear about the nature of the family decision process and willing to introduce it in his school, he referred implementation to his family support team. The referral process involves the school team identifying a child having difficulties and referring to the school outreach worker. This worker then meets with the family, presenting a brief overview of the family decision process. If the family expresses an interest, the worker has them sign a consent to refer them to the coordinator, who makes contact with the family and starts the process that will ultimately lead to the meeting.

After getting off to a slow start educating school personnel and community and family members about the objectives of the family decision process, momentum began to build. Four families were referred and participated in the project by the end of the school year, four months after implementation of the project. To date a total of twenty-two families have participated and five are awaiting conferences. Seven families offered the model declined. These refusals occurred early in implementation, but as the word got out in the community that this is a positive process, participation increased. Since beginning in one elementary school, another elementary school and a middle school have joined as referral sources.

The family decision process can effectively be employed as a method community organizers use to engage in a discussion of the community itself. It offers an elegant way to shift the focus of discussions from dysfunction to strengths, producing clear and specific action plans. The family decision process makes it difficult to simply conduct a strengths-based assessment and stop. Intrinsic to its structure is a plan for action based on community recognition of strengths and assets.

In Stanislaus County there are eighteen community collaborative organizations primarily composed of local residents. All of these programs have community building in their neighborhoods as one of their primary tasks. This commitment to organizing is rooted in the belief that the welfare of children is intimately bound to the welfare of families and the communities they live in. They all are designed to encourage service system reform through establishing relevant and accessible services in the neighborhoods. These projects have come together and created a community building alliance for children, currently called the Community Building Project. This project is working to unify the eighteen community collaboratives into a powerful organization that can direct existing services and produce services on its own. The project is directed by the coordinators of the eighteen collaboratives. Family decision process, in addition to being seen as a way of working with families, is being conceptualized as a countywide organizing methodology that looks at each community collaborative as if it were a "family member." All of these members come together to plan for the well-being of all the children in the county.

Employing the family decision process in this way creates a consistent context for the regular reexamination of services and their relationship to the overall health of the larger community. It provides a functional and accessible method of realizing the rhetoric of giving a community what it asks for by providing a way for communities to ask. The family decision process also drives a revitalization of natural community supports and a reorganization of service system programs. As the community is engaged in the self-reflection that is central to the family decision process, it parallels the experience of individual families going through the same process. As the individual family decision process produces plans that require support, the community is also examining its ability to provide primary support to its families and children. This leads to enfranchising and mobilizing natural supports that long outlive transient service system supports.

PRINCIPLES AND ROLES

The development of family decision-making processes in the northern central valley of California has been referred to as the Stanislaus model and has followed some basic definitions and principles. This model calls for three distinct service provider roles: coordinator, facilitator, and cofacilitator.

The coordinator makes contact with the referred family, establishes a relationship, and works to educate the family about the process. In the context of this discussion, the coordinator encourages the family to tell their story. As the family story is elaborated, those people who will be on the initial invitation list are identified. The coordinator then makes contact with the entire extended network of family and service providers to educate prospective participants and coordinate meeting logistics, time, and location. The coordinator is a full time, non–case-carrying position to allow for the work necessary to properly engage family in the premeeting phase of the family decision process.

The facilitator is a trained "nonprofessional." The belief is that the traits that make a good facilitator are basically social, and a wide variety of people could have these traits. Professional degrees have never been an assurance that an individual is competent to work with people. The role of the facilitator is to encourage and support communication in the meeting. This includes getting through the initial stages of the meeting so that the family is prepared to have their private time discussion and directing the process to stay on task. This role is handled in a way that enfranchises family rather than undermining them, based on a respect for the family. Facilitators are expected to gather at least once a month to engage in critical reflection of their experience and educate themselves. Facilitation is done in the family's natural language. Any interpreting is from natural language into English, for the English-only service providers. The ultimate responsibility of the facilitator is to close the facilitated part of the meeting and leave the family for its production of the plan. The family time is absolutely nonnegotiable. The facilitator is never given the power to remain or allow service providers or unapproved nonfamily to remain with the family. The facilitator's final responsibility is to return to the family to hear and facilitate adoption of the family's plan.

The cofacilitator plays the role of recorder. All the strengths and concerns identified in the first part of the conference are written on chart paper and posted for the family to use during their private time. This is also done in the natural language of the family. This is an active role with the cofacilitator actively engaging the family to ensure that the spirit of their communication is captured.

These roles all function within the context of some basic principles. First among these is that nuclear families are part of the whole family. In order to begin the transformation toward partnership we must realize that the group that we refer to as the family is only the local representation of an extended and multigenerational network that is usually not local and often difficult to connect with. We believe that central to the Stanislaus model is a redefinition of the concept of family so that we are prohibited from considering the local representation of the family as the entire family. This is not simply making an effort to find "other" family members, but is a fundamental shift in definition. It means that we are not working with the family unless we are working with the extended network. We have also learned from experience that we must go beyond blood kin. Although kin networks form the basis of this notion of family, we must work with the local family to create a definition of family that is based on their particular culture and experience. We have discovered that this often transcends typical kin relationships.

This requires that the worker lead a process in which the family members can tell the story of their family. The basic process is much like gathering an oral history. The worker leads with very open-ended questions to encourage an elaboration of the life experiences of the members of the local family. As the story is told the worker must listen closely for themes to emerge that indicate how this family "defines" itself. As these themes emerge, the worker re-presents them to the family for validation. This process of thematization and re-presentation has several important functions. It illuminates for the family the themes that are present in their own histories. These themes will be a mixture of those aspects of experience that have contributed to the family's survival and those that have contributed to the family's isolation. This illumination and the awareness born in the re-presentation will assist in the discussion of the importance of moving toward inclusion of the entire extended network. The process also helps the family gain a clear and conscious understanding of the boundaries of their family. The role of the worker is also transformed in this process from an investigator who is trying to identify the problem to a service provider who demonstrates genuine curiosity and interest in the life of the client family. Once a clear definition of the family is created, all people who fit into the definition will be invited to the meeting. All individuals who fit the definition of family emerging from the story must be invited. The only exclusion is in situations where a member may pose a serious physical or emotional threat to other family members. In these cases it is incumbent upon the coordinator to be creative in attempting to include these people in some way that protects the vulnerable parties. This may include, but is not limited to, having written input, suggesting locations that maximize safety, inclusion of advocates or protectors. All options should be considered and involve very active decision-making by the family. The concept of inclusion is held to be important because of the need to examine the reconstruction of the natural supports that make the conference so powerful.

The one feature that appears to unite all local families that emerge in serious trouble is isolation from a meaningful and self-conscious support network. We know that there is dysfunction in the local network. Once the notion of family has been expanded to include the entire network it becomes clear that we can discuss the functional nature of family. The relationships of the extended network present new or renewed possibilities, history, and resources not available in the isolated local family group. Working with and supporting this functionality becomes the center of the service provider role.

The fact that this approach to families is a strengths-based approach is self-evident. Underlying this fact, however, is an assumption that families are functional. This assumption flows from the notion of the extended family discussed above and goes to the heart of the transformation that is required to implement this model. Central to implementation of this concept and practice is the understanding and belief that families care for their own children better than strangers and systems do. Once we begin operating from the position of functionality we must be willing to admit that families are also more invested in their children's well-being than any service system could ever be. Recent legislation has acknowledged the role that kin has always played and is moving us toward easing the ability of kin networks to care for their children with system supports. This movement is of great assistance to the transformation. There will be times and circumstances that require a child to be absent from his or her family. Families must be able to invoke this option as an expression of their love and caring for their child. But the family and service providers are partners in such a decision.

Transformation is the key element of this process. One of the essential expressions of this transformation is the belief that all families have a right to privacy. We have, in many of our service systems, demanded that families and individuals share their deepest secrets with us, the service system. The reason, we tell them, is that we can only truly help them if they tell us. They are to trust that we will honor their privacy as they do and act only in their interests. This assumption has not been a good one. Families, however, learned to comply, but the family only lets us know what it wants us to know. Families must be respected and trusted to use their own intimate knowledge of themselves to plan for a safe environment for their children. This belief in the right of families to keep their secrets from the service system is central to the family being left alone to deliberate. The commitment to respecting the family's right to privacy does not in any way support the maintenance of the shroud of secrecy that covers over family violence. These "secrets" are usually exposed in this process of inclusion of family.

While maintaining that families have a right to privacy, it is important to recognize that service providers have an obligation to provide the family with all the information they have regarding the family. It is not appropriate for providers to keep "secrets." It is vitally important that the entire family have all the information contained in the service provider experience. This experience contains experiences and information, guided by very specific training and a point of view to which the family otherwise does not have access. Armed with this information, combined with their own experience and concern, the family is in the best position to create thorough, supportive, and focused support plans.

Basic to our understanding is also the knowledge that service systems and their representatives are extremely transient. Successful implementation of this model requires that we see the necessity of connection to the natural system of supports both inside the family network and outside in the community that surrounds them. We see that service supports are functional only in as much as they respond to the needs of families as understood by them. When the family creates a plan to protect their children, they create a role for service providers. These roles are designed by a family's struggle to provide a safe and nurturing environment. Because any service identified by the family is what they want, the services delivered will be in support of the family. This approach entails a basic shift in the notion of family as consumer of services toward a view of the family as producer. As families create their own plans, service providers can join them as coproducers of the services and supports necessary to nurture the children.

TRANSFORMING AGENCY SETTINGS

The transformation process and the development of policy and procedures for the family decision process is, in essence, a change in the culture of an agency. Education to stimulate and support transformation is radically different than training in a new technique. Training people in a technique is designed to teach different ways of behaving within the existing paradigm. Transformative education requires not only that learners (both teachers and students) acquire new information and skills, but that they learn new ways of processing and integrating them. Employing the principles and practices basic to the family decision process as a template for the educational process produces a set of experiences that educate while providing the catalyst for the transformation effort. This process requires that the learners re-create the new information in their reality. This is the same re-creation that the client family is encouraged to do in the family conference. This parallel process demonstrates the system's commitment to change and self-reflection. It also creates experiences for mangers and workers that are mirrors of the experience families will have.

In practice, a full day of training is conducted that leads agency staff through a critical reflection on current practice, points out the dilemmas, and identifies the need to change. After this identification, a presentation and discussion of the family decision process occurs. This experience and exercise gives all agency participants a common language and experience. It also identifies the reason and context for the transformation. Following this intense critical reflection, a series of facilitated discussions with the agency "family" are conducted to create policy and procedures for implementing the family decision process. Each policy and procedure discussion is declared safe so that all levels of staff can participate honestly without fear. Managers and staff experience each other in very different ways, seeing each other's real strength and ability. They develop and incorporate a new set of beliefs about themselves and the families they work with. In this process all participants, while learning about themselves, are also learning through direct experience about the family decision process. They are re-creating it in a way that reflects who and what they are and owning it in a way that is impossible in traditionally dictated policy and practice.

This process takes time. Experience suggests that initiating this transformation in an agency can take from six to ten months. The history of attempts at cultural change has taught that it is never achievable by coup or by declaration. The use of a family decision process is voluntary for both workers and families. Those workers who understand and desire to change in this way lead the implementation process. As they experience the new way of working, others join in, not because they are required to but because they have chosen it. This process does have its difficulties and complexities, but the resulting transformation is dynamic and healthy.

One of the most powerful lessons in the experience thus far is that top- and middle-level leadership is absolutely crucial. This support and guidance can be demonstrated through a commitment to self-reflection, redirection of resources, and a changed set of relationships between mangers and workers. Local projects have reverted to old practices almost immediately without clear, devoted supervision. Those in leadership positions can then take on the role of educators, monitors, and supporters of best practice. These roles are important to mitigate the inevitable tendency toward relapse and absorption of the initial transformation into old structures and beliefs.

IMPLEMENTATION ISSUES

The issues that follow appear to be basic to any organization that plans to create a family decision process protocol. Informed consent is at the center of an agency's ethical obligations when considering a move toward the family decision meeting practice model. In the Stanislaus model, selected families are provided the option of utilizing the family decision meeting. Parents can choose not to engage this process and will be provided with standard child welfare services. Parents who express interest in a family decision meeting will have the entire process explained to them by a coordinator and have all information provided in writing in their primary language. If the family is already involved in the court process, they are referred to their legal counsel. All attorneys involved in a case are also provided written notice of the meeting.

In order to share the specific details of the child welfare case, the parents must be willing to waive confidentiality. Because there are usually multiple service providers involved with the family, a release form accepted by governmental and community organizations must be designed. The release should be time limited and specify that it is solely for the purpose of the family decision meeting.

It is critical that a definition be established to determine family. For instance, one family may believe that only blood relations are considered family, while another family considers a much broader network of fictive kin. Once a definition is established, everyone who fits is invited to the meeting. A veto of any person fitting the definition is not allowed. Security procedures are provided if personal safety is a concern for any participant. It is particularly important that the search for family is diligent in locating both branches of each child's extended family.

The length of time a parent has been absent from the relationship is not considered in creating the invitation list.

In order to provide family decision meetings to families that face removal of their children due to substantiated allegations, agencies may need to design emergency placement provisions that can legally avoid invocation of the court process. In the Stanislaus model, court diversion placements were created so that parents could opt for voluntary placement of their child with kin or in foster care for up to thirty days while a family decision meeting was coordinated. At the family decision meeting, planning for the safety of the children and rehabilitation of the parents can be done in an environment free of the court-imposed boundaries and time lines.

All agencies and communities that implement conferencing will have to consider funding. Through a combination of creative use of agency dollars and grants we have been able to sustain the implementation as described here. There are potent arguments that must be part of the general education of policymakers. These arguments include the savings in out-of-family placement, diversion from high-cost services in the future, maximizing the utilization of community and family support systems, and savings generated by less staff burnout. Improved agency relations in the community, ability to genuinely support families and strengthen community, and increased well-being of children are also powerful arguments for implementing the model.

The agency must make provisions for flexible funding to support the family decision meetings. Funds must be readily available to provide for assistance to allow family members to attend the meeting. This may include transportation, childcare, lodging, and assistance with food. It is also essential that the agency have a mechanism in place to provide immediate support to the family's plan. This may include flexible funding to purchase services or goods to enable a family member care for the children. These funds must be readily accessible so that family plans do not fall apart while waiting for promised services.

Any community that chooses to implement a family decision meeting protocol must create its own version that reflects community values and culture. It is important that communities understand that the process of transformation takes time and thoughtful planning. Any process created to assist in this transformation must attend to the power dynamics in the community and attempt to truly empower both workers and families. This is not a "quick fix" or a new way to do what we have always done. Involvement of every level of staff as well as community stakeholders is critical to the success of the program and will decrease the resistance that any new program is likely to face. This type of individualization of the protocol will help transform agency practice in a way that empowers and supports families in the task they do best: loving and protecting their children.

Family Group Decision-Making
in Oregon

TED KEYS and ANNA ROCKHILL

The Family Unity Meeting (FUM) model of family group decision-making was developed in Oregon in 1990 and is the version of family meetings used most frequently by state child welfare workers. Use of the model has increased rapidly over the past few years and over four thousand FUMs were conducted in 1998. This chapter draws on this extensive experience, along with two recently completed research projects. Highlighted are some of the challenges associated with attempting to implement its use.

INTRODUCTION TO THE FAMILY UNITY MEETING MODEL

Family Unity Meetings are similar to family group conferences, with family members and their supports as well as service providers and other community members invited to come together and plan for their children. Although the format of FUMs varies somewhat, meetings typically do not call for private family deliberation time. Family Unity Meetings facilitate a process of joint decision-making by creating a partnership of family, extended family (including nonrelated kin), community, and authorities for the safety of children and other victims of family abuse. Engaging the family in this way is thought to increase their sense of ownership and investment in decisions. Also, authorities are able to draw on the knowledge and strengths of family members and make better plans.

A number of variations exist as to the precise format of a FUM and a few of these will be explored below. The original format for FUMS follows:

1. **Introduction.** All persons present should be introduced in a manner respectful to the family, including the relationship of each person to the child(ren).
2. **Purpose of the meeting.** This should have been clarified with all participants during the preparation phase and now restated; everyone present is asked to agree if this is their understanding of the meeting purpose. Any misunderstandings or changes in the purpose should be discussed and agreed upon before proceeding further.
3. **Concerns.** The concerns of the agency and those of the family are listed. Caseworkers might say, for example, "I am concerned for the safety [safety

from physical abuse, sexual abuse, verbal abuse] of this child in this home."

4. **Options.** The family is first asked for their best thinking on how to deal with the concerns that have been raised. Additional options can be suggested by professionals and other participants for the family to consider.

5. **Touch Points Partnership.** The final plan reached by the participants at the FUM is outlined in a Touch Points Partnership agreement. This agreement can then be monitored by the agency and family.

EVOLUTION OF FUM PRACTICE

In the early years the model was recommended for use in two types of low-risk situations: in cases where the worker felt there was a good chance that removal of a child could be avoided and when the worker felt there was a good chance that a child could be returned home. FUMs were not originally intended to be used when a worker felt that the only possible solution was an alternative home for a child because of safety concerns. Cases involving domestic violence or sexual abuse were also seen as inappropriate for a Family Unity Meeting. As experience with the model grew, workers began using the model in new ways and a survey conducted by the American Humane Association (1997) found that FUMs were frequently used with cases near termination of parental rights.

Use of meetings has increased dramatically in the last five years, largely as a top-down process driven by legislation and agency policy. In the mid-1990s, pressure to build more collaborative relationships with families came from child advocates concerned that permanent placements for children needed to be resolved sooner. Attorneys from the Juvenile Rights Project representing the interests of children in state custody joined to together with Oregon child welfare officials, other child welfare experts, and educators to create a System of Care agreement in 1995. Three stated goals of this agreement were:

1. The basis for service planning should be on achieving agreement between the State Office for Services to Children and Families and the family about the needs of the child(ren).
2. The collaborative planning process should build on family strengths and the family's perspective in identifying needs and planning services.
3. Services should be developed to meet specific needs, supported by flexible funding, to ensure that services can be found or created as necessary to meet the identified needs.

FUMs became the main way caseworkers implemented the System of Care agreement, with meetings used to join with families to identify the child's needs and plan services. The agenda of FUMs evolved with this policy initiative. The meeting focus on presenting child welfare concerns was now seen as counterproductive. Parents might be more likely to collaborate in services if they felt less defensive about their prior care of the children. Since planning was to be centered on the children's needs for safety and attachment, the concerns phase of the meeting evolved toward a step for creating a list of the child's needs. Likewise, policy and training focused the work with families toward the needs of the child since it was felt that the family and state office would more quickly come to agreement on services for the future protection and care of the children. The move away from a more frank discussion of concerns was not accepted without reservation, however. Reservations surfaced from child protective services consultants who felt that the original child safety concerns were too quickly put away in order to achieve agreement with families.

A second policy initiative with important implications for the use of FUMs is the Oregon Family Group Decision Meeting law of 1997. The law requires consideration of a family group decision meeting whenever a child has been placed in state custody for longer than sixty days. If the agency does not hold a meeting, the reasons are to be documented in the written service plan. The law refers to family-focused interventions facilitated by professional staff designed to build and strengthen the natural caregiving system for the child. This includes family group conferences, FUMs, family mediation, or other professional interventions that include extended family and rely on the family to make decisions about planning for the children. According to the law, parents, grandparents, and any other family members who have had significant, direct contact with the child in the year prior to the substitute care placement must be notified, including a child twelve years of age or older, or a child younger than twelve years when appropriate. Family members may be excluded if they compromise the safety of other participants; however, they may submit recommendations that address the subject of any family group decision meeting.

The family plan is to be incorporated into the state office service plan if it protects the child, builds on family strengths, and is focused on achieving permanency for the child within a reasonable time. If the family plan is not incorporated into the state office service plan, the reasons are to be documented in the service plan narrative. The plan developed at the meeting shall include the expectations of the parents and other family members, services the child welfare agency will provide, timelines for implementation, benefits of compliance and consequences of noncompliance, and a schedule of future meetings, if appropriate. A copy of the family plan is to be sent to all participants within twenty-one days of the family decision-making meeting.

The practice implications of the new Oregon Family Group Decision Meeting Law are far-reaching. Pressure on workers to conduct meetings has increased dramatically. Parents are no longer able to exclude family members if relatives have had significant direct contact with the child in the past year. This came about due to considerable lobbying of the legislature by grandparents and other relatives of children in state custody. However, participants can be excluded if an individual would compromise the safety of other participants. In addition, the law includes the provision for concurrent planning. This requires simultaneous consideration of both a return home plan *and* an alternative placement plan for a child if he or she cannot return home. Child welfare agencies are now required to plan for both eventualities at once and parents must be notified of this at the meeting. The parents must also be notified of the benefits and consequences for achieving or not achieving the goals of the plans created at meetings. The plan developed at the meeting must be incorporated into the agency's service plan to the extent that it "protects the child, builds on family strengths and is focused on achieving permanency for the child within a reasonable time." This is potentially a major new right for parents and for relatives of the child(ren). For the first time the agency cannot impose plans on the family if the family plan meets the child's needs.

RESEARCH FINDINGS

Two studies conducted within the past two years shed some light on actual practices. Both studies were undertaken by the Child Welfare Partnership at Portland State University. The first is an evaluation of strengths-/needs-based services outlined in the System of Care agreement, while the second study (Rockhill & Rodgers, 1999) is aimed at identifying key elements of successful meetings that engaged the family in decision-making. This study provides information on major practice issues associated with FUMs in the larger, more urban centers of the state.

Overall the research results were mixed. Most importantly, FUMs appear to have the potential to be an effective vehicle for engaging family and extended family in a collaborative decision-making process with the caseworker and other service providers. For example, over a third of the parents surveyed in the family decision-making study felt that they had just the right amount of "say" in decision-making at the meeting, and nearly 60 percent of relatives ranked their own level of influence the same way. In addition, family members' level of participation and "say" seemed to increase when a series of meetings were held. FUMs appear to serve a variety of other goals as well. The outcome most frequently mentioned by caseworkers and service providers was that of service coordination. The opportunity to get everyone "on the same page" regarding the services being provided to various family members was seen as an important benefit of the FUM. On occasion, input from the family regarding the time or location of the service was also taken into consideration. In general, however, meetings in which the coordination of services was a primary focus did not entail a great deal of involvement on the part of family members.

One of the benefits of FUMs mentioned most frequently by family, including birth parents and extended family, was the information they received about expectations of the state child protection agency. Other notable comments concerned information received by parents about how their children were doing in foster care. At times, families reported having little knowledge about the specific problems their children were facing, and FUMs were an opportunity to access some of this information. Findings from the System of Care study suggest that families who had participated in a FUM were more knowledgeable about the process and rationale behind the planning and had more positive feelings about themselves and a more favorable image of the agency.

Both studies also point to many practice challenges. The family decision-making study suggested that a lack of preparation underlay most of the problems identified by meeting participants. Preparation was perceived to be lacking in the opinion of all types of participants including family, service providers, caseworkers, and facilitators. Preparation for meetings frequently consisted of little more than a message on an answering machine with the time, date, and location of the meeting. As a result, the quality of family participation was affected. For example, family members were often unfamiliar with the "strengths/needs" language commonly employed at meetings and therefore were reticent to talk. Many family members reported being unclear about the purpose of the meeting and therefore unsure about their role. They also expressed concern about how information would be used outside the meeting. Extended family members were reluctant to share information that might potentially be used against their relative. The cursory discussion at the beginning of the meeting about the purpose did little to allay these types of concerns and confidentiality issues were rarely covered. Service providers also complained about the lack of preparation and reported not knowing ahead of time what information they would be asked to provide.

Parents did not often contribute to decisions about who should be invited to the meeting, and when they were given an opportunity, they reported not knowing enough about the meeting to decide who might be appropriate to invite. Some parents reported not being aware that they could invite people other than immediate family members or service providers already working with their case. Information was not always shared freely at the meetings. This was due to the lack of preparation along with other factors. One inhibiting factor was that family members distrusted the system and feared that what they said might be used against them or against other family members. Many participants, including service providers and facilitators as well as family members, expressed concern about the lack of confidentiality. On occasion, family members reported that they thought decisions of consequence had already been made prior to the meeting. An even more frequent complaint was that the agency was unwilling to be clear about the conditions under which the children would be returned home or, in some cases, free to live with relatives. Although the Oregon legislation requires that any family member having significant contact with the child be invited to the meeting, this did not happen consistently. Moreover, in addition to the mixed results concerning how much "say" family members had in the decision-making process, kin did not appear to be involved in service delivery other than as a placement resource, nor were they involved in the monitoring and evaluation of plans in any meaningful way. While the legislation requires that timelines be included in plans and that parents be informed about the benefits and consequences of compliance, timelines were rarely incorporated in plans and the benefits and consequences were not identified in any meaningful way.

DISCUSSION

The implementation of family group decision meetings in Oregon has been fairly extensive in terms of numbers, but shallow in practice. What would contribute to a more successful implementation of FUMs in light of these concerns? One important need is training. Facilitation for FUMs is provided by agency staff or contracted facilitators. While training is available, FUM facilitators may not have participated in any formal training beyond observing coworkers conduct meetings. Many caseworkers feel overloaded and workload was the most common explanation given for the lack of meeting preparation. Legislation requiring that family meetings be considered for all children placed in out-of-home care after sixty days of placement was mentioned as a workload concern by caseworkers. From their perspective there are not enough resources to handle the number of meetings required. The fact that FUMs are legislatively mandated contributes to worker ambivalence. Efforts to reform practice imposed from above meet with a lukewarm reception from the field without new funding. Extensive preparation for FUMs is not required by the legislation and until recently was not outlined in detail in policy. Workers are not required to document efforts to prepare participants.

CONCLUSION

FUMs were designed to facilitate joint decision-making by creating a partnership of family, extended family, community, and child welfare authorities for the safety of children, while promoting family participation and "say" in planning for their children. Agency expectations were often clarified to families over a series of meetings and they also helped family members have a more positive image of themselves. They also helped family members to have a more favorable image of the agency.

Challenges remain with respect to better preparation of family participants, better training of facilitators, and better communication of agency expectations of parents. Confidentiality and family reluctance to speak openly with everyone present also need to be addressed. The use of private family time in FUMs could help increase the family's contributions to the planning process.

REFERENCES

American Humane Association (1997). *Innovations for children's services for the 21st century: Family group decision making and Patch.* Englewood, CO: Author.

Rockhill, A., & Rodgers, A. (1999). *Family decision meetings, final report.* Portland: Graduate School of Social Work, Portland State University.

Section IV   Introduction: Evaluating Family Group Conferences

JOE HUDSON and GALE BURFORD

Chapters in this section deal with the evaluation of conferencing programs, presenting evaluation approaches, methods, and case studies. While many of the chapters in Part III presented evaluation research findings in support of the observations about implementing conferencing programs in different countries, states, and provinces, the focus here is on planning and conducting conferencing evaluations.

Gordon Bazemore and Jeanne Stinchcomb begin by describing an approach for evaluating family group conferences and circles in a way they propose does justice to their unique programming characteristics while providing useful information about what works and why. These authors argue for using program models, maps, or intervention theory to more clearly understand the underlying premises on which family group conference and circle programs are based. Evaluation research methods can then be used to monitor program practices against the theoretical model or map. An illustrative conferencing model is presented, one related to conferencing with young offenders. The following chapter by Yvonne Unrau, Jackie Sieppert, and Joe Hudson presents a case study that supports and illustrates points made by Bazemore and Stinchcomb. Particular attention in this chapter is given to the variety of data collection approaches employed in a conferencing program carried out in Calgary, Alberta. Key principles of a user-oriented approach to evaluation are described and illustrated by Unrau and her colleagues, with emphasis on involving and empowering project stakeholders. As these authors demonstrate, the stakeholder or client group for the evaluation of the Calgary project was involved in making all key decisions about the research questions to be addressed, methods used, and the timing and use of evaluation information produced. Principles of inclusiveness, teamwork, and partnership are described in these first two chapters as being central to a user-oriented approach to evaluation. These are the same principles identified throughout the book as central to a conferencing approach. From this perspective, the work of an evaluator amounts to serving as a facilitator or helping person.

William Vesneski and Susan Kemp report in their chapter on research carried out on a family group conference project in the state of Washington. Questions addressed by this study included the characteristics of persons participating in the conferences, nature of the conference plans, and immediate results of the conferences. Particular attention is given to the relationships of conferencing to family-centered and strengths-based practice. The main data collection procedures involved in this project were interviews, questionnaire, and analyses of conferencing plans and intake forms. The major study results reported by Vesneski and Kemp are that conference plans reflected principles of a family-centered and strengths-based approach, with high rates of kinship placements and use of professional and community resources.

The final chapter in this section, by David Crampton and Wendy Lewis Jackson, describes evaluation work conducted on a conferencing program in Michigan. Like the other chapters, emphasis is given to stakeholder involvement in planning and conducting the evaluation and the use of evaluation findings to make ongoing program modifications throughout program implementation.

The Nature of Program Evaluation

Running through these chapters is a view of program evaluation as amounting to the systematic collection, analysis, reporting, and use of information for making decisions about a program. Evaluations have both descriptive and judgmental purposes and the key is designing a study that fits with the information needs of designated users. Important questions to be addressed in evaluation planning are:

- Who are the stakeholders or users of the evaluation?
- What do they want to know about the program to be evaluated, when do they want this information, with what degree of rigor, and at what cost?
- What program decisions will be made on the basis of the information collected and reported?
- What is the program to be subject to evaluation in respect to key elements and set of linking assumptions?

As these chapters illustrate, the focus of evaluations is on examining a program, intervention, or set of activities aimed at addressing identified problems or needs. In the case of conferencing, the focus of an evaluation might be on a total program, or a single project. For example, an evaluation might focus on a regional or national program such as the New Zealand conferencing initiative. Alternatively, the focus of an evaluation might be on local projects. Besides the different levels of aggregation that could be the focus of an evaluation, these chapters see conferencing initiatives as composed of a set of program elements and linking assumptions. While the terms that are used may differ, key elements going to make up a program are usually seen to include inputs or resources, activities or interventions, and the outputs, outcomes, and effects achieved as a result of using the identified resources to carry out the specified activities or interventions.

These chapters note that an important initial task of an evaluation is to gain an understanding of the program, its structure and logic. As Bazemore and Stinchcomb and Unrau, Sieppert, and Hudson note, failing to obtain a clear program definition will likely lead to evaluations being misdirected, failing to provide useful information to improve program operations. The chapters also illustrate that the focus of a family group conference evaluation might be on any element of program structure and logic—inputs or resources, activities or interventions, results, as well as the problem, need, or condition the program is intended to ameliorate or meet.

Evaluation studies focused on questions about problem conditions are usually referred to as needs assessments, addressing questions about the extent, size, and distribution of problems addressed by conferencing programs. Limited information is presented in these chapters on the needs assessments that, presumably, led to the design and implementation of the conferencing programs. Evaluation studies that address program inputs or resources commonly focus on such questions as the number and characteristics of persons served, the extent the target population is reached, and costs. Each of the studies reported here describes characteristics of the populations served by the conferencing programs and some cost information is provided in the chapter by David Crampton and Wendy Lewis Jackson. Evaluations can also focus on the activities or interventions actually carried out in the conferencing program, including the frequency, timing, and duration of interventions, as well as the assumptions linking activities to results. Program results are the final set of program elements and include immediate results or outputs, as well as longer-term outcomes and unintended effects. Examples of program outputs addressed in these chapters include participant satisfaction ratings, stakeholder views, and characteristics of conference plans. Longer-term program outcomes are not discussed mainly because of the purpose set for the studies.

Evaluation Purpose

These chapters emphasize using evaluation to improve program performance, referred to as formative evaluation, as distinguished from evaluations carried out to achieve a summative purpose. Formative evaluations aim to provide for the ongoing feedback of information to decision-makers for use in modifying programs. Usually, the focus of a formative evaluation is on program implementation and immediate results—the way the program gets located and operates within a particular setting. Evaluation information is routinely provided back to program decision- makers for use in modifying the program to improve performance. In contrast, a summative purpose for an evaluation aims at assessing long-term program effects to make decisions about continuing, expanding, or terminating the program. In a summative evaluation, information is not fed back to decision-makers until the program has completed a full cycle and determinations can then be made about outcomes and effects. Evaluation information is not fed back to decision-makers because summative evaluations require that the program remain stable; otherwise problems of attribution will occur—was it the program as it operated at this point in time, or that point, that caused the outcomes and effects? Preconditions that should be met for conducting a summative evaluation include a clearly defined program, clearly specified goals or effects, and a rationale linking the program to the goals or effects. It is rare for newly implemented family group conference programs to meet these preconditions for a summative evaluation, and therefore studies aimed at testing program effectiveness are likely to be seen as premature. As these chapters note and illustrate, a formative purpose of attempting to discover the program, its operations, and immediate results is more likely the preferred approach.

Role of the Evaluator

These chapters emphasize the role of the evaluator as one of collaborator or helper providing a service to help improve programs. This contrasts with the more traditional view of the evaluator as researcher, standing apart from the program to ensure objectivity and using rigorous research methods to test program outcomes and effects. Independence and objectivity are emphasized in the researcher model of evaluation practice, with the evaluator seen as an outside technical expert. In contrast, these chapters present a picture of the evaluator as a helper and facilitator, not judge or neutral observer. This fits with the approach to evaluation as a service activity requiring active collaboration by the evaluator with program stakeholders.

Stakeholder Involvement

Two key messages are presented in these chapters in respect to the role of program stakeholders in planning, conducting, and reporting evaluations. One message is the importance of closely involving the various stakeholders or persons directly affected by the evaluation in making decisions about all aspects of the study. This means that program clients, managers, practitioners, and other interested parties have an important role to play in the evaluation. People can learn best from an evaluation on the basis of having been actively involved in the process. They can have confidence in the information produced, see it as relevant and useful, and more readily come to accept the need for change and improvement. To make change in programs requires the agreement of many stakeholders, and therefore involving them in the evaluation process is an important way to increase the likelihood that program improvements will actually be put into effect. The challenge for evaluators then is to involve and work with stakeholders in planning, conducting, and reporting the evaluation, while still retaining the ability to question, challenge, and produce objective and credible evaluation findings.

Another important point made in these chapters about the role of program stakeholders is the importance of evaluators marketing and communicating the evaluation findings to the stakeholders. Facts do not speak for themselves and learning about program improvements means involving people and assisting them through their involvement to understand the evaluation findings to the extent of having enough confidence to put them into effect. This means integrating the evaluation process into program decision-making, as well as decision-making in organizations such as state child protection agencies that may have direct responsibilities for conferencing programs.

Data Collection Methods

These chapters describe and illustrate the use of a variety of quantitative and qualitative methods to collect information on family group conference programs. Underscored is the view that procedures used for collecting program data are tools to be used to help answer specific questions. It therefore makes no more sense to view one method as being superior to another than it would to argue the superior merits of a saw over a hammer. Tools should be used according to the work to be done. In the case of evaluations, data collection tools should be used according to the questions to be addressed, resources available, and constraints imposed. The great danger is that evaluators trained in the use of particular techniques see all the problems they encounter as requiring the use of techniques in which they are skilled. Some tools are denied and a narrow-minded approach is followed.

27   Restorative Conferencing and Theory-Based Evaluation

GORDON BAZEMORE and JEANNE B. STINCHCOMB

The elusiveness of measuring an intervention like family group conferencing (FGC) is perhaps best expressed in the observation that we will know restorative justice is working "when the sun shines more brightly." As this tongue-in-cheek statement suggests, doubts can be raised about the feasibility of measuring what seems to be very intangible, or even the necessity to scrutinize something that appears to be so self- evident that we simply "know it when we see it." On the other hand, there are very real concerns that the application of traditional evaluation techniques may distort or trivialize FGC practice by forcing it into conventional textbook models of evaluation. By challenging rigid thinking rather than rejecting evaluation altogether, there is hope for some middle ground between these two extremes. That is, innovations like circles or FGC can be evaluated in a way that does not sap the very life out of them, while still helping practitioners and theorists learn more about what works most effectively.

Practitioners themselves are demanding rigorous research that will help them improve operational practices while maintaining intervention integrity. In order to do so, better techniques for measuring overall effectiveness are needed, along with the capacity to monitor the extent to which conferencing practices are being implemented in a manner consistent with restorative principles. Evaluators have been somewhat slow to respond, at least in part because of the intellectual challenge presented by the diverse and untraditional goals of an evolving movement whose objectives are not always clearly defined.

The challenges that conferencing presents for evaluators are not primarily technical. Rather, they are for the most part the same problems facing conferencing practitioners: developing consensus about just what conferencing *is*; what kinds of cases are most appropriate for various kinds of conferencing interventions; what conferencing is intended to accomplish; what among competing goals should receive priority; what the most appropriate techniques are to achieve these goals; and why these techniques should be expected to do so. In research terms, these issues can be characterized as lack of clarity about a number of key ingredients—ranging from what the "independent variable" (i.e., conferencing) actually is, to what eligibility criteria should be, what clients or conditions should be targeted by the intervention, what outcomes are being sought, and how various conferencing techniques are believed to produce intermediate and long-term results.

Both practitioners and researchers are in need of "maps" to help them locate the various components of a conferencing process and diagram the relationships that link them together. Because they logically advance from one hypothesis to another in chain-link fashion, such maps can be expressed as "logic models" (Hawkins & Nederbood, 1987). By mapping the anticipated relationship between theoretical assumptions on which the intervention is based, related inputs (i.e., the nature of the intervention itself), and expected outcomes, logic models help us think more clearly about the paths along which cases are expected to move in an effort to bring about the kinds of conflict resolution, repair, or other transformations sought in various conferencing processes. They likewise enable us to more clearly articulate underlying theoretical premises by illustrating the nature of expected causal relationships between operational processes and resulting outcomes.

The presumed logical connections between assumptions about the problem, responses to it, and anticipated outcomes are what we refer to here as *intervention theory*. Essentially, such theories should provide a common understanding of why conferencing might be expected to "work." Although there are certain conventional strategies that apply across disciplines for developing, updating, and refining intervention theory, the process can take on some unique twists when applied specifically to conferencing.

The purpose of this chapter is to consider how strategies for conducting theory-driven evaluations can be employed within the context of conferencing. While not a technical "how to" guide to evaluating conferencing, some conceptual tools are suggested for developing intervention theories that practitioners and researchers can use to increase the likelihood that evaluation will lead to improved practice. Consideration is given both to how conferencing is *similar* to conventional evaluation processes, as well as how such evaluations are likely to *differ* when applied to this nontraditional setting.

WHY RIGOROUS EVALUATION?

At a time when practitioners are often in the early stages of developing conferencing as an intervention, some might question how important it is to focus on systematic, theory-driven evaluation. Some would maintain that it is premature, or might argue that an intensive effort to define, map, and specify outcomes could threaten the very creativity and adaptability that have characterized the conferencing movement thus far. But failure to specify and empirically test the intervention theories underlying conferencing models poses several risks. First, as an increasing number of programs jump on the bandwagon, there is a danger that conferencing interventions will be watered down or misconceived to the point that the integrity of the entire concept is threatened. Theory-based evaluation demands a critical focus on inputs into the conferencing process. This does not preclude viewing the "independent variable" (i.e., conferencing) as dynamic and continually evolving. But accurately documenting what practitioners are really doing and trying to accomplish is essential in judging the success or failure of a particular conferencing model. Another concern is assuring that both negative and positive outcomes are appropriately attributed to *conferencing,* rather than to some very different intervention or to faulty implementation of the kind that has plagued many prior community-based reform efforts (Harris & Smith, 1996). In the absence of implementation integrity, it is impossible to draw meaningful conclusions about either the intervention's practical impact or its theoretical implications. Coherent evaluation models should make clear what conferencing is and is not trying to accomplish and should provide standards for gauging the extent to which conferencing is being implemented according to principles.

HOW IS CONFERENCING EVALUATION SIMILAR AND DIFFERENT?

In many ways, conferencing represents a departure from the evaluation challenges presented by most intervention programs in child welfare. The first and more persistent challenge has to do with the nature of the dependent variable, or intervention outcome. The second, a challenge related to the independent variable, or the intervention itself, is more temporary and is due in part to the fact that conferencing is currently such a dynamic and emergent practice.

Regarding the dependent variable, conferencing moves beyond concern with changing children and other family members. The question, Does it work? or Is it working? must be addressed in a different way. In essence, the appropriate response to this issue is another question: Work for whom? The commitment must be to involve and meet the needs of different stakeholders by, for example, measuring community impact and identifying systematic ways to monitor and document meaningful involvement of the stakeholders. This means conceptualizing and measuring collective as well as individual outcomes. Community members, for example, may express disapproval or even outrage at the youth or family's actions in order to affirm communal norms, but may also need to connect in some way with other families and neighbors. Citizens may themselves benefit from the support they provide others and from the new connections established. Multiple outcomes are becoming more explicit as field experience evolves.

Regarding the independent variable in conferencing, the danger is that evaluators unfamiliar with practice principles will assume that interventions focused primarily on "shaming" or confrontation, for example, are illustrative of conferencing principles. Additionally, a key need is to promote the idea that the "restorativeness" of an intervention such as conferencing must be assessed along a continuum. This calls for measures to assess dimensions such as the community's role and the nature of citizen involvement (Bazemore, 1998).

Assessing the integrity and strength of conferencing interventions is further complicated by the fact that, according to its fundamental principles, conferencing programs must be community-driven. This means, of course, that the independent variable may shift as community demands change, thus making adherence to principles—one of which is community involvement in decision-making (Van Ness & Strong, 1997)—a key evaluation criterion.

Simply because the substantive nature of a particular intervention is unusual, untested, or even outright unorthodox, however, does not necessarily mean that the process used to assess it must be equally untraditional. In fact, standardized evaluation approaches are generally more likely to be applicable than inapplicable to even the most unique interventions. Just as the essential techniques of good driving apply regardless of whether the motorist is operating a typical Chevy or a top- of-the-line Cadillac, there are likewise basic principles that are fundamental to good evaluation design. In examining how the evaluation of conferencing should be similar to any other well-designed evaluation, we briefly consider tasks related to two evaluation principles that are essential regardless of the research topic: (1) determining relevant evaluation strategies, and (2) establishing a collaborative, consumer-based orientation.

Determining Relevant Evaluation Strategies

If evaluation can be defined in a practical, stakeholder-focused manner as *the systematic collection and use of information to answer performance-related programmatic questions,* it becomes apparent that its central purpose is to assist with improving practice and, ultimately, shaping public policies. The issue then becomes what it is that practitioners, policymakers, and community stakeholders want to know about a program intervention. The response is usually reflected in two fundamental questions—the simplicity of which stands in direct contrast to the difficulty of providing the answers: Does it work? Why or why not? Answering the former calls for an impact or outcome evaluation, whereas the latter is better addressed through a process assessment.

Impact evaluations deal with the "does it work?" question by analyzing intended long-term effects. By stimulating dialogue about what outcomes are expected to be achieved as a result of the intervention, outcome evaluations help to target program efforts. In the absence of such dialogue, agencies can fall into the trap of maintaining unrealistic expectations or becoming so "program-driven" that they lose sight of their intended goals and client needs. Yet useful impact evaluations can only be conducted when a program has achieved a sufficient degree of operational stability to justify holding it accountable for results. Program interventions experience "growing pains" as practitioners experiment with various alternatives, and many require time to develop a coherent focus. Thus, it is premature to hold them accountable for long-term outcomes in the early developmental stages—when conducting an untimely outcome assessment could produce very misleading results.

Program initiatives that have not yet reached a sufficient degree of maturity are best assessed through an *implementation* or *process* evaluation, which addresses the question of whether the initiative is being operationalized as originally designed. The focus in such an evaluation is on whether the intervention, in its developmental stages, is doing what it was intended to do. Typically, process-oriented evaluations will address such issues as whether the program is targeting appropriate participants, is functioning in a manner consistent with relevant principles and intervention theory, is operating with an appropriate infrastructure, and is utilizing properly qualified staff. Such evaluations can also examine qualitative and quantitative indicators of the program implementation progress, including the extent to which initial plans were actually carried out, whether key stakeholders were identified and involved, and the extent to which political or turf issues may be inhibiting progress. Questions of initial or immediate (vs. long-term) impact on families and communities might also be included.

Process evaluation is not so much concerned with the question of "what works" as with "why" and "how" it works (or fails to work). Without addressing these questions, impact evaluation has little meaning, because researchers are unable to say why one program or reform failed, or why another succeeded. Such exploration of the integrity and intensity of implementation is the most neglected part of the evaluation process—despite its essential role in interpreting outcome findings and its utility in providing feedback for programs that are not sufficiently stabilized to justify conducting an impact evaluation. Ultimately, effective replication and generalization will require that evaluators help practitioners "tell the story" of intervention successes and failures in the emergent stages of conferencing initiatives in an unbiased way.

Establishing a Collaborative, Consumer-Based Evaluation Orientation

Evaluations yield information, and information provides the power to make change. Informed members of the public, informed policymakers, and informed decision-makers have substantial potential to make progressive change—change that is based on empirical evidence rather than the emotional enticement or political grandstanding that has more often fueled contemporary public policy developments (Lehman & Labecki, 1998; Stinchcomb & Fox, 1999, pp. 650–51). But information is power only when it is relevant to those who have the desire and ability to use it (Patton, 1986, p. 110). This means that evaluators who aspire to bridge the gap between knowledge and action must assure that the identified stakeholders are active participants in an ongoing, collaborative strategy that combines established principles of evaluation research with utilization-focused implementation strategies.

Just as it is imperative to select an appropriate evaluation strategy, it is equally essential to consider from the outset who will ultimately utilize the findings (Patton, 1986). If, for example, evaluation research is expected to influence the direction of future policymaking, it must incorporate issues of concern to policymakers. If it is expected to improve future program operations, it must address the priorities of practitioners. Moreover, to inform a meaningful, sustained restorative process, it must be based on a collaborative process involving key stakeholders, e.g., family members and community groups. Since the very fabric of conferencing rests on a foundation advocating balanced participation among family, child protection, and community, it stands to reason that these same principles of collaborative partnerships should be incorporated into the research design applied to evaluate such efforts. The more these stakeholders are assigned active roles in the process from the outset, the more likely it will be that their interests are accommodated and that the outcome will be relevant to their needs.

Evaluators—no matter how technically proficient—cannot provide agencies with useful information if managers, staff, and other stakeholders fail to fulfill their roles in the evaluation process. Traditional methodological training has often emphasized the need for researchers to remain detached from the program implementation process in order to maintain scientific objectivity. But this "hands-off" approach is more appropriate to laboratory experiments, where researchers tend to have full control of subjects and the treatment "can usually be precisely manipulated" (Chen, 1990, p. 32). In the social sciences, collaboration need not bias results and, in fact, when targeted toward meeting the needs of key stakeholders, evaluation virtually demands mutual collaboration.

Because assessing the integrity and intensity of implementation is a *practice* concern, as well as a research concern, it is entirely appropriate that nontechnical stakeholders play a key role in the formative phase of the evaluation process. On an operational level, managers actually will need to take the lead role in certain respects, such as ensuring the availability of baseline information and creating a supportive organizational climate in which results are used objectively and productively to improve performance. Whereas the outside evaluator plays the lead role in analyzing data and making casual inferences about impact, practitioners and community stakeholders should play a significant role by providing input into determining what research questions will be explored, clarifying what the program intends to accomplish, and suggesting how "success" can be measured. Outside evaluators can be of most assistance in the process evaluation phase by helping to identify what data are needed to answer questions about the success of implementation, designing management information systems to collect this data, and assisting with or conducting preliminary data analysis. They can also assume leadership in developing an intervention theory that provides all stakeholders with a shared understanding of the conferencing model in question.

INTERVENTION THEORY AND LOGIC MODELS

The extent to which evaluation findings are able to enlighten future decisions and policymaking depends not only on how well they meet stakeholders' initial needs, but also on how well grounded they are in a plausible theoretical framework. That is not to say that theories driving program operations are always explicitly referenced in formulating the program's design. To the contrary, practitioners may well view social science theory as functioning at too high a "level of abstraction" to be useful to guide the specific elements of their program operations (Weiss, 1997, p. 509). However, practitioners generally have some implicit assumptions, even if not explicitly stated, that might be considered "theories-in-use" (Argryis, 1982) about the anticipated cause-and-effect relationship between taking certain actions and producing certain outcomes. In the case of conferencing, for example, it may be assumed that involving family members and the community more intimately in the process will produce greater satisfaction and achieve better results.

Such expected relationships, based on past experience, practical knowledge, or simply intuition (Weiss, 1997, p. 503), could be considered as a form of *experientially based, speculative theory*. Though such theorizing might not meet rigorous academic standards, the point is that without some logical basis from which to operate, evaluators are inhibited from providing very useful analyses of their findings. It is one thing to determine from the outcome of a well-controlled, quasi-experimental study that a particular initiative produces positive (or negative) results. But the question then becomes, Why? What exactly was it about the initiative that accounted for the outcome?

An intervention theory is essentially a simple statement about why stakeholders believe a service or activity should lead to a positive change in current conditions, or in the situation or behavior of specific clients. Intervention theory helps to explain why a program or policy worked or did not, and also indicates what information is needed to determine effectiveness. Without a solid theoretical anchor, results cannot be logically explained—researchers cannot accurately specify just what accounted for the program's success, or precisely where it was that things broke down. In fact, such "black box" approaches to evaluations tend to produce a dichotomous type of "thumbs up/thumbs down" assessment of success or failure. But interventions are rarely either completely ineffective or totally without merit. Even the best programs have weaknesses, and even those that appear to be utter failures may have some virtues. Yet without guidance from evaluators pinpointing specifically what worked and what failed, practitioners are helpless to understand how to build on strengths and overcome weaknesses. In evaluating family group conferencing, for example, without information on the nature of the process, we would be unable to say whether the underlying theory is flawed or whether some critical part of the process is being handled in a way inconsistent with the theory. Pragmatically, clear program theory helps practitioners maintain consistent operations that are coherent, set priorities among competing program emphases, and specify the conditions under which a program is likely to work well. Intervention theory helps managers and staff rationally assess whether their conferencing program is truly outcome-oriented or is in danger of becoming a "strategy in search of a problem." Intervention theory also helps to pinpoint what data are needed to determine if the program is being implemented with integrity and is producing the initial effects believed to precede intended long-term results.

For scholars, such theories provide an initial basis for *generalization*. For practitioners, they provide the primary bases for *replication*. Whereas scholars may draw on a wide infrastructure of research-based knowledge in an effort to make broad generalizations to multiple settings, practitioners usually draw on a considerably more finite foundation of experientially based knowledge that is generally relevant to a much more restricted environment. While the academic researcher is attempting to develop macrolevel theories to explain universal social phenomenon, the program practitioner is attempting to develop microlevel interventions to elevate operational functions in a particular setting. Thus, the task of the evaluator is often to uncover these experiential theories and connect them to relevant social science theories that permit the broader generalizations ultimately needed both for replication and for expanding program relevance. When clearly articulated, intervention theory should therefore provide the ultimate bridge between theory, practice, and research.

LOGIC MODELS AND CAUSAL RELATIONSHIPS IN CONFERENCING

Whether grounded in scholarly research, field experience, speculative predictions, or some combination of all three, interventions with a theoretical foundation are targeting their efforts toward achieving specified outcomes. Theory, therefore, provides a guiding framework for taking goal-oriented action. Precisely what is expected to be accomplished and how that will happen is not, however, always crystal clear. Unless explicitly stated and carefully depicted, the theoretical underpinnings of a program's operations may not be readily apparent, or they may be unknowingly based on faulty assumptions. Anticipated cause-and-effect relationships can be visually outlined in a rational, step-by-step progressive sequence that was referred to earlier as a "logic model." Mapping a logic model enables specification of how theoretical assumptions, operational interventions, and expected outcomes are causally related. As shown hypothetically in Figure 1, a chain of related events is postulated, i.e.: "If A, then B. If B, then C. If C, then D."

Development of a logic model forces thinking about the presumed cause-and-effect relationships between independent and dependent variables. But even when

(A) If...

> ...youths engage in crime as a result of a sense of personal detachment and psychological immunity from concern about their victims;

(B) then...

> ...they are likely to alter their behavior to the extent that they are psychologically sensitized to the personal suffering of their victims;

(C) and with sufficient psychological sensitivity...

> ...their detachment and immunity can be expected to break down, producing greater concern about the impact of their actions;

(D) and with increased sensitivity and concern...

> ...it is less likely that they will continue victimizing others.

Figure 1. Chain of related events in a logic map.

developmental expectations are clearly outlined in this format, the presumed link between theory and results may not be completely definitive—or it may be completely wrong. In that case, depicting causal relationships in a logic model helps to reveal possible conceptual flaws. For instance, in the example shown in Figure 1, it is extremely unlikely that *all* youths engage in *all* forms of criminal behavior as a result of a sense of personal detachment and psychological immunity from concern about their victims. Obviously, this theory would not explain drug use, gambling, economically motivated thefts, or any other number of offenses (particularly those traditionally labeled "victimless"). While this does not imply that a theory is "completely wrong" simply because it is not universally applicable, it would certainly be inappropriate to attempt to apply it in response to problems it was not intended to address. In the social sciences, one size does not necessarily fit all—a realization that becomes more apparent with the visual delineation provided by a logic model.

By clearly specifying links in the anticipated causal chain of events, researchers and practitioners can review the theoretical premises of conferencing interventions and ensure that each linkage is connected with the next in a rational developmental sequence. But while these basic concepts of logic modeling are certainly applicable to evaluating conferencing initiatives, the multiplicity of intervention targets and intended outcomes involved in this endeavor adds a unique dimension. Using family group conferencing as an example, Figures 2, 3, and 4 map interventions based on the theory of "reintegrative shaming" (Braithwaite & Mugford, 1994) in the form of three generic models representing the various perspectives of victim, offender, and community.

As these figures suggest, elaborating intervention theory in the form of a logic model helps staff and evaluators think through the connection between programs, processes, and intended outcomes. In that regard, the first step requires consideration of what clients (or conditions/problems) are actually most appropriate for the intervention. The second step calls for defining what events must transpire before

Assumption – *The offender's personal confrontation with the victim and the consequences of his/her actions for victims and community, along with willingness to make amends for wrongdoing, will strengthen the offender's bond to the community and produce positive outcomes.*

Client → (Target group)	*Intervention →* (Reintegrative shaming)	*Intermediate Outcomes →* (Changes in client that must occur to achieve impact)	→*Impact* (Long-term consequences)
OFFENDER			
* Must admit guilt or be adjudicated delinquent *Must be prepared to face victim and community respectfully.	*Community members, family, and intimates of offenders discuss impact of crime *Victim(s) describes personal effects of crime and discusses obligation of offender for reparation *Offender describes crime and reasons for involvement *Offender hears the behavior is wrong and harmful but that she/he is not a bad person *Offender participates in developing plan for making amends.	*Awareness of harm to others and disappointment of family and supporters; may experience shame *Awareness of suffering and of real person hurt by his/ her crime *Expression of apology and remorse *Hearing positive expressions of support for her/ him as a person. *Possibly obtaining forgiveness * Fulfilling plan, meeting obligations	*Sense of justice and fairness *Increase in empathy and awareness *Greater sense of bonding or connectedness *Reduced recidivism
	Question: What is being done that is different from the typical process (e.g., court diversion)? What do youth participating in the FGC experience get that others do not?	*Question:* Why, according to the theory, (e.g., reintegrative shaming), would these changes be expected to result from the FGC intervention?	*Question:* Why would intermediate outcomes be expected to produce these results?

Figure 2. Family group conferencing (FGC): Offender-focused intervention theory.

Assumption – *Victims who are empowered to take an active role in adjudicating their case and confronting those who harmed them will experience a greater sense of satisfaction that justice was achieved.*

Client → (Target group)	Intervention → (Reintegrative shaming)	Intermediate Outcomes → (Changes that must occur to achieve impact)	→ Impact (Long-term consequences)
		VICTIM	
* Must volunteer to participate *Must understand purpose of conference	*Tells story to community and offender *Gets information abut the offender and hears offender's story *May receive apology * Negotiates agreement for restitution	*Increased sense of support and empowerment *Decreased fear of offender *Increased understanding of offender and family factors *Restitution for damages	*Sense of justice and fairness *Sense of closure *Satisfaction with the process *Less overall fear and greater sense of order
	Question: What is being done that is different from the typical process (e.g., court diversion)? What do victims participating in the FGC experience get that others do not?	*Question:* Why, according to the theory, (e.g., reintegrative shaming), would these changes be expected to result from the FGC intervention?	*Question:* Why would intermediate outcomes be expected to produce these results?

Figure 3. Family group conferencing (FGC): Victim-focused intervention theory.

Assumption – *Broader involvement of supportive members of the community will expand participation in the justice process and enhance effectiveness of its outcomes.*

Client → (Target group)	Intervention → (Reintegrative shaming)	Intermediate Outcomes → (Changes that must occur to achieve impact)	→ Impact (Long-term consequences)
		COMMUNITY	
* Family or supporters of offender and victim *Must understand purpose of conference	*Participates in discussion about disposition *Expresses concern about crime and denounces offense *Supports offender in effort to repair harm	*Greater responsibility for sanctioning and establishing tolerance limits *Increased involvement of other citizens in the process *Improved capacity to settle disputes *Increased desire to participate in justice process	*Sense of justice and fairness *Reduced fear *Greater willingness to become involved in civic responsibilities *Safer communities
	Question: What is being done that is different from the typical process (e.g., court diversion)? What do community members participating in the FGC experience get that others do not? How is the process different because of their participation?	*Question:* Why, according to the theory, (e.g., reintegrative shaming), would these changes be expected to result from the FGC intervention?	*Question:* Why would intermediate outcomes be expected to produce these results?

Figure 4. Family group conferencing (FGC): Community-focused intervention theory.

one can conclude that an intervention such as FGC has moved from beginning to end. Clarifying theory in the form of a logic model helps to set standards for the quality of interventions and for the process of engaging stakeholders, who are necessary to produce desired results. As the questions in the bottom row of column two suggest, an initial task is to specify what, if anything, about this process is truly different from business as usual. As the question at the bottom of column three suggests, actual practice may not always be consistent with the theory of change. For example, some might view staff phone contact with victim and offender as "conferencing," while others might insist on several additional components in a setting involving a face-to-face encounter. Likewise, if an intervention theory pointed toward work experience as important because it was believed to promote prosocial youth-adult bonding, it would be questionable whether employment in a fast food restaurant (where very few employees are adults) would fulfill theoretical intentions (Bazemore, 1991) and therefore could be expected to produce the intermediate outcomes specified. In any event, by clearly incorporating these inputs into a logic model, it becomes readily apparent just what service the client is or is not receiving, as well as the extent to which program operations adhere to both overall FGC principles and the particular intervention theory that is being operationalized.

The third step then focuses on identifying what initial changes are expected in the attitudes, behavior, and/or situation of the client. Here we are defining what specifically constitutes "successful program completion." The idea is that if the underlying theory is accurate, and if the specified resources and services are provided, certain intermediate changes can be expected upon completion of the process (e.g., more positive attitudes, safety of children and other family members, reduced fear, closer prosocial bonding), which in turn are anticipated to result in certain ultimate long-term outcomes (e.g., care and protection, safer neighborhoods, family well-being). Again, the potential strengths or weaknesses of the linkages between intermediate outcomes and projected long-term impacts become more readily apparent when visually outlined in the form of a logic model.

DISCUSSION

A collaborative effort to develop a theory-based approach to the evaluation of conferencing is sensitive to the distinctive aspects of FGCs, while also acknowledging important similarities with all sound evaluation processes. Although we have encouraged the development of rigorous standards, it is also important to consider evaluation of conferencing in the context of current child welfare evaluation and appropriate standards of comparison.

Jessie Jackson once said, "When you're down on the floor, you don't need to worry so much about falling off the bed." The popularity of conferencing today is largely due to the fact that the child protection system has been "down on the floor" for a long time. Putting conferencing evaluation into context therefore requires that we evaluate FGCs not by some ideal standard, but alongside the real performance of the current social service system (Stuart, 1995). Similarly, while we have argued for development and use of intervention theory, it is also important to acknowledge that relatively little *current* intervention practice is based on firm theoretical foundations. Moreover, some of the most popular social welfare programs have not been evaluated at all—or in some cases have been negatively evaluated (Finkenauer & Gavin, 1999). The most common child protection practices have had decades to refine and develop safeguards, yet they continue to fall short both in ensuring fairness and in achieving effective outcomes. While FGCs will certainly produce some failures, the track record of the current system should be the standard by which success and failure are gauged.

Social service professionals are often captives of the priorities of bureaucracies that protect "business as usual" by insulating current practices from the critical scrutiny that inevitably seems to be focused on new interventions such as conferencing. Moreover, the potential in FGC programs for multiple benefits suggests that a fair assessment of policies and practices must also consider family, community, and alternative child protection outcomes. The appropriate standard of comparison is with more *formal decision-making processes* on outcomes such as fairness, client satisfaction, safety, and reduced fear.

CONCLUSIONS

The preliminary status of the developmental progress of conferencing programs, combined with the dynamic nature of their ongoing refinement efforts, argues for a greater investment in a process evaluation strategy that is initially focused more on implementation than impact. Additionally, the multipronged objectives of conferencing initiatives demand taking the interests of multiple stakeholders into account. Not only does this call for involving key decision-makers and information-users in the evaluation process, it also points to the need to map interventions and related outcomes from varying perspectives. Intervention theory can serve as an effective tool for accomplishing these essential objectives, with clear implications for immediate and long-term improvement in practices, as well as for improved theory development and evaluation utility. The challenge is to develop testable theories that link inputs with intervention processes and intermediate outcomes in a causal chain of events—and then to link intermediate outcomes with long-term indicators of strengthened communities. When that causal chain is effectively articulated and operationalized, the sun surely will be shining more brightly.

REFERENCES

Argryis, C. (1982). *Reasoning, learning and action.* San Francisco: Jossey-Bass.

Bazemore, G. (1991). New concepts and alternative practice in community supervision of juvenile offenders: Rediscovering work experience and competency development. *Journal of Crime and Justice, 14*(2), 27–52.

Bazemore, G. (1998). Evaluating community youth sanctioning models: Neighborhood dimensions and beyond. In *Crime and place: Plenary Papers of the 1997 Conference on Criminal Justice Research and Evaluation. National Institute of Justice Journal,* 23–49. Washington, DC.

Braithwaite, J., & Mugford, S. (1994). Conditions of successful reintegration ceremonies: Dealing with juvenile offenders. *British Journal of Criminology, 34*(2), 139–71.

Chen, H. (1990). *Theory-driven evaluations.* Newbury Park, CA: Sage.

Finkenauer T., & Gavin, P. (1999). *Scared straight: The panacea phenomenon revisited.* Prospect Heights, IL: Waveland.

Harris, P., & Smith, S. (1996). Developing community corrections: An implementation perspective. In A. Harland (Ed.), *Choosing correctional options that work. Defining the demand and evaluating the supply.* Thousand Oaks, CA: Sage.

Hawkins, J. D., & Nederbood, B. (1987). *Handbook for evaluating drug and alcohol prevention programs.* Rockville, MD: Office for Substance Abuse Prevention, U.S. Department of Health and Human Services.

Lehman, J., & Labecki, L. (1998). Myth vs. reality: The politics of crime and punishment and its impact on correctional administration in the 1990s. In T. Alleman & R. Gido (Eds.), *Turnstile justice: issues in American corrections.* Upper Saddle River, NJ: Prentice Hall.

Patton, M. (1986). *Utilization-focused evaluation* (2nd ed.). Beverly Hills, CA: Sage.

Stinchcomb, J., & Fox, V. (1999). *Introduction to corrections.* Upper Saddle River, NJ: Prentice Hall.

Stuart, B. (1995). Sentencing circles—Making "real" differences. Unpublished paper presented at Territorial Court of the Yukon.

Weiss, C. (1997). How can theory-based evaluation make greater headway? *Evaluation Review, 21*(4), 501–24.

Van Ness, D., & Strong, K. (1997). *Restoring justice.* Cincinnati, OH: Anderson.

28

Data Collection in a Family Group Conference Evaluation Project

YVONNE UNRAU, JACKIE SIEPPERT, and JOE HUDSON

INTRODUCTION AND PURPOSE

Family group conferencing (FGC) is becoming recognized as useful intervention for families implicated in child welfare and juvenile justice systems. The core notion of conferencing is relatively simple—bring together family members, helping professionals, other significant people in the child's life, and the child for the purpose of preparing a service plan to ensure the child's immediate and long-term safety and well-being. Implementing the concept of conferencing is more complex, requiring involvement of persons with knowledge and skills in working with involuntary clients, scheduling, group dynamics, conducting large group meetings, treatment planning, cultural diversity, and available social services and community resources.

Evaluating FGC programs is an essential part of refining and developing their use as an intervention approach. In general, systematic monitoring of a FGC process and outcomes helps us understand whether programs were implemented as designed, and whether they achieved their stated purpose. Evaluation findings can yield information on distinctive features of individual programs such as client profiles, worker qualifications, and group processes. Gaining a detailed understanding of an FGC program not only assists in program development, but also helps when implementing other similar programs.

This chapter discusses evaluation options for FGC programs, with particular focus on data collection, using a Canadian FGC demonstration program, "the Calgary project," as a case example. Data collection methods used in the Calgary project are described, along with discussions about the information yield from each.

PERSPECTIVE ON PROGRAM EVALUATION

The field of evaluation has come a long way since the 1960s when evaluation research was commonly seen as the application of social science research methods to test the effectiveness of social programs. A great deal of attention was paid to the development of sophisticated quantitative measurement tools and statistical procedures for measuring program effects and testing cause-effect relationships between program interventions and outcomes. However, during the 1970s and into the 1980s and 1990s, a different perspective on evaluation emerged. Increasingly, practitioners and researchers raised questions about the relevance of evaluation studies designed in isolation of the "real" program. Too often these evaluations measured artifacts of behavior or phenomena that had little to do with day-to-day program operations and the decisions to be made about them. Many researchers and practitioners also realized that a strict reliance on quantitative methods was not appropriate. Attention shifted to using qualitative methods and approaches to describe and assess programs.

In its early years, evaluation was seen primarily as a method to arrive at conclusions about the effects of a program. There is growing appreciation, however, that what happens in a program is at least as important as outcomes. As such, evaluations now are emphasizing the exploration of program processes in addition to addressing questions about how these might affect program outcomes. Evaluation is now commonly seen as amounting to the systematic collection, analysis, reporting, and use of information to describe and explain, and improve and develop a program. Increasingly, there is a broader perspective on the purpose of evaluation, moving away from an emphasis on a summative purpose aimed at rigorously testing program effects, to formative evaluations aimed at providing a continuous feedback of information on the program.

Program evaluations are increasingly seen as meeting administrative purposes, to assess the appropriateness of program changes and promote continuous development and improvement of innovative interventions. Evaluations are also used to assess the degree to which programs have deviated from intended operations and the factors that contribute to such deviations. They may be used to "discover" programs, including the unintended or side effects of interventions. In this vein, evaluations are instruments of organizational change.

The past two decades have also seen a shift in perspective about the role of program stakeholders in the evaluation process. Increasingly the view is held that evaluations should be conducted in ways that empower stakeholders, enhancing their power and voice in all phases of the evaluation study. The role of evaluator has shifted from one of objective researcher making most of the decisions about the planned study, to one of a facilitator or advisor assisting program stakeholders to make key decisions about the focus, scope, and use of the evaluation.

The Calgary project is one example of this dramatic shift in the roles that stakeholders and evaluators play in planning and implementing programs. In this project, stakeholder decision-making, information for routine program operations, and formative evaluation took precedence over evaluator control and a narrow focus on outcome data.

THE CALGARY FGC PROJECT

The Calgary project was established as a child welfare demonstration program. As such, it was important to design the project's evaluation procedures in keeping with the developmental nature of the project. This meant that the evaluation focus was to be on documenting services delivered and describing program implementation. A critical first task involved identifying the key stakeholders and then convening a meeting of the stakeholder group. At the first meeting the stakeholders had to agree on the role of the group, along with the schedule and agenda for future meetings. Attention then shifted to reach agreement on the FGC program and the focus of evaluation work. A description of the proposed FGC program had been presented in the original project proposal based largely on the conferencing literature. This amounted to a description of required resources, expected activities, and results. The model is presented in Figure 1.

Figure 1 shows the major type of resources expected to be used in the Calgary project, key activities, as well as the expected results or outcomes. This model amounts to a set of expectations held by the stakeholders about the Calgary project. The next step was designing and using data collection procedures to address stakeholder questions about program operations. The data collection and reporting efforts to be carried out amounted to testing whether the assumptions underlying the program logic were sound.

Having some clarity about the program focus of the proposed evaluation, attention then shifted to working with the stakeholder group to further refine this focus by developing specific evaluation questions. Generic questions were first suggested including:

- Is the program being implemented as designed?
- Is the target population being served?
- Are client services likely to achieve the program's specified goals?

Each of these generic questions was then broken down into more precise and operationalized questions that were used in developing the data collection instruments.

Central to this work by the stakeholders was a consideration of cost. Each evaluation question has an associated cost, largely consisting of staff time to collect, enter, and analyze data. The Calgary project, with a very limited evaluation budget, developed eight general questions to guide evaluation activities in its pilot year of operation:

1. What key events are necessary to establish a FGC program?
2. What is the profile of families referred to the program?
3. How much effort is needed to set up FGCs?
4. Who participates in FGCs, and what is the nature of this participation?
5. What process is used to carry out FGCs?
6. What is the nature of participant communication patterns at FGCs?
7. What client outcomes are achieved as a result of FGCs?
8. How satisfied are participants with FGCs?

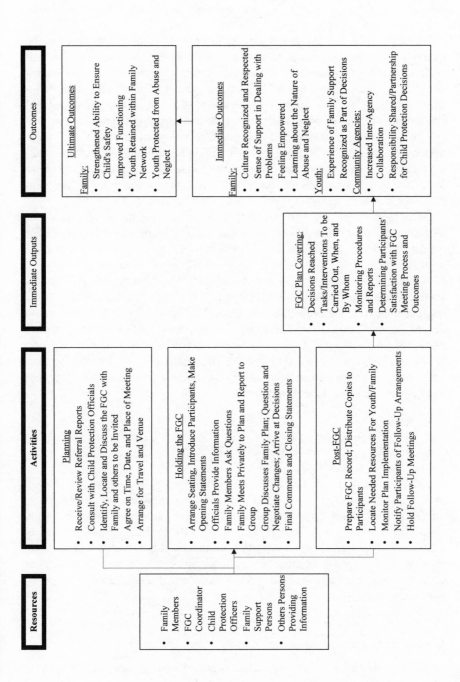

Figure 1.

These questions are similar to the questions asked of many programs, and the methods available to answer them are not specific. In fact, the variety of data collection and analysis methods used in social science research are described in most introductory research textbooks. The methods are not specific to program evaluation. Instead, it is the purpose for which data are collected and analyzed that characterizes formative evaluation. As planned and carried out in the Calgary project, the evaluation was designed to provide decision-makers with timely feedback on the program as implemented, and to provide information useful in making necessary modifications to the program as it unfolded. Evaluation results were to be used to determine whether the program was on target in terms of its operations, not to make conclusive statements about effectiveness.

Once the program structure and logic were defined and stakeholder questions identified, attention shifted to selecting the data collection methods and designing data collection instruments. Most evaluation questions can be answered using a variety of data collection methods. Just which method is chosen depends on a number of factors, most notably the nature of the questions the decision-makers want answered, the resources available, and the amount and type of data to be brought to bear on the evaluation questions. The "ideal" data collection method depends upon the unique circumstances of individual FGC programs. Smaller FGC programs with limited resources and a client database that consists of paper-and-pencil recordings will likely select a different data collection method than larger programs with a client data base that is computerized. The Calgary project most closely resembled the former.

DATA COLLECTION

A variety of data collection methods were used in the Calgary project, with each providing different types of data and giving different perspectives on FGC operations. In line with the aim of formative evaluations to serve programs—not stand in judgment of them—the data collection methods used in the Calgary project were carefully designed to fit well with operations, not disrupt them. At the same time the data collection methods had to fit within definite budget restraints. The Calgary project used six data collection methods, which supplied various types of data about the program.

Minutes of Stakeholder Meetings

In an ideal world every meeting would begin with an agenda and an accurate record of minutes. The agenda would provide a list of topics for discussion, while the minutes would carefully record key discussion points, decisions, actions taken, and new tasks or topics generated for future meetings. While agendas and minutes can vary in degree of formality, they serve the primary purpose of facilitating communication and understanding among meeting participants to achieve specific results. As such, they are helpful sources of data that could be used to track decision-making and establish a valuable timeline of key meeting events. Such data can assist in achieving the formative purpose of understanding how the program design got implemented in the form of daily operations.

Minutes of stakeholder meetings were recorded for all planning sessions held for the Calgary project. These provided a historical timeline of key events. The original concept paper presented the "idea" of a FGC program and successfully generated interest from key stakeholders, who eventually had a role in developing the program. The stakeholder group was varied and included representatives from the child welfare regional office, the child placement committee in the region, child welfare supervisors, the Office of the Children's Advocate, the Faculty of Social Work at the University of Calgary, and family court judges. This group, which later formed the steering committee, met monthly to get the Calgary project operating.

The steering committee's minutes provide a useful accounting of key events leading up to program operations. They also provide means for reflection. Looking back, one might ask whether nineteen months was a reasonable amount of time to get the program started, or what key events appeared to have the greatest impact in establishing the program. Such reflection could be helpful for further development of the Calgary project, or provide "lessons learned" for other programs in their preimplementation stage.

Contact and Communication Log

A central task of conferencing is getting family, professionals, and other significant people in a child's life to attend a meeting. The Calgary project developed a contact and communication log to be completed by the conference coordinator after each attempted or successful contact with a prospective participant. This form required the coordinator to record the type and number of contacts, along with travel time. Data were later entered into a computerized database and summarized to identify and track patterns of contact and communication between the coordinator and prospective conference participants.

As expected, the Calgary data showed that conferences require considerable time and effort to set up. The coordinator made a total of 950 attempted contacts for 23 conferences over one year. Just over half (531) of these contacts were successful at reaching the desired party. Put another way, the conference coordinator made, on average, 41 attempted contacts in setting up a conference. Although most (76 percent) of the successful contacts were made by phone, the coordinator still spent considerable time traveling. While only 11 percent of contacts were made in person, the average amount of travel time spent per conference was 1 hour and 12 minutes, ranging from 15 minutes to 2.5 hours.

Client Intake Forms

Intake forms are germane to most social service programs and are typically used to collect the first set of data for clients entering a program. The main purpose of intake is to determine if the referred client meets program eligibility requirements. The Calgary project had four eligibility requirements and each was included as part of a checklist on the project intake form. Other data collected on the form included: parent contact information; children's names, birth dates, and current placements; specific issues to be addressed at the FGC; and other professional organizations or individuals involved with the family. The project intake form recorded only data used for client service delivery, fitting on one legal-sized paper and taking approximately fifteen minutes to complete. Data collected on the intake form provided a basic profile of the families receiving services from the program. In total, twenty-three families, with fifty-one children meeting program eligibility requirements, were conferenced.

A major mistake made on many social service intake forms is asking too much. Not uncommonly, agency intake forms extend up to five or six pages. While it would have been interesting to collect additional client data for the Calgary project, it was not necessary given the evaluation questions and small budget. Data about household income, family composition, and child abuse history, for example, would have given a more detailed picture of clients referred to the program. On the other hand, they also would have resulted in more time for data collection, more intrusiveness, and increased cost.

Observation of FGC Process

Observation is a data collection method that involves an observer being present throughout a conference meeting. The role of the observer might range from being detached to being a full conference participant. A completely detached observer might watch the conference from outside the conference circle. A fully participating observer, on the other hand, would have a dual role at the conference. Besides having a role as conference participant, such as conference coordinator, he or she would also observe the process according to the data collection tools.

The Calgary project employed a nonparticipant observer to gather data about conferencing. The observer was provided a structured data collection instrument, covering a series of questions: Who participates at FGCs, and what is the nature of this participation? What process is used to carry out FGCs? What are the communication patterns of participants at FGCs? In keeping with the growing recognition of the value of qualitative evaluation methods, observations were recorded during the conference in the form of handwritten notes. These notes were later transcribed. This text data consisted of rich descriptions of key events and impressions about the conference process, allowing for both quantitative and qualitative analyses.

Extracting key observations from the data produced quantitative data. With respect to the question of communication patterns, for example, information was collected on who dominated conference discussions. The observer's notes revealed that, in eleven of nineteen conferences, adult participants dominated the discussion. In five conferences, it was a single adult family member, in four it was two adult family members, and in one it was the coordinator. At no time was a child observed to dominate the discussion.

While the quantitative data give a rough count of who is likely to dominate discussion in a FGC, the qualitative data provide more insight into how this occurred. One example occurred in the planning stage of a conference, that is, the portion of the meeting where problems and issues to be resolved were defined. In this conference, a prospective adoptive mother (AM) and one of the two great aunts (GA) were observed to dominate the discussion. This FGC included eleven participants: birth mother, grandmother, two great aunts (current caregivers for the child), great uncle, the prospective adoptive mother, a child protection worker, a private adoption agency, a clergyman, the coordinator, and the observer. Below are the observer's notes about how the discussion was dominated and by whom.

Both the AM and the GA were very verbal. It is estimated that between the two of them, they talked about 70% of the time. In estimation, the AM talked about 40% of the time and the GA talked 30% of the time. The AM seemed eager to relay three points to the group.

1. She was very excited and felt very fortunate to be able to have this opportunity to adopt the child. She had already met him and had him over for a visit. She reiterated many positive things about him including: the fact that she felt he was a very clever boy, the fact that he appeared to be in such good health and the fact that he got along so well with her children. . . . Although she never explicitly stated she was excited or felt fortunate to have this opportunity to adopt the child, it was evident through her body language, tone of voice, and her face positively beaming happiness from the beginning of the meeting to the end.

2. The second item . . . was that in her opinion the natural family was not relinquishing all contact with the boy. She mentioned many times over that the natural family was welcome in her home, and that she and her husband would not be threatened by their continued contact with the child. Rather, contact with the birth family was something that she and her husband encouraged.

3. The third item . . . was that although she and her husband were fine with the natural family coming over as much as they wanted, she believed that the experts in adoption should probably decide how much interfamily visiting was appropriate. She said that making this transition from one home to the other as smooth as possible was paramount. "After all," she said, "we are all adults and he is a small child, his welfare has to be our number one concern."

4. GA basically played the combined role of the family advocate and facilitator of the planning portion of the meeting. She encouraged the birth mother (BM) to give the AM a

recounting of some of the positive events that the BM and child had shared together. She also encouraged the AM and the BM to talk about what they saw as the ideal solution to this situation. It was during this part of the discussion that the BM revealed she wanted to see her child's report cards, pictures of him as he grew up and possibly even some of his school work and projects as he got older. She said that she did not want any contact with him, however, she changed her mind a few times on this during the meeting. GA mentioned at least twice how fortunate she felt that the child was going to be living with the AM and how she felt that this was a difficult situation for the BM but that she (GA) knew in her heart it was the right decision for the child. As an interesting aside the BM avoided eye contact with her family members most of the time, but was quite comfortable about maintaining eye contact with the AM.

Care Plan

Like the intake form, the care plan used in the Calgary project served program operations first and the evaluation second. The care plan is a principal product of conferences, having two components. First, it records conference logistics, including date, time, location, and proposed review dates. It also describes key components of the service plan, including goals, the persons responsible for tasks, and monitoring procedures. In the Calgary project, each participant signed the care plan and noted whether or not they agreed with the plan.

Each care plan for the twenty-three families in the Calgary project reflected the unique needs of the target child and his or her family. A review of the service goals for the families revealed seven themes: contact among family members, parent follow-through of specified treatment and legal tasks, children's living arrangements, safety, well-being, legal status, and culture.

Satisfaction Questionnaires

Client or consumer satisfaction questionnaires are often used to gather data about perceptions of the conference. These data provide one type of quality assurance measure. The Calgary project used a simple satisfaction questionnaire, consisting of seventeen questions. Each conference participant rated satisfaction questions on a five-point scale. The dimensions of satisfaction measured included:

- **conference setup** (i.e., conference location, overall preparation for the conference, and having the right people in attendance to make decisions);
- **participation** (i.e., being seen as an equal participant, amount of information provided at the conference, and feeling free to speak one's mind);
- **decision-making** (i.e., involvement in reaching decisions, having some control over decision-making, having time to make decisions, the decisions made, and the service plan);
- **comfort** (i.e., feeling supported and feeling safe);

- **coordinator role** (i.e., knowledge of child protection, knowledge of family, and helpfulness);
- **overall satisfaction** with the conference.

The tally of satisfaction scores showed that the vast majority of conference participants were satisfied with the conferences. For example, 79 percent of conference participants indicated being highly satisfied with the way conferences were run. The results also showed that a small percentage of participants were highly dissatisfied. This leads to questions about what makes some participants satisfied and others dissatisfied. Two open-ended questions were included as part of the satisfaction questionnaire and provide some insights about what participants did and did not like about the conference. Handwritten responses were transcribed and analyzed for common themes. A total of seventy-five participants responded to the question: In your opinion, what was the best thing about the FGC? Of these, sixty-eight responded positively, one negatively, and one with reservation. Five individuals did not respond at all. The negative comment was made by a youth who expressed dissatisfaction by saying, "Nothing [was good] because I didn't get to see my dad!"

Several themes were noted in the many positive comments made about the conferences. One theme centered on healthy communication. Participants said, "Everyone had a chance to speak," "[They] were able to air the situation," "Communication was open and honest." And they were able to "say what had to be said." Praise was given by some to the coordinator. "Having the rules set down beforehand," and "good facilitation" were thought to be helpful in bringing parties together to talk about problems. A second theme coming out of the satisfaction questionnaire was family participation in planning the future of the young person. Having all parties together and in one location seemed a feat that had not been accomplished before by some families. People remarked that conferences helped in "getting some headway." For one family, "A deal was worked out after of period of fighting in the past."

A third theme was a strong sense that the conferences resulted in "empowerment of the family." This empowerment was realized as decisions were made. For example: "[The family] reached an agreement," "Closure [was reached] for a continuous issue of permanent guardianship," "The family owned and tried to solve their own problems." A fourth theme centered on information shared at the conferences. For some it was worthwhile to learn general information about the youth's care plan and the family's problems. In other instances, more specific information was valued.

A second open-ended questionnaire item asked: In your opinion what was the worst thing about the FGC? The responses ranged from "**everything** because of one person" to "nothing." Of seventy-five participants, nine said there was nothing wrong with the conference and nine did not report their views. The remaining fifty-seven provided a variety of responses, producing three themes for use in the Calgary project. First, there was some frustration expressed at participants who were seen as acting inappropriately. In some cases key family members were late, left early, or did not show up despite their expressed willingness to attend. In other cases, participants expected that certain conference participants should have "taken charge" of the situation but did not. For example, comments from one conference focused on a mom needing to take more responsibility, while another focused on a youth failing to do so. In another, one participant commented that "professionals failed to provide resource/background information."

While discussion among participants at the conference was identified as a theme for one of the *best* things about the FGC, there were also concerns expressed about how discussions took place. Individuals remarked that there was "yelling," "fighting and hurt feelings," and "hard feelings." One person said the worst thing about a conference was "having to speak honestly and hurting some people at times." Other responses to this question suggested that some participants wanted more structure. For example, one person remarked that "sometimes [there was] no "judge" to stop confrontation and things get off topic." Another observed that the discussion "got into past subjects instead of working on the present."

Interviews

Interviews were another data collection method used in the Calgary project. Child protection workers were contacted by a research assistant and invited to give their perceptions about the project. A structured interview schedule included questions such as: Did you have concerns about the coordinator? What changes would you make to the project? What information was needed to better prepare child welfare workers for the project? What are your reasons for making referrals to the program?

Ten child welfare workers participated in these interviews and their responses were recorded and transcribed. The data produced an itemized list of comments and suggestions for the program. For example, the following are some of the most common reasons given for making continued referrals to the program:

- FGC is very empowering for families;
- FGC is a very effective and efficient use of time for problem solving.
- FGC is a great opportunity to hold families accountable for their responsibilities.
- The process gives families more opportunities for input and involvement in the decision-making process and in a safe place.

UTILITY OF RESULTS FOR PROGRAM DECISION-MAKING

The final phase of formative evaluation is making use of the results for program development. There are two ways to think about the meaning of utilization. One is using evaluation findings to make program adjustments, enhance program understanding, and reduce uncertainty. For example, if the evaluation results show that after forty FGCs, the average duration was two hours with little variation between individual conferences, decision-makers could project the number of FGCs that could be feasibly held over a specified time period. This might assist in setting workload targets based on empirical evidence. Another way to think about evaluation utilization is the knowledge gained about the program by evaluation stakeholders as a result of engaging in the evaluation process. In this sense, evaluation is a learning opportunity whereby stakeholders gain a greater understanding of a program's operations, clientele, and outcomes.

The data collection methods used in the Calgary project produced different types of data for program stakeholders to consider. The communication and contact log, for example, provided a detailed accounting of how many contacts were made (attempted and successful) to schedule a conference. The satisfaction questionnaire provided an estimate on how satisfied participants were with the experience, along with some written impressions about the *best* and *worst* aspects of the conferences. Observations produced the richest data in the sense that they offered a portrait of what actually went on in each conference. Observations also facilitated a better understanding of how patterns and processes developed within the conferences.

Data collection also addressed questions about the project's goals and objectives. By observing conferences and reviewing care plans it is possible to detail the types of outcomes sought. Through follow-ups these outcomes can be monitored. For example: Are the tasks and behaviors in the care plan being completed and by whom? What types of practice objectives are frequently achieved? Additional interview data from referring child welfare workers also add to this picture. These types of information are useful for learning about the dynamics of conferences and the types of outcomes achieved. Using multiple data collection methods gives stakeholders the flexibility to examine data from various perspectives in an effort to gain a better understanding of program operations.

A FINAL NOTE

While evaluation data are useful for facilitating decision-making about program operations and the understanding of stakeholders, setting up a reliable data collection system is no easy task. Whether for therapeutic or evaluation purposes, data collection is an activity included in the job descriptions of most human service workers. However, it is a job that is not always well done. To increase the likelihood of receiving accurate and timely data collected by workers, it is helpful to establish basic monitoring protocols and feedback loops. Monitoring protocols are a set of "check-and-balance" procedures that help ensure quality data collection. For example, a procedure might involve a FGC program administrator selecting client files at random on a monthly basis to check for data completion. Information gained from this evaluation of staff compliance with program policy could than be shared in supervision meetings. The aim would be to improve program operations.

An important principle for consideration when designing data collection procedures is to ensure they, at worst, minimally interfere with program operations and, at best, enhance them. Formative evaluations are undertaken to serve the program, not the program to serve evaluation. The key to designing feedback loops of useful evaluation information is ensuring that the information meets the needs of designated users. If a FGC coordinator is charged with collecting client history data for each family, for example, then a feedback strategy might include providing the coordinator with a summary client profile at agreed-upon times. This leads to the work of deciding on data analysis and reporting strategies.

A data analysis strategy is usually determined through a deductive process. Once the evaluation questions have been operationalized, data collection instruments designed, and decisions made about who receives what evaluation information and when, the data analysis strategy becomes obvious. For example, if the evaluation stakeholders want to know how long it takes to conduct a FGC, a data collection instrument might be designed to record start and end times of each phase of conferences. The stakeholders might also decide to have a summary report prepared after every ten conferences. The summary report could include minimum and maximum times, average time, and variance to give a picture that answers stakeholder questions.

So what are some possible next steps in the current evaluation study? Certainly many of the original questions posed remain relevant. In a few years, for example, stakeholders might still want information about the profile of families referred to the program; the nature and amount of effort required by coordinators to set up, hold, and follow up conferences; participation patterns at conferences; communication among participants; and satisfaction levels. While answering these questions is essential for monitoring program operations, determining what is not working as intended, and making modifications to program activities, future data collection might place more emphasis on following up FGC participants to answer questions about program effectiveness.

Simplicity, which was a major feature of the Calgary project, is another element that would remain consistent over time. The evaluation model used in the Calgary project was based on a simple framework, one that involved limited resources and a focus on stakeholder questions. Consequently, some of the evaluation tools, such as the client intake form and care plan, would continue to be useful. They address key questions and are simple to use, recording essential information. Furthermore, additional questions can be added or deleted to these forms to address stakeholder questions as they change over time. Information generated from these forms allows evaluators to identify important client trends and issues, as well as gaps in service delivery.

SUMMARY

The Calgary project is an example of a pragmatic program evaluation. In contrast to older evaluation models that focused on summative outcomes and methodological rigor, this newer model of evaluation strives to provide information for continuous program improvement. This inevitably entails developing a different relationship between evaluators and other program stakeholders. The evaluator is no longer considered an outside expert parachuted in at a critical point to determine if the program is "working." Program personnel are active participants in evaluation planning, implementation, and reporting. In formative evaluation, evaluators and program stakeholders work collaboratively. The evaluator offers advice about research methods, data collection, and analysis, while other stakeholders make decisions about the scope, focus, and timing of evaluations, as well as the amount and type of resources to be used.

A major lesson learned from the Calgary project is the value of multiple data sources and data collection techniques that are simple in nature. Few programs have the resources or expertise to develop sophisticated and complex data collection tools. Trying to develop such tools without appropriate resources or expertise will often lead to incomplete data, or data collection techniques that are quickly abandoned by program personnel. It is much better to incorporate simple data collection procedures that serve both administrative and evaluation purposes. Systematic recording of client intake information and progress on care plans are examples of obtaining relevant information for program development and improvement.

Three basic principles should be kept in mind when designing evaluations of FGC programs. First, stakeholders ought not to prematurely focus evaluations on program outcomes. At a minimum, a relatively precise description of program operations is required for outcome evaluations. Second, data collection strategies should be simple and fit within available resources. Third, stakeholders are encouraged to incorporate a diverse range of data sources and methods to maximize the types of information available for program development and improvement.

29

Families as Resources

The Washington State
Family Group Conference Project[1]

WILLIAM VESNESKI and SUSAN KEMP

INTRODUCTION

In the study reported here, data were analyzed from one hundred family group conferences (FGCs) in Washington State to examine the links between conference decisions, the content of conferencing plans, and two widely adopted practice frameworks: family-centered practice and the strengths perspective. Our results suggest that both the content and the outcomes of family group conferences are consistent with family-centered and strengths-based practice, aspects of which appear to be inherently supported by family group conferencing methods.

Washington State embraced family group conferencing because of the positive reputation it had gained in its country of origin, New Zealand. From modest beginnings as a small demonstration project in a suburban Seattle office of the state's Department of Child and Family Services (DCFS), conferencing expanded statewide throughout 1997. This expansion was driven by collaboration between DCFS officials and staff members of the Northwest Institute for Children and Families, a child welfare training institute located within the University of Washington School of Social Work. The expanded project was administered by the Northwest Institute and supervised by an MSW-level social worker with extensive child welfare practice experience.

The administrative structure of the FGC project was straightforward. Conference coordinators were employed by the DCFS and "loaned" to the project. These coordinators were responsible for organizing and facilitating conferences in each of the state's six administrative regions. A coordinator worked in each of these regions and received referrals for conferences from social workers employed within the region. Referred cases ranged from those in the early stages of an abuse or neglect investigation to those where parental rights had been legally terminated and the children were legally free for adoption or other permanent family placement.

In addition to administering the program and working with the conference coordinators, the project's supervisor provided case consultation, facilitated communication and information sharing among coordinators through a monthly "roundtable," and conducted training sessions on conferencing. Finally, a graduate student was employed to design and complete a descriptive evaluation of the project.

METHODS

The evaluation of Washington's FGC project was designed to answer the following questions:

1. Who was served by the project?
2. What were the outcomes for children and families participating in the project?
3. Does conferencing engage families in the delivery of child welfare services?

A number of research methods were used to answer these questions.

First, descriptive data were gathered on all conferences known to have been held in the state between October 1996 and March 1998 ($n = 100$). Data were obtained from intake sheets completed by FGC coordinators and copies of family plans produced during conferences. These documents proved to be rich sources of data on both the circumstances of a family's case and the services the family outlined for itself during the conference meeting. Not surprisingly, they contained less information on the feelings of participating families about the intervention itself.

Second, we conducted two surveys of workers involved with family group conference projects. The first was a telephone interview with fourteen social workers who had referred cases to the FGC program. Social workers were selected at random from the fifty-six case sample existing on October 1, 1997, and interviewed during the fall and winter of 1997. The second survey was a written instrument administered to all nine conference coordinators in May 1998. Both surveys were designed to identify the practice approaches that social workers believed were associated with conferencing as well as the impact they thought conferences had on families receiving child welfare services.

The third research method was a qualitative analysis of the family plans generated during the conferences and of the coordinators' intake sheets. The qualitative analysis provided a more nuanced understanding of the FGC project's impact and the links between family group conferencing practice and underlying theoretical frameworks.

To analyze the qualitative data, a grounded-theory approach was used, specifically, the constant comparison method (Glaser & Strauss, 1967; Strauss & Corbin, 1990). As recommended by Strauss and Corbin (1990), a three-stage process of open coding, axial coding, and selective coding was used. Coordinators' intake sheets, their case notes written on the sheets, and the family's plans—all appropriate subjects for grounded-theory analysis—were coded according to this three-stage methodology. During the analysis, data were first divided into two large groups (case facts and case plans) and subsequently divided into meaning units. The case facts group included all references to a participant family's strengths or challenges. Data in this group were obtained largely, but not exclusively from the intake sheets and case notes. In contrast, the case plan group contained all data related to *products* of the family group conference. Data for the case plan group were taken largely, but not exclusively, from the family plans.

A limitation of the study is that the sample includes a disproportionate representation of plans and intake sheets from particular coordinators. Although all coordinators were asked to submit documents to the evaluator for analysis, some facilitated more conferences than others, and therefore contributed a greater number of intake sheets and family plans during the study period. The work of these coordinators is thus more fully represented in the evaluation, with consequences that cannot be fully determined. Those who are overrepresented tended, however, to be those with the longest experience with conferences. If length and degree of experience is correlated with greater investment in family group conferencing methods, the data may have a positive skew.

In interpreting these data, it is also important to note that over the course of the family group conferencing project no attempt was made by the project's administrator, evaluator, or FGC coordinators to limit the types of cases referred for a conference. The state's child welfare social workers were simply asked to refer families they thought might benefit from a conference. The coordinator then worked to arrange a conference. This lack of referral criteria stems from the early history of the project. Washington's FGC program was originally designed to determine whether frontline child welfare workers were comfortable with the intervention and whether they thought it helped their work. The creation of referral criteria would have detracted from answering these questions.

DESCRIPTION OF CHILDREN

Between October 1996 and March 1998, 229 children were the subjects of family group conferences in Washington. Although these children had varying levels of involvement with the state's child welfare system, 71 percent had reached the point of supervision by the juvenile court system. The remaining 29 percent were not sufficiently urgent to require court supervision. Court supervision took one of two forms: either a child was placed in shelter care or short-term custody of the state (11 percent of the entire sample), or the child had been declared dependent and was in the long-term custody of the state awaiting a permanent placement (60 percent of the entire sample). Children whose cases were not supervised by the juvenile court experienced a mean case duration of 4.1 months, whereas those with court supervision and who were in shelter care had a mean case duration of 4.8 months. Children whose cases were supervised by the court and for whom a dependency had been filed (the largest group in the sample) had the longest mean case duration—17.8 months.

The age distribution of the children in the sample was consistent with data on children in out-of-home care more generally, with over half (55 percent) the sample made up of children aged six or younger. One of the more interesting aspects of the sample's demographics is the proportion of children in different racial and ethnic groups. Children of color, who already are overrepresented in the child welfare population in Washington, represent an even larger proportion of the children in this sample (49 percent of the sample vs. 33 percent statewide). Conversely, Caucasian children are underrepresented in this sample compared with their representation among children in out-of-home care (51 percent of the sample vs. 67 percent statewide).

In the sample of conferences, family members attended in significant numbers and participated in ways that differed from typical patterns of family involvement in child welfare services. The mean number of family participants per conference was 6.9, compared to 5.2 participants for professionals. Fathers, who typically are less involved in the child welfare processes relating to their children than mothers (Kahkonen, 1997; O'Donnell, 1995), participated in 49 percent of the conferences.

The family members attending conferences brought with them a number of personal and interpersonal concerns, including difficulties with substance abuse, challenges in meeting basic needs, and concerns over physical safety. Nevertheless, the evaluation data indicate that conference participants created thoughtful and detailed plans for keeping their children safe following a conference. These plans skillfully leveraged both personal and environmental resources in developing solutions to family problems and concerns.

FAMILY-CENTERED PRACTICE

Family-centered interventions both validate and respect the knowledge and strengths already present in families, and create opportunities for family members to become more competent, independent, and self-sustaining (Dunst, Deal, & Trivetle, 1997). Such interventions strengthen families and their natural support networks while also bolstering their decision-making abilities. Family-centered interventions also emphasize enhancing individual and family environmental and social competencies. As in empowerment practice, these competencies include those skills necessary for effective interaction with others and the larger world, such as problem solving, parenting, job seeking, and self-advocacy (Dodd & Gutierrez, 1990).

Analyses of family plans produced during FGCs in Washington State reveal that not only is the *process* of family group conference consistent with family-centered practice principles, but that the commitments made by family members to activities *following* conferences also reflect core principles of a family-centered approach, particularly those related to building capacity in the family for effective parenting. For example, family members frequently committed to postconference activities that would provide them with additional competencies in key life domains.

During the qualitative analysis, a metacategory emerged from the data entitled *Achieving Competency.* Two subcategories are contained within this metacategory: (1) *Education* and (2) *Parenting Education.* The *Education* subcategory included references to GED preparation, school programs, and job training for parents and family members. The *Parenting Education* subcategory included references to parenting classes, programs, and skill development courses for families. The emergence of these two subcategories supports the notion that family group conferencing sets the stage for the acquisition of important social and environmental competencies by family members. Unlike many mandated services, however, conferences address the need for competency building by way of organic, nonstigmatizing, and family-driven processes.

Consistent with other research studies, competency building was not the only family-centered practice principle found to be reflected in conferencing. In one study of FGCs in the United Kingdom, for example, more than 90 percent of conferences were characterized by family members offering supportive resources to a maltreated child's immediate family in novel and unexpected ways (Crow & Marsh, 1997). The data from this evaluation similarly provide support for conferences as an important mechanism for expanding the options available for problem solving by both families *and* professionals. Unsolicited comments on survey instruments used during the evaluation reveal, for example, that Washington's coordinators thought "families often brought in their own [or] new resources to the meetings—resources the social worker didn't know about." Other comments indicate that the services families request might be "different at times" but "about the same quantity" as those initially outlined by the family's social worker before the conference.

A salient feature of services requested by families was that they had a "different priority" than those accorded by the social worker. At least one of Washington's coordinators was "always surprised" by the services families requested during a conference. These comments support the belief that conferencing provides family members an opportunity to use their immediate, personal (and indeed idiosyncratic) knowledge when identifying and accessing services for their children. They are also consistent with family-centered philosophy, which emphasizes the central importance and validity of the family's knowledge and expertise. A more detailed description of one Washington family plan further illustrates these ideas.

The "Doe" family attended a conference in 1998. Although the family had a history of involvement with the state's child protective services department, there was no court involvement in the family's case at the time of the conference. It appears that the conference was held because the family's children were at risk of being removed from their relative placement. It is not known whether this relative placement was a legacy of prior governmental involvement.

Eleven family members attended the conference and, after hearing reports from eight professionals, devised a plan for their children. The written plan begins with a frank discussion of each family member's feelings about the children's situation as well as each member's opinion on returning the children home. Following this section, the plan specifies the children's future placement.

The plan indicates that the children would continue living with their relatives while slowly making the transition back into the home of their parent. The family clearly sought to strengthen the relative placement by attending to the caregivers' needs because their plan outlines a detailed respite care schedule. This schedule includes a monthly weekend stay for the children with a foster family, monthly overnight visits with the parent, and the plan lays the groundwork for hiring a part-time home care aide to assist the caregivers.

In addition to specifying the children's placement and parental visitation, the family addressed other important issues in their planning process. For example, they outlined mental health services, such as counseling and medication management for the children. They also addressed the parent's unresolved family law case and identified a family spokesperson. This spokesperson was charged with maintaining regular contact with the family's social worker and transmitting information from the social worker to other family members. Finally, the family arranged transportation for the children to their various appointments, capitalizing on the services of two community agencies as well as three different family members acting as volunteer drivers.

In some ways, the Doe family plan is similar to traditional casework plans. Many of the services called for, such as mental health counseling and respite foster care, are staples of child welfare social work. However, the plan also includes a frank and affirming recitation of family members' feelings about the case and a depth and breadth of focus uncommon in conventional child welfare practice. Perhaps most significantly, the plan differs from traditional case planning in its nuanced knowledge of the children and their needs. This understanding is particularly evident in the plan's closing section. Here, the family states that it wants to involve the children in church activities, and it suggests possibly enrolling them in a Big Brother/Sister program. The plan details each of the children's extracurricular activities, interests, and hobbies and pays attention to their educational plans. In fact, the plan specifically calls for family encouragement of one child's art activities.

The expertise of the Doe family, no doubt gained from its members' close, personal knowledge of one another, is demonstrated throughout the plan. The family seems as adroit at recommending medication management for the children as it is at listing the children's hobbies and encouraging their creative endeavors. The family's ability to use its own knowledge and expertise, in combination with traditional child welfare services, reinforces family competence and affirms their independence—both hallmarks of family-centered practice.

The qualitative analysis likewise demonstrates that participating families found unique ways of using their own resources when meeting the needs of their members. In fact, the use of family resources and strengths was so prominent in family plans that five important subcategories emerged from the qualitative analysis. All of these subcategories concern the family and are contained within the *Facilitating Interpersonal Connections* metacategory:

1. *Arranging visitation and family contact.* Analysis of the 100 family plans revealed significant reference to family visitation, telephone contact, and letter writing among and between family members.
2. *Family decision making.* Includes family requests for follow-up family group conferences and other formal means of family decision-making.
3. *Family meetings/gatherings.* This subcategory describes the various ways families arranged to come together and connect with one another informally, including the creation and use of "family councils."
4. *Fostering communication.* Explains how families decided to facilitate communication among their members and with others. Examples include "communication/collaboration among caregivers" and "family members to speak with one another when issues arise."
5. *General family support and help.* This subcategory details the methods families used to help one another, such as monitoring a parent's progress ("relatives to keep Dad on track"), assisting with child care ("family to assist with kids' activities"), and arranging family assistance ("Mom to move in with Dad to help stabilize family").

These findings are consistent with reports that conferencing encourages "family commitment" and allows families to make better decisions about their children (Lupton, Barnard, & Swall-Yarrington, 1996). One of the reasons conferencing appears to support family decision-making is its ability to foster a family's use of professional social work services while also encouraging use of their own resources. During a conference families not only have their own personal resources to select from when addressing problems, but also those services traditionally provided by the child welfare system.

Qualitative analysis of the Washington data suggests that families participating in conferences choose traditional social work and health care services when addressing personal concerns such as anger management and attention deficit/hyperactivity disorder. This conclusion is reflected in family plans, such as the one for the Doe family, which recommend professional counseling and medical assistance for these concerns. The use of formal interventions is, however, counterbalanced by the families' decisions to use family and community resources when trying to improve interpersonal relationships. For example, families chose to engage in church activities, participate in support groups, or visit one another in order to strengthen their interpersonal ties.

Research in the United Kingdom (Lupton et al., 1996) indicates that families participating in conferences request more assistance from social service agencies than families not participating in conferences. From the survey data, about half of Washington's coordinators thought families requested more professional services because of their conference participation. None of the coordinators thought families requested fewer services as a result of a FGC. Rather than simply replacing professional services with the use of individual and community resources, family group conferences may therefore promote better integration between formal and informal services. This finding appears to relate to the work of Berger and Neuhaus (1977), who describe the salience of informal systems of support as "mediating structures" between families and formal social systems. These and other similar findings underscore the role of FGCs in building connections between marginalized families, and the range of services that are essential to maintaining family integrity and well-being.

The findings on the services identified by families also suggest that it is not necessarily the services offered to families in traditional child welfare practice, but the assumptions and power hierarchies embedded within them that may be problematic. In short, using family group conferencing to restructure the process of delivering services does not eliminate either the need for services or a family's desire for them. Rather, it incorporates a family's valuable knowledge into the decision-making process, widens the array of informal and formal services the family has to choose from, and places the family in charge of identifying the services to be incorporated into the plan.

KINSHIP PLACEMENTS

Given the extent to which family group conferencing fosters family decision-making, it is perhaps not surprising that it also appears to foster the use of kinship placements. Not only are such placements consistent with family-centered practice principles, but rates of kinship placement can also be interpreted as indicators of an extended family's engagement in child welfare service delivery.

Data on the extent to which children in this sample were placed with relatives following a family group conference are displayed in Table 1. This table shows that of the 192 children for whom placement data were available, more than three-quarters (78 percent) remained in their current placement. Data on placement types for the forty-three children experiencing a placement change following the conference show that all children except one were placed with parents or relatives. The importance of this finding can be more fully appreciated when it is considered in relation to the placement data for the "no moves" children. These placements are described in Table 2.

These data indicate that the majority of "no moves" children remained in either parental or relative care, suggesting that the FGCs either facilitated or strengthened opportunities for placement within children's biological family systems. In this sample, 86 percent of all children who were the subject of conferences were placed either with relatives or parents at the conclusion of the conference, whether or not their cases were supervised by the court. To better interpret this finding, it

Table 1. Placement Moves Following Conference ($n = 192$)[a]

Type of placement move	No. of children	Percentage of total[b]
No moves	149	78
Foster care to relative care	22	11
Relative care to parental care	12	6.1
Foster care to parental care	4	2.1
Parental care to relative care	3	1.5
Juvenile rehabilitation to relative care	1	0.5
Relative care to foster care	1	0.5

[a]Thirty-seven children had placement changes missing from their intake sheets and family plans.
[b]Percentages reflect rounding error.

is helpful to compare it to more general data on children in out-of-home placement in Washington State.

For the year ending June 1998, there were 9,938 children in out-of-home placements in Washington State (Children's Administration, 1998). All of these children were the subject of abuse and neglect cases supervised by the juvenile court. Just over 2,700 (27 percent) were placed with relatives. In the family group conference sample, 103 children were placed outside the home and under supervision of the juvenile court. Of this group, 77 percent were placed with relatives. This number stands in marked contrast to the 27 percent relative placement rate statewide and raises interesting questions concerning conferencing's role in maintaining, strengthening, and fostering kinship placements..

STRENGTHS-BASED PRACTICE

Strengths-based social work practice emphasizes the positive attributes, resources, capacities, potentialities, and competencies of clients and communities (Kemp, Whittaker, & Tracy, 1997). Rather than focusing primarily on pathology, risk, and dysfunction, strengths-based practice underscores family resilience and

Table 2. Placements for Children Not Moved after a Conference ($n = 149$)

Type of placement	Number of children	Percentage of total[a]
Parental care	58	38.9
Relative care	65	43.6
Foster care	25	16.8
Group care	1	0.67

[a]Percentages reflect rounding error.

focuses on the development of partnerships with families that build on the ways in which clients cope, survive, and thrive. Surveys of FGC coordinators in Washington show that they believe conferencing is solidly strengths-based. When asked to identify the extent to which knowledge of the strengths approach was important in carrying out their jobs, coordinators uniformly indicated that this knowledge was "always important." Coordinators also strongly agreed with the statement that "FGCs are a strength-based intervention."

The defining elements of strengths-based practice parallel the fundamental tenets of family group conferencing outlined by Elizabeth Cole (1996). Cole argues, first, that conferencing supports the principle that families have primary responsibility for their children and that their ability to carry out this responsibility should be respected and protected. Second, she notes that conferencing generally assumes that families can make sound decisions about their children's care and that they are able to make needed changes in behavior. Third, she points out that conferencing puts into action the idea that where possible children should live with their families even though most abuse and neglect occurs within the family. Because of their shared commitment to honoring and respecting clients, family group conferencing and the strengths approach both aim to provide empowering and responsive services to clients.

The qualitative analysis of intake sheets and family plans reinforces Cole's assertions. A robust *Strengths* metacategory was clearly evident in the data. Indeed, this was the largest and most dynamic category to emerge during the analysis. In evaluating this, it should be noted that any references coordinators made to individual or family strengths on their intake sheets were wholly unsolicited. Nor were coordinators directed to take a strengths inventory as part of their conference preparation. In this context, the emergence of a *Strengths* metacategory is even more telling, for it suggests that conferencing is inherently associated with a strengths approach and that this association can be directly activated in child welfare practice. The *Strengths* metacategory consisted of eight subcategories. A detailed description of each subcategory provides a rich appreciation for the variety of strengths possessed by families participating in conferences:

1. *Child/Family Relationships.* This subcategory included the following references in case-notes and family plans: "Child lived with relatives his whole life," "Children happy in relative home," and "Children need to be connected to family."
2. *Child/Parent Relationships.* Subcategory included "Good parenting," "Mom and Dad eager and willing to parent," and "Kids know their parents and want to maintain contact."
3. *Engagement with Service Providers.* Subcategory included "Regular domestic violence [treatment] attendance," "Complied with DSHS recommendations," and "Mom making wonderful progress in drug treatment."

4. *Family Support of Permanent Plan.*   Subcategory included "Fathers agree to guardianship" and "Family believes adoption is best for child."
5. *Family Support of Individuals.*   Subcategory included "Many relatives willing to help," "Family working well together," and "Paternal side rich and stable environment."
6. *Child Functioning.*   Subcategory included "Child doing pretty well," "Making social, academic, and emotional progress," and "Child hasn't run away."
7. *Interpersonal Functioning.*   Subcategory included "Mom not associating with old friends," "Parents agreed to put differences aside and make joint decisions regarding kids," and "Work well together."
8. *Sibling Relationships.*   This subcategory includes the following references: "Siblings being together" and "Want siblings together."

The identification of this dynamic group of strengths confirms the belief held by Washington's coordinators that family group conferencing is a strengths-based intervention. More importantly, these findings support the notion that conferencing incorporates strengths-based practice values and contributes to child welfare practice that values family resources, supports their use, and strengthens their effectiveness.

CONCLUSION

The quantitative data from this evaluation add to the growing body of knowledge on the impact of family group conferencing on children and families receiving child welfare services. Most significant is the finding that relative and parental placements appear to be robustly supported by family group conferences. The low number of children who moved out of placements with family or kin supports this conclusion, as do the data that conferences frequently result in children moving from foster care into parental and relative care. Indeed, very few children in the Washington sample were placed in nonrelative care or group care at the conclusion of a conference.

We speculate that a primary reason for the reinforcement that family group conferencing provides for the use of kinship placements (beyond its obvious value in convening potential family caregivers) is the extent to which it is consistent with family-centered and strengths-based practice. Support for this conclusion can be found in the results of the qualitative analyses. These show that conferencing provided these families with an opportunity to inventory, utilize, and strengthen their own individual and community resources to solve problems. In addition, the findings suggest that conferencing sets the stage for the acquisition of the environmental and social competencies that family members need to support their caregiving. This emphasis on maximizing family potential within a social and environmental context constitutes a "radical rethinking" of child welfare service delivery (Lupton, 1998). Most importantly, it holds the promise of improving developmental outcomes for abused and neglected children by maintaining their safety *and* fostering the connections between children, their extended family systems, and an array of formal and informal resources and supports.

NOTE

1. Support for this research was provided by the Washington State Department of Child and Family Services and the Northwest Institute for Children and Families, University of Washington.

REFERENCES

Berger, P., & Neuhaus, R. (1977). *To empower people: The role of mediating structures in public policy*. Washington, DC: American Enterprise Institute.

Children's Administration, Washington State Department of Social and Health Services (1998). *Out of home placement statistics, July 1997–June 1998*. Fact Sheet, Olympia, Washington.

Cole, E. (1996). Key policy decisions in implementing family group conferences: Observations drawn from the New Zealand model. In M. Hardin (Ed.), *Family group conferences in child abuse and neglect cases: Learning from the experience of New Zealand* (pp. 121–52). Washington, DC: ABA Center on Children and the Law.

Crow, G., & Marsh, P. (1997). *Family group conferences: Partnership and child welfare*. Sheffield, UK: University of Sheffield.

Dodd, P., & Gutierrez, L. (1990). Preparing students for the future: A power perspective on community practice. *Administration in Social Work, 14*(2), 63–78.

Dunst, C., Deal, A., & Trivetle, C. (1994). *Supporting and strengthening families*. Cambridge, MA: Brookline.

Glaser, B., & Strauss, B. (1967). *The discovery of grounded theory: Strategies for qualitative research*. Chicago: Aldine de Gruyter.

Kahkonen, P. (1997). From the child welfare trap to the foster care trap. *Child Welfare, 76*(3), 429–45.

Kemp, S., Whittaker, J., & Tracy, E. (1997). *Person-environment practice: The social ecology of interpersonal helping*. Hawthorne, NY: Aldine de Gruyter.

Lupton, C. (1998). User empowerment or family self-reliance? The Family Group Conference model. *British Journal of Social Work, 28*(1), 107–28.

Lupton, C., Barnard, S., & Swall-Yarrington, M. (1996). Family planning? An evaluation of the family group conference model (Report No. 31). Portsmouth, UK: University of Portsmouth.

O'Donnell, J. (1995). Casework practice with fathers in kinship care. Unpublished Ph.D. thesis, University of Illinois, Chicago.

Strauss, A., & Corbin, J. (1990). *Basics of qualitative research*. Newbury Park, CA: Sage.

30 Evaluating and Implementing Family Group Conferences

The Family and Community Compact in Kent County, Michigan

DAVID CRAMPTON and WENDY LEWIS JACKSON

Successful conferencing can be facilitated by a process evaluation that identifies implementation barriers and solutions. This chapter describes the evaluation and implementation of the Family and Community Compact (FCC) program in Kent County, Michigan. Highlighted is the role of participatory action research.

PARTICIPATORY ACTION RESEARCH

Lisbeth Schorr has noted that traditional program evaluation is focused on narrowly defined programs so that the effects can be precisely measured (Schorr, 1997). By contrast, the "new" program evaluation focuses on finding out what works through a theoretical-conceptual base developed with program participants. Evaluators are no longer auditors from a distance. They work with program staff and promote self-evaluation. Evaluation theorists advocate looking for categories, patterns, footprints, and/or "successful failures" that help develop a theory of how a program works, how well it works, and when it does not work (Glaser & Strauss, 1967; Mohr, 1995; Patton, 1997; Ristock & Pennell, 1996; Scriven, 1976; Weiss, 1998).

This approach to evaluation is well suited for family group conferencing because it allows community and family members to help decide what the outcomes should be and how they should be measured. For example, the Newfoundland and Labrador researchers described their approach as follows:

> The study used a collaborative action research approach that was viewed as congruent with its philosophy of forming partnerships. The study was designed: (a) collaboratively by involving a range of project participants as well as external consultants, (b) sequentially by drawing upon learning from earlier phases of the project, and (c) formatively by revamping procedures on the basis of feedback from participating families, community representatives, government officials and project staff. (Burford & Pennell, 1995, p. 7)

The Kent County evaluation follows the Newfoundland-Labrador example. A "core team" made up of people from the county public child welfare agency, foundations, the Family Court, and the larger community guides the evaluation and facilitates program implementation. The core team reviews evaluation findings as they are presented and considers program changes. The emphasis of the evaluation is on continuous improvement.

INITIATING FAMILY GROUP CONFERENCING
IN KENT COUNTY

Located in Western Michigan, Kent County has maintained a commitment to permanency for children affected by abuse and neglect for over twenty-five years. This commitment has resulted in a child welfare model that is based on strong collaboration and a sense of shared responsibility. As a result, 90 percent of children in care achieve permanency within six months. The Kent County system has been able to accomplish this due to: (1) a shared commitment to timely permanency by child welfare professionals, (2) state legislation that supports safety, well-being, and early permanence for children, (3) a financial investment by county government to support necessary prevention, in-home care, and intensive family-based foster care services, and (4) a strong local child welfare management team from the Kent County Family Independence Agency, Kent County Circuit Court—Family Division, and private foster care and adoption providers. In this team approach, a data management system comprised of performance standards and quality measures is used to track all children in the system and monitor their progress through the courts and agencies.

Community interest in family group conferencing in Kent County began in 1994 when, as part of the W. K. Kellogg Foundation's Families for Kids Initiative, concerned citizens undertook a year-long community visioning process to develop a comprehensive plan for the local child welfare system. Families for Kids centered on the achievement of five outcomes:

1. **Family Support.** Assistance to help families stay together and meet the challenges of daily life.
2. **Coordinated Assessment.** A single, coordinated process that evaluates a family's needs in a comprehensive way.
3. **Consistent Casework or Casework Team.** Casework continuity through the permanency planning process.
4. **Stable Foster Care.** Children cared for in their own communities by a single, stable foster family.
5. **Timely Permanency.** One year at most until placement in a permanent home.

What made Families for Kids unique was that people who used the child welfare system were approached about how service delivery could be improved. Until this effort, consumers and advocates in Kent County were not equal partners in planning for reform in child welfare. The heart of this unprecedented planning process involved a dialogue with four hundred citizens, representing eighteen different stakeholder groups. It was a simple concept—to have a conversation with people who use the system and find out what they think. Adoptive parents, foster parents, persons who were denied foster or adoptive placements, child welfare professionals, and civic leaders were consulted. Most importantly, children waiting for permanent families were asked what needed to be changed. More than anything else, the voices of the children shaped the direction of the strategic plan and the development of what ultimately became the Family and Community Compact.

Kent County's commitment to permanency for children had significantly reduced the number of children in foster care and the time they spent in care. However, the visioning process revealed that people were concerned about the over-representation of minority children in foster care and the lack of meaningful inclusion of extended family and community members in the care of maltreated children. With more than half of the foster care placements and adoptions in the county involving relatives, it was clear that families were taking care of their own. However, the visioning process revealed an uncoordinated approach to relative caregiver selection, service delivery, and placement. Many relative caregivers believed the system was intrusive and not addressing their needs. Community leaders wanted to develop a process for including extended family and community members in the care and protection of children. Inspired by the use of family group conferencing in New Zealand, funds were applied for and received from the W. K. Kellogg Foundation to develop the Family and Community Compact program (FCC).

HOW FAMILY GROUP CONFERENCING WORKS
IN KENT COUNTY

The design of the Family and Community Compact program directly addresses the community's concern about the overrepresentation of children of color in foster care and the need to involve extended families in the decision-making process from the beginning. The process seeks to provide care, protection, and support for children faced with entering the foster care system by means of a culturally competent family and community network intervention that strengthens the connections of every child to their family and community. A team made up of Children's Protective Service workers and the Family and Community Compact staff identifies concerned members of the child's kinship and community network; convenes a family and community compact meeting; develops a plan for the child's safety;

and provides supports to kin and/or community caregivers and parents. The process ensures that children in need of permanent families will receive timely support, assessment, and casework services with minimal court involvement.

Substantiated child protection cases are referred to the Family and Community Compact program only when the CPS worker who investigated the case determines that the child must be removed from home and the following conditions have been met: the case does not involve sexual abuse; the parents agree to participate in the program; and family preservation service attempts have been unsuccessful. Community representatives decided that the Family and Community Compact should not accept cases involving child sexual abuse because programs that already exist in the community are meeting the needs of these children. Since the court cannot require a parent to participate in any program without opening a legal case, and the goal of the FCC is to keep court intervention at a minimum, it was necessary to make the program voluntary. Due to community concerns about the overrepresentation of children of color in the Kent County child welfare system, from 1996 to 1998 the FCC first targeted this population for participation in the program. Beginning in January, 1999, however, the program began to serve all children, regardless of race or ethnicity, who meet the criteria described above.

Preparation prior to the Family and Community Compact meeting is essential. Family Community Compact staff provide as much information as possible to ensure that everyone who participates in the program or who will be attending a Compact meeting understands they are to make critical decisions regarding the care and protection of a child. Once the parent(s) agree(s) to participate, the FCC staff begin to organize a Compact meeting by:

1. Conducting a family and child assessment, which includes a comprehensive assessment of social support, education, employment, health, legal history, substance use, extended family, child-rearing practices, home environment, and attitudes toward taking in a child).
2. Completing background checks of potential caregivers, with the assistance of the child protective service worker assigned to the case.
3. Contacting family members and others connected with the family.
4. Contacting professionals who are involved with the case (e.g., child protective service workers, teachers, ministers, public health nurses, attorney, and physicians).

After this preparation is completed, the family and community members who have an interest in the welfare of the child are invited to participate in a Compact meeting.

The FCC staff convenes the Compact meeting and reviews the agenda and the objectives of the process. The primary goal of the compact meeting is to develop a plan for the care and protection of the children that guarantees their safety and timely permanency, and that ideally keeps them with their extended family. Family Community Compact staff describe the process in terms of five phases: *intro-duction, information, decision-making, review,* and *follow-up.* In the introduction phase, everyone introduces themselves and explains their relationship to the children. Often, extended family members and professionals do not know each other. Family Community Compact staff also use this time to explain the importance of confidentiality, and ask participants to sign an agreement that they will not disclose what is discussed in the meeting. In the information phase, biological relatives, fictive kin (such as church members, godparents, and neighbors), and support people (such as public health nurses, teachers, and ministers) first hear from the CPS worker and other involved professional staff about their concerns regarding the welfare of the children. This involves reading the findings from the child protection investigation by the CPS worker. The FCC staff report that while the family is often aware of the concerns identified in the investigation, they need to hear directly from child protection staff about any problems with potential caregivers or permanency plans. Families can make informed decisions only if they have all the available information. During the case presentation, family members have an opportunity to ask questions of the professionals present and contribute their own concerns about the case. Family Community Compact staff may add information, perhaps by reading a letter or statement from family members who could not attend. Following the information phase is the Decision-Making phase or private family time, during which the professionals leave the meeting and the family develops a plan for the care, safety, and protection of the children—the Family and Community Compact Agreement. The family also identifies a "recorder" to record the plan and report it back to the professionals in the next phase. Although professionals leave the meeting, they are asked to remain nearby in case the family needs more information or clarification. Family members can, and sometimes do, invite professionals to remain in the meeting.

In the review phase, the recorder and family report to the FCC staff what the family plan is, and the FCC staff have an opportunity to ask questions, clarify procedures, and give feedback on the plan. The Family and Community Compact Agreement is treated as a family contract. If the family cannot develop a plan, the case is referred back to child protection and the children placed in traditional foster care. The agreement outlines which family members will take in which child, any services the caregivers will need, how other family members can support each placement, and if reunification is a possibility. In addition, it includes what the parents must do in order to regain custody of their children and how visitation will be arranged. During the meeting, FCC participants are asked to develop a contingency plan for each placement. The Compact agreement is written up after the meeting by FCC staff, signed by all participants, and mailed to the family and the child protection worker assigned to the case. In the follow-up phase, the FCC Family Advocate staff person explains her role in helping the family secure the services and resources they will need to support their plan.

Safety of the children is the primary consideration of the Family and Community

Compact process. After the children are placed according to the decisions made in the FCC agreement, staff meet with the family every three months for up to one year, at which time a permanent plan must be developed. The goal of monitoring the FCC agreement is to ensure that permanency is achieved. If at any time FCC staff are concerned about the welfare of the children, they can contact child protection staff and recommend foster care placement.

KEY FINDINGS

In June 1995, six months before the FCC received their first case, a research team from the University of Michigan School of Social Work was identified to help the community develop an extensive process and impact evaluation of the program, using a participatory action approach. The evaluators provided each member of the core team of community representatives with a list of traditional child welfare measures. Core team members indicated the relevance of these measures and suggested ways to define and implement them for the Kent County evaluation (Crampton, 1998). Data are collected from several sources. Administrative computer files for every temporary court ward in Kent County are captured and put in a database that allows the evaluators to trace their placement into out-of-home care and permanent placement. This database is used to compare the experiences of children placed through the traditional system with those who participate in a FCC and monitor whether all eligible children are referred to the FCC. In the first year of the program, the evaluators discovered that not all eligible children were being referred to the FCC. After consulting with the child protection workers, they found that workers were not referring cases in which they planned to attempt immediate termination of parental rights as well as children who had previously been in foster care. The FCC and public child welfare agency staff then worked together to clarify and monitor the referral criteria. As a result, it is no longer possible for a child to be placed in foster care without considering the case for referral to the FCC program.

The evaluators also collect data on all FCC referrals, the written agreements and reports, terminated cases, as well as those closed successfully. Data entered into a database allow for tracing the disposition of all program referrals. A total of 254 families were referred to FCC from December 1995 to December 1998 and 96 (38 percent) of them proceeded with a meeting. Of these, 58 (60 percent) developed a plan that kept the children out of foster care and court involvement. The 58 diverted cases represent 23 percent of the 254 referred, suggesting that the FCC reduced by 23 percent the admission of children into foster care over the three-year period. Although the evaluation does not include a comparison group, the evaluators use the caseflow patterns and "successful failures" as suggested by Weiss (1998) and others, to determine if children placed by the FCC program would otherwise have gone into foster care. For example, of the forty cases that did not have a meeting because the parents refused to sign into the program, all of them show up in the court database as being placed in foster care.

Although the FCC has proven to be an important addition to Kent County's efforts to reduce child maltreatment, it is not appropriate for every family. Forty-six cases did not meet the removal criteria. In another forty cases, parents declined to participate in the FCC program because they either believed their children required services that could only be offered through the child welfare and court systems, disputed the CPS petition, had mental health issues preventing them from adequately understanding the program, or were adoptive parents who no longer wanted to care for the children.

A very simple benefit-cost analysis (Gramlich, 1990) suggests that the estimated foster care and court savings for children diverted by the FCC exceeded program costs. This analysis is based on the assumption that all the children diverted by FCC would have been removed from home and made court wards, as well as the assumption that all of the children would have been placed with relatives who would not have received a foster care per diem. Following these assumptions, the only cost to the county public child welfare agency would be the payments to a private agency to monitor the cases. If the children were placed with a family who received a per diem, the costs would be almost double. This is a conservative assumption since it could be argued that at least some of the relatives who agreed to take in the children because of the FCC process would not have taken them through the traditional process. As a result, the children would have been placed in a licensed home. A conservative estimate of the cost of monitoring a relative placement is $5,000 per child. The American Bar Association estimates the cost of monitoring a case in the Kent County Juvenile Court as $1,000 per child (Hardin, Rubin, & Baker, 1995). In fiscal year 1998, the Family and Community Compact received 107 referrals. Of the 107 cases, 39 (36 percent) proceeded with a meeting. Of these, 24 cases developed a plan that diverted the children from out-of-home placement and court involvement. A conservative estimate of the cost of those 50 children entering foster care is $6,000 each ($1,000 for court supervision, $5,000 for foster care case management). Therefore, the Family and Community Compact is estimated as having saved $300,000 at a program cost of about $220,174.

Attendance at meetings has ranged from two to thirteen participants with an average of six, although the number of people supporting each plan is increasing slightly over time. On average, four kin members attend and one professional is present, in addition to the FCC staff. During the first three years of the program, the investigating Children's Protective Services (CPS) workers attended 37 percent of the compacts. In January 1999 when the program was expanded to serve all children, the importance of CPS attendance was emphasized to staff, and attendance increased to 69 percent. In the majority of Compacts (73 percent), one or more parents attend. When a meeting is held, the participants are usually (60 percent) able to come to an agreement. In most agreements (85 percent), the permanency plan developed by the family is reunification. Substantiated child abuse and neglect concerns included substance abuse (69 percent), neglect (60 percent), physical abuse (24 percent), mental health issues for the parent (21 percent), parent in jail (15 percent), and abandonment (14 percent). Service needs of the selected caregivers identified at the meetings included financial (68 percent), medical (52 percent), clothing (40 percent), counseling for the children (23 percent), child care (16 percent), and housing (8 percent). Not surprisingly, the Compacts with an above average number of people supporting the plan are more likely to keep the children out of foster care. Similarly, the more people who attend the meeting, the more likely the placement will last. This probably relates to the fact that the more people at a meeting, the more support for the child. Plans developed at meetings where one or both parents attend are also more likely to keep the children out of foster care.

IMPLEMENTATION BARRIERS ADDRESSED

The evaluation helped the core team identify some ways the program can be improved. For example, the program designers assumed that conferencing would most often be used to facilitate the long-term placement of children with their relatives in a legal guardianship. In practice, most of the families wanted to develop a plan for reunification. As a result, the program was modified to ensure that resources were put in place to help families realize their reunification plans. The evaluation also discovered early on that attendance at family conferences was less than reported in other sites. Through discussion with the core team and FCC staff, a consensus was reached that the goal was not to maximize the number of participants but to ensure that everyone who is prepared to help care and protect the children attends the conference. The evaluation also revealed implementation problems such as children not being referred to the program and Children's Protective Services workers not attending the compact meetings. These were then addressed by the core team.

FUTURE DIRECTIONS

The Family and Community Compact of Kent County has exceeded its goals to meaningfully involve families and communities in the child welfare decision-making process. Governor John Engler's 1998–99 state budget included $3 million for pilot programs like the Family and Community Compact in other Michigan counties. The success of the Kent County program was used in support of this funding request. Six sites were selected, with plans to serve 325 families in the first year. Staff from Kent County assisted in the training of the selected sites in

April 1999. A second Kent County site was added in October 1999. A federal grant was awarded to allow the Family and Community Compact to serve Caucasian families. The expansion has more than doubled the number of referrals to the program.

Next steps in the Kent County evaluation include a more detailed analysis of FCC outcomes and case characteristics, interviews with family members, and establishing a self-evaluation system. The growing number of cases will allow the evaluators to look more closely at key case characteristics and see how they relate to case outcomes. Because there are now enough closed FCC cases, evaluation can compare the outcomes of FCC cases to other foster care cases, as well as other kinship cases. These comparisons will include measures that were identified by the core team, such as prevention of additional maltreatment, placement stability, and timely permanency, and will be examined by using the court database to look at all out-of-home placements one year before the FCC started to the present. The evaluators also plan to collect more information from the families themselves to better understand, for example, whether families truly believe they are making the decisions.

REFERENCES

Burford, G., & Pennell, J. (1995). *Family group decision making: New roles for "old" partners in resolving family violence: Implementation Report Summary*. St. John's: Institute of Social and Economic Research, Memorial University of Newfoundland.

Burford, G., Pennell, J., MacLeod, S., Campbell, S., & Lyall, G. (1996). Reunification as an extended family matter. *Community w: International Journal of Family Care, 8*(2), 33–55.

Crampton, D. (1998). Evaluating family group decision making: What are the expected outcomes and how can they best be measured? In L. Merkel-Holguin (Ed.), *1997 National Roundtable Series on family group decision making: Summary of proceedings*. Englewood, CO: American Humane Association.

Glaser, B., & Strauss, A. (1967). *The discovery of grounded theory: Strategies for qualitative research*. Chicago: Aldine.

Gramlich, E. (1990). *A guide to benefit-cost analysis* (2nd ed.) Englewood Cliffs, NJ: Prentice-Hall.

Hardin, M., Rubin, H. T., & Baker, D. (1995). *A second court that works: Judicial implementation of permanency planning reforms*. Washington, DC: American Bar Association Center on Children and the Law.

Mohr, L. (1995). *Impact analysis for program evaluation*. Thousand Oaks, CA: Sage.

Patton, M. (1997). *Utilization-focused evaluation: The new century text*. Thousands Oaks, CA: Sage.

Pennell, J., & Burford, G. (1998). Evaluating family group decision making: What are the expected outcomes and how can they best be measured? In L. Merkel-Holguin (Ed.), *1997 National Roundtable Series on family group decision making: Summary of proceedings*. Englewood, CO: American Humane Association.

Ristock, J., & Pennell, J. (1996). *Community research as empowerment: feminist links, postmodern interruptions*. Toronto: Oxford University Press.

Schorr, L. (1997). *Common purpose: Strengthening families and neighborhoods to rebuild America*. New York, NY: Anchor.

Scriven, M. (1976). Maximizing the power of causal investigation: The modus operandi method. In G. Glass (Ed.), *Evaluation studies review annual* (Vol. 1; pp. 120–39). Beverly Hills, CA: Sage.

Weiss, C. (1995). Nothing as practical as good theory: Exploring theory-based evaluation for comprehensive community-initiatives for children and families. In J. Connel, A. Kubisch, L. Schorr, & C. Weiss (Eds.) , *New approaches to evaluating community initiatives: Concepts, methods and contexts*. Washington, DC: Aspen Institute.

Weiss, C. (1998). *Evaluation: Methods for studying programs and policies* (2nd ed.). Upper Saddle River, NJ: Prentice-Hall.

Index